World Economic Situation and Prospects 2017

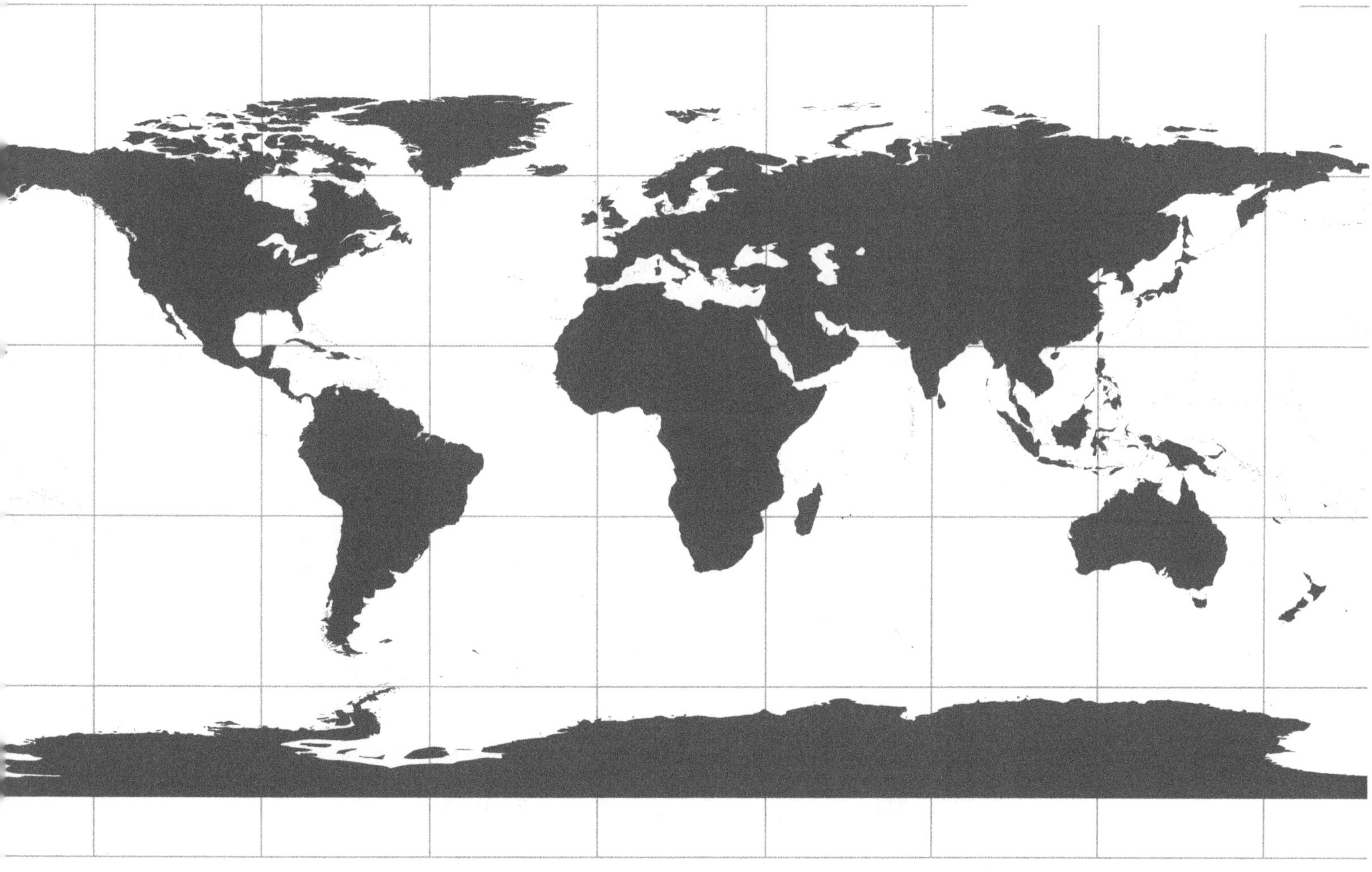

United Nations
New York, 2017

The report is a joint product of the United Nations Department of Economic and Social Affairs (UN/DESA), the United Nations Conference on Trade and Development (UNCTAD) and the five United Nations regional commissions (Economic Commission for Africa (ECA), Economic Commission for Europe (ECE), Economic Commission for Latin America and the Caribbean (ECLAC), Economic and Social Commission for Asia and the Pacific (ESCAP) and Economic and Social Commission for Western Asia (ESCWA)). The United Nations World Tourism Organization (UNWTO) also contributed to the report.

For further information, see http://www.un.org/en/development/desa/policy/wesp/index.shtml or contact:

DESA

Mr. Wu Hongbo, *Under-Secretary-General*

Department of Economic and Social Affairs
Room S-2922
United Nations
New York, NY 10017
USA

☎ +1-212-9635958
✉ wuh@un.org

UNCTAD

Dr. Mukhisa Kituyi, *Secretary-General*

United Nations Conference on Trade and Development
Room E-9042
Palais de Nations
1211 Geneva 10
Switzerland

☎ +41-22-9175806
✉ sgo@unctad.org

ECA

Dr. Abdalla Hamdok, *Executive Secretary*

United Nations Economic Commission for Africa
Menelik II Avenue
P.O. Box 3001
Addis Ababa
Ethiopia

☎ +251-11-5511231
✉ ecainfo@uneca.org

ECE

Mr. Christian Friis Bach, *Executive Secretary*

United Nations Economic Commission for Europe
Palais des Nations
CH-1211 Geneva 10
Switzerland

☎ +41-22-9174444
✉ info.ece@unece.org

ECLAC

Ms. Alicia Bárcena, *Executive Secretary*

Economic Commission for Latin America and the Caribbean
Av. Dag Hammarskjöld 3477
Vitacura
Santiago, Chile
Chile

☎ +56-2-22102000
✉ secepal@cepal.org

ESCAP

Dr. Shamshad Akhtar, *Executive Secretary*

Economic and Social Commission for Asia and the Pacific
United Nations Building
Rajadamnern Nok Avenue
Bangkok 10200
Thailand

☎ +66-2-2881234
✉ unescap@unescap.org

ESCWA

Ms. Rima Khalaf, *Executive Secretary*

Economic and Social Commission for Western Asia
P.O. Box 11-8575
Riad el-Solh Square, Beirut
Lebanon

☎ +961-1-981301
@ http://www.escwa.un.org/main/contact.asp

ISBN: 978-92-1-109175-5
eISBN: 978-92-1-059945-0

United Nations publication
Sales No. E.17.II.C.2

Acknowledgements

The *World Economic Situation and Prospects 2017* is a joint product of the United Nations Department of Economic and Social Affairs (UN/DESA), the United Nations Conference on Trade and Development (UNCTAD) and the five United Nations regional commissions (Economic Commission for Africa (ECA), Economic Commission for Europe (ECE), Economic Commission for Latin America and the Caribbean (ECLAC), Economic and Social Commission for Asia and the Pacific (ESCAP) and Economic and Social Commission for Western Asia (ESCWA)). The United Nations World Tourism Organization (UNWTO) contributed to the report. The report also benefited from inputs received from the national centres of Project LINK and also from the deliberations in the Project LINK meeting held in Toronto on 19-21 October 2016. The forecasts presented in the report draw on the World Economic Forecasting Model (WEFM) of UN/DESA.

Under the general guidance of Lenni Montiel, Assistant Secretary-General for Economic Development in UN/DESA, and the management of Pingfan Hong, Director of Development Policy and Analysis Division (DPAD), this publication was led by Dawn Holland, Matthias Kempf, and Ingo Pitterle in the Global Economic Monitoring Unit of DPAD.

The contributions of Grigor Agabekian, Helena Afonso, Hoi Wai Cheng, Peter Chowla, Ann D'lima, Cordelia Gow, Andrea Grozdanic, Dawn Holland, Kenneth Iversen, Arend Janssen, Matthias Kempf, Erik Klok (visiting fellow), Poh Lynn Ng, Lara Palmisano, Ingo Pitterle, Gabe Scelta, Oliver Schwank, Nancy Settecasi, Krishnan Sharma, Shari Spiegel, Alex Trepelkov, Sebastian Vergara, Qian Wan (intern) and Jie Wei from **UN/DESA**; Bruno Antunes, Stephanie Blankenburg, Alfredo Calcagno, Stefan Csordas, Samuel Gayi, Taisuke Ito, Mina Mashayekhi, Nicolas Maystre, Alessandro Nicita, Janvier Nkurunziza, and Julia Seiermann from **UNCTAD**; Yesuf Mohammednur Awel, Hopestone Chavula, Adam Elhiraika and Khaled Hussein from **ECA**; José Palacín from **ECE**; Claudia De Camino, Michael Hanni, Daniel Titelman and Cecilia Vera from **ECLAC**; Hamza Ali Malik, Jose Antonio Pedrosa Garcia, Matthew Hammill, Dorothea Lazaro, Swayamsiddha Panda, Nyingtob Pema Norbu and Vatcharin Sirimaneetham from **ESCAP**; Abdallah Al Dardari, Moctar Mohamed El Hacene, Mohamed Hedi Bchir, Nathalie Khaled, Maroun Laoun, John Robert Sloan and Yasuhisa Yamamoto from **ESCWA**; Michel Julian, John Kester and Javier Ruescas from **UNWTO** are duly acknowledged.

The report was edited by Carla Drysdale.

Explanatory notes

The following symbols have been used in the tables throughout the report:

..	**Two dots** indicate that data are not available or are not separately reported.
–	**A dash** indicates that the amount is nil or negligible.
.	**A full stop** is used to indicate decimals.
-	**A hyphen** indicates that the item is not applicable.
-	**A minus** sign indicates deficit or decrease, except as indicated.
/	**A slash** between years indicates a crop year or financial year, for example, 2015/16.
–	**Use of a hyphen between years**, for example, 2016–2017, signifies the full period involved, including the beginning and end years.

Reference to "dollars" ($) indicates United States dollars, unless otherwise stated.

Reference to "billions" indicates one thousand million.

Reference to "tons" indicates metric tons, unless otherwise stated.

Annual rates of growth or change, unless otherwise stated, refer to annual compound rates.

Details and percentages in tables do not necessarily add to totals, because of rounding.

Project LINK is an international collaborative research group for econometric modelling, coordinated jointly by the Development Policy and Analysis Division of UN/DESA and the University of Toronto.

For **country classifications**, see statistical annex.

Data presented in this publication incorporate information available as at **11 November 2016.**

The following abbreviations have been used:

AAAA	Addis Ababa Action Agenda
ADB	Asian Development Bank
AfDB	African Development Bank
AIIB	Asian Infrastructure Investment Bank
BIS	Bank for International Settlements
BoJ	Bank of Japan
BOP	balance of payments
CFTA	Continental Free Trade Area
CIS	Commonwealth of Independent States
CPA	country-programmable aid
DAC	OECD Development Assistance Committee
DSR	debt service-to-income ratio
EBRD	European Bank for Reconstruction and Development
ECB	European Central Bank
EEU	Eurasian Economic Union
EIB	European Investment Bank
ETFs	exchange-traded funds
EU	European Union
FDI	foreign direct investment
Fed	United States Federal Reserve
G20	Group of Twenty
GCC	Cooperation Council for the Arab States of the Gulf
GDP	gross domestic product
GNI	gross national income
GVCs	global value chains
HIPC	heavily-indebted poor countries
IBRD	International Bank for Reconstruction and Development
ICT	information and communication technology
IDA	International Developement Association
IEA	International Energy Agency
IFC	International Finance Corporation
IIC	Inter-American Investment Corporation
ILO	International Labour Organization
IMF	International Monetary Fund
ITA	Information Technology Agreement
LBMA	London Bullion Market Associations
LDCs	least developed countries
LIBOR	London Interbank Offered Rate
LME	London Metal Exchange
MC10	tenth Ministerial Conference of the WTO
MDBs	multilateral development banks
MFN	most favoured nation
NDB	New Development Bank
NTMs	non-tariff measures
ODA	official development assistance
OECD	Organisation for Economic Co-operation and Development
OIS	overnight indexed swap
OOF	other official flows
OPEC	Organization of the Petroleum Exporting Countries
PPP	purchasing power parity
QE	quantitative easing
R&D	research and development
RTAs	regional trade agreements
SDGs	Sustainable Development Goals
SIDS	small island developing States
SMEs	small and medium-sized enterprises
SOEs	State-owned enterprises
SWFs	sovereign wealth funds
TFP	total factor productivity
TISA	Trade in Services Agreement
TOSSD	Total Official Support for Sustainable Development
TPP	Trans-Pacific Partnership Agreement
UN/DESA	Department of Economic and Social Affairs of the United Nations Secretariat
UNCTAD	United Nations Conference on Trade and Development
UNWTO	United Nations World Tourism Organization
WDI	World Development Indicators
WGP	world gross product
WTO	World Trade Organization

Executive summary

Prospects for global macroeconomic development

The global economy remains trapped in a prolonged episode of slow growth

In 2016, the world economy expanded by just 2.2 per cent, the slowest rate of growth since the Great Recession of 2009. Underpinning the sluggish global economy are the feeble pace of global investment, dwindling world trade growth, flagging productivity growth and high levels of debt. Low commodity prices have exacerbated these factors in many commodity-exporting countries since mid-2014, while conflict and geopolitical tensions continue to weigh on economic prospects in several regions.

World gross product is forecast to expand by 2.7 per cent in 2017 and 2.9 per cent in 2018, with this modest recovery more an indication of economic stabilization than a signal of a robust and sustained revival of global demand. The slight increase in gross domestic product (GDP) growth projected for developed economies in 2017 is largely driven by the end of the destocking cycle in the United States of America and additional policy support in Japan.

Economies in transition are expected to expand by 1.4 per cent in 2017, following two consecutive years of decline, as the region has largely absorbed the sharp terms-of-trade shock that several countries suffered in 2014-2015. Commodity exporters in developing countries are also expected to see some uptick in growth, as commodity prices stabilize and inflationary pressures driven by sharp exchange rate depreciations ease. East and South Asia will continue to grow more rapidly than other regions, benefiting from robust domestic demand and space for more accommodative macroeconomic policy. The outlook remains subject to significant uncertainties and downside risks. If these downside risks were to materialize, the moderate acceleration in growth currently projected would be derailed.

Given the close linkages between demand, investment, trade and productivity, the extended episode of weak global growth may prove self-perpetuating in the absence of concerted policy efforts to revive investment and foster a recovery in productivity. This would impede progress towards the Sustainable Development Goals (SDGs), particularly the goals of eradicating extreme poverty and creating decent work for all.

Weak investment is at the foundation of the slowdown in global growth

Investment growth has slowed significantly in many of the major developed and developing economies, as well as in many economies in transition. Protracted weak global demand has reduced incentives for firms to invest, while economic and political uncertainties have also weighed on investment. Since 2015, many countries have seen sharp contractions in investment in the oil and extractive industries, although these declines are mostly cyclical, rather than signalling significant structural progress towards a less fossil fuel-intensive economy. Lack of access to finance has also acted as a constraint in some cases, especially in countries where banks remain undercapitalized or where financial markets are under-developed. Despite record-low, often negative bond yields, Governments in developed countries have made steep cuts in public investment since 2010, reflecting fiscal adjustment policies implemented in response to high levels of government debt. Since mid-2014, Governments in many commodity-exporting countries have also curtailed much-needed investment in infrastructure and social services, in response to the sharp loss of commodity revenue. In some other developing countries in East and South Asia and parts of Africa, on the other hand, weaker private sector investment has been partially offset by an expansion of government infrastructure projects.

The extended period of weak investment is a driving factor behind the slowdown in productivity growth

Labour productivity growth has slowed markedly in most developed economies, and in many large developing and transition countries. Investment in new capital can affect factors such as the rate of innovation, labour force skills and the quality of infrastructure. These in turn drive the technological change and efficiency gains underpinning labour productivity growth in the medium term.

Government support for public goods, such as combating climate change, remains crucial, as private investors tend to evaluate risk and return over a short-term horizon and under-invest in public priorities. Investment in key areas, such as research and development, education and infrastructure, would serve to promote sustainable development and social and environmental progress, while also supporting productivity growth. While fiscal space to support an expansion of investment remains limited in many countries, especially commodity exporters that have suffered a sharp loss of commodity revenue, some large economies do have the scope to take advantage of low borrowing costs to finance investment.

Aggregate growth in the least developed countries (LDCs) remains well below the Sustainable Development Goal target of "at least 7 per cent GDP growth"

Aggregate growth in the LDCs will remain well below the SDG target in the near term, but is expected to rise modestly from an estimated 4.5 per cent in 2016 to 5.2 per cent and 5.5 per cent in 2017 and 2018, respectively. The below-target growth poses a risk to critical public expenditure on healthcare, education, social protection and climate change adaptation. The latter is all the more critical since the LDCs remain highly vulnerable to natural catastrophes and weather-related shocks.

Further efforts are also needed to diversify exports of the LDCs, which remain highly concentrated in a few primary products vulnerable to price volatility and external shocks. Under the current growth trajectory, nearly 35 per cent of the population in the LDCs may remain in extreme poverty by 2030. Without an acceleration in both GDP growth and progress towards improving income inequality, eradicating the high levels of extreme poverty in the LDCs by 2030 is a formidable challenge.

Garnering the resources to finance the investment needed in the LDCs remains difficult. Investment in these countries would need to expand at an average annual rate of at least 11 per cent through 2030, a significant acceleration relative to recent trends. Foreign direct investment (FDI) continues to bypass many LDCs and remains concentrated in extractive industries. Greater efforts are needed to mobilise domestic and international, public and private resources for achieving the SDGs of these countries.

Sustained improvements in carbon emissions mitigation will require concerted efforts to improve energy efficiency and promote renewable energy

The level of global carbon emissions has stalled for two consecutive years. This positive development reflects the declining energy intensity of economic activities, a rising share of renewables in the overall energy structure, and slower economic growth in major emitters.

However, the world remains some distance from achieving a sustained decoupling between economic growth and carbon emissions growth. Despite advancements, especially in developing countries, where the level of new renewable energy investment exceeded that of developed countries in 2015, renewable energy still accounts for only a small share of global power generation. New renewable investment dropped sharply in the first half of 2016, and the improvements to emissions mitigation witnessed in recent years could easily reverse without concerted efforts from the public and private sectors to improve energy efficiency and promote renewable energy, supported by international cooperation on clean technology transfer and climate finance.

International trade and finance

World trade at a standstill

Dwindling world trade growth is both a contributing factor and a symptom of the global economic slowdown. World trade volumes expanded by just 1.2 per cent in 2016, the third-lowest rate in the past 30 years. Cyclical factors — such as the composition of global demand and heightened uncertainty — continue to restrain global trade growth, while the impact of a number of structural shifts that favoured the rapid expansion of global trade in the 1990s and 2000s have started to wane, coupled with slower progress in trade liberalisation. The ratio of world trade growth to world gross product growth has declined significantly since the 1990s. While global import penetration is expected to exhibit a modest recovery, world trade growth is unlikely to outpace world gross product significantly in the coming years. World trade is projected to expand by 2.7 per cent in 2017 and 3.3 per cent in 2018.

Closing the investment gap to achieve the SDGs by 2030 requires the mobilization of significant financial resources

The prolonged slowdown in global economic growth makes generating the long-term investment necessary for achieving the SDGs particularly challenging. International finance is a critical complement to domestic revenue mobilization, which has grown steadily in developing countries over the last 15 years, but has yet to close investment financing gaps.

However, international capital inflows remain volatile, and net flows to developing countries are estimated to remain negative at least through 2017, underscoring the challenges of financing long-term sustainable development.

Since the global financial crisis, low interest rates have prompted sovereign bond issuance by developing countries in international capital markets. However, in some cases, concerns over debt sustainability are now being realised, especially where repayment burdens are subject to significant exchange rate movements. The provision of international public finance, including official development assistance (ODA) from Members of the OECD Development Assistance Committee, increased in 2015, but remains below United Nations targets. The increase in ODA to a large extent reflects the resources spent on refugees in host countries. Lending by multilateral development banks and through South-South cooperation also increased in 2015. Nonetheless, available domestic and international financial resources remain insufficient to fill investment financing gaps for sustainable development, particularly in the poorest countries.

Aligning institutional investment with sustainable development requires a change in the incentive structure

Aligning investment with the SDGs, including building sustainable and resilient infrastructure, requires policies and regulatory frameworks that incentivize changes in investment patterns. Current FDI patterns are not fully aligned with sustainable development, and the bulk of recent flows have been directed towards cross-border mergers and acquisitions, which may have limited impact on jobs and development. A reallocation of 3 to 5 per cent of institutional investor assets towards long-term investment in sustainable development could have an enormous impact. Yet to date, investment by institutional investors in the long-term illiquid assets necessary for sustainable development has been limited. Investment by institutional investors has tended to be short-term oriented, as reflected in the volatility of cross-border portfolio flows. Volatile international portfolio and banking flows can undermine sustainable development rather than support it.

Aligning incentives in capital markets with long-term investment in sustainable development and also incentivizing greater direct investment can be addressed through the financial governance architecture, and supported through various policy mixes including pricing externalities, effective regulatory frameworks, blended finance and guarantees and leveraging private investment through public intermediaries, such as development banks.

Uncertainties and risks

The materialization of several key downside risks could prolong the period of weak global growth

Global economic prospects remain subject to significant uncertainties and risks that are weighted on the downside, with the potential to obstruct the modest acceleration in growth that is currently forecast for 2017-2018. Some of these risks stem from monetary policy actions in major developed economies. The impact of introducing untested monetary policy instruments — such as the negative interest rate policies in Japan and Europe — remains unclear. There is a risk that such measures could lead to a deterioration of bank balance sheets, causing credit conditions to tighten, with the potential to destabilize fragile and undercapitalized banks. The timing of interest rate rises in the United States is another area of uncertainty. As interest rate differentials relative to other developed economies widen, this has the potential to trigger financial volatility, reversal of capital inflows to developing economies, and abrupt adjustments in exchange rates. Such volatility would exacerbate vulnerabilities associated with high levels of debt and rising default rates in a number of developing countries, with the potential to push up borrowing costs, raise deleveraging pressures, and increase banking sector stress.

Policy uncertainty in the United States and Europe has widened the confidence bounds around global economic forecasts

There are also considerable uncertainties in the international policy environment. For example, uncertainties remain high with respect to the forthcoming changes by the new Administration of the United States to important policies in international trade, immigration, and climate change. The decision by the United Kingdom of Great Britain and Northern Ireland to leave the European Union, or "Brexit", and its potential implications for the free movement of goods and workers in Europe, also poses considerable regional uncertainty. All of these uncertainties have the potential to undermine any projected recovery in business investment, impede international trade growth and even derail the already weak global growth.

Policy challenges and the way forward

A more balanced policy mix is needed, moving beyond excessive reliance on monetary policy

Many economies continue to place excessive dependence on monetary policy to support their objectives. In order to restore the global economy to a healthy growth trajectory over the medium-term, as well as tackle issues in the social and environmental dimensions of sustainable development, a more balanced policy approach is needed. In addition to a more effective use of fiscal policy, balanced achievement of the SDGs requires moving beyond demand management, to ensure that macroeconomic policy measures are fully integrated with structural reforms and policies that target, for example, poverty, inequality and climate change.

A broader policy toolkit is called for, to be adapted as appropriate to individual country circumstances. For example, structural reforms could encompass a broader use of income policy to tackle inequalities and sustain demand, as well as active labour market policies to support vulnerable or marginalized sectors of the labour market. Effective financial regulation and incentives should mobilize resources and encourage investment in inclusive and resilient infrastructure, social services and green technology. In addition, investment in education, worker training and the research base will promote workforce skills and foster innovation. Policies should encourage a dynamic business environment aligned with sustainable development, including inclusive access to finance, transparent administrative procedures and effective regulatory frameworks.

With domestic resource mobilization limited by structural factors, additional concessional international public financing is needed to support developing countries, especially the LDCs.

Enhancing international policy coordination under the new 2030 Agenda

International coordination is needed to ensure consistency and complementarities among trade policy, investment policy and other public policies and to better align the multilateral trading system with the 2030 Agenda for Sustainable Development, ensuring inclusive growth and decent work for all. These efforts would be supported by a transparent international services market that facilitates the participation of service providers from developing countries in particular. International cooperative efforts are also needed to reduce high trade financing gaps, especially among the poorest countries in Africa, developing Asia, and the small island developing States. To ensure that development concerns are addressed by the global trading system, a stronger role for the World Trade Organization is warranted.

Deeper international cooperation is also needed in many other areas, such as expediting clean technology transfer, supporting climate finance, expanding international public finance and ODA, strengthening international tax cooperation and tackling illicit financial flows, providing a global financial safety net and coordinating policy to address the challenges posed by large movements of refugees and migrants. These issues were recognized at the Hangzhou G20 Summit, where the need for deeper international policy coordination was duly stressed.

Table of contents

Page

Chapter II

International trade

Chapter III

Finance for sustainable development

Chapter IV

Regional developments and outlook

Boxes

Figures

Tables

Statistical annex

Annex tables

Chapter I
Global economic outlook

Prospects for the world economy in 2017–2018

Global growth prospects

In 2016, growth in both world gross product and world trade dropped to their slowest pace since the Great Recession of 2009

The global economy remains trapped in a prolonged period of slow economic growth and dwindling international trade growth. Since 2012, world gross product (WGP) has expanded at an average annual rate of 2.5 per cent, much lower than the average of 3.4 per cent observed in the decade prior to the financial crisis (figure I.1). In 2016, growth in both WGP and world trade dropped to their slowest pace since the Great Recession of 2009. WGP is estimated to have expanded by just 2.2 per cent, reflecting a downward revision of 0.7 percentage points relative to forecasts a year ago (table I.1). The weaker-than-expected growth performances in Japan, the United States of America and in several countries in Africa, the Commonwealth of Independent States (CIS) and Latin America and the Caribbean have contributed to this downward revision relative to forecasts presented in the *World Economic Situation and Prospects* (*WESP*) *2016* (United Nations, 2016a).

The prolonged sluggishness in the global economy has been characterized by a widespread slowdown of productivity growth in many parts of the world, weak investment, low wage growth, low inflation and rising debt levels. Low commodity prices have exacerbated these trends in many commodity-exporting countries since mid-2014, while conflict and geopolitical tensions continue to weigh on economic prospects in several regions.[1]

Sluggish economic growth poses a challenge for the Sustainable Development Goals

While some of the exceptional factors that restrained global growth in 2016 — such as the destocking cycle in the United States and adjustment to the sharp terms-of-trade shock faced by commodity-exporters — can be expected to ease, the longer-term pressures restraining the global economy continue to prevent more robust growth. WGP is forecast to expand by 2.7 per cent in 2017 and 2.9 per cent in 2018, with this modest recovery more a reflection of stabilization in the aftermath of negative short-term shocks than a signal of a dynamic revival of global demand. In per capita terms, this equates to average global growth of just 1.5 per cent per annum in 2016-2018, compared to an average of 2.1 per cent in 1998-2007 (figure I.2). The relatively slow pace of economic growth will hamper progress towards achieving the Sustainable Development Goals (SDGs), as defined in the 2030 Agenda for Sustainable Development, which was adopted by the Member States of the United Nations in 2015. If downside risks to the outlook were to materialize, this could push global growth rates down even further, with additional setbacks towards achieving the SDGs, particularly the goals of eradicating extreme poverty and creating decent work for all.

1 According to the Global Conflict Tracker, conflict in 28 countries was either worsening or unchanged in 2016. In addition to the devastating humanitarian crises, conflict zones and neighbouring regions have suffered heavy economic losses.

Figure I.1
Revision of world gross product forecast since WESP 2016

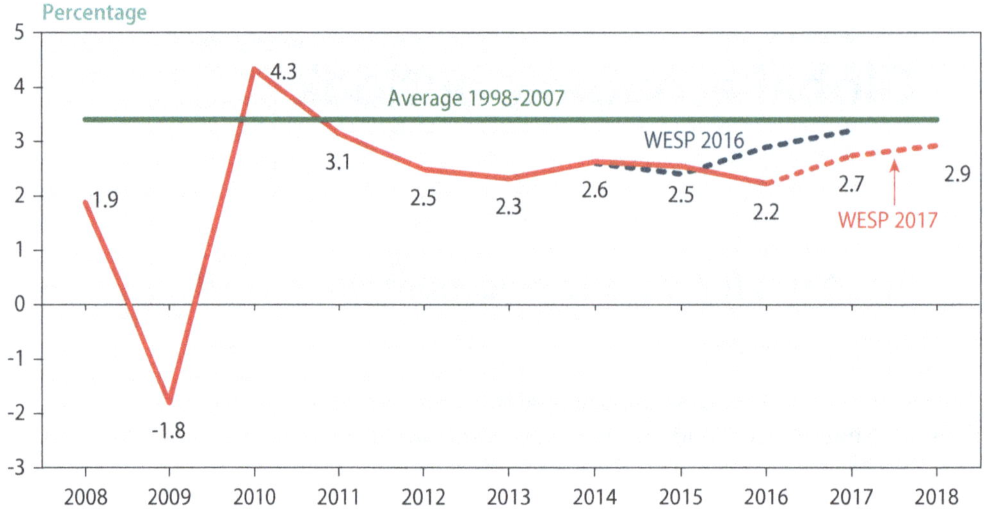

Source: UN/DESA, based on United Nations Statistics Division National Accounts Main Aggregates Database and UN/DESA forecasts.

Figure I.2
Gross domestic product per capita growth by region

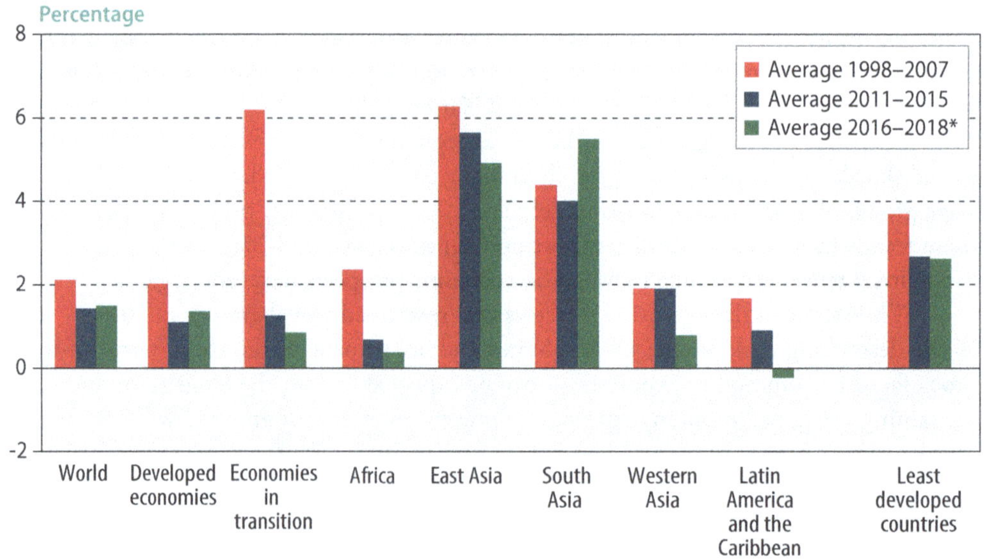

Source: UN/DESA, based on United Nations Statistics Division National Accounts Main Aggregates Database, United Nations Population Division World Population Prospects and UN/DESA forecasts.

* Includes estimates for 2016 and forecasts for 2017-2018.

Factors underpinning sluggish economic growth are self-reinforcing, prolonging the slowdown

The factors underlying the protracted economic slowdown have a tendency to reinforce one another, through the close linkages between demand, investment, trade and productivity. Firms are unlikely to invest in new projects and expand production when demand is weak or expected profits are low. This reluctance has been particularly acute in extractive industries since 2015, as adjustment to the lower level of commodity prices has intensified the weakness in aggregate demand.

Economic and political uncertainties have also weighed on investment demand in many countries, while the nexus between profits and investment has weakened in both developed and developing countries (UNCTAD, 2016a). The declining demand for capital goods associated with weak investment restrains global trade, which in turn curtails

Table I.1
Growth of world output, 2014–2018

Annual percentage change	2014	2015	2016[a]	2017[b]	2018[b]	Change from WESP 2016	
						2016	2017
World	2.6	2.5	2.2	2.7	2.9	-0.7	-0.5
Developed economies	1.7	2.1	1.5	1.7	1.8	-0.7	-0.6
United States of America	2.4	2.6	1.5	1.9	2.0	-1.1	-0.9
Japan	-0.1	0.6	0.5	0.9	0.9	-0.8	0.3
European Union	1.5	2.2	1.8	1.8	1.8	-0.2	-0.4
EU-15	1.4	2.0	1.7	1.6	1.7	-0.3	-0.5
EU-13	2.8	3.6	3.0	3.2	3.3	0.0	0.0
Euro area	1.1	1.9	1.6	1.7	1.7	-0.3	-0.3
Other developed countries	2.5	1.6	1.7	2.0	2.2	-0.4	-0.5
Economies in transition	0.9	-2.8	-0.2	1.4	2.0	-1.0	-0.5
South-Eastern Europe	0.2	2.0	2.6	3.1	3.3	0.0	0.1
Commonwealth of Independent States and Georgia	1.0	-3.0	-0.3	1.4	2.0	-1.0	-0.4
Russian Federation	0.7	-3.7	-0.8	1.0	1.5	-0.8	-0.2
Developing economies	4.3	3.8	3.6	4.4	4.7	-0.7	-0.4
Africa	3.8	3.1	1.7	3.2	3.8	-2.7	-1.2
North Africa	1.8	3.2	2.6	3.5	3.6	-1.5	-0.6
East Africa	7.0	6.6	5.5	6.0	6.3	-1.3	-0.6
Central Africa	5.4	1.5	2.4	3.4	4.2	-1.9	-0.8
West Africa	6.1	3.2	0.1	3.1	4.1	-5.1	-2.2
Southern Africa	2.7	1.9	1.0	1.8	2.6	-2.0	-1.5
East and South Asia	6.1	5.7	5.7	5.9	5.9	-0.1	0.1
East Asia	6.1	5.7	5.5	5.6	5.6	-0.1	0.0
China	7.3	6.9	6.6	6.5	6.5	0.2	0.0
South Asia	6.2	6.0	6.7	6.9	6.9	0.0	-0.1
India[c]	7.3	7.3	7.6	7.7	7.6	0.2	0.2
Western Asia	2.6	2.7	2.1	2.5	3.0	-0.3	-0.5
Latin America and the Caribbean	0.7	-0.6	-1.0	1.3	2.1	-1.7	-1.4
South America	0.1	-1.9	-2.3	0.9	2.0	-2.2	-1.5
Brazil	0.1	-3.9	-3.2	0.6	1.6	-2.4	-1.7
Mexico and Central America	2.5	2.7	2.3	2.3	2.2	-0.6	-1.1
Caribbean	3.1	4.0	2.7	2.7	2.8	-0.9	-0.6
Least developed countries	5.7	3.7	4.5	5.2	5.5	-1.1	-0.4
Memorandum items							
World trade[d]	3.8	2.6	1.2	2.7	3.3	-2.8	-2.0
World output growth with PPP weights[e]	3.3	3.1	2.9	3.5	3.7	-0.7	-0.4

Source: UN/DESA.
a Estimated.
b Forecast, based in part on Project LINK.
c Fiscal year basis.
d Includes goods and services.
e Based on 2012 benchmark.

investment further. Meanwhile, the extended period of weak investment is a driving factor behind the more medium-term phenomenon of a slowdown in productivity growth. Weaker productivity growth may be compounded by the broad slowdown in global trade growth, as international trade, supported by a universal, rules-based, open, non-discriminatory and equitable multilateral trading system, has the potential to speed the rate of technological diffusion between countries and improve the efficiency of resource allocation. Weak productivity growth has also curbed wages and progress in poverty reduction, aggravating the slowdown in aggregate demand. In the absence of concerted policy efforts to revive productive investment and foster a recovery in productivity, there is a risk that the protracted episode of weak global growth may linger for several more years.

Policy uncertainty in the United States and Europe has widened the confidence bounds around global economic forecasts

Stable private consumption will remain the mainstay of growth in the developed economies (figure I.3). The slight increase in gross domestic product (GDP) growth that is forecast for 2017 is driven primarily by the end of the destocking cycle in the United States and additional policy support in Japan, including an expansion of government investment spending. Uncertainty related to the withdrawal of the United Kingdom of Great Britain and Northern Ireland from the European Union (EU) has led to downward revisions to growth forecasts for the United Kingdom and several other countries in Europe in 2017. Meanwhile, the lack of clarity about the future direction of policy in the United States, with potentially far-reaching spillover effects on both domestic and global economic prospects, has increased the margin of uncertainty around global baseline forecasts.

The economic downturn in Brazil may have turned a corner

GDP growth in developing countries, especially in East and South Asia, is expected to remain driven by domestic consumption. China's expansion is expected to remain stable, supported by the strong policy stance, but the rebalancing of the economy continues to weigh on global trade flows. India is expected to remain the fastest growing large developing economy, as the country benefits from strong private consumption and the gradual introduction of significant domestic reforms. The downturn in Brazil may have turned a corner, following the sharp decline in output in 2015 and 2016. Political uncertainty in Brazil has declined and the foundations of a programme for macro-management have been introduced. However, high unemployment and a relatively tight fiscal policy stance will

Figure I.3
Projected contributions to GDP growth, 2016–2018

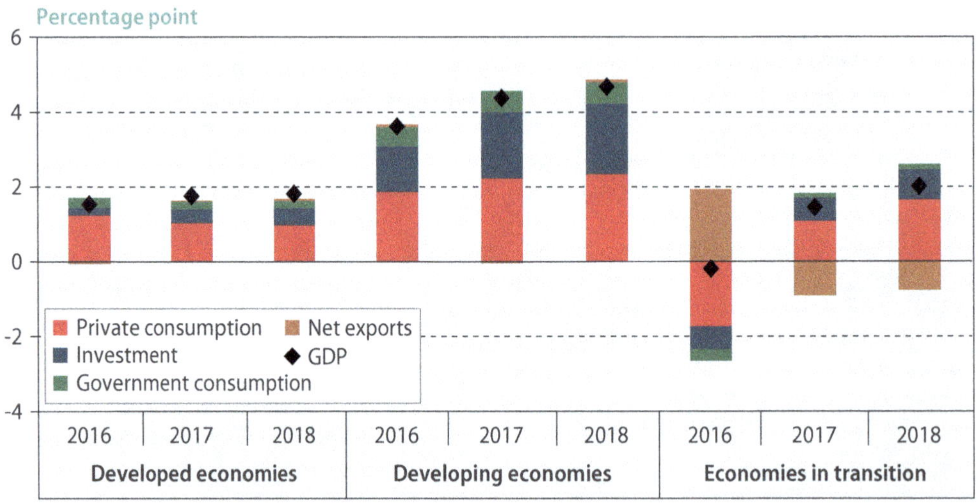

Source: UN/DESA forecasts.

continue to weigh on the economy. Meanwhile, growth in the least developed countries (LDCs) is expected to rise modestly from an estimated 4.5 per cent in 2016 to 5.2 per cent and 5.5 per cent in 2017 and 2018, respectively (box I.1).

Box I.1

Prospects for the least developed countries

Aggregate growth in the LDCs will remain well below the Sustainable Development Goal (SDG) target of "at least 7 per cent GDP growth" in the near term, but is expected to rise modestly from an estimated 4.5 per cent in 2016 to 5.2 per cent and 5.5 per cent in 2017 and 2018, respectively, with the rise in per capita GDP averaging just 2.6 per cent between 2016 and 2018. The below-target growth poses a risk to critical public expenditure on healthcare, education, social protection and climate change, which may in turn constrain improvements in living standards and limit progress on poverty reduction.

Among the LDCs, growth performance varies significantly. Fuel and metal exporters have been adversely affected by persistently low global commodity prices, and the loss of commodity-related revenue has induced significant deterioration in the fiscal balance of countries such as Angola, the Democratic Republic of the Congo, Equatorial Guinea, Mozambique and Zambia. Rising inflationary pressures, fueled in part by weaker domestic currencies, have also weighed on private consumption and business investment in these economies. For Angola, where oil accounts for almost 95 per cent of its total exports, growth decelerated to 0.8 per cent in 2016 and is expected to only improve modestly to 1.8 per cent in 2017.

Growth in many LDCs also remains highly vulnerable to natural catastrophes and weather-related shocks. In 2016, LDCs in the East and Southern African regions, including Ethiopia, Lesotho, Malawi and Uganda, experienced the worst drought in decades, dampening agriculture production and overall growth. A prolonged and severe drought also hit agriculture output in Haiti, where the economy also remains constrained by political uncertainty and institutional weaknesses. Meanwhile, the Nepalese economy is still recovering from the aftermath of the devastating earthquake of 2015. Amid ongoing reconstruction efforts, growth in Nepal strengthened in the second half of 2016 and is forecast to exceed 4.0 per cent in 2018.

A few LDCs are expected to achieve a growth rate close to or above the 7 per cent target in 2017-2018, including Bangladesh, Bhutan, Cambodia, Djibouti, Ethiopia, Lao People's Democratic Republic, Myanmar, Rwanda and the United Republic of Tanzania. Myanmar is set to be the fastest growing LDC, with a projected expansion of 8.0 per cent in 2017, supported by accommodative monetary and fiscal policies, as well as the implementation of growth enhancing reforms. Growth in Bangladesh is likely to remain robust at 6.8 per cent in 2017 and 6.6 per cent in 2018, driven by buoyant domestic demand and a more proactive fiscal stance. As the impact of drought dissipates, growth in Ethiopia is expected to rebound to above 7.0 per cent in 2017 and 2018, supported by investment to improve power supply, and the recent completion of a cross-border railway connecting Ethiopia and Djibouti, where growth is forecast to average 6.8 per cent in 2017-2018. Strong infrastructure investment, particularly in the energy and transport sectors, is also supporting growth in Cambodia, the Lao People's Democratic Republic, Rwanda and the United Republic of Tanzania.

For many LDCs, weak productivity growth, amid poorly diversified economic structures and insufficient levels of investment, remains a challenge to achieving stronger medium-term growth prospects. If the current pattern continues, related shortfalls in essential investment also put at risk many other economic, social and environmental targets set in the SDGs.

Figure I.1.1 decomposes the medium-term projections for GDP growth in a selection of LDCs into the expected average annual contributions from labour input growth and labour productivity growth over the period 2015-2030.

Productivity growth in most countries is expected to fall well short of what is needed to achieve the targeted level of GDP growth in the LDCs. Tackling the shortfall in productivity growth will require an increase in the rate of investment in order to upgrade the existing capital stock and increase the available capital per worker in the economy.[a] A model simulation exercise to assess the magnitude of additional investment needed to close the productivity gaps, and approach an average GDP growth rate of 7 per cent per annum in the LDCs, suggests that investment growth in the LDCs as a whole would need to average 11.3 per cent per annum through 2030, an increase of roughly 3 percentage points relative to

a See discussion in United Nations (2016b).

(continued)

Box I.1 (*continued*)

baseline projections. While this exceeds the average rate of investment growth of 8.9 per cent recorded between 2010 and 2015, it is in line with the investment rate recorded during the period of rapid growth of 2000-2005, when GDP growth in the LDCs as a whole averaged 6.8 per cent per annum. However, the external environment is expected to be much less supportive to growth in the LDCs than it was in 2000-2005, when export growth for the group averaged 6.5 per cent per annum.

Figure I.1.1

Decomposition of average annual GDP growth projections, 2015–2030

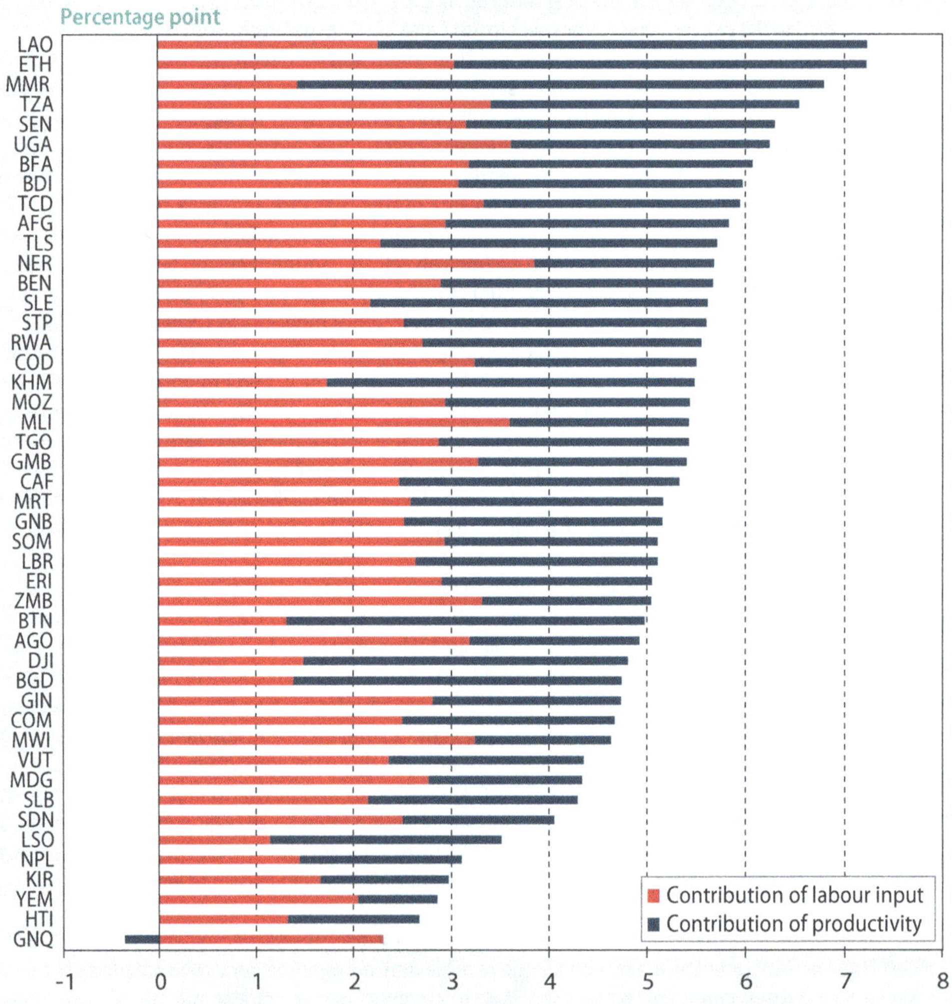

Source: UN/DESA forecasts.
Note: See Table J in the Statistical Annex for definitions of country codes.

Figure I.1.2 illustrates the expected rate of convergence in GDP per capita between the LDCs and the developed economies under two different scenarios. The baseline scenario represents prospects according to the current forecast, which sees GDP growth in the LDCs averaging 5.2 per cent per annum to 2030. At this rate of growth, GDP per capita can only be expected to converge marginally towards average levels in the developed economies, rising from just 2 per cent of the developed economy average in 2015 to just under 2.5 per cent in 2030.

If, on the other hand, the shortfalls in productivity growth could be closed through an acceleration in investment, there would be a more rapid pace of convergence. This would allow GDP per capita in the LDC to rise from 2 per cent of the developed country average in 2015 to 3 per cent by 2030.

(*continued*)

Box I.1 (*continued*)

Garnering the financial resources required to finance the necessary investment to put the LDCs on a more rapid growth path remains a key challenge for achieving the SDGs. With private financing and domestic resource mobilisation limited by structural factors, additional concessional international public financing may be needed to close this financing gap (see Chapter III for further discussion of sources of finance).

Authors: Dawn Holland and Poh Lynn Ng

Figure I.1.2
GDP per capita in LDCs relative to developed country average, 1995–2030

Source: UN/DESA forecast and World Economic Forecasting Model (WEFM) scenarios.

Russian Federation to register positive growth in 2017

The economies in transition suffered a sharp collapse in domestic demand in the CIS region in 2016, while net trade made a positive contribution to GDP growth, reflecting the impact of lower imports as a result of steep exchange rate realignments in several countries. In 2017, the economy of the Russian Federation is expected to register its first year of growth since 2014, as the country has largely absorbed the sharp terms-of-trade shock suffered in 2014-2015 (see Chapter IV for more detailed discussion of regional prospects).

Downside risks could undermine any projected recovery in business investment, impede international trade growth and prolong the self-propagating cycle of weak global growth

Global economic prospects remain subject to significant downside risks, with the potential to obstruct the modest acceleration in growth that is currently forecast for 2017-2018. Considerable uncertainty shrouds both the path and impact of monetary policy actions in major developed economies. The effects of introducing untested monetary policy instruments — such as the negative interest rate policies in Japan and Europe — remains unclear, with a risk of unintended consequences, such as a deterioration of bank balance sheets and tightening of credit conditions, which could destabilize fragile and undercapitalized banks.

While the path of policy interest rates in the United States remains unclear, interest rate differentials relative to other developed economies are expected to widen, potentially triggering financial volatility, capital outflows from developing economies and abrupt adjustments in exchange rates. The future direction of certain international policy stances is uncertain. There is a lack of clarity over the shape and timing of future changes by the new Administration of the United States to crucial policies in international trade, immigration, and climate change. The decision by the United Kingdom to leave the EU, or "Brexit", and its potential implications for the free movement of goods and workers in Europe, also poses considerable regional uncertainty.

Finally, risks facing developing countries include vulnerabilities associated with high levels of debt and rising default rates in a number of countries, with the potential to push up borrowing costs, raise deleveraging pressures and increase banking sector stress. Such risks are exacerbated by the volatility of international capital flows. All of these uncertainties have the potential to undermine any projected recovery in business investment, impede international trade growth and prolong the self-propagating cycle of weak global growth.

Inflation prospects

Inflation is low in most countries, but exceeds official targets in parts of Africa, South America and the CIS

In 2016, average global inflation edged up slightly to an estimated rate of 2.4 per cent from 2.1 per cent in 2015, which was the lowest level registered since the global financial crisis.[2] Inflation in the developed economies remained below 1 per cent, reflecting the impact of the drop in global energy prices, persistently weak wage growth and the generally high level of economic slack. Inflation forecasts for both the EU and Japan have undergone significant downward revisions in the last 12 months, and both economies dipped back into deflation in the first half of 2016. The low level of inflation is broad-based across developed economies, and also prevalent in many developing countries in Asia.

Figure I.4 compares estimated consumer price inflation to central bank targets for inflation in 2016.[3] More than two-thirds of the countries in the sample are experiencing inflation rates below their targeted level. The countries exceeding official inflation targets are predominantly in Africa, while a few countries in South America and the CIS are also experiencing high inflation relative to targets. Higher inflation in these regions largely reflects the impact of currency depreciations, and in some cases food price spikes related to El Niño.

Oil price will put upward pressure on inflation in 2017

By the end of 2016, the contribution of the oil price to year-on-year inflation reached a turning point, and will have a significant upward impact on inflation in most countries in early 2017 (figure I.5). The spike in inflation driven by the oil price is likely to be short-lived, and the impact on headline inflation and wages is likely to remain contained in most coun-

Figure I.4
Inflation relative to central bank target in 2016

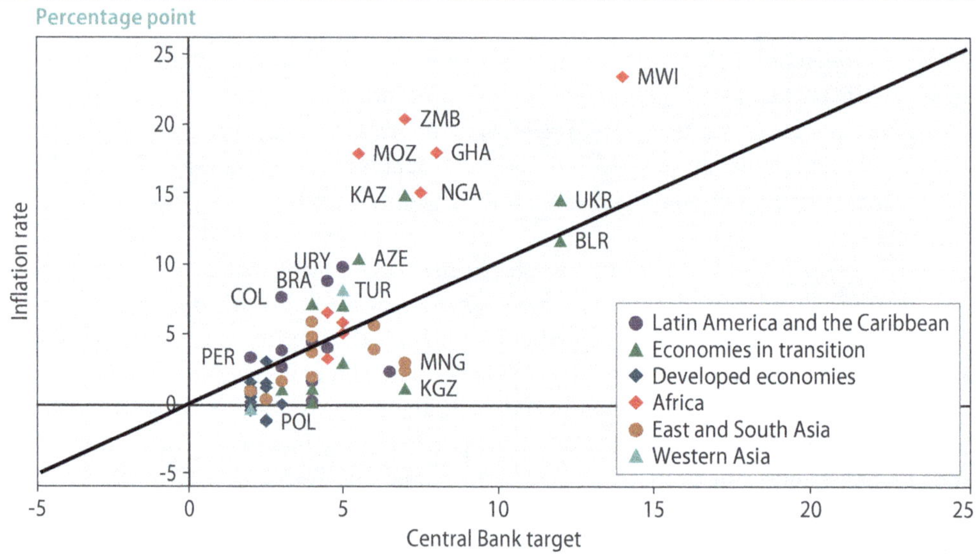

Source: Central Bank News, UN/DESA estimates for inflation.
Note: See Table J in the Statistical Annex for definitions of country codes.

2 Aggregate figures for inflation reported throughout this report are weighted averages based on GDP in 2010, denominated in US dollars. They exclude Venezuela (Bolivarian Republic of), due to the distortionary impacts of very high inflation in a single country.

3 The sample only includes countries that have an explicit or implicit target rate for inflation.

Figure I.5
Price of Brent crude, January 2014–December 2018

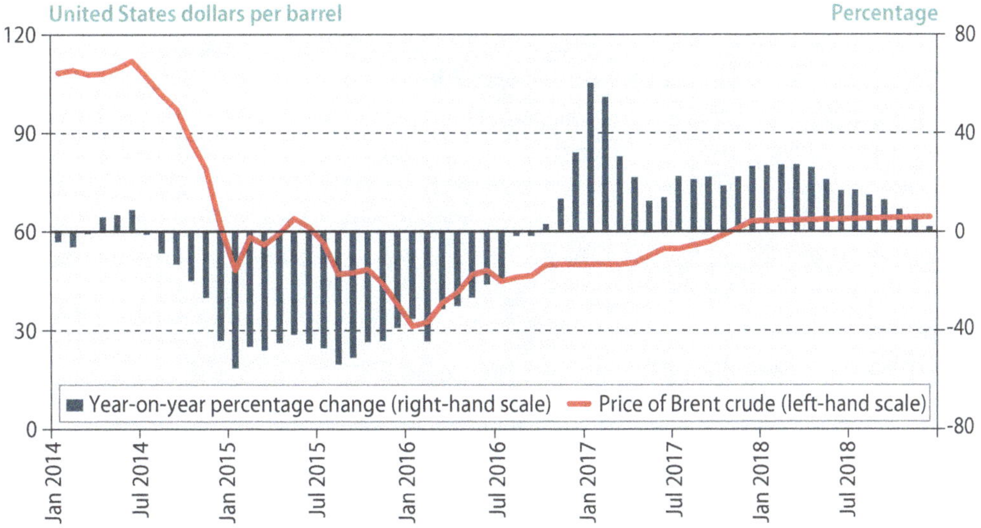

Source: US. Energy Information Administration retrieved from FRED and UN/DESA projections.

tries. However, if there is a more sustained pass-through, inflation could rise above target in more countries in 2017, which may in turn prompt a more significant rise in interest rates than currently expected.

Employment and labour productivity

More than 27 million additional people are unemployed today compared to before the financial crisis

The protracted period of weak global growth has also impacted employment, wages and household welfare, leading to a slowdown in household consumption growth. At the global level, growth in household consumption has averaged 2.2 per cent per annum since 2012, compared to an annual average of 3.3 per cent in the decade prior to the global financial crisis, exhibiting a marked slowdown despite the greater resilience of consumer spending relative to other components of demand. According to estimates by the International Labour Organization (ILO), there are over 27 million more unemployed people today than before the financial crisis, an increase of about 0.5 per cent of the working age population (ILO, 2016).

While the unemployment rates in some large developed countries, including Germany, Japan, the United Kingdom and the United States, have receded towards or below pre-crisis levels, most other members of the EU continue to struggle with high unemployment rates. Unemployment rates are generally low in East Asia, but rising unemployment in parts of South America, including Argentina, Brazil and Colombia, is raising concerns. Western Asia also suffers high unemployment, particularly among youth.

Youth unemployment is a global concern, with significant longer-term social and economic costs

Youth unemployment is a widespread global concern, impeding progress towards the SDGs. In 2016, 35 per cent of unemployed people globally were aged 15-24, although this cohort represents only 15 per cent of the world's labour force. Youth unemployment remains high in Western Asia, and it is rising in Latin America and the Caribbean, as well as in parts of the CIS and South-Eastern Asia. High levels of youth unemployment can have significant longer-term social and economic costs, resulting in labour force withdrawal, outward migration, disincentives to pursue education and social unrest.

Job security is also a widespread global concern. Vulnerable employment — defined as own-account work and contributing family employment, which are typically subject to low levels of job security and volatile income – accounts for 46 per cent of employed people worldwide, and is especially high in South Asia and many parts of Africa.

Wage growth is weak, including in countries where the unemployment rate is low

Nominal wage increases in most developed economies have slowed since the financial crisis. The incidence is widespread, including in countries where the unemployment rate is low. Despite low headline inflation, real wages have been stagnant or declining in many countries, and have for the most part lagged behind productivity growth. This is illustrated in figure I.6, where two-thirds of the developed countries in the sample have seen smaller gains in real wages than in productivity since the financial crisis. This is a reflection of the quality of jobs that have been created over this period, which have been dominated by low quality, low paid jobs, and a rise in the incidence of part-time and temporary contracts.

Figure I.6
Average annual labour productivity and real wage growth, 2008–2015

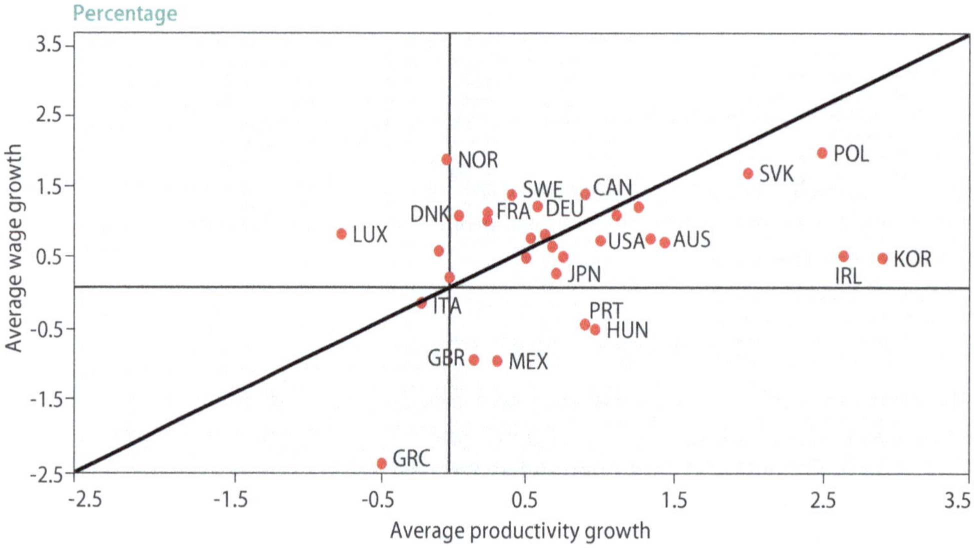

Source: UN/DESA, based on data from OECDStat.
Note: See Table J in the Statistical Annex for definitions of country codes.

Labour productivity growth has slowed markedly in most developed economies, and in many large developing and transition economies

Labour productivity growth in the majority of developed economies has slowed markedly since the global financial crisis, with an even more pronounced slowdown in real wages. Many large developing economies and those in transition have also experienced a significant decline in labour productivity growth, including Brazil, China, the Russian Federation and South Africa. GDP growth can be decomposed into the contribution from growth in labour inputs and the contribution from growth in labour productivity.

In terms of welfare, the input of labour productivity to GDP growth is particularly important. Changes to labour inputs are largely driven by demographic developments, although they may also reflect shifts in labour force participation, the average number of hours worked and shifts in the unemployment rate. If GDP growth is spurred entirely by a rise in labour from an expanded population, income per capita remains stagnant. Therefore, in order to raise average incomes in the economy, labour productivity growth is essential. This growth may need to be supported by policies to ensure that the benefits are more equitably shared, as evidenced by the recent tendency for real wages to lag behind productivity growth. The links between productivity growth, decent wages and reduction of poverty are recognized in the 2030 Agenda for Sustainable Development, which underscores the importance of generating full employment and decent work for all.

Figures I.7 and I.8 parse average GDP growth in the largest economies by contributions from labour input and from labour productivity, which is further broken down into contributions from the capital intensity of production (capital deepening) and total factor productivity (TFP).

Figure I.7
Decomposition of average annual GDP growth in major developed economies

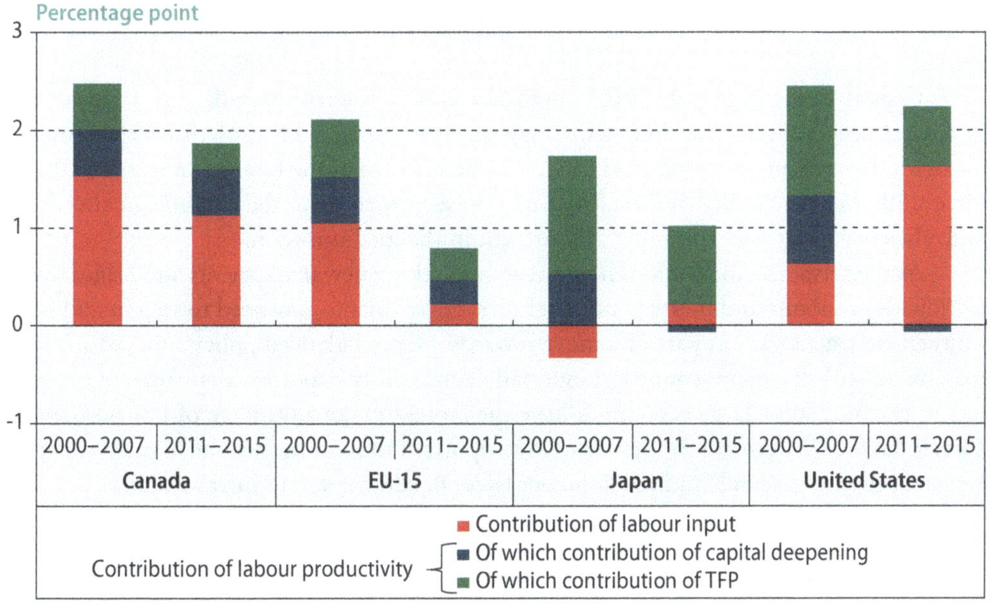

Source: UN/DESA derived from OECDStat, Annual macro-economic database of the European Commission's Directorate General for Economic and Financial Affairs and United Nations Statistics Division National Accounts Main Aggregates Database.

Figure I.8
Decomposition of average annual GDP growth in major developing economies and economies in transition

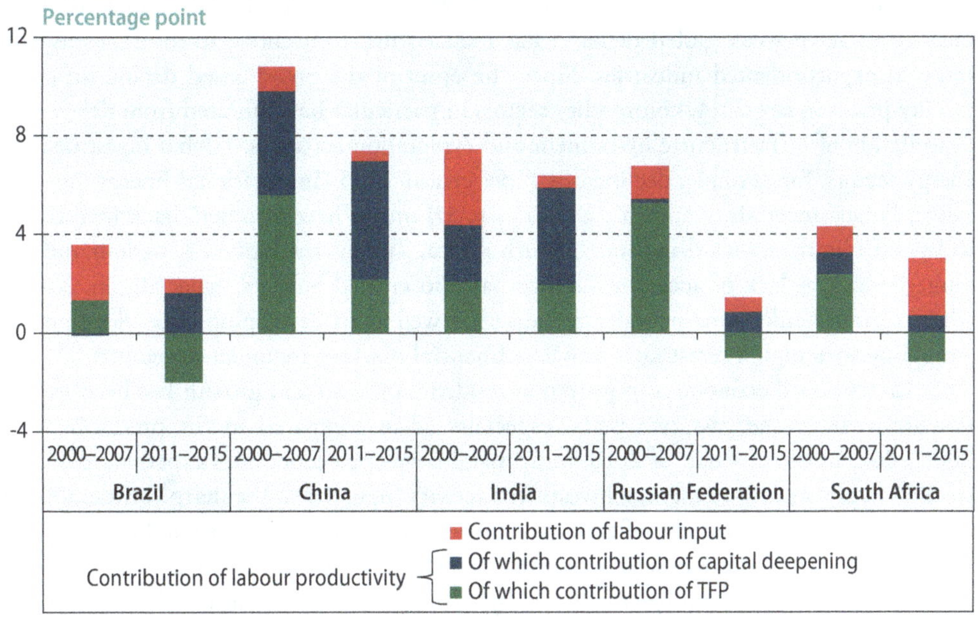

Source: UN/DESA derived from Penn World Tables 9.0 retrieved from FRED, The Conference Board Total Economy Database and United Nations Statistics Division National Accounts Main Aggregates Database.

Germany, Japan and the United States have undergone a period of 'capital shallowing', reflecting a collapse in investment growth

In the large developing and transition countries, the falling contribution of productivity to GDP growth is primarily attributable to a decline in TFP growth, whereas the slowdown in labour productivity growth in the major developed economies has been also driven by the very low rate of capital deepening. Germany, Japan and the United States have, in fact, undergone a period of 'capital shallowing' since 2011, as the volume of productive capital stock per hour of labour input has actually declined. This is indicative of the collapse in investment growth in developed economies post-crisis, which has allowed the existing capital stock to decay. The widespread slump in capital deepening in developed economies reflects low rates of both private and public investment, as discussed in the next section.

Investment in R&D, education and infrastructure is essential to support productivity growth in the medium term

Capital deepening and TFP growth are closely interconnected, and a slowdown in capital deepening in the short-term may presage weaker TFP growth over the medium-term. Investment in new capital can affect factors such as the rate of innovation, labour force skills and the quality of infrastructure. These in turn drive the technological change and efficiency gains underpinning TFP growth in the medium-term.

As the private sector remains hesitant about making new investments amid significant worldwide economic and political uncertainties, governments may need to step in and help fill the investment gaps as part of a move towards a more balanced policy mix. While this may be difficult for many countries, especially commodity exporters that suffered a sharp loss of revenue, some large economies have the scope to take advantage of low borrowing costs to finance investment. It is particularly important to stem the decline in investment in key areas such as research and development (R&D), education and infrastructure.

Investment

Weak investment underpins the sluggish global economy, through its close linkages with demand, productivity and international trade

Weak investment has been at the foundation of the mediocre global economy, through its interplay with demand, productivity and international trade. The contribution of investment to global growth has declined from an average of 1.4 percentage points per annum in 2003-2007 to 0.7 percentage points per annum since 2012.

Since late-2014, commodity sectors, in particular, have experienced declining investment

Both global and country-specific factors have contributed to the weakening of investment. Protracted weak global demand has reduced firms' incentive to invest, especially those in export-oriented industries. Since the onset of the broad-based decline in commodity prices in late-2014, commodity sectors in particular have suffered from delays and cancellation of infrastructure investment and exploration activities. Global investment in energy sectors, for example, declined by 8 per cent in 2015 (International Energy Agency, 2016). Policy uncertainty and in some cases social unrest have also held back investment in several countries, including Brazil, South Africa, Turkey, the United Kingdom and the United States. A lack of access to finance has also created barriers, especially in Europe where certain banks remain undercapitalised as well as in developing countries that are struggling with high interest rates or where financial markets are under-developed.

Contractions in investment in extractive industries do not necessarily signal progress towards a less fossil fuel-intensive economy

In developed economies, private non-residential investment growth has been exceptionally weak in the past two years, especially when compared to the pre-crisis years 2005-2007. In the first half of 2016, most major developed economies experienced a contraction in private non-residential investment activity (figure I.9). The sharp contractions in Australia and Canada largely reflect large cutbacks in mining-related capital expenditure, while the United States has seen a significant decline in investment in the shale-oil sector. These declines have not been matched by a commensurate expansion of investment in renewable energy, and are likely to prove temporary, rather than signal significant structural progress towards a less fossil fuel-intensive economy.

In the United States, in particular, an expansion of investment in fossil fuel industries would be expected in 2017, should the new Administration lift certain environmental restrictions on production in the shale, oil, natural gas and clean coal sectors, risking setbacks to environmental targets in the SDGs and the Paris Agreement on climate change.

Investment in manufacturing sectors in Japan and the United States has been discouraged by the strength of their currencies, which is suppressing exports and the earnings of companies operating abroad. Private investment growth in France and Germany has seen more resilience, reflecting modest improvement in the euro area. However, the heightened levels of uncertainty following the Brexit vote in June 2016 may have restrained investment in Europe in the second half of 2016.

Figure I.9

Average year-on-year change in private non-residential investment in developed economies *(constant prices)*

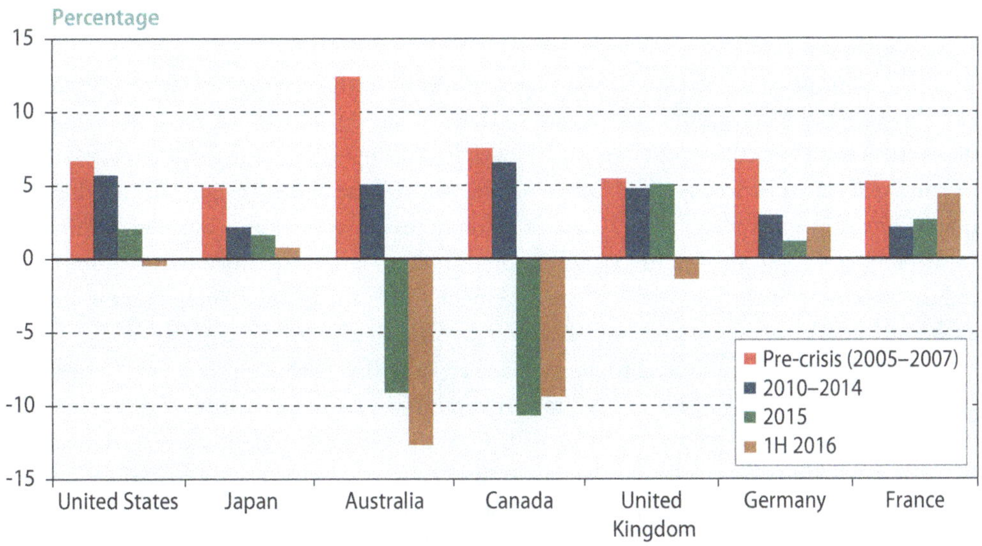

Source: National statistics offices.

Public sector investment has contracted significantly in many developed countries since 2010

Despite record-low, often negative bond yields, Governments in developed countries have been reluctant to increase public sector investments to fill the gap in private investment. Steep cuts in government investment largely reflect fiscal adjustment policies that have been implemented in many developed economies since 2010 in response to soaring levels of government debt (figure I.10). In recent quarters, Australia, France, Germany and the United States have experienced some recovery in public investment, although the ratio of public investment to GDP remains low. Fiscal stimulus programmes in Canada and Japan will revive government investment in 2017, while policy measures in Australia are expected to stem the decline in investment by small and medium-sized businesses, which will support a modest increase in the contribution of investment to GDP growth in the forecast period. While the policy outlook for the United States remains highly uncertain, proposals to boost infrastructure spending would support a revival of investment in the fiscal year starting October 2017 if implemented.

Figure I.10
Average annual change in general government investment (*constant prices*), **2011–2015**

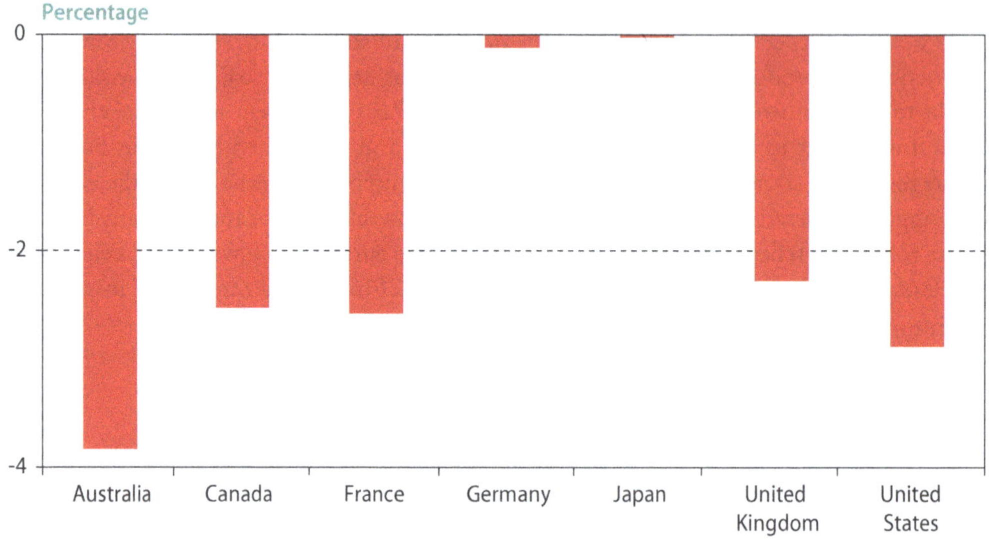

Source: OECD Quarterly National Accounts, National statistics offices.

Investment growth has also slowed notably in many developing countries and economies in transition

In major developing countries and economies in transition, investment growth has also slowed notably in recent years (figure I.11). As in developed economies, a sharp decline in investment in the commodity sector has weighed on investment growth, particularly in Brazil, the Russian Federation and South Africa. In the Russian Federation, the decline also reflects the impact of international sanctions on access to capital and business sentiment. In the case of China, weaker investment growth reflects large overcapacity in a number of industrial sectors, including iron and steel, cement and even the solar energy sector, as well as sluggish market demand and higher corporate financing costs.

Policy shifts and elevated financial market volatility, including large exchange rate depreciations, have led to greater investor uncertainty in several countries. For example in Nigeria, the currency peg removal in June 2016 resulted in a sharp depreciation of the naira of more than 40 per cent, with a consequent impact on investment. In some other parts of Africa, however, investment remains more robust, reflecting major infrastructure projects and structural policies to improve the domestic business climate.

Government investment in infrastructure has offset weaker private sector investment in several countries in Africa and East and South Asia

Slower investment growth in major developing economies has been largely driven by the private sector. In line with their greater scope to exploit fiscal space, East Asian and South Asian economies have generally seen stronger growth in public investment, especially in infrastructure. State-owned enterprises have expanded infrastructure investment in China, while in India public investment has also been critical to avoid a further deterioration in investment growth. Growth in some of the smaller economies in South-Eastern Europe and Central America has also been supported by large public sector investments in infrastructure. However, public investment has fallen considerably in many of the commodity-reliant economies, including Brazil and the Russian Federation, as well as several other economies in the CIS, South America and Western Asia.

High corporate debt burdens may increase risks of debt distress in some developing countries

The slowdown in private sector investment growth in many developing economies raises some concerns, as it suggests that the significant increases in corporate debt burdens, particularly in East Asia, have failed to deliver a comparable increase in productive capital stock. Going forward, these high debt burdens may begin to restrain access to finance or

Figure I.11
Average year-on-year change in gross fixed capital formation in developing and transition economies (*constant prices*)

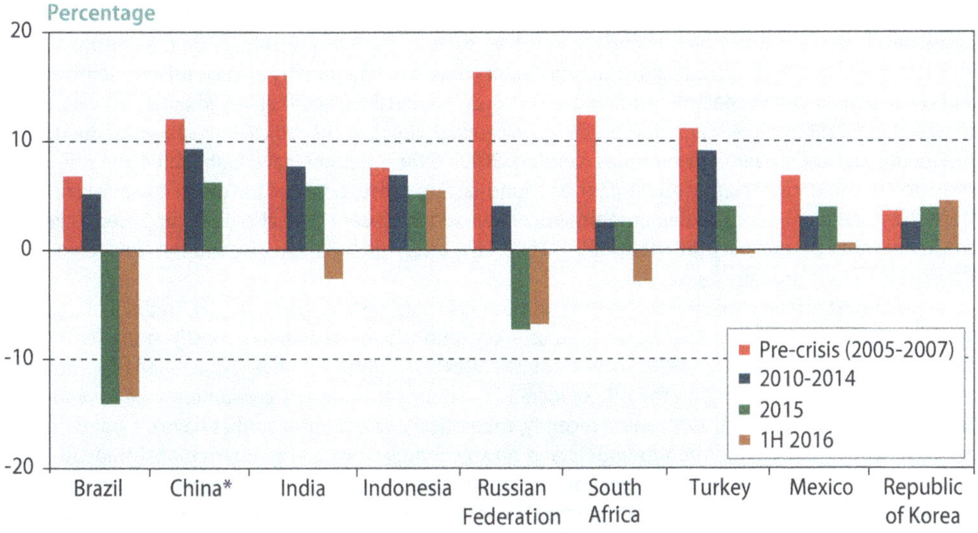

Source: OECD Quarterly National Accounts, United Nations Statistics Division National Accounts Main Aggregates Database.
* Data for 1H 2016 is not available.

prompt firm deleveraging, perpetuating the slowdown in investment growth, and may also increase the risks of debt distress and financial instability in some developing countries.

Trade, capital flows and remittances

International trade flows

Dwindling world trade growth is both a contributing factor and a symptom of the global economic slowdown. Trade and investment are strongly interconnected and mutually reinforcing. The current weak investment trends in major developed and developing economies have constrained trade in capital goods, while at the same time, the weakness in trade is propagating and reinforcing the slump in investment, especially in other export-oriented sectors. There may also be spillovers from weak global trade to productivity, especially in developing countries (box I.2).

Dwindling world trade growth is both a contributing factor and a symptom of the global economic slowdown

The 2030 Agenda for Sustainable Development recognizes the important role of trade as an engine of inclusive and sustainable growth (e.g. SDG 17 calls for significantly increasing the exports of developing countries). The appropriate design of policies to support these objectives requires an understanding of the factors behind the slowdown in world trade growth, distinguishing between temporary cyclical factors and more permanent structural factors.

While global trade growth has been volatile over the past four decades, the prolonged downturn is exceptional, suggesting that not only cyclical factors are at play. The volume of world trade in goods and services is estimated to have expanded by just 1.2 per cent in 2016, the slowest growth rate since the financial crisis, marking a significant downward revision of nearly 3 percentage points compared to projections in the WESP 2016. In first half of 2016, world merchandise trade virtually stagnated, continuing the downward trend — both in historical terms and also relative to GDP growth — of international trade growth observed

World trade volumes expanded by just 1.2 per cent in 2016, the third-lowest rate in the past 30 years

Box I.2

The slowdown in productivity growth: a view from international trade

Despite measurement concerns, there is a growing consensus that productivity growth has slowed down across developed and developing countries. However, there is much less unanimity on the reasons behind this trend, and both cyclical and structural factors have been suggested as main drivers. Some authors have argued that the pace of technological progress has declined and that incremental innovations observed in recent decades have smaller effects on productivity than the radical innovations of the late nineteenth and early twentieth centuries (Gordon, 2012). Others authors have highlighted the role of weak demand and lower capital investment, as a long-lasting consequence of the global financial crisis. More structural factors such as demography, education and inequality have also been proposed as key drivers for lower productivity growth (OECD, 2015a). Less attention has been given to the slowdown in international trade growth as a cause.

In the last fifteen years, the analysis of international trade has changed radically. Traditional trade theories emphasized comparative advantages as a key rationale for trade flows, mostly in the form of inter-industry trade. Since the 1980s, new trade theories have given intuitive explanations for intra-industry trade flows, focusing on the role of increasing returns to scale and consumers' love for variety (Krugman, 1981; Helpman, 1981). More recently, theoretical and empirical studies have included firm heterogeneity as a key dimension to understand how economies respond to international trade (Bernard and others, 2011). The seminal model by Melitz (2003) shows how firm heterogeneity, even within narrowly defined industries, affects aggregate outcomes, including productivity growth, when trade barriers diminish or transportation costs fall. This model is key. In particular, high-productivity exporting firms survive and expand, while low-productivity non-exporting firms shrink or exit, leading to within-industry productivity gains. Furthermore, the increase in operational scale in foreign markets leads to investments in technology and innovation. Firms specialize by adjusting the extensive margins of products and destinations (Melitz and Redding, 2015). This reallocation of resources related to international trade raises aggregate productivity.

The current subdued export flows and slowing pace of trade liberalization are constraining productivity growth. Exports can boost productivity growth by creating economies of scale and introducing new production techniques, inputs and product designs from international contacts. Empirical evidence for countries such as Canada, Chile, India, Slovenia and many economies in Africa has supported this causal link (Lileeva, 2008; Van Biesebroeck, 2006; De Loecker, 2007; Alvarez and Lopez, 2005 and Mukim, 2011).

An aggregate analysis at country level also illustrates this relationship. Figure I.2.1 displays labour productivity growth and export gains for developed and emerging economies during 2003-2007 and 2013-2015. Noticeably, the data illustrates a positive correlation between export and labour productivity growth within countries. In addition, the period between 2013 and 2015 is characterized by lower productivity and export growth in most developed countries and emerging economies.

In addition to the export channel, the slowing pace of trade liberalization, coupled with the rising protectionist measures recently, also restrain productivity growth. Trade liberalization is associated with productivity gains from variety and economies of scale, resource reallocation within industries and from exporters innovating for a larger market (Melitz and Trefler, 2012; Alvarez and Vergara, 2010; Bustos, 2011; Amiti and Konings, 2007). However, trade liberalization usually entails a significant exit of firms and worker displacements. The reallocation of resources can encounter huge difficulties, as experienced in some African and Latin American countries during the 1980s.

The dynamics of trade are closely connected to investment behaviour. A firm's decision whether to enter or expand in foreign markets is ultimately made jointly with its decisions on investment, technology, product-mix and R&D (Lileeva and Trefler, 2010). At the firm level, productivity growth arises from a number of decisions taken jointly with trade participation (Aw and others, 2011; Bustos, 2011; and Bloom and others, 2011).

(continued)

Box I.2 (*continued*)

Country-level analysis also illustrates the relationship between investment and productivity growth. Figure I.2.2 depicts the growth of labour productivity and of private investment for developed countries and emerging economies during 2003-2007 and 2013-2015. There is a positive correlation between labour productivity gain and private investment growth within countries. In addition, between 2013 and 2015, most developed countries and emerging economies have seen significantly lower growth of both productivity and investment than in the period before the financial crisis.

Recent theoretical and empirical studies on international trade and heterogeneous firms offer interesting insights to understand the productivity slowdown. Subdued global trade and weak investment, together with the slowing pace of trade liberalization, are constraining productivity growth, highlighting some of the self-propagating forces behind slow global growth.

Author: Sebastian Vergara

Figure I.2.1

Growth of labour productivity and growth of exports, 2003–2007 and 2013–2015

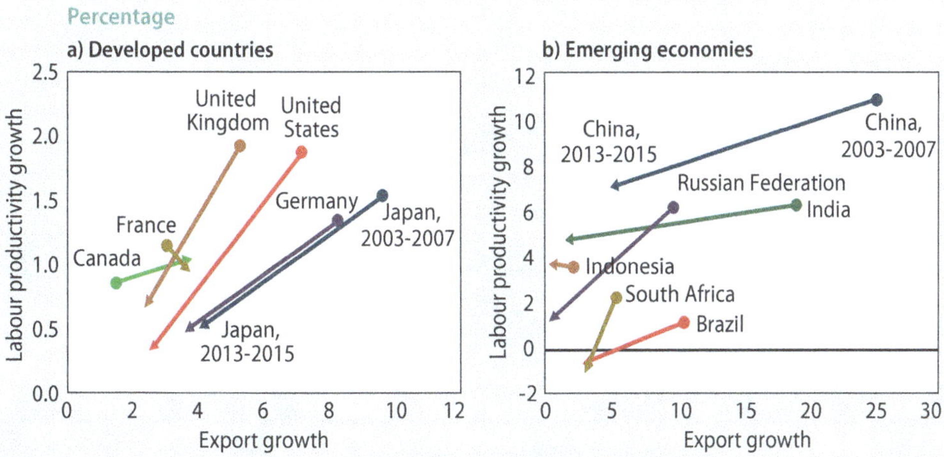

Source: UN/DESA, based on data from CEIC Data and IMF (2016a).

Figure I.2.2

Growth of labour productivity and growth of private investment, 2003–2007 and 2013–2015

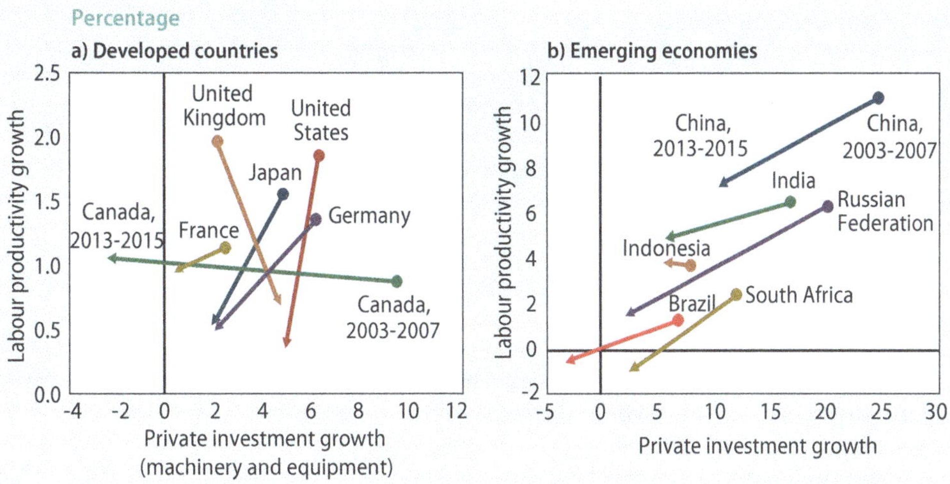

Source: UN/DESA, based on data from United Nations Statistics Division National Accounts and CEIC Data.

in recent years. The estimated global trade growth of only 1.2 per cent in 2016 will stand out as the third-lowest rate of growth in the past 30 years.

Weak global trade extends across developed, developing and transition economies

The weakness in trade flows is broad-based, encompassing developed, developing and transition economies, although there are notable regional differences between the developments in imports and exports. Merchandise imports were exceptionally weak in developing economies in the first half of 2016. Asia, Africa and the Middle East and Latin America have seen contractions compared to the previous year (figure I.12). This reflects weak domestic demand (in the cases of Latin America and Africa), significant currency depreciations and, in some cases, a gradual transformation and rebalancing of the economic structure, as observed in the case of China. The slowdown in global manufacturing output has also played a role, as it is very import-intensive. On the merchandise export side, emerging Asia and the United States — affected by the strong dollar — have seen contractions over the previous year, whereas Latin America benefited from much weaker domestic currencies (figure I.13).

Figure I.12
Average year-on-year change in merchandise imports *(volume)*

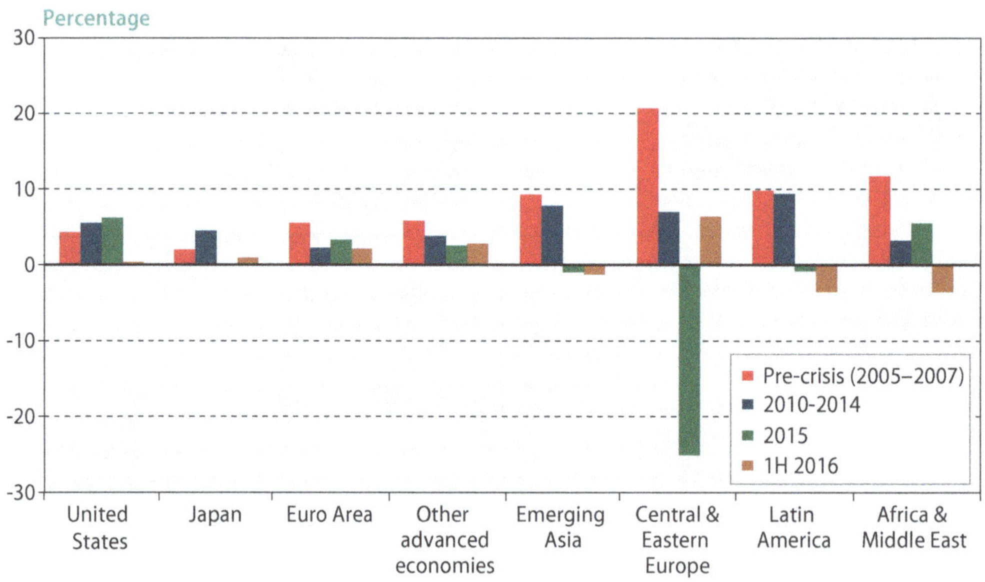

Source: CPB World Trade Monitor, Netherlands Bureau for Economic Policy Analysis.

Ratio of world trade growth to WGP growth has declined significantly since the 1990s

Trade growth is not only weak from a historical perspective, but also in relation to overall GDP growth (figure I.14). The ratio of world trade growth to WGP growth has fallen gradually since the 1990s, from a factor of 2.5 to 1. In 2016, WGP grew at a significantly faster pace than global trade, and the ratio of world trade growth to WGP growth is estimated to be only about 0.5.

The key question is whether the current weakness in trade is a temporary (cyclical) or a longer-lasting (structural) phenomenon. In other words, can the world economy expect a return to stronger trade growth in the coming years or is the current very low level of trade growth the "new normal"?

A number of recent studies identify several factors contributing to the falloff in global trade. These studies are discussed in more detail in Chapter II, and conclude that while cyclical factors — such as the composition of global demand and heightened uncertainty — continue to restrain global trade growth, the impact of a number of structural shifts that

Figure I.13

Average year-on-year change in merchandise exports *(volume)*

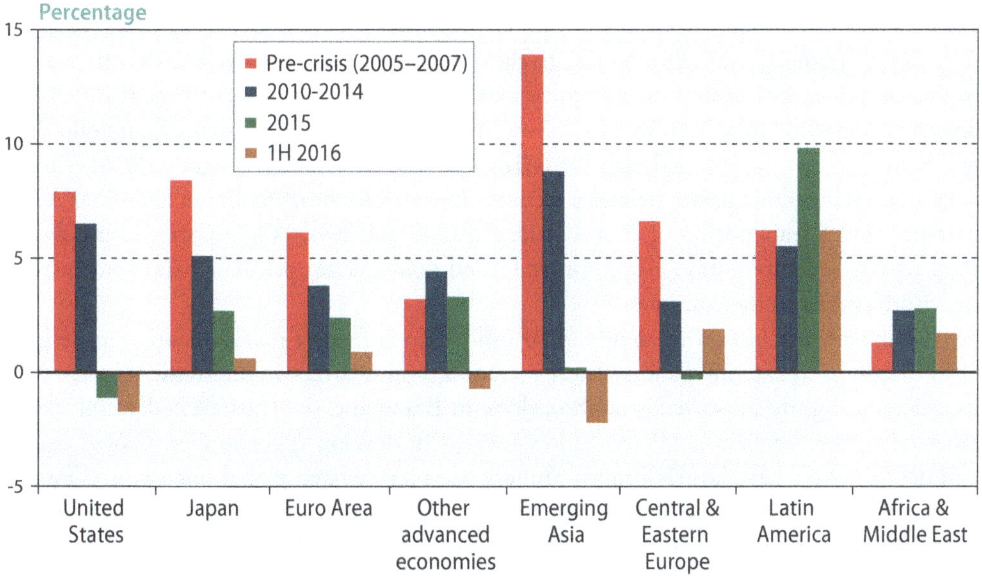

Source: CPB World Trade Monitor, Netherlands Bureau for Economic Policy Analysis.

Figure I.14

Average annual change in world trade and world gross product by decade *(constant prices)*

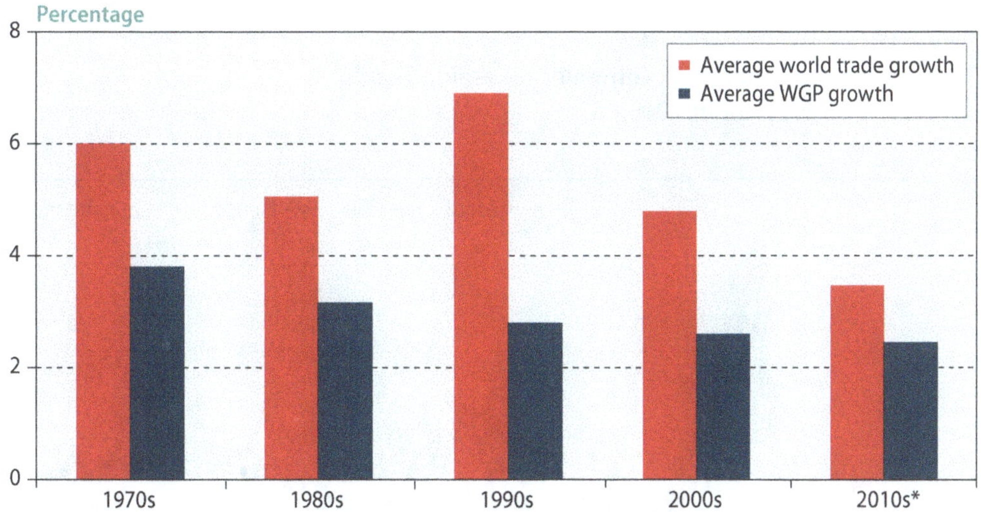

Source: United Nations Statistics Division National Accounts Main Aggregates Database.

* Includes UN/DESA estimates for 2016.

favoured the rapid expansion of global trade in the 1990s and 2000s have started to wane. These structural shifts include, for example, the reduction in transportation costs supported by information and communications technology (ICT) advancements; the integration process of the economies in transition and China into global trade networks; deeper integration in Europe with the European Single Market; and the expansion of global value chains (GVCs).

World trade growth will track WGP growth more closely in the coming years

Global import penetration is expected to stabilize in 2017, and exhibit a partial recovery in 2018 of some of its recent losses. However, the elasticity between trade and GDP growth is likely to remain closer to 1 over the next several years.

Capital inflows to emerging economies

Private non-resident capital inflows to emerging markets recovered some losses in 2016

Amid a slower-than-expected pace of interest rate rises in the United States and a further expansion of unconventional monetary policy measures in other developed economies, international financial markets were relatively stable for the most part in 2016, after a tumultuous January of selling-off in equity markets. Private non-resident capital inflows to emerging markets[4] have seen some recovery, after experiencing outflows of portfolio debt and banking flows in 2015 and early 2016 (Institute of International Finance, 2016). The revival of capital inflows partly reflects a recovery in portfolio flows to China and other Asian markets, and a stabilisation of cross-border banking outflows. While portfolio inflows to the Russian Federation have also improved, total non-resident private capital continues to be withdrawn from the country.

Global equity and debt markets have largely proven resilient, despite elevated global uncertainty

The recovery in non-resident capital inflows to emerging market economies reflects both internal and external factors. These include a mild recovery in international commodity prices, a slightly improved growth outlook in Brazil and the Russian Federation and a renewed search for yield amid record-low returns in developed economies. Global equity and debt markets have largely proven resilient, despite elevated global uncertainty. Financial markets recovered quickly from the unexpected outcome of the Brexit referendum in June 2016, in large part due to the rapid and forceful response of central banks in developed countries.

About 25 per cent of global bonds are offering negative yields

The recovering capital inflows have resulted in significantly lower government and corporate bond yields in emerging economies (figure I.15) and higher equity prices (figure I.16). Meanwhile, developed country bond yields declined to record lows in the third quar-

Figure I.15

Yield spreads on emerging economies sovereign bonds, January 2007–November 2016

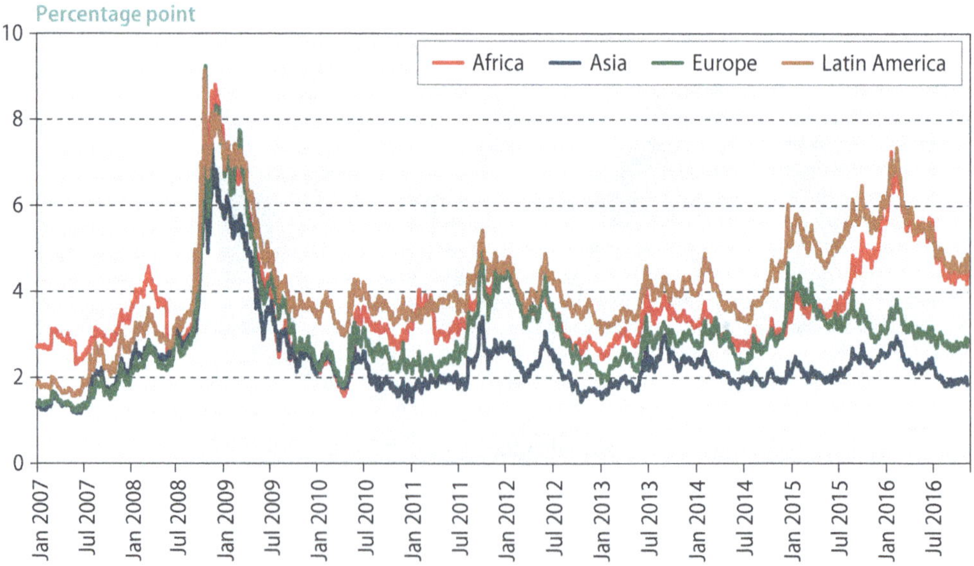

Source: JPMorgan Chase.

4 This definition differs from data presented in Chapter III, which apply the 'net net flows' concept, which is net inflows less net outflows. The use of 'net inflows' focuses on the effects of volatility in foreign capital inflows, while the use of 'net net flows' focuses on the balance of payments effects.

ter of 2016. The total face value of negative-yielding corporate and sovereign debt stood at $11.6 trillion as of 30 September.[5] This is slightly below the peak of $11.9 trillion at the end of June and represents about 25 per cent of the total value. Japan and Western Europe each account for about 50 per cent of the bonds offering negative yields, of which roughly 85 per cent are sovereign bonds.

Figure I.16
Equity market indices in selected developing countries, January 2014–October 2016

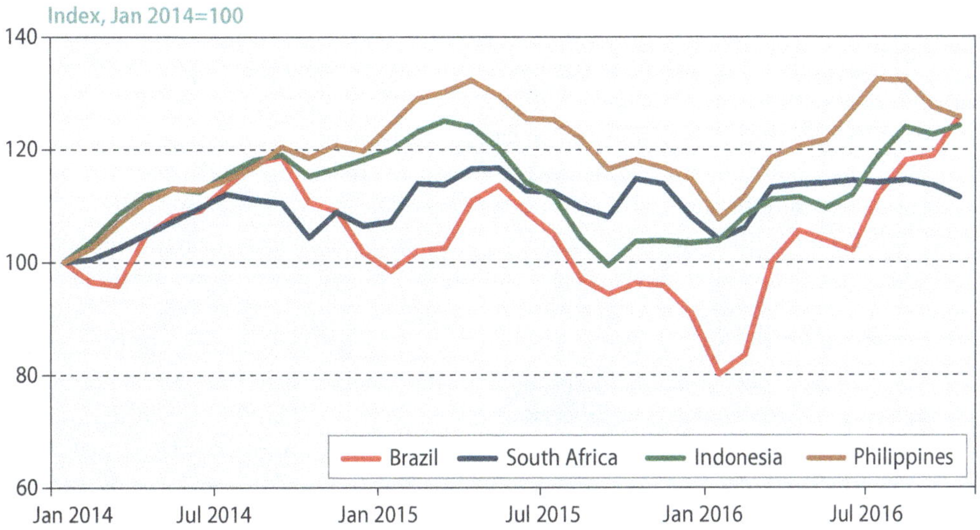

Source: UN/DESA, based on CEIC Data.

Widening divergences in global policy rates may heighten asset price volatility and trigger capital withdrawal from developing countries

Looking ahead, significant fragilities in the international financial system pose major risks to developed and developing economies. The main underlying factor is the widening divergence between buoyant — and complacent — financial markets and persistently weak global economic growth resulting from the over-reliance on monetary policy to stimulate economic activity.

Years of expansionary monetary policy coupled with the lack of support on the fiscal side encouraged excessive risk-taking and considerable distortions, leading to very high equity and asset prices, without ensuring a robust growth trajectory. Significant uncertainties and risks persist in the financial market, which may suddenly alter the volume, destination, composition and pace of international capital flows.

As global divergences in policy rates and yields continue to widen, this may trigger disorderly adjustments in asset prices and change capital flows, with significant adverse effects on the real economy, especially in large developing countries with high openness to foreign capital, such as Mexico, South Africa and Turkey.

In the first days following the election in the United States, emerging market assets dropped noticeably, along with a sharp depreciation in several emerging market currencies. A further surge in risk aversion — driven, for example, by concerns related to the possible introduction of protectionist measures by the United States or the implementation of Brexit — could destabilize financial markets worldwide.

5 Bloomberg Barclays Global Aggregate Index, covering 24 developed and emerging economies.

Remittances

Remittance flows to developing countries virtually stagnated in 2015

Remittances are resource transfers between residents and non-residents, generally in the form of wages transferred from migrant workers to their families. In several countries they comprise a significant share of disposable household income. Amid subdued global economic growth, remittance flows to developing countries in dollar terms virtually stagnated in 2015. Officially recorded remittances to developing countries amounted to $431.6 billion in 2015, an increase of only 0.4 per cent from 2014 — the lowest rate of increase since the global financial crisis.[6] Preliminary data for 2016 underscore large differences not only across major geographic regions, but also within regions.

Declining remittance flows from the Russian Federation weighed on household income in other CIS countries

The appreciation of the dollar and the low oil price constrained the growth in the dollar value of remittances in 2015, and continued to weigh on remittance flows in the first half of 2016. The CIS countries that receive most of their remittance inflows from the Russian Federation have suffered particularly steep contractions, reflecting the sharp decline in the rouble's value, amid the challenging labour market conditions and economic outlook in the Russian Federation. The contraction in domestic currency terms was much more moderate, as the CIS currencies also weakened versus the dollar, but still weighed on households' purchasing power and private consumption of extra-regional goods and services.

Low oil prices have also constrained remittances from other oil-exporting countries

Outflows from the Cooperation Council for the Arab States of the Gulf (GCC) have also slowed, negatively impacting Egypt in North Africa and South Asian economies, notably Bangladesh, India and Nepal. In certain cases, the flow of remittances in the "reverse direction" increased in 2016, for example, from Asian to Gulf countries or from the Caucasus to the Russian Federation, as families in home countries tried to provide some support to the migrant workers facing temporary difficulties.

The outlook for remittance flows from the United States may be impacted by policy changes

Remittance-receiving economies with a strong exposure to the United States and euro area countries have generally performed well, thanks to positive labour market trends. Remittance flows to Mexico, for example, increased by over 8 per cent year-on-year in the first half of 2016 in US dollar terms, and by even more in terms of domestic currency. At $13.2 billon, remittance inflows far exceeded oil export revenues. The outlook for remittance flows from the United States is highly uncertain, depending on whether any of the proposed changes to immigration policies and taxation are introduced by the new Administration of the United States.

Countries with a higher concentration of remittance sources tend to have more volatile remittance inflows

The post-2014 experience in CIS economies, including Kyrgyzstan, Tajikistan and Uzbekistan, illustrates the risks for countries whose inflows come almost exclusively from one country. Among the major remittance-receiving developing countries, the degree of source country concentration varies significantly (figure I.17). Countries with a higher concentration of remittance sources tend to have more volatile remittance inflows.

A weaker British pound will weigh on remittances from the United Kingdom

The weakening of the British pound in the wake of Brexit will have a considerably negative impact on countries for which the United Kingdom provides a large share of total remittance inflows. Figure I.18 depicts the 10 countries with the largest share of inflows from the UK in total inflows, which includes four African countries.

The Addis Ababa Action Agenda (AAAA) includes a commitment to reduce, by 2030, the average transaction costs of migrant remittances to less than 3 percent, recognizing the important role that remittances can play in reducing poverty. While remittance costs have continued to decline, they remain higher in sub-Saharan Africa, where remittance transac-

6 World Bank Migration and Remittances Data(http://www.worldbank.org/en/topic/migrationremittancesdiasporaissues/brief/migration-remittances-data).

Figure I.17
Degree of concentration of remittance sources for selected countries, 2015

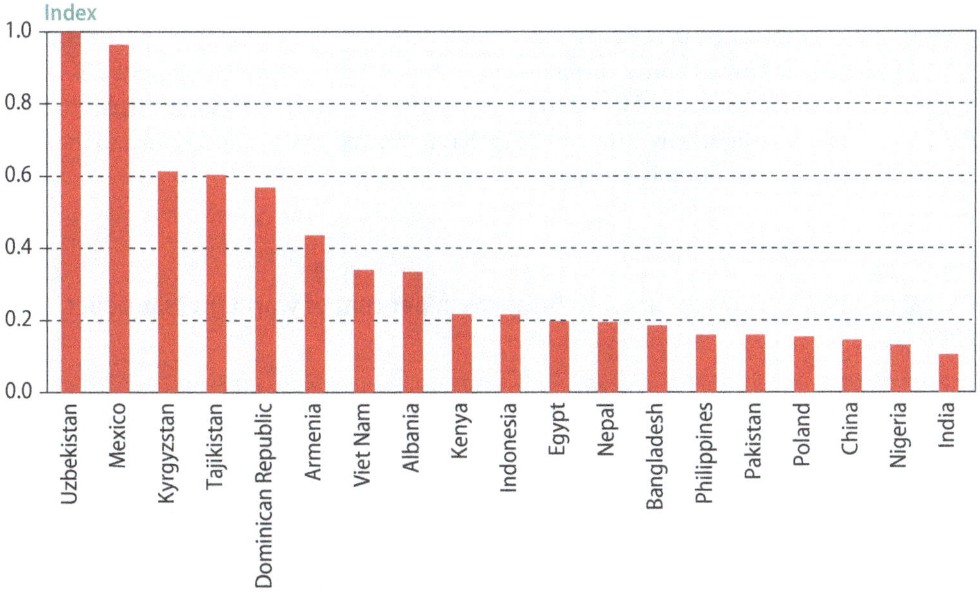

Source: UN/DESA derived from World Bank Bilateral Remittances Matrix 2015.
Note: A higher index refers to more concentrated remittance sources. The remittance concentration index is measured as the sum of squared shares of each source (remittance-sending country) in the total inflow of remittances into the recipient country.

Figure I.18
Share of remittances from the United Kingdom in total remittance inflows, 2015

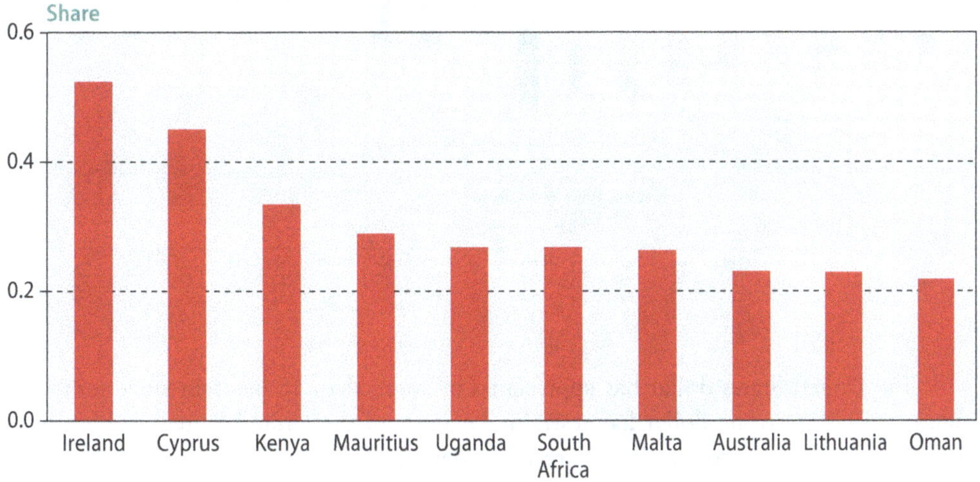

Source: World Bank Bilateral Remittances Matrix 2015.
Note: Ten top countries depending on remittances from the United Kingdom.

tion costs averaged 9.5 per cent in the fourth quarter of 2015, with costs in some corridors between South Africa and nearby countries as high as 18–20 per cent.

Better access to financial services, and more effective use of formal providers, can facilitate speedier and safer remittance flows, and lower the high remittance transaction costs in underserved areas, as called for in the AAAA.

Global imbalances

Global current account imbalances have narrowed, but may still pose a risk to global financial stability

While the dispersion of global current-account deficits and surpluses has narrowed somewhat from the peaks leading up to the global financial crisis, a significant degree of imbalance still persists, posing a potential risk to global financial stability. The United States current-account deficit narrowed from 1.6 per cent of WGP in 2006 to 0.5 per cent in 2013, combined with a decline in China's current-account surplus from 0.5 per cent of WGP to 0.2 per cent over the same period.

However, the United States current account deficit has been widening since 2014, and is expected to widen further in 2017-2018 (figure I.19). The current account surplus in East Asia, after widening slightly in 2014 and 2015, has narrowed again, and a return to the level of global imbalances in 2006 is unlikely.

Figure I.19
Global imbalances: Current account balances in per cent of world gross product, 2000–2018

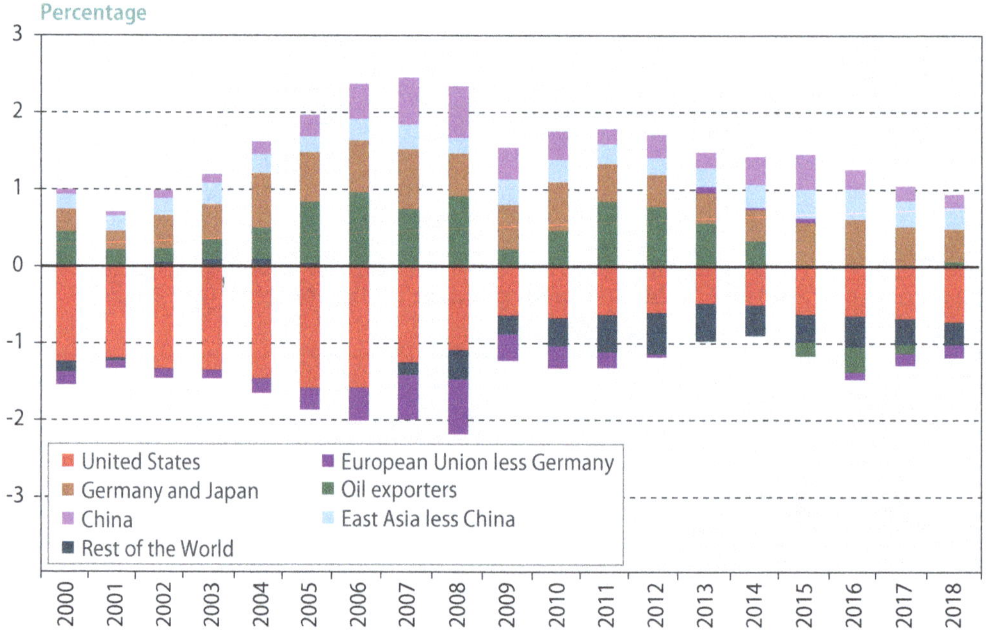

Source: UN/DESA derived from IMF International Financial Statistics. Includes UN/DESA estimates and projections for 2016-2018.

The strong US dollar has underpinned a widening of the current account deficit in the United States

The United States dollar has appreciated by more than 15 per cent since mid-2014 (figure I.20). The strong dollar has restrained exports of the United States, and has been an important factor underpinning the recent widening of the current account deficit of the United States. As interest rates in the United States are expected to rise relative to other major developed economies in 2017-2018, some upward pressure on the dollar is expected to continue, further unwinding some of the improvement in the current account deficit of the United States since 2006.

Many commodity exporters are now running large external deficits due to the steep loss of export revenue

The drop in oil prices in 2015 helped contain greater imbalances, as the majority of fuel exporters have historically run persistent current-account surpluses. However, many commodity exporters are now running large external deficits due to the steep loss of export revenue. The partial recovery in oil and other commodity prices in 2017-2018 will ease some of these pressures. Nonetheless, if global imbalances were to begin to deteriorate, this could pose an additional risk to the already modest global economic recovery.

Figure I.20
Nominal effective exchange rate of the United States dollar, January 2010–October 2016

Source: UN/DESA estimates of nominal effective exchange rate, measured against a weighted average of 175 trading partners.

Sustainability and inclusiveness of economic growth

Poverty and inequality

Over the last few decades, the world has witnessed rapid progress in poverty reduction. The proportion of the world population living in extreme poverty, as defined by the international poverty line of $1.90 a day, declined from 44.3 per cent in 1981 to 10.7 per cent in 2013.[7]

Slow global growth poses a risk to achieving the target of eradicating extreme poverty by 2030

The dramatic declines at the global level are largely a reflection of sustained rapid growth in a few large countries, most notably China and India. However, the current global environment of slow growth poses significant risk to the achievement of SDG 1, which sets a target to "eradicate extreme poverty for all people everywhere" by 2030. In order to achieve this goal, the world would collectively need to lift more than 800 million people above the extreme poverty line within a time frame of 15 years.

Poverty reduction in the current economic environment will require countries to tackle inequality issues more rigorously

Poverty reduction in a given country can be attributed to a "growth effect" and a "distributional effect", although these two effects are not strictly independent (Datt and Ravallion, 1992). The global decline in the incidence of extreme poverty since 1981 has relied heavily on the "growth effect". The broad slowdown in global economic growth may linger for several more years. In this environment, curtailing poverty will require countries to make greater use of the "distributional effect", by addressing income distribution and inequality issues more rigorously.

Under the current growth trajectory, nearly 35 per cent of the population in LDCs may remain in extreme poverty by 2030

Figure I.21 illustrates projections for poverty reduction by 2030, based on an extension of the baseline forecasts,[8] under an assumption that income distribution remains

7 World Bank Poverty and Equity Database.

8 See Altshuler and others (2016) for a detailed description of the model underlying the longer-term forecast projections.

unchanged.[9] The results paint a worrying picture. Without reducing income inequality, current growth projections would leave 6.5 per cent of the global population trapped in extreme poverty by 2030. While the poverty rate in East Asia can be expected to fall to very low levels, nearly 35 per cent of the population in LDCs may remain in extreme poverty by 2030.[10]

Figure I.21
Extreme poverty headcount ratios in 2012 and projections for 2030, holding inequality constant

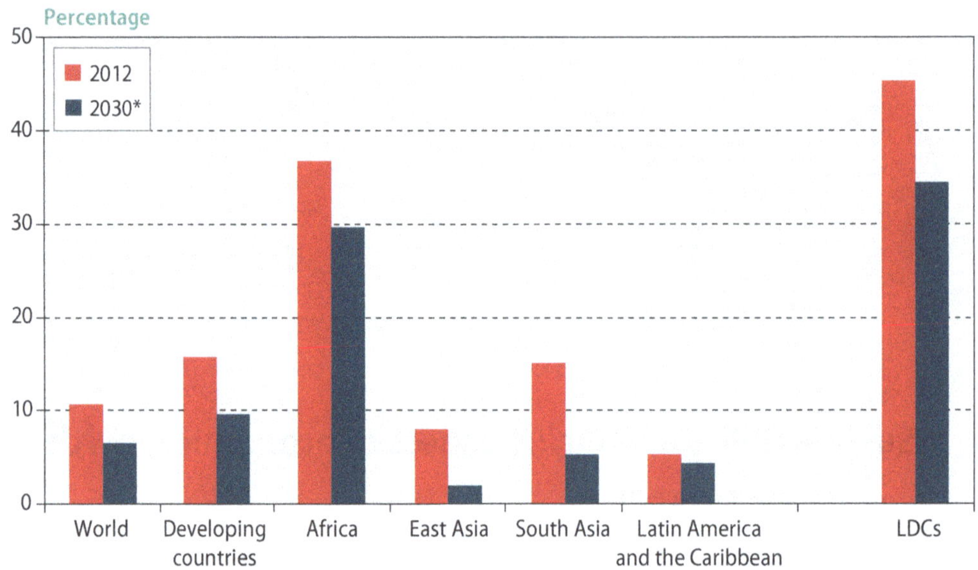

Source: UN/DESA.
* See Holland and Jayadev (2016) for discussion of the forecast models. The 2030 projection is based on the simple average of projections from the three forecasting models presented. Projections are done at the country level and aggregated for the region. Discrepancies at the regional level in the three projections are less than 2 percentage points in all regions.

Under current projections, relying on the growth effect alone will clearly not be sufficient to eradicate poverty within the time frame specified in the SDGs. Policy makers will need to make additional efforts, both to foster an environment that will accelerate medium-term growth prospects and to tackle the "distributional effect" of poverty reduction through the implementation of redistributive policies to address inequality in income, opportunity and outcomes.

The historical evolution of income distribution suggests that tackling income inequality will be difficult, given that inequality within countries has not seen much improvement in many regions for the past 30 years (figure I.22). The exception is Latin America and the Caribbean, which has seen a broad-based decline in inequality since the early 2000s. This improvement can be largely attributed to the reduction in the earning gaps between skilled and low-skilled workers — a result of expanding basic education — and significant changes in labour and social policies, including an increase in public transfers.[11]

9 The projections rely on the relationship between mean household income from surveys and national consumption per capita, as well as prospects for labour force participation.

10 These projections are generally consistent with the more pessimistic scenarios reported in Ravallion (2013) and Yoshida, Uematsu and Sobrado (2014) and Hoy and Sumner (2016).

11 For more detailed discussions, please refer to López-Calva and Lustig (2010).

Figure I.22
Evolution of income distribution, by region, 1984–2014

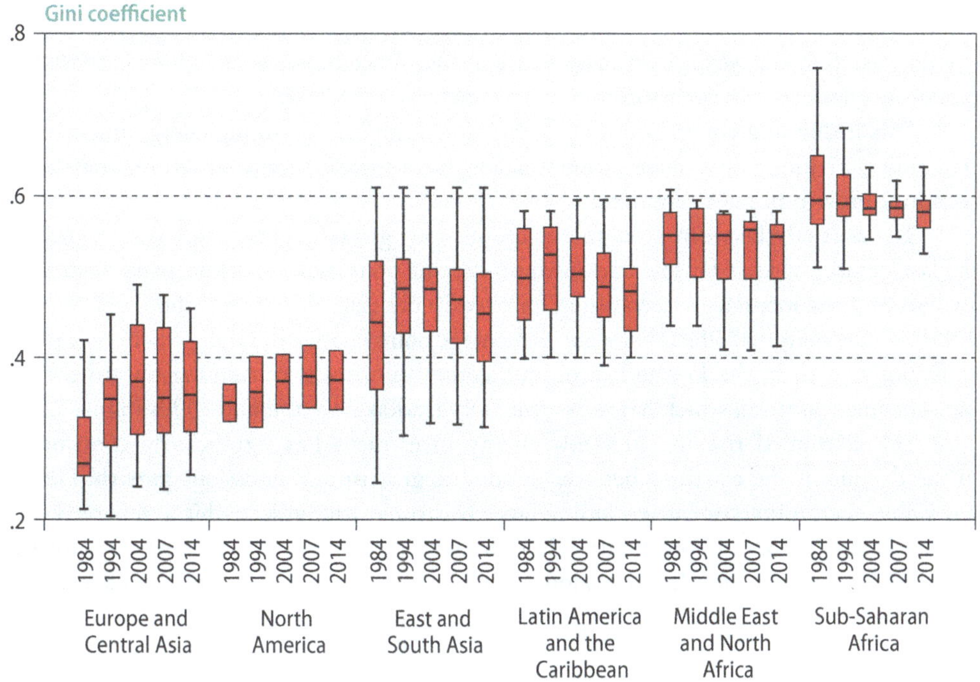

Source: UN/DESA, based on data from the Global Consumption and Income Project.
Note: The box plots used here are standard box plots. The ends of the whiskers indicate the highest (lowest) observations within 1.5 interquartile range of the third (first) quartile.

Reallocation of public spending can strengthen support for poverty reduction in many developing countries

Hoy and Sumner (2016) argue that there are sufficient public resources at the national level — at least in upper middle income countries — to end three-quarters of extreme global poverty even in the absence of acceleration in economic growth. While Ravallion (2009) concluded that the marginal tax rates needed to fund the fight against poverty in the mid-2000s were prohibitively high, updated estimates by Hoy and Sumner (2016) suggest that this may no longer be the case. According to the study, many national Governments in developing countries have the financial capacities to support those in extreme poverty through well-targeted cash transfers, funded either via new taxation on those not facing poverty or through the reallocation of public spending away from fossil fuel subsidies or military spending. The scope for poverty reduction via tax funded public transfers remains — for the most part — restricted to upper middle income countries[12] and will do little to redress the persistently high rates of poverty in the LDCs. However, the removal of fossil fuel subsidies — which often disproportionately benefit rich and middle-class households — could provide national resources to reduce extreme poverty levels in several of the LDCs as well.

Eradicating extreme poverty will require commitments to share prosperity both within and across national borders

Without accelerated GDP growth and progress towards improving income inequality, eradicating the high levels of extreme poverty in the least developed economies by 2030 will remain a formidable challenge. While policies aimed at reducing inequality must play a crucial role, mobilizing resources to support investment and productivity growth, as well as a commitment to share prosperity both within and across national borders, are also essential to achieving the SDG targets.

12 It is estimated that a marginal tax rate of less than 10 per cent would be sufficient to support the tax-funded public transfers in upper middle income countries.

Energy and environment

The level of global carbon emissions stalled for two consecutive years

At approximately 32 gigatons, global energy-related carbon emissions stalled for two consecutive years during 2014-2015 despite positive economic growth (figure I.23). It strengthens the case that the world is starting to see a divergence between emissions growth and economic growth — an observation that was made in *WESP 2016*.

This is due to a combination of factors, including the declining energy intensity of economic activities, rising share of renewables in the overall energy structure, and slower economic growth in major emitters.

The elasticity between economic and emissions growth appears to have declined in the last decade, at least for low and medium-income countries. Based on panel regression analysis of 35 economies — accounting for over 80 per cent of world's carbon emissions in 2015[13] — the marginal effect[14] of a one percentage point change in GDP growth on carbon emissions growth in the low and medium-income countries is converging toward that in high-income countries, which has seen some stabilization since the mid-1990s (figure I.24).

The level of new renewable energy investment in developing countries surpassed that of developed countries in 2015

The continued rise in renewable energy investment has significantly contributed to the decline in the elasticity between economic growth and emissions growth. Global renewable energy investment (excluding large hydro-electric projects) hit a new record in 2015, totaling $285.9 billion (figure I.25). Notably, developing countries have — for the first time — surpassed developed economies in new renewables investment. China leads the

Figure I.23
World gross product growth and carbon emissions growth, 1991–2015

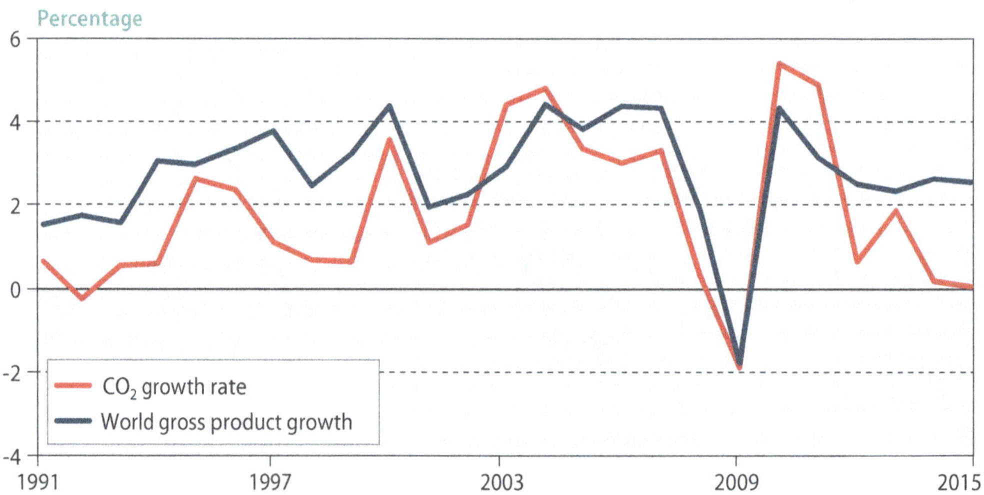

Source: International Energy Agency and United Nations Statistics Division National Accounts Main Aggregates Database.

13 The 35 countries examined are: Algeria, Argentina, Australia, Austria, Bangladesh, Brazil, Chile, China, Colombia, Ecuador, Egypt, Finland, France, Germany, India, Indonesia, Iran, Japan, Republic of Korea, Malaysia, Mexico, the Netherlands, New Zealand, Norway, Pakistan, the Philippines, Russian Federation, Saudi Arabia, Singapore, South Africa, Sweden, Thailand, Turkey, United States, and Venezuela (Bolivarian Republic of).

14 The marginal effects are estimated using a moving-window panel regression from 1980 to 2015, with 10-year windows. The model regresses carbon emissions growth on real GDP growth, GDP per capita, interaction between real GDP growth and GDP per capita, renewable energy's share in primary energy consumption, industry value-added's share in GDP, population growth, and share of urban population in total population. It also controls for year effects and country-specific fixed effects, and allows for correlation of observations within the same country.

Figure I.24

Marginal effect of one percentage point change in GDP growth on carbon emissions growth, 1980–2015

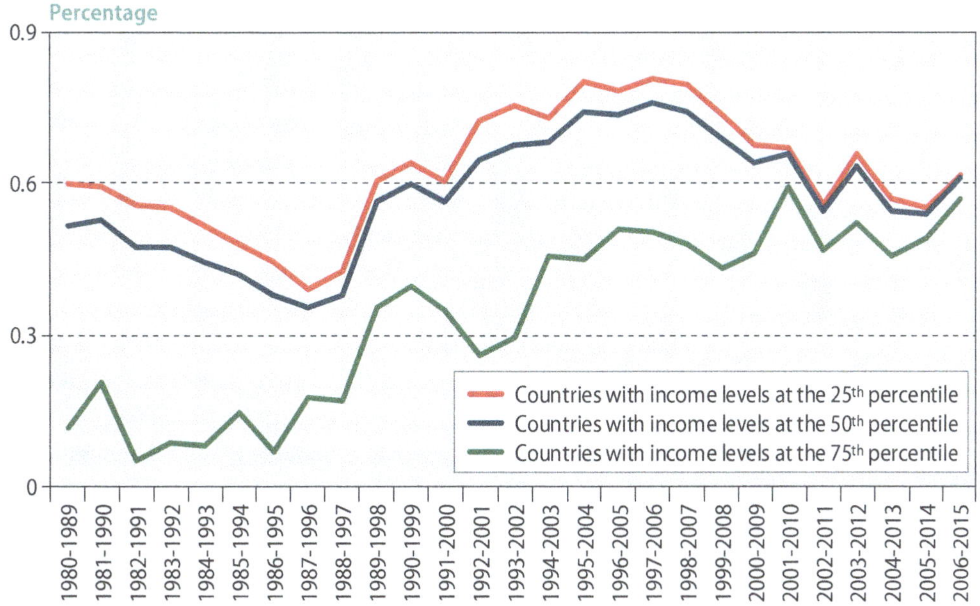

Source: UN/DESA staff estimation.

trend with investment of $102.9 billion in 2015, which accounted for 36 per cent of global new renewables investment in that year.

Despite advancements, renewable energy still only accounts for a small share of global power generation

Approximately 134 gigawatts of renewable power capacity (excluding large hydro) were commissioned globally in 2015, meaning that renewables account for over 50 per cent of all newly installed power generation capacity for the first time. Renewable energy (excluding large hydro), however, still accounts for only 16.2 per cent of global power capacity and 10.3 per cent of global power generation. The current share of renewables in global power generation is thought to have prevented the emission of 1.5 gigatons of carbon dioxide-equivalent, i.e. 4.7 per cent of total carbon emissions in 2015 (Frankfurt School–UNEP Centre/BNEF, 2016).

New renewable investment dropped sharply in the first half of 2016

Despite significant progress in 2015, the early 2016 data indicates a slowdown in renewables investment. In the first half of 2016, new renewables investment in clean energy dropped by around 23 per cent year-over-year.[15] Around half of the year-over-year decline in clean energy investment in the first half of 2016 can be attributed to China, which is facing weak electricity demand and uncertainty regarding the country's feed-in tariff policy, which pays users for generating their own sustainable energy. At the global level, the weaker investment also partly reflects the sustained low fossil-fuel energy prices, which might start to weigh on renewables investment.

Without further efforts to improve energy efficiency and promote renewable energy, recent progress could reverse

The world is still some distance from achieving a sustained decoupling between economic growth and carbon emissions growth and ensuring sustainable consumption and production patterns (SDG 12). While China's carbon emissions have stabilized in the past two years, other developing countries are still seeing them rise. The improvements witnessed in recent years could easily reverse if there is a lack of concerted effort from the public and

15 Bloomberg New Energy Finance. Clean energy investment differs from renewable energy investment, as the former also include low carbon services (e.g. carbon markets) and energy smart technologies (e.g. energy storage and fuel cells). Renewable energy investment accounts for around 82 per cent of global clean energy investment in 2015.

Figure I.25
Global new investment in renewable energy, 2004–2015

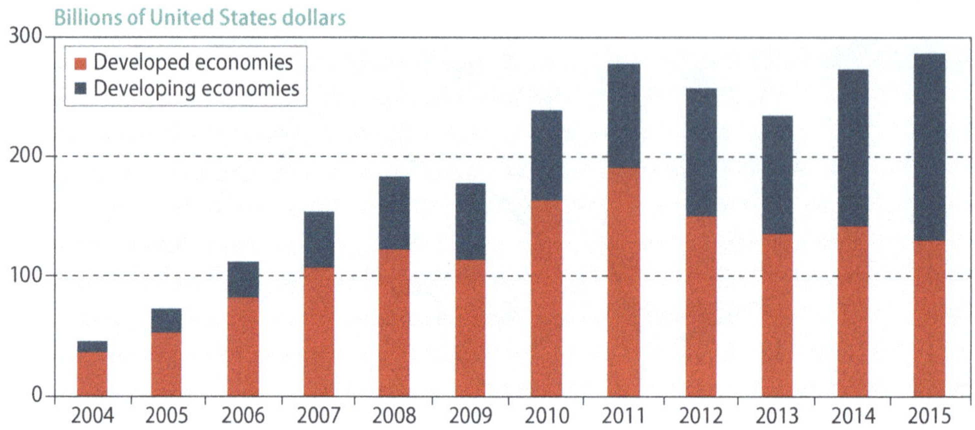

Source: Frankfurt School-UNEP Centre/BNEF (2016).

private sectors to improve energy efficiency and promote renewable energy. There must be international cooperation on clean technology transfer and climate finance. Countries will have to continue to pursue nationally-appropriate low-carbon development paths that are sustainable on economic, social and environmental fronts.

Major uncertainties and risks in the global economy

Uncertainties about major changes in the international policy environment

The new Administration in the United States has proposed policy changes in a number of spheres

There is considerable uncertainty related to the evolution of international policy. For example, the new Administration in the United States has discussed far-reaching changes to the current direction and stance in policy related to macroeconomics, trade, immigration, foreign affairs and the environment, as well as the nature of its participation in multilateral organizations and institutions. Should some of these changes be implemented, the substantial economic impact would mostly manifest itself beyond the forecasting period of this report, but heightened uncertainty could weigh on investment decisions in the short-term as well. This uncertainty may also trigger capital withdrawal from developing economies with open capital markets, such as Mexico, South Africa and Turkey, in a general "flight to safety".

The potential economic impact of any new measures remains unclear

Some measures recently proposed by the incoming Administration in the United States may have the potential to accelerate GDP growth in the short-run, such as a large expansion of infrastructure investment coupled with significant cuts in taxation, although it is not clear whether Congress would agree to the rise in government debt levels that such a move would entail. The introduction of *ad hoc* tariff barriers to some important trade partners, such as China and Mexico, on the other hand, would be counterproductive and slow economic growth, especially if such actions trigger retaliatory measures that could potentially spread to other countries.

Any backtracking in energy and environmental policy may endanger the environmental targets in the SDGs and the Paris Agreement on climate change.

Brexit raises a number of uncertainties in Europe

The decision by the United Kingdom to leave the EU also raises questions regarding international policy, which can be broadly grouped into three different levels: uncertainties about the future trade, financial and migration arrangements between the United Kingdom and the EU and between the United Kingdom and other countries; the likelihood that similar actions will be taken by other EU members; and the extent to which this signals a change in the trend of global economic integration at large (box I.3).

From a global perspective, the shifting direction of policy in the United States and the United Kingdom partly reflects increasing discontent with the imbalanced distribution of the burdens and gains that deepening global economic integration has brought in the past few decades. For example, more open international trade has indeed generated substantial

Should protectionism escalate, it could prolong slow growth in the world economy

Box I.3

Uncertainties associated with Brexit

In June 2016, the electorate of the United Kingdom unexpectedly voted to leave the EU. The initial shock to global financial markets was precipitous, but faded quickly, partly because central banks responded promptly to stabilize markets. However, significant uncertainties remain regarding how economic structures and relations will evolve.

The United Kingdom is expected to trigger Article 50 of the Lisbon Treaty by March 2017 — formally declaring its intention to withdraw from the EU. Under Article 50, the timescale for negotiations is two years, and the United Kingdom will leave the EU in 2019. However, two years may not be sufficient to finalise long-term agreement with the EU and all 27 other Member States, given the scale of agreements and contentious issues involved. Policy clarity in the period immediately after departure is crucial, in the event that further negotiations are needed.

Questions about the future trade, financial and migration arrangements between the United Kingdom and the EU, as well as arrangements between the United Kingdom and other countries which the EU holds agreements with, could restrain investment in the short-term. These uncertainties may also affect where multinational firms locate as well as the development of global value chains, both of which may have longer-term impacts. Estimates of the longer-term economic impact for the United Kingdom — and also for countries with close ties to the United Kingdom, such as Ireland and Spain — tend to be negative, although the magnitude of any output loss will ultimately depend on the final terms of these agreements.

The United Kingdom will seek to limit the free movement of EU workers. If the EU does not offer the United Kingdom the ability to restrict migration unilaterally while retaining full access to the single market, or remaining in the European Economic Area (EEA), the pattern of non-tariff barriers (NTBs) facing the United Kingdom may change considerably. The NTBs can be in various forms, such as quotas, voluntary export restraints, rules of origin, and technical and administrative barriers, including product standards.

Potentially high stakes are also at play in the financial sector. As a key global financial center, London plays a critical role in banking, accounting for large global shares in cross-border lending, investment banking, wholesale banking, interest rate trading, European equity trading, and foreign exchange trading, as well as in other market functions such as infrastructure, insurance and asset management. Under future arrangements, banks may incur additional expenses associated with moving operations out of London. Banks may also have to bear the cost of additional capital, liquidity, and total loss-absorbing requirements. The sector may be subject to changes in financial services rules, depending on negotiations.

Brexit has already triggered outflows from the London real estate market, and more significant declines in foreign investment in commercial real estate of the United Kingdom are likely in the coming years. Meanwhile, the complex process of the exit negotiations itself could erode household and business confidence, although to date confidence indicators have held up relatively well.

Brexit has also highlighted a problem in the EU governance structure — the conflict between the supranational institutions (the European Commission and the European Parliament) and the intergovernmental institution (the Council of Ministers). In the 1990s and early 2000s, supranationalism was on the rise with the creation of the European Economic and Monetary Union (EMU), a new supranational institution in the European Central Bank (ECB), and the increased power of the European Parliament. However, after the sovereign debt crisis in 2011, intergovernmentalism has revived and a number of intergovernmental arrangements were created, such as the Fiscal Compact, the Single Resolution Fund and the European Stability Mechanism. Many people viewed the existing supranational institutions as elitist, remote, and slow-moving. With Brexit, it is uncertain how the EU governance structures will evolve.

economic gains for many countries through improved efficiency in allocating resources worldwide. At the same time, more open trade has been associated with widening income inequality in many countries, along with job losses and declining wages for certain categories of workers, although these developments also reflect factors such as technological progress. These concerns have enhanced the appeal of protectionism and inward-looking policies in many countries. More concerted international efforts to improve global governance, along with more effective domestic redistribution policies, are needed to ensure that the gains from global economic integration are more inclusive. In the absence of such efforts, protectionist tendencies may escalate, which could prolong the slow growth in the world economy and lead to a less-efficient allocation of resources and slower pace of technological diffusion.

Uncertainties and risks associated with unconventional monetary policy

Developed economies continue to rely heavily on monetary policy to support their macroeconomic objectives. As the scope for conventional monetary stimulus was to a large extent exhausted when interest rates were cut to near zero levels in the aftermath of the global financial crisis, central banks have made greater use of unconventional policy, such as quantitative and qualitative easing, negative interest rate policies and yield curve targeting. Proposals have also been made to explore new tools such as "helicopter money", which is essentially a fiscal expansion financed by a central bank. The longer-term impacts of these measures, which have limited historical precedence, remain unclear.

Several central banks in Europe and Japan have introduced negative interest rate policies

Currently, at least six central banks (five in Europe, plus Japan), with the GDP of these economies accounting for 25 per cent of the world total, have set negative policy interest rates. Moreover, the yields of many long-term bonds, which are not set by central banks but determined by capital markets, are also below zero. This shows investors are willing to accept a loss by holding these bonds, as the price paid by investors today is greater than the interest payments and principle repayment in the future.

Negative policy rates in these economies have produced some intended effects through interest rate, credit, portfolio, and exchange rate channels — declines in money market rates and lower bank lending rates, although inflation expectation continued to decline in these countries. However, in the longer run, a number of risks are associated with the negative policy rates and yields on longer term bonds.

An extended period of negative interest rates may erode bank profits and tighten lending conditions, rather than encourage bank lending as intended

If central banks hold negative policy rates for a protracted period and/or push rates further below zero, risks to financial stability could escalate. Financial institutions rely on lending at higher rates than they borrow. As central bank deposit rates drop below zero, there may be contractual or market constraints on the ability to pass these negative interest rates on to customers. This would erode the profitability of banks and other financial intermediaries, undermining their financial resilience and curbing their lending capacity.

Moreover, the negative yields on longer term bonds, as well as the broad low interest rate environment, pose risks to the solvency of certain types of financial institutions, including insurance companies and pension funds (IMF, 2016b). The business models of insurance companies are very sensitive to low interest rates. During 2016, equity prices for many insurance companies declined more than that of other sectors and credit default swap spreads for these companies increased. A rising systemic risk of the insurance sector could trigger contagion to the broader financial sector.

Risks associated with debt overhang in emerging economies

The significant rise of corporate debt in emerging markets in recent years has emerged as an important risk to the global growth outlook. This trend has been largely driven by loose financing conditions in the post-crisis period, facilitated by capital inflow seeking higher-yield assets. Some of the larger developing economies, including China, have continued to see rising leverage in non-financial firms in recent years. Rising leverage does not necessarily pose a risk if it reflects the deepening of financial markets, which is natural as economies progress. However, in some cases — most recently especially in firms operating in commodity sectors — profitability has deteriorated in conjunction with the accumulation of debt, putting balance sheets on a more fragile footing. This has been associated with a rise in default rates among firms in some emerging markets, notably in Latin America and the Caribbean. If these pressures were to develop into a disorderly deleveraging process, this would expose banking sector fragilities with the potential to introduce banking sector stress.

Loose financing conditions have encouraged a significant rise in corporate debt in emerging markets

In addition, productive investment in many developing countries has slowed in recent years, with much of the accumulated debt channeled into financial sector and real estate assets (see discussion in box III.1), escalating risks of assets bubbles, rather than boosting overall productivity.

Government debt has also risen in many developing countries, reflecting the deterioration of fiscal positions related to slower growth, subdued commodity prices and higher financing costs, especially in countries that have suffered sharp currency depreciations. Foreign currency-denominated debt has been gaining importance in pockets of the developing countries, leaving borrowers exposed to exchange rate risk. Since the United States dollar is expected to continue to strengthen as interest rate differentials relative to other developed economies widen, this will continue to raise the debt servicing burden in countries where significant levels of debt are issued in dollars.

The rise in foreign currency-denominated debt may pose risks as the US dollar strengthens

Should widening interest rate differentials in the developed economies heighten financial volatility, including an abrupt depreciation in currencies of emerging economies, the risks associated with debt overhang in emerging economies would escalate.

Other risks to the outlook

Other risks and uncertainties in the world economic prospects include banking sector fragilities, especially in Europe, but also in some developing and transition economies, which could trigger financial distress in response to a further squeeze on bank lending margins or rising defaults related to exchange rate shocks; the response to recovery in commodity prices, which could lead to a stronger pass-through to inflation than currently forecast; as well as the political, geopolitical and security risks which continue to weigh on regional prospects in many parts of the world.

On the upside, non-oil commodity prices have shown some signs of revival. If sustained, this recovery can be expected to ease the pressure on several countries, especially non-oil commodity exporters in Africa, which may trigger a recovery in investment and act as an upside risk to the regional prospects. However, as much of the upward pressure on commodity prices has been related to supply pressures, for example due to the impact of El Niño on agriculture, and the suspension of production in certain metal industries, the rise in commodity prices may have a greater impact on inflation than on aggregate demand.

Policy challenges

Reorienting towards a more effective policy mix

The macroeconomic policy stances discussed in the Appendix to this chapter are mostly based on the policy announcements made by the authorities of individual countries. These policy stances are, however, not necessarily the optimal options for these economies, nor for the global economy as whole. They may not be sufficient to extricate the world economy from the protracted quagmire of subdued growth, stagnated trade flows, feeble investment, flagging productivity, rising inequality and ballooned debt levels in the aftermath of the global crisis.

Policy measures must target a wide range of objectives to meet the economic, social and environmental dimensions of sustainable development

In order to restore the global economy to a healthy growth trajectory over the medium-term, as well as tackle poverty, inequality and climate change, policy measures need to target a wide range of objectives, including, for example, improving education; investing in worker training; promoting investment, including in inclusive and resilient infrastructure, social protection and green technology; and progressive reform of the regulatory environment.

Currently, many economies depend excessively on monetary policy alone to support their objectives. Although it played an important role in the aftermath of the global crisis and remains an important policy tool, a much broader approach is needed, incorporating a more effective use of fiscal policy (box I.4), as well as moving beyond policies of demand management to include structural reforms. As revealed at the Hangzhou G20 Summit, there is a consensus on the need for a more balanced policy mix in the global economy.

A more balanced policy mix is needed, moving beyond excessive reliance on monetary policy

A much broader policy toolkit is demanded, adapted as appropriate to country circumstances. For example, structural reforms to the business environment can increase transparency in administrative processes and support effective protection of property rights. A broader use of income policy may be introduced to tackle inequalities and sustain demand, as well as active labour market policies to support vulnerable or marginalized sectors of the labour market. Micro- and macro-prudential policies can be employed to contain financial risks while supporting inclusive access to finance, especially for small- and medium-sized firms, while financial regulation and incentives along the investment chain should encourage long-term and sustainable investment, including in green technology and environmental protection. Finally, industrial policies can remedy market failures and science and technology polices may be introduced to increase investments in R&D and foster innovation.

Fiscal and monetary policy space is restricted in many commodity-exporting economies

Weak growth, rising inflationary pressures and low commodity prices have complicated the conduct of policy in many commodity-exporting developing economies and economies in transition, notably in Africa, the CIS and Latin America and the Caribbean. Several countries have introduced pro-cyclical interest rate rises to stem capital outflows, mitigate currency depreciation, and contain rising inflation, at the expense of higher borrowing costs that weigh on domestic activity.

Additional concessional international public financing may be needed to ensure LDCs reach the levels of investment needed to achieve the SDGs

Low global commodity prices have also intensified fiscal pressures in commodity-dependent economies. As a result, cutbacks or delays occurred in much needed investment in infrastructure, social protection and social services, energy and transport. This has in turn constrained productivity growth and undermined social and environmental progress.

In order to achieve the SDGs, policy makers will need to step up efforts. Garnering the resources required to finance investment levels needed to put the LDCs on a more rapid growth path remains a key challenge. Tackling the high levels of poverty requires acce-

Box I.4

Measuring fiscal space

While the term "fiscal space" is widely used by government officials and economists alike, there is no clear consensus on its definition and measurement. The most widely-used definition provided by Heller (2005) describes fiscal space as the "availability of budgetary room that allows a government to provide resources for a desired purpose without any prejudice to the sustainability of a government's financial position." Other definitions of fiscal space focus more specifically on countries' potential to expand their financing capacity in support of pursuing development objectives (Roy and others, 2009).

Given the lack of a clear and unique definition, a range of alternative measures have been proposed. Conventional measures rely on the concept of debt sustainability, defining fiscal space as the distance between the current levels of public debt and estimated sustainable public debt levels. Three of the most common and widely used approaches to estimate a country's sustainable debt level are:

1. The median or mean debt-to-GDP ratio of a defined group of countries, e.g. regional groups or income groups, which are associated with the country of interest (World Bank, 2015).
2. The classic approach of calculating the present discounted value of all future projected primary balances of a country (IMF, 2013). Debt levels below that level would be considered sustainable.
3. The ability-to-pay model, which estimates a non-linear response function of the primary balance to public debt levels and an effective interest payment schedule that depends on public debt levels (Ghosh and others, 2013). Within this framework, sustainable debt levels are defined as those beyond which the primary balance adjustment would not be sufficient to offset growing debt service.

An alternative fiscal space measure is de facto fiscal space (Aizenman and Jinjarak, 2010), defined as the ratio of the public debt level to the "de facto tax base", or the number of tax years a Government needs to repay its debt. This differs fundamentally from conventional fiscal space measures in that it does not involve estimation of sustainable debt levels.

It is perhaps not surprising that estimates of fiscal space vary significantly with the methodology that is used. We illustrate this by applying the following four measures to a sample of 27 economies:

1. Gross general government debt;
2. De facto fiscal space;
3. Ability-to-pay-model fiscal space; and
4. Effective ability-to-pay-model fiscal space. This measure corresponds to the ability-to-pay-model fiscal space scaled by a country-specific fiscal multiplier based on the most recent estimates found in the literature. The motivation for this adjustment is to capture the main objective of fiscal space assessments, namely measuring the fiscal capacity to support economic growth.

For each of these four measures, figure I.4.1 depicts an economy's percentage deviation from the group mean of the 27 selected economies. It is evident that for a number of economies, not only the relative distance from the group mean changes with the fiscal space measures, but also the ordinal position in the group. The latter is particularly the case for countries in the middle of the pack.

Countries with higher public debt-to-GDP ratios do not necessarily have smaller fiscal space according to the ability-to-pay model. For example, Singapore and the United States have bigger ability-to-pay-model fiscal space than many economies with lower public debt-to-GDP ratio. This can at least partly be attributed to their relatively sanguine economic outlook and institutional stability. When taking fiscal spending effectiveness into account, further changes to the landscape can be seen.

According to the effective ability-to-pay-model, the United States has considerable fiscal space, whereas Singapore has effectively none. This result stems from the significant differences in the two countries' estimated fiscal multipliers and underscores the fact that a Government has a much weaker case to engage in fiscal stimulus if its estimated fiscal multiplier is small or, as in the case of Singapore, even negative. De facto fiscal space often paints a different picture than the other measures since it mainly reflects a Government's revenue collection capacity.

(continued)

Box I.4 (*continued*)

Figure I.4.1
A comparison of different fiscal space measures in 2014

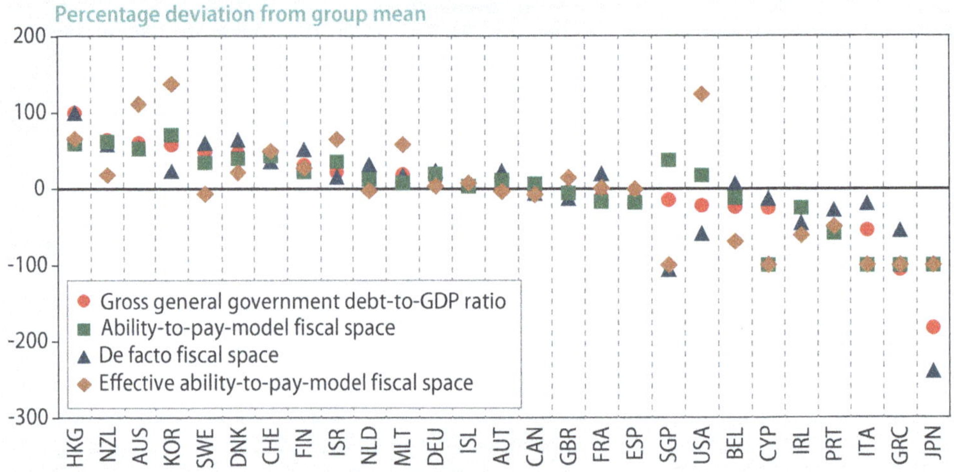

Source: UN/DESA calculations, based on data from IMF (2016a), Moody's Analytics, and estimates of country-specific fiscal multipliers taken from the literature.

Note: The signs on the percentage deviation of each economy's gross general government debt-to-GDP ratio and de facto fiscal space from the group mean have been reversed to ensure comparability with the other two measures.

See Table J in the Statistical Annex for definitions of country codes.

This simple empirical exercise illustrates that relying on any single fiscal space measure leads to an incomplete, and potentially biased assessment of the fiscal resources available to a Government. A comprehensive approach to assess fiscal space for policy decisions would instead require a scoreboard of measures. Such a scoreboard should not only include the above-mentioned measures — along with some modifications — but other indicators that capture important aspects of fiscal sustainability. This includes, for example, the extent to which a country issues debt in its own sovereign currency, the geographical composition of debt and the determinants of interest rates.

Authors: Hoi Wai Cheng and Ingo Pitterle

lerating medium-term growth and implementing redistributive policies to address multidimensional inequalities. Governments, particularly in developing countries, need to augment public investments in education, health and infrastructure to ensure that those with low-income enjoy equal opportunities for a decent livelihood. With private financing and domestic resource mobilisation limited by structural factors, additional concessional international public financing is needed to support developing countries (see chapter III for further discussion).

Enhancing international policy coordination under the new 2030 Agenda

Macroeconomic policy measures to support economic growth should be integrated with social and environmental policies to promote balanced achievement of the SDGs

The year 2016 marked the beginning of the implementation of the 2030 Agenda for Sustainable Development, which includes 17 SDGs and 169 targets, cross-cutting economic, social and environmental dimensions of sustainable development.

It is imperative to recognize that any efforts to revitalize global economic growth, attain full employment and maintain macroeconomic stability are integral to overall efforts to implement the 2030 Agenda. Sustained, inclusive and sustainable growth, full employment and macroeconomic stability are already included in the SDGs. Therefore, macroeconomic policy measures to support economic growth should be integrated with social and environmental policies so as to promote balanced achievement of the SDGs. These issues were recognized at the Hangzhou G20 Summit, where the need for deeper international policy coordination in the areas discussed below was duly stressed.

While a systematic integrative policy approach to realising the 2030 Agenda can only be developed through the engagement of Member States and international organizations in years to come, some ad hoc measures can be taken to improve international policy coherence and consistency in a number of areas.

Boosting international trade

International trade will not revive independently of a recovery in aggregate demand. However, the process can be encouraged through a number of measures at the global and the national levels.

To ensure development concerns are addressed by the global trading system, a stronger role for the World Trade Organization is needed

The central role of the World Trade Organization (WTO) in the global economy must be strengthened. As the WTO provides a unique rules-based, transparent, non-discriminatory, open and inclusive multilateral trading system, its central role should be strengthened through the conclusion of the negotiations on the Doha Development Agenda. Concerted efforts should be made to curb the rising number of restrictive measures on trade in goods and services since the global financial crisis, and to roll back old protectionist measures, subsidies and tariffs that are particularly damaging to developing countries' exports.

WTO members should expedite the implementation of the Trade Facilitation Agreement (TFA), in order to lower global trade costs. In this regard, international efforts are needed to provide capacity building and technical assistance for developing countries in their implementation of TFA.

International cooperation is needed to align the multilateral trading system with the SDGs, integrate export sectors with domestic economies and reduce trade financing gaps

International coordination is needed to ensure consistency between trade, investment and other public policies so as to prevent the dismantling of GVCs, which have been important drivers of international trade and investment flows, and align the multilateral trading system with the 2030 Agenda for Sustainable Development, ensuring inclusive growth and decent work for all.

Accordingly, efforts are needed to support an open, transparent, and competitive services market, so as to facilitate the participation of service providers, especially from developing countries and low income countries in GVCs. Countries need to link their export-oriented sectors to the rest of the economy, developing backward, forward and income linkages, avoiding the generation of enclave economies.

International cooperative efforts are also needed to reduce trade financing gaps, which are found to be highest among the LDCs, notably in Africa, developing Asia and small island developing States, as well as small and medium-sized enterprises.

International cooperation on clean technology transfer and climate finance is also necessary. Countries will have to continue to pursue nationally-appropriate low-carbon development paths that are sustainable on economic, social and environmental fronts.

Promoting infrastructure investment

Building sustainable and resilient infrastructure requires a realignment of incentives to ensure that investment is widespread across countries and sectors

Increased investment in sustainable and resilient infrastructure is a prerequisite for achieving the 2030 Agenda, and at the same time can also stimulate short-term global growth and boost potential growth in the longer run.

In the AAAA, an integral part of the 2030 Agenda, countries agreed on actions to help overcome barriers to infrastructure investment on both the demand and supply sides. The Addis Agenda encourages long-term institutional investors to allocate a greater percentage of their investment to infrastructure, particularly in developing countries. Policy frameworks should be geared toward long-term investment, so as to mitigate the risk that global efforts for increased investment in infrastructure will focus on a limited number of countries, and only on sectors with potential cash flows. Incentive structures of private investors need to be aligned with the long-term investment horizon necessary for many infrastructure projects.

Development banks play important roles in infrastructure investment. The Global Infrastructure Forum launched by the World Bank Group, in cooperation with other multilateral development banks (MDBs) and UN-DESA in April 2016 can help coordinate the efforts among MDBs, so that they can work together on infrastructure financing in project preparation and improving data and information, keeping their focus on LDCs and ensuring resilient and sustainable infrastructure investment.

In addition, international policy cooperation and coordination need to be strengthened in international public finance and official development assistance (ODA), international tax cooperation, illicit financial flows, global financial safety nets, governance reform of the International Monetary Fund (IMF) and World Bank Group as well as refugees and migrants.

Appendix
Global assumptions

Baseline forecast assumptions

This appendix summarizes the key assumptions underlying the baseline forecast, including monetary and fiscal policies for major economies, exchange rates for major currencies and the international prices of oil. Key assumptions include:

- The United States Federal Reserve Board (Fed) will raise its policy rate by 50 basis points and 75 basis points in 2017 and 2018, respectively.
- The price of Brent crude oil is projected to average $52 per barrel in 2017 and $61 per barrel in 2018.
- Most major currencies are expected to depreciate against the US dollar in 2017-2018.

Monetary policy

Monetary policy in major developed economies is expected to remain broadly accommodative in 2017-2018, despite further divergence in interest rates among these economies (figure I.A.1).

Figure I.A.1
Key policy rates, March 2012–December 2018

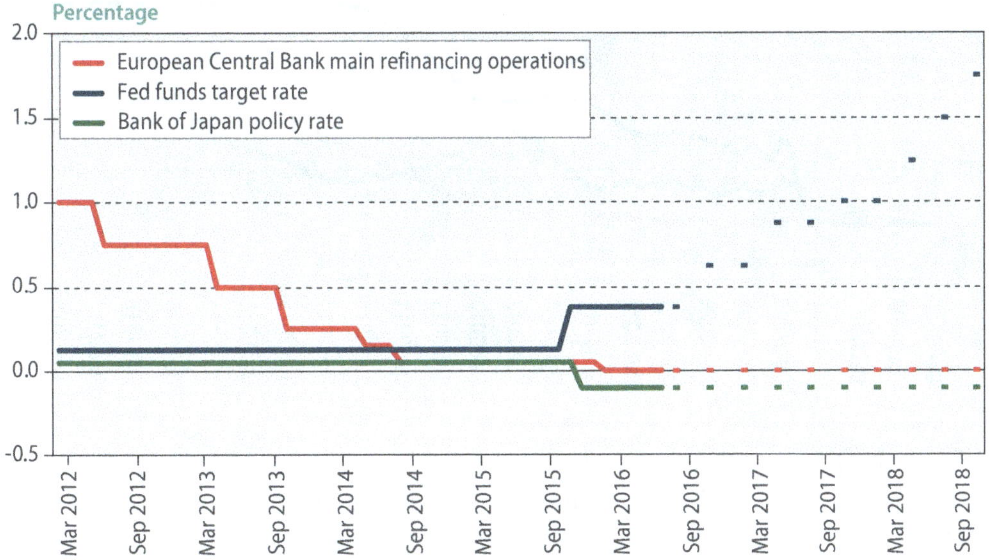

Source: National central banks and UN/DESA forecast assumptions.

United States: The Fed is expected to have raised its key policy rate by 25 basis points by the end of 2016. The target for the federal funds rate will then increase gradually, by 50 basis points and 75 basis points in 2017 and 2018, respectively. The Fed is expected to maintain its policy of "reinvesting principal payments from its holdings of agency debt and agency mortgage-backed securities in agency mortgage-backed securities and of rolling over maturing Treasury securities at auction" until the end of 2018 (figure I.A.2).

Japan: The Bank of Japan (BoJ) is expected to continue applying a negative interest rate on the Policy-Rate Balances in current accounts held by financial institutions at the BoJ and maintain the set of unconventional monetary policy measures announced in September 2016 until at least the end of 2018. These measures include two components: (1) a "quantitative and qualitative monetary easing with yield curve control" framework to anchor 10-year Japanese Government Bond yields at around 0 per cent; and (2) an explicit commitment to increase the monetary base until inflation overshoots the 2 per cent target.

Euro area: The European Central Bank (ECB) will continue to maintain an extremely accommodative monetary policy stance that comprises three elements: policy interest rates at or below zero; quantitative easing (QE) in the form of monthly asset purchases; and targeted longer-term refinancing operations (TLTROs) intended to move banks to lend more money.

Figure I.A.2

Total assets of major central banks, December 2006–December 2018

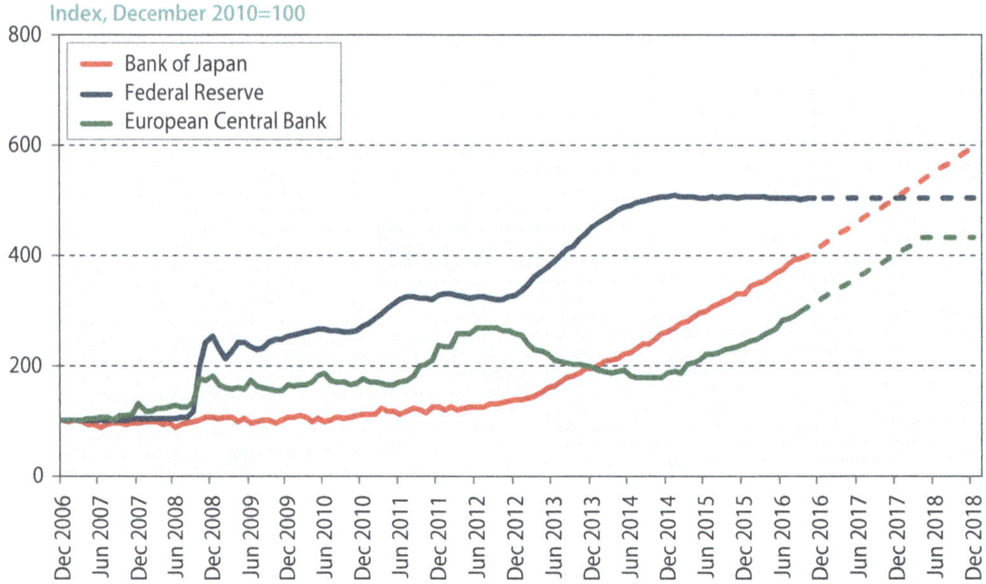

Source: National central banks and UN/DESA forecast assumptions.

United Kingdom: The Bank of England (BoE) reacted to the decision of the United Kingdom to leave the EU by cutting its policy interest rates by 25 basis points to 0.25 per cent and by increasing the volume of its QE measures. In the outlook, monetary policy in BoE is expected to be responsive to uncertainties and risks arising from new institutional arrangements in the process of exiting the EU.

Monetary policy stances vary significantly among developing countries and economies in transition. Figure I.A.3 illustrates the share of each major global region that has increased and reduced interest rates since the Federal Reserve's first interest rate rise in December 2015.

Figure I.A.3
Global divergence in policy rates since December 2015

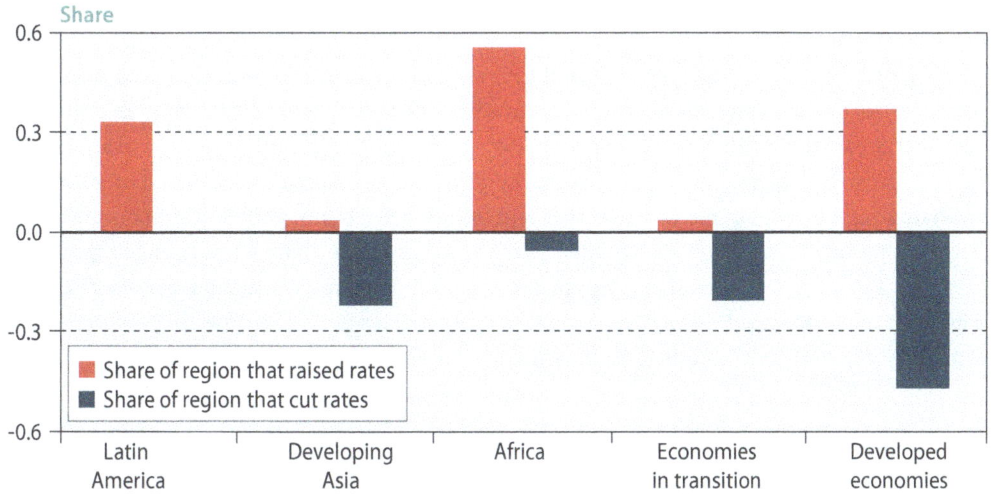

Source: UN/DESA.

There has been a clear tendency towards tightening in Africa and Latin America and the Caribbean, despite deteriorating economic prospects in these regions. In many cases (Angola, Azerbaijan, Egypt, Mexico, Mozambique, Namibia, Nigeria, South Africa and Sri Lanka), recent interest-rate increases followed sharp exchange-rate depreciations, and the rates of return for international investors have declined despite higher domestic interest rates. This leaves countries exposed to capital withdrawal, as investors seek higher rates of return elsewhere.

CIS: Most central banks in the CIS reduced interest rates during 2016 in view of slowing inflation; however, in the largest economies of the region, monetary easing will remain cautious.

East Asia: Policy rates across major economies in developing East Asia are approaching or have reached historic low levels. With few exceptions, there remains some — albeit limited — room for further rate cuts given the overall low inflationary environment. However, central banks will remain sensitive to the potential impact on capital outflows, private sector leverage and bank profit margins. The People's Bank of China (PBoC) is expected to make at most two 50 basis-point reserve requirement ratio cuts in 2017 and continue to pursue a prudent monetary stance. Credit growth will continue to outpace GDP growth in 2016-2018, but at a rate lower than in 2015.

South Asia: Monetary policy in South Asia continues to be moderately accommodative, on the back of subdued inflationary pressures and remaining output gaps in some economies. The accommodative stance is expected to continue in the forecast period, with further easing in some countries.

Western Asia: GCC countries will continue to follow the movement of the Fed, due to the pegging of their currencies to the dollar, and inject liquidity into the banking system through measures such as repurchase agreements. In Turkey, after cuts in interest rates in the second half of 2016, room for further monetary easing is limited in the face of the weak currency and high inflation.

Latin America and the Caribbean: The monetary tightening cycle in South America is mostly over and some easing is expected for 2017-2018. In Mexico, the central bank increased interest rates three times in 2016 as the peso tumbled to a record low, and further rate rises are likely.

Africa: In Africa, policy is expected to remain constrained by inflation and currency pressures in many economies. However, in some countries, including Botswana, Kenya and Morocco, where inflation is relatively low, some additional policy space is available to support growth. Nigeria removed its currency peg to the dollar in mid-2016 in an effort to alleviate severe foreign currency shortages and reduce price distortions in the economy. The Nigerian naira subsequently depreciated sharply, losing more than 40 per cent of its value over just a few months. Similarly, Egypt devalued its domestic currency by more than 30 per cent and announced a move to a more flexible exchange rate regime, as persistent foreign currency shortages weighed on business activity and investor sentiments.

Fiscal policy

Fiscal policy in developed economies is expected to be somewhat less restrictive in 2017-2018, moving away from the tight fiscal austerity programmes that have been in place for the most part since 2010. A few countries have announced expansionary measures, including Australia, Canada and Japan.

United States: The new Administration has indicated an intention to significantly expand government investment in infrastructure and introduce substantial tax cuts for corporations. However, there is a lack of clarity and specificity at the time of writing. Given the uncertainty, the forecasts presented in this report are predicated on a broadly neutral fiscal stance in 2017-2018.

Japan: The new fiscal stimulus programme announced in mid-2016 is expected to increase spending by national and local governments by 7.5 trillion yen, which includes 4.6 trillion yen in additional spending in the 2016 fiscal year (FY2016). The additional spending allocated for FY2016 is equivalent to around 0.9 per cent of GDP and a 4.8 per cent expansion from the original government budget for the fiscal year. The Government has postponed the next consumption tax increase to 2019 at the earliest, and announced a significant expansion of public works spending.

EU: Fiscal policy in the EU maintains a tightening stance overall, given institutional requirements such as the excessive-deficit mechanism of the EU. However, the fiscal stance has become less restrictive for the most part. Some countries, such as Austria and Germany will see significant fiscal spending requirements in view of the large number of migrants and the challenge of integrating them into their societies and labour markets. In the United Kingdom, the decision to leave the EU has important implications for fiscal policy, with an expected increase in its budget deficit in coming years.

Among developing countries and economies in transition, fiscal policy stance continues to vary significantly from region to region.

CIS: Energy-exporting countries are expected to tighten government spending, while energy-importing countries will maintain largely a neutral or slightly expansionary fiscal stance. In the Russian Federation, while the budget for 2017-2019 is still under discussion, spending is likely to be reduced in nominal terms, implying an even deeper real contraction. The authorities are planning to increase domestic borrowing and to mobilize household savings to channel them into investment.

East Asia: The fiscal stance was mostly expansionary and countercyclical in 2015-2016, amid weak regional growth and limited room for furthering monetary easing. China is expected to maintain a mildly expansionary stance in 2017-2018, with more active intervention in infrastructure investment and promotion of new strategic industries. The on-budget deficit increased in 2016 and will remain at similar levels in 2017-2018. In addition, significant fiscal support will also be provided through off-budget channels, such as policy banks, public-private partnership, and deployment of rising local government revenues from land sales.

South Asia: Fiscal policies are officially expected to be in a moderately tight stance in most economies, but in reality, some economies have implemented more expansionary policies. Budget deficits are expected to remain high in most economies. The region needs to increase its efforts to strengthen the tax base.

Western Asia: Fiscal policy is under consolidation in GCC countries, including significant cuts in spending and subsidies and increases in taxes, as well as new issuance of debt. In October 2016, Saudi Arabia raised $17.5 billion in its first international bond issuance to finance its large budget deficit, which reached a record high of about 15 per cent of GDP in 2015. In some cases, privatization plans are also underway. The fiscal situation in conflict-affected countries worsened in 2016, particularly in Iraq, the Syrian Arab Republic and Yemen. Meanwhile, weak revenue prospects continue in Jordan and Lebanon, and public debt levels look set to expand. Both countries continued to require international financial support for their efforts to accommodate Syrian refugees. In Turkey, fiscal policy is expected to remain relatively tight.

Latin America and the Caribbean: Fiscal policy will remain tight in Latin America in the outlook period as Governments respond to lower commodity prices and macroeconomic imbalances. The fiscal adjustment will generally be gradual, to minimize the downward pressure on aggregate demand.

Africa: Persistently low commodity prices have intensified fiscal pressures in the commodity-dependent economies. As a result, many African countries announced budget cuts or fiscal reform measures. For example, Algeria, Angola and the Congo announced significant budget cuts during 2016. Nigeria and Zambia have sought financial assistance from international organisations amid deterioration in their external and fiscal positions.

Exchange rates

The dollar/euro exchange rate is assumed to average 1.112 in 2016, and to depreciate in line with the widening differential between ECB and Fed interest rates to 1.104 in 2017 and 1.079 in 2018.

The yen/dollar exchange rate is assumed to average 107.46 in 2016, 105.41 in 2017 and 105.99 in 2018.

Figure I.A.4
Data and assumptions on major currency exchange rates

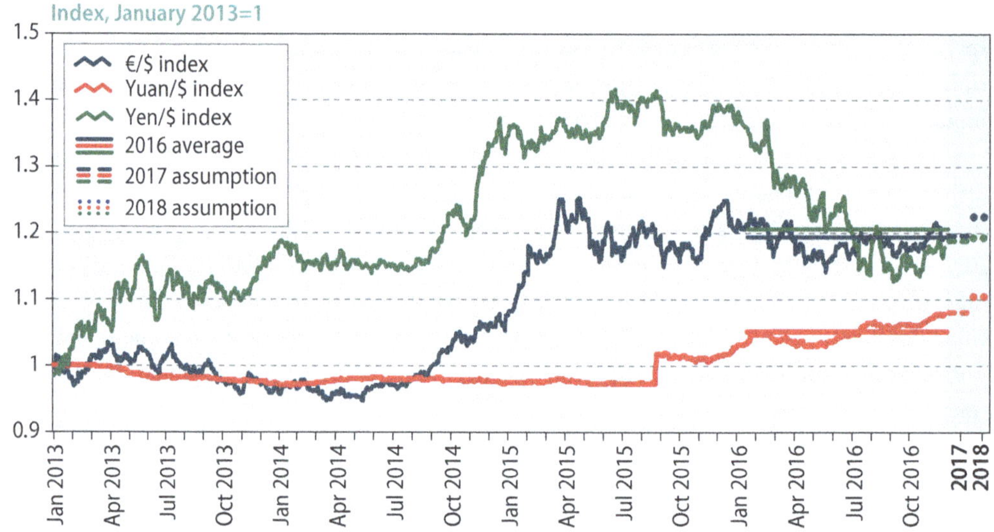

Source: IMF Exchange Rate Query Tool and UN/DESA forecast assumptions.

The renminbi/dollar exchange rate is assumed to average 6.61 in 2016, 6.79 in 2017 and 6.92 in 2018.

Oil price

The price of Brent crude oil is assumed to average $43 per barrel in 2016, $52 per barrel in 2017 and $61 per barrel in 2018.

Figure I.A.5
Data and assumptions for the price of Brent crude

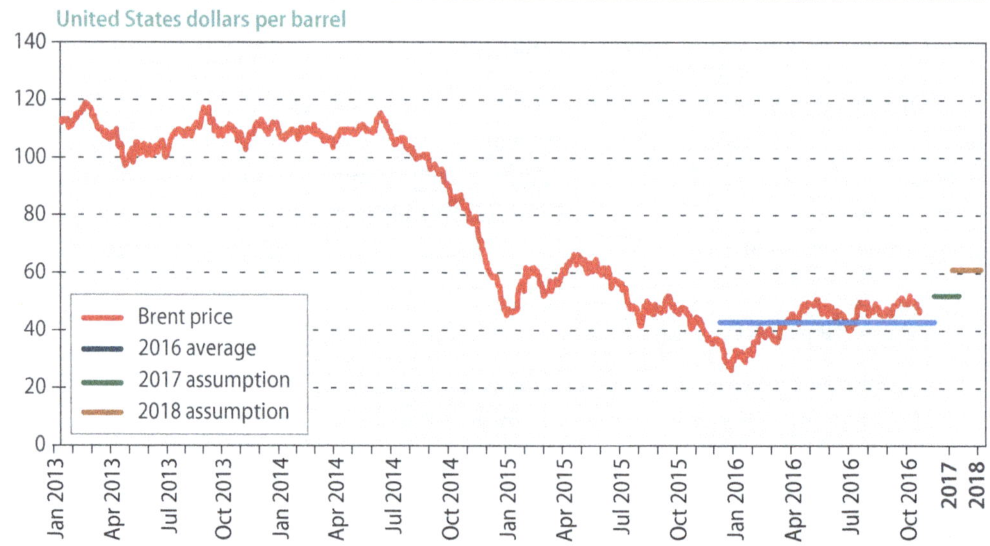

Source: Energy Information Administration and UN/DESA forecast assumptions.

Chapter II
International trade

Trade flows

General trend in trade flows

Global trade flows weakened further in 2016. At the slowest pace since the Great Recession of 2009, the volume of world trade is estimated to have grown by a meagre 1.2 per cent. The downward shift in world trade growth in recent years has been significant: in the two decades prior to the global financial crisis, the average growth of the volume of world trade was about 7 per cent, but it slowed down to below 3 per cent between 2012 and 2016 (figure II.1). More worrisome is the substantial decline in the ratio of global trade growth to world gross product (WGP) growth, dropping from an average of 2:1 in 1980-2008 to 1:1 recently, and even lower in 2016.

Figure II.1
Growth of volume of world trade and growth of world gross product, 1990–2018

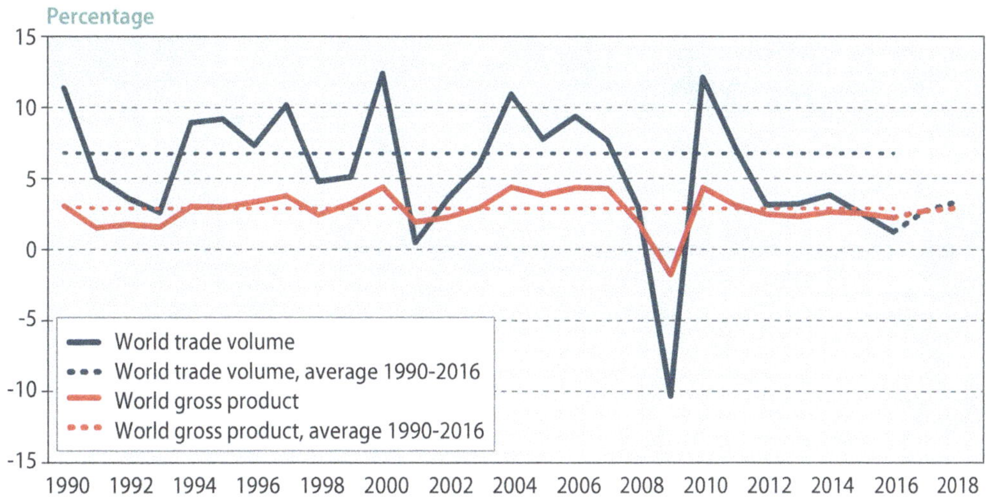

Source: UN/DESA.
Note: Growth for 2016 is partially estimated; growth for 2017 and 2018 are forecasts.

A demand composition effect contributed to the slowdown in trade

A number of factors are behind the slowdown of global trade flows in recent years. Some of these are cyclical and others structural (see Constantinescu and others, 2015; European Central Bank, 2016; International Monetary Fund, 2016c). Since the global financial crisis, the subdued gross domestic product (GDP) growth and the change in the composition of aggregate demand in many countries seem to have significantly impacted trade flows. In particular, a substantial weakening in fixed investment growth in both developed countries and emerging economies in the aftermath of the crisis appears to be highly correlated with the slowdown in global trade flows (figure II.2).

Import demand is more sensitive to fixed investment in many countries

On average, capital goods account for about 39 per cent of world merchandise trade. Consequently, in many countries, import demand is more sensitive to fixed investment than other expenditure components of GDP. For instance, for a sample of 18 OECD countries, the average import intensity of investment, exports, private consumption and public consumption are respectively 32, 28, 25 and 10 per cent (figure II.3). According to some studies, the compositional effect explains a significant part of the plummet of imports during the financial crisis and the subsequent decline in the ratio of import growth to GDP growth for major developed countries (Bussière and others, 2013).

Figure II.2
Year-on-year change in global gross fixed capital formation and growth of world trade, 1990–2015

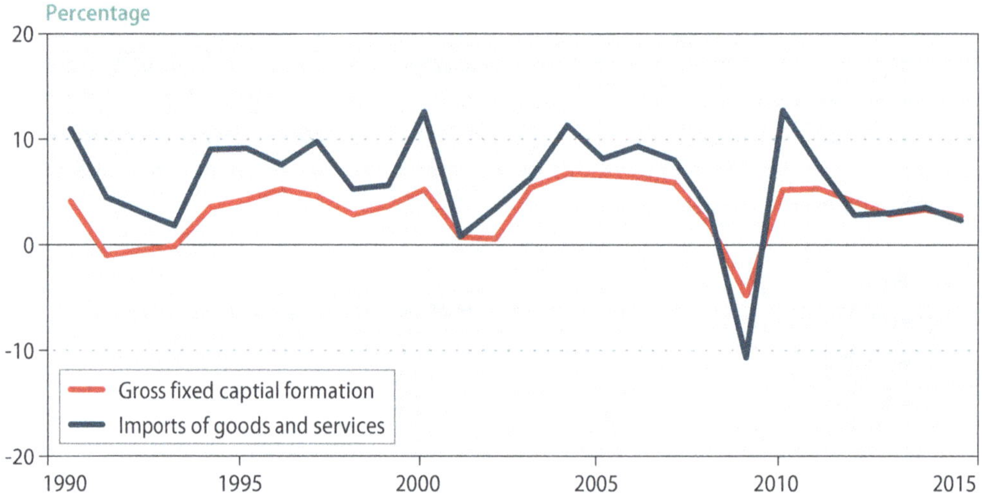

Source: UN/DESA.

Figure II.3
Import intensity of the expenditure components of GDP

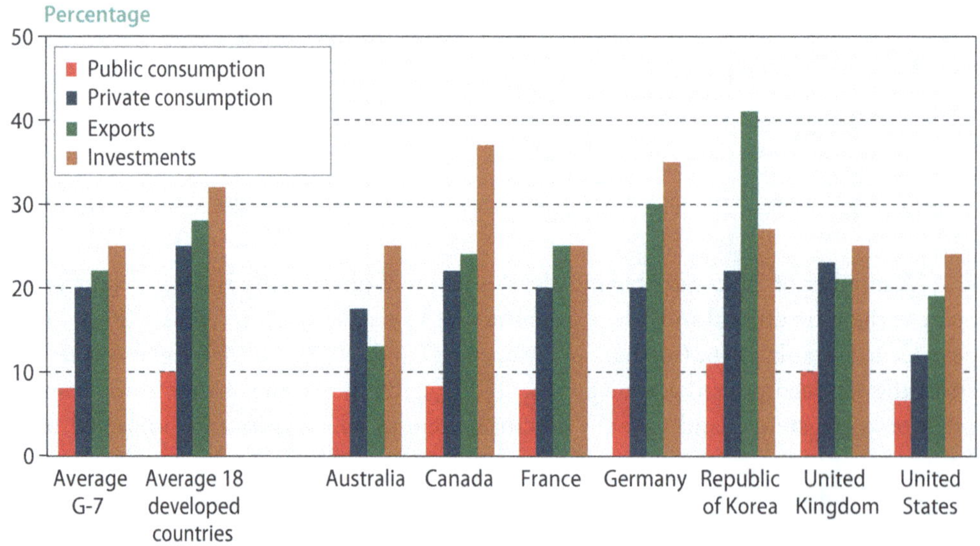

Source: UN/DESA, based on Bussière and others (2013).

Empirical studies also show that heightened uncertainties in the aftermath of the global financial crisis, in terms of increased volatility in financial markets, including equities, bonds, currencies and commodity prices, may have had a direct adverse impact on international trade flows. For instance, Novy and Taylor (2014) show that in response to uncertainty shocks, firms adjust their orders to foreign intermediaries more strongly than to domestic ones, given differences in their cost structure. As a result, heightened uncertainties lead to a larger contraction of international trade flows than of domestic sectors.

Heightened uncertainties also have a negative effect on trade

Diminished expansion of international global value chains (GVCs) has also significantly subdued trade flows. GVCs expanded substantially during the 1990s and 2000s, driven by "efficiency-seeking" foreign direct investment to establish International Systems of Integrated Production (ISIP) in sectors such as automobiles, electronics and apparel. This led to a boom in international trade flows in the 1990s and early 2000s, but has noticeably decelerated in the last decade. As a case in point, the share of Chinese imports of parts and components in merchandise exports has decreased from 60 per cent in 2000 to less than 35 per cent in recent years (Constantinescu and others, 2015). This is partly because a number of manufacturing plants have moved their operations into other countries such as Bangladesh and Viet Nam due to increasing labour costs in coastal areas of China.

A slower expansion of global value chains also tapers trade growth

In addition to waning GVC expansion, the pace of dismantling trade barriers between countries has also diminished. The World Trade Organization (WTO) Doha Round of multilateral trade negotiations has not progressed in supporting trade flows in recent years, and the effects of Regional Trade Agreements (RTAs), such as the possible Trans-Pacific Partnership, remain uncertain. Moreover, the rise of trade-restrictive measures observed since the financial crisis is becoming more widespread across both developed and developing countries (WTO, 2016a; European Commission, 2016). These restrictive measures have mainly appeared as non-tariff barriers. Between October 2015 and May 2016, the Group of Twenty (G20) countries implemented 145 new trade-restrictive measures, marking the highest monthly average since 2009. Trade-restrictive measures in place increased from 324 in 2010 to 1,196 in 2016 (figure II.4), and 75 per cent of all trade-restrictive actions executed since the financial crisis are still in place (WTO, 2016a).

Slower progress in trade liberalisation likewise leads to a more tepid trade expansion

Figure II.4
Trade-restrictive measures, G20, October 2010–May 2016

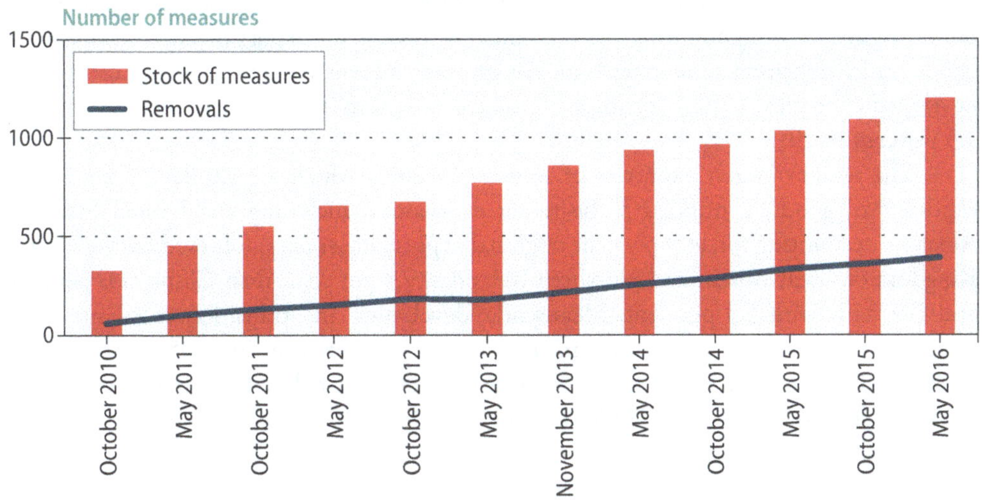

Source: WTO (2016a).

The rising number of trade restrictions is mostly explained by the rise in anti-dumping actions, safeguard actions and countervailing duty measures

Trade covered by these restrictive measures is about 6 per cent of G20 imports and about 5 per cent of global imports. Anti-dumping actions, safeguarding actions and countervailing duty measures account for most of the rise in trade-restrictive measures, as well as the creeping demand for local content. Meanwhile, bailouts and subsidies continue to represent a large proportion of trade-distortive measures in place. While the empirical evidence on the linkage between the recent upswing in trade-restrictive measures and the observed slowdown in global trade growth remains limited, if protectionist tendencies persist and intensify, this will likely weigh on global trade prospects.

The recent rise of local content requirements, or the so-called "localisation measures",[1] can change the balance between trade and foreign direct investment (FDI) strategies of transnational firms. Some firms are implementing more aggressive localisation strategies worldwide, favouring the FDI approach to serving external markets (Evenett and Fritz, 2016; Bathia and others, 2016). Interestingly, in 2015, cross-border mergers and acquisitions in the manufacturing sector peaked at an historical high of $388 billion (UNCTAD, 2016b).

Strong trade growth in the past was also due to exceptional historical events

From a long-run perspective, the strong trade growth relative to world gross product (WGP) growth in the 1990s and 2000s, at a ratio of 2:1, was also driven by historical events which are not repeatable. This includes the integration of the economies in transition, China and other developing economies into the global economy, which significantly reduced barriers to international trade and investment. China's export growth surged at the annual rate of 20 per cent for about two decades during and after its accession to the WTO. Similar one-off events include increased trade and monetary integration within the European Union, especially the adoption of the euro. In addition, the revolution in information and communication technology (ICT)and other technologies led to lower global transportation costs.

Trade growth is expected to rebound slightly

A slight rebound is expected for global trade growth, at a pace of 2.7 per cent in 2017 and 3.3 per cent in 2018, along with some improvement in WGP growth (see chapter I), but the ratio of global trade growth to WGP growth is not expected to return to its historical highs in the foreseeable future.

Trade in services

Trade in services has been more resilient than trade in goods

Services remain a key avenue to realising international trade potential. Although the value of global exports in services decreased by about 6 per cent from $5.1 trillion in 2014 to $4.8 trillion in 2015, trade in services has been more resilient than trade in goods, as observed after the global financial crisis. This trend holds for both developed and developing economies (figure II.5), highlighting the relevance of services for export diversification. As in goods trade, transition economies took the greatest decline, exceeding 15 per cent. Least developed countries (LDCs) constitute a notable exception, with trade in services growing 1.3 per cent in 2015.

Major economies were the main services exporters

The world's largest exporters of services in 2015, which are similar to the largest exporters of goods, continued to be major economies, including the United States of America, accounting for 14.9 per cent of global exports in services, followed by the United Kingdom of Great Britain and Northern Ireland at 7.3 per cent, then China at 6 per cent and Germany with 5.3 per cent. Meanwhile, developing and transition economies have increased their share in global trade in services, from 23 per cent in 2005 to 31 per cent in 2015. The share of LDCs in global services trade still lies below 1 per cent and has only expanded from 0.5 per cent in 2005 to 0.8 per cent in 2015.

1 Localisation measures include not only local content requirements but also tax, tariff or price concessions in local procurement, and tailoring import licensing procedures to promote domestic purchases and reserve lines of production to domestic firms, among others.

Figure II.5
Trade in goods and services, global and by country groups, 2005–2015

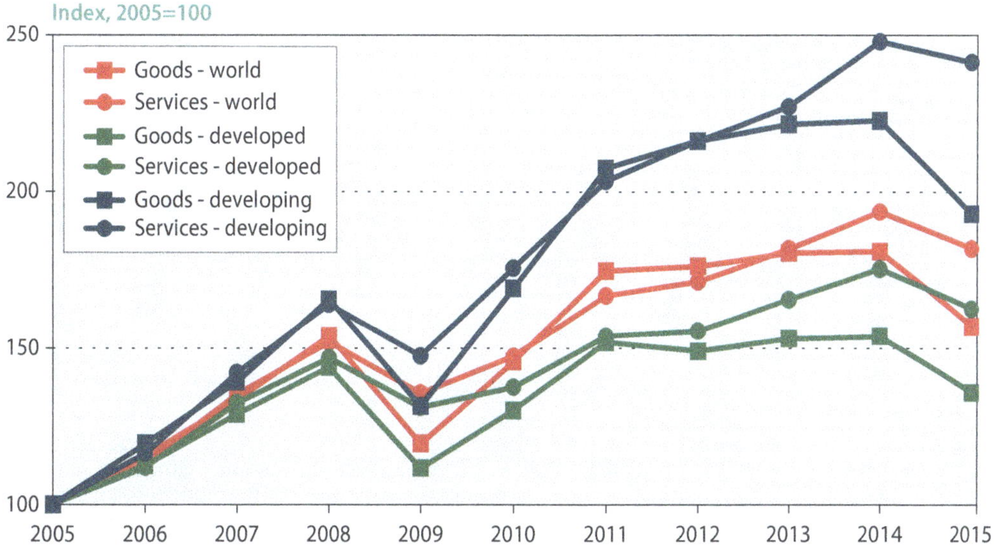

Source: UNCTADstat.

Exports of services growth was stronger in developing and transition economies

Exports of services from developing and transition economies grew more than that of developed economies in almost every sector between 2005 and 2015, including some higher value-added sectors, such as financial services, telecommunication, computer and information services, and other business services. Between 2014 and 2015, trade in telecommunication, computer and information services and intellectual property grew in developing economies, due to growth in Asia and Latin America and the Caribbean, in contrast to a decline in developed economies (figure II.6).

Nonetheless, developing economies still show a pattern of specialization in traditional services such as transport and travel, especially in Africa and LDCs, while developed economies continue to lead in higher value-added services, such as financial and insurance services (figure II.7).

The share of services in trade remains lower than in domestic output

The share of services in international trade is significantly lower than the shares of services in domestic output and employment. The services sector accounts for roughly three-quarters of value-added and employment in developed economies, and close to half in developing countries and economies in transition. However, the share of services in trade is only about one-quarter for developed economies and 15 per cent for developing countries and economies is transition. This is partly due to an underestimation in statistics of trade in services.

Data insufficiently reflect the value of services embedded in goods

In addition, data on cross-border trade in services do not capture the significant value-added of services embedded in goods, particularly in sectors such as energy, chemicals, machinery and transport equipment. In 2011, services accounted for 59 per cent of the gross value-added of exports in developed economies and 43 per cent in developing and transition economies.

This is much higher than the contribution of services to total exports, as measured by traditional cross-border data. Even in a simple jacket, physical components, including labour, fabric, lining, buttons, sleeve heads, shoulder pads, labels and hangtags, account for only 9 per cent of the price; the remaining 91 per cent of the value is for intangible assets, including a wide range of services such as retail, logistics, banking and marketing (see Low, 2013).

Figure II.6

Growth rate in trade in services by country groups and sectors, 2005–2015 (*CAGR*) and 2015

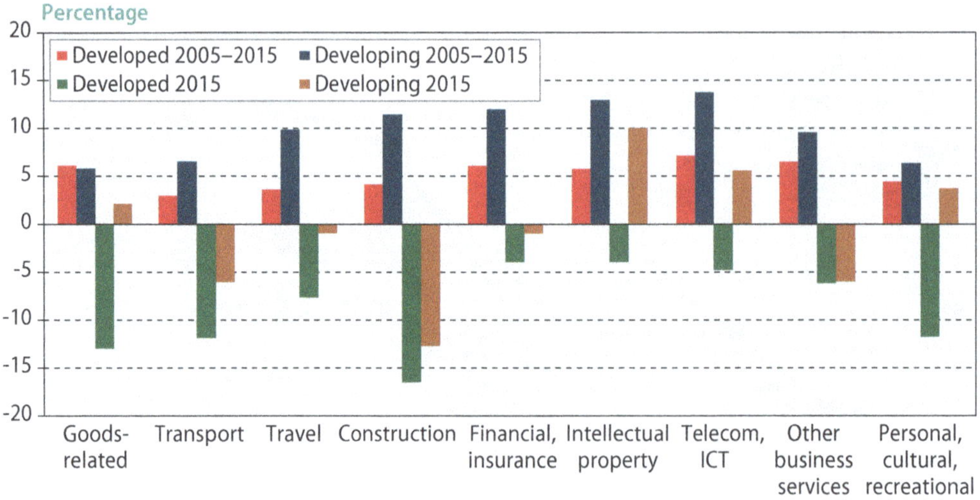

Source: UNCTADstat.

Figure II.7

Developing economies, share in global services exports by sector, 2005 and 2015

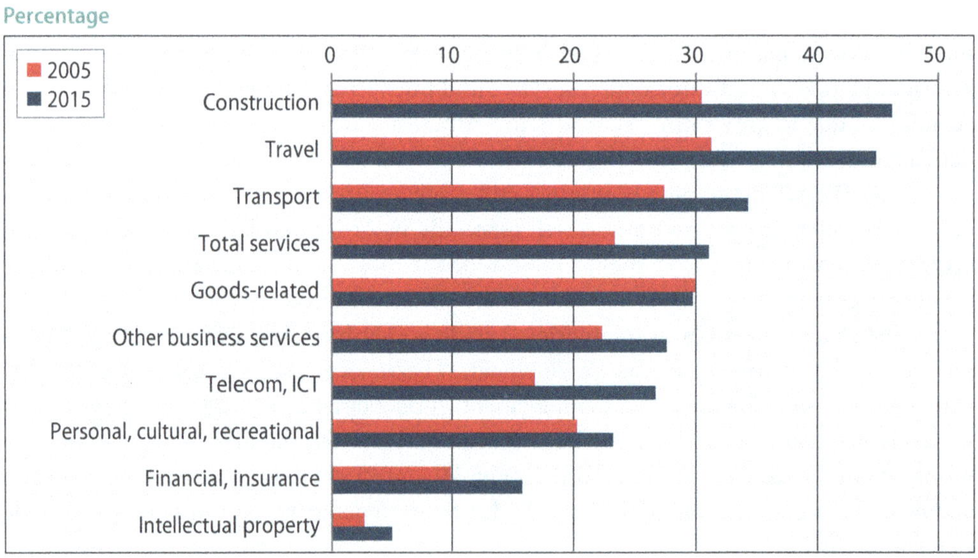

Source: UNCTADstat.

Services are a vital enabling factor for trade

This illustrates the vital role of services, including those related to infrastructure, as enablers of trade in all economic sectors and as direct determinants of economic productivity and competitiveness (see UNCTAD, 2012). All economic sectors combine a services element at all stages in GVCs, including pre-production, production, and post-production. Back-office services in the form of financial, communications, business services and utilities account for 33 per cent of all services activities in the whole value chain; production services such as quality control, engineering, security and medical services for 26 per cent; pre-production services for 18 per cent; post-production and sales services for 9 per cent; post-sales services for 8 per cent and establishment services for 6 per cent (see Low, 2015).

Transport, for example, plays a key role in linking consumers and producers, and integrating markets by facilitating exports and imports. Improving transport infrastructure, logistics and cross-border trade facilities is central to reducing delivery times and costs, and therefore for the integration into GVCs. For developing countries which are short on transport infrastructure, especially for landlocked developing countries, this is particularly important. Telecommunications, computer and information services drive economic and social activity and lead to greater productivity and competitiveness. Cross-border trade also gets a boost (box II.1).

Transport and ICT are key service sectors

Financial services promote domestic and international transactions, mobilise and channel domestic savings and open up credit for small and medium-sized enterprises (SMEs) and households. This fosters supply and export capacity, supporting entrepreneurship and linking SMEs to GVCs. Another benefit of financial inclusion is speedier, safer and less costly remittances.

Financial services are driving economic activity

Box II.1

Digital economy and ICT services-enabled trade

Telecommunications and ICT services are crucial in facilitating modern economic and social activities, contributing to productivity and competitiveness. As infrastructure services, they provide inputs to the overall economy, strengthening supply capacity for other sectors. For example, two billion people currently do not have access to a bank account but, of these, 1.6 billion have access to a mobile phone; therefore, telecommunications and ICT services can play a key role in supporting financial inclusion through digital financial services (UNCTAD, 2016c; UNCTAD, 2016d), with reduced costs and increased coverage.

The benefits of telecommunications and ICT services are further enhanced in the context of international trade, where information and connectivity barriers are traditionally higher. ICT-enabled solutions improve connections between providers and customers, enhance knowledge on the traded product and alternatives, provide payment solutions and in some cases facilitate distribution services.

Cross-border trade is enhanced by ICT-induced efficiencies, such as reductions of transport costs and electronic means of delivery. Online activities often have backward and forward linkages involving all modes of services. The e-commerce, and ICT-enabled trade in general, is crucial for SMEs, enabling them to access new domestic and international markets and participate in global value chains (GVCs) (UNCTAD, 2016c; UNCTAD, 2016d) .

E-commerce became an issue on the Doha Development Agenda and gained new dynamism at the WTO even without a negotiating mandate (WTO, 2016b). The global value of e-commerce in 2013 was estimated at $15 trillion in business-to-business (B2B) transactions and at $1.2 trillion in business-to-consumer (B2C) transactions (UNCTAD, 2015a).

There are several conditions for developing e-commerce, including a comprehensive enabling ecosystem. For example, in China, the e-commerce company Alibaba established a diverse ecosystem to enable trade through a network of services, including an e-payment system which soon expanded to banking, investment, and clearing house for cross-border trade. One of its affiliates, Alipay, has approximately 400 million users of its online payment services.[a] Alibaba's platform integrates consumers, manufacturers, customs clearing, transport and several financial services such as credit, foreign exchange and insurance (UNCTAD, 2014a).

Furthermore, SMEs account for a larger share of businesses trading through Alibaba than in traditional markets. Chinese companies trading through Alibaba can reach up to 98 export destinations, almost double that in other markets. A 10 per cent rise in Internet use within a country increases the number of products traded internationally by 1.5 per cent and raises the average trade value per product by 0.6 per cent (World Bank, 2016a).

E-commerce has not gone far enough in narrowing the digital divide. This divide has not decreased in recent years in terms of the number of Internet users, and low and middle-income economies are still lagging behind in fixed broadband subscriptions (figure II.1.1). SDG target 9.c calls for a boosted access to ICT and for universal and affordable access to the Internet in LDCs by 2020, where 85 per cent of

a https://intl.alipay.com/ in 2016-10-05

(continued)

Box II.1 (*continued*)

Figure II.1.1
Digital divide: gap of low and middle-income economies from the world average, 2007–2014 (*per 100 users or subscriptions*)

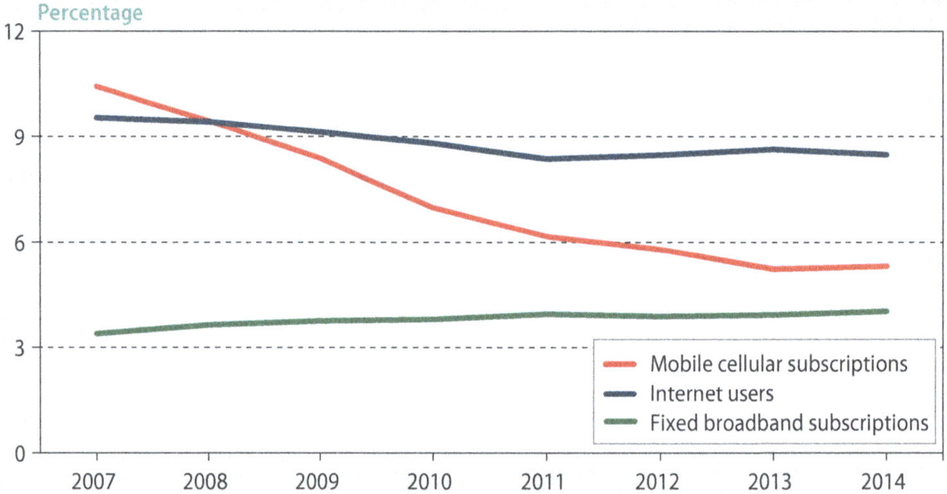

Source: UNCTAD calculations based on the World Bank WDI.
Note: Based on World Bank classification; low and middle-income economies are those in which 2015 GNI per capita was $12,475 or less.

people are offline (WTO, 2016b). In 2016, the e-commerce index of UNCTAD was 71 for developed economies and 24 for Africa (UNCTAD, 2016e), confirming an e-commerce divide wider than the digital divide.

As already mentioned, a customized and coherent regulatory and institutional framework must work in conjunction with e-commerce, especially in the context of exponential technological change, increasing convergence of telecommunication, computer and broadcast technologies, blurring between content and carriage and overlap between telecommunication and financial services in some segments (UNCTAD, 2016c). In this regard, UNCTAD developed Services Policy Reviews (SPRs). The SPR of Rwanda, for example, identified cyber security and data protection regulatory issues that needed to be dealt with by legislative processes.

The global trade dimension of e-commerce requires an examination of undue barriers to trade and regulatory divergence, with a view to enhancing transparency, objectivity and coherence between regulatory and international trade agendas. This should support e-business activities. The sequencing of regulatory reform and liberalization is critical (UNCTAD, 2016f).

The Republic of Korea has set a good example with higher Internet access, where 98.5 per cent of households had Internet access at home in 2014 (ITU, 2016). This is partly explained by public policies prioritizing ICT and earmarking the universal fund from the sector in telecom infrastructure development. Additionally, telecom liberalization has been pursued multilaterally and through RTAs while seeking coherence with national regulations. The country has established coordination mechanisms, including the State Council chaired by the President or by the Prime Minister to settle disputes.

Cross-border commitments in telecommunications and ICT services are still limited in the context of the General Agreement on Trade in Services (GATS). Unbound market access is higher than full market access in developed economies and higher than full and partial market access in developing economies (WTO, 2016c). While RTAs increased binding commitments, controversial regulations, such as commercial presence and localization requirements, still exist.

A Trade in Services Agreement (TISA) may propose that data protection issues be addressed by mutual recognition of consumer protection systems instead of local presence requirements. There are also concerns regarding overly aggressive e-commerce provisions in some trade agreements. In India, a cautious, gradual, and learning-by-doing approach to services liberalization allowed the country to become a successful exporter. Policy space was preserved by first initiating unilateral liberalization and rolling it back at times.

Authors: Mina Mashayekhi, Taisuke Ito and Bruno Antunes

Crucially, from a development perspective, a 10 per cent rise in remittances may contribute to a 3.5 per cent reduction in the share of people living in poverty (UNCTAD, 2014b; UNCTAD, 2015b). This is recognised by target 10.c of the Sustainable Development Goals (SDGs) on reducing transaction costs on migrant remittances to less than 3 per cent. Financial services such as savings, loans and insurances play a vital development role in remittances by providing options for investing these private funds in productive activities, social services and infrastructure (UNCTAD, 2013a). These options may comprise diaspora funds which could be enhanced through financial education and tax and credit incentives. Remittances also represent a promising source of demand for financial services and may thus contribute to financial inclusion.

In general, efficient business, professional and infrastructure services are a must in supporting GVCs. Research and development, product design and marketing services can also bolster export diversification and increase export and supply capacities.

The 2030 Agenda reflects the importance of services

The 2030 Agenda for Sustainable Development, including the SDGs themselves, needs well-functioning infrastructure and basic services in order to succeed. Infrastructure services are reflected in SDG 5 on gender equality and in SDG 9 on infrastructure, industrialization and innovation. Specific infrastructure services are reflected in other goals and targets: energy in SDG 7; ICT services in SDG 4 on education, as well as SDGs 5 and 9; transport services in SDG 11 on cities and human settlements; and financial services in SDG 1 on ending poverty, SDG 2 on ending hunger, and SDG 5 as well as SDG 8 on economic growth.

Policy frameworks are a condition for realizing gains from services

Policy, regulatory and institutional frameworks which ensure efficient and competitive markets while supporting available, affordable, convenient, equitable and high-quality services are also necessary to achieve development gains, especially from infrastructure.

These frameworks should address external and coordination issues so that service sectors and the economy at large are aligned and complement each other. However, devising frameworks best fit to national circumstances and priorities is a difficult challenge. They need to function within rapidly evolving national regulatory landscapes to ensure that they better respond to new models in ICT services; to seek a pro-development outcome between financial stability, security and inclusion; and to address climate change and energy efficiency goals through transport and energy regulations. Challenges are especially acute for some developing countries with fiscal and institutional constraints, including issues related to the political commitment, accountability and independence of regulators and regulatory capacity.

Regulations are more and more subject to trade liberalization processes

Regulatory and institutional frameworks are also increasingly subject to trade liberalization requirements under multilateral, plurilateral and regional trade negotiations which aim to address the potential trade-restrictive effects of domestic regulation. Policy coherence must be established between services regulation and liberaization so that the benefits of opening markets are balanced with the need to implement regulatory measures in support of public policy objectives. In other words, smart regulations should cohere with development needs and minimize inadvertent trade-restrictive effects. Regulatory and institutional frameworks should be built in advance to accommodate the content, pace and sequencing of liberalization and be equipped to adapt to new challenges, including those from liberalized markets (UNCTAD, 2016c). Lessons can be drawn from the UNCTAD Services Policy Reviews.

Another notable sector in trade in services, international tourism, has shown some resilience amid an overall sluggish trend in international trade (box II.2).

Box II.2
Trends in international tourism

International tourist arrivals up 4 per cent in the first half of 2016

International tourist arrivals (overnight visitors) increased by 5 per cent in 2015, reaching a record 1,186 million, up from 1,134 million in 2014. Demand for international tourism remained robust, with growth exceeding the long-term average for the sixth year in a row, following the 2009 global economic crisis. China, the United Kingdom and the United States led outbound tourism in their respective regions, fuelled by their strong currencies and economies, driving intraregional demand. This trend continued into the first nine months of 2016, with January-September arrivals increasing by 4 per cent compared to the same period last year, in line with the estimate by the World Tourism Organization (UNWTO) of 3.5 to 4.5 per cent for 2016.

By regions, in the first nine months of 2016, international arrivals increased by 9 per cent in Asia and the Pacific, 4 per cent in the Americas, 2 per cent in Europe and 8 per cent in Africa, with Sub-Saharan destinations rebounding strongly, while North Africa continued to report weak results. Limited data for the Middle East points to an estimated decrease of 6 per cent, though results vary from destination to destination (UNWTO, 2016a; UNWTO, 2016b).

Global factors affecting tourism flows

Three major factors influenced tourism flows in 2015 and the first half of 2016: strong exchange rate fluctuations, the decline in prices of oil and other commodities, and ongoing global concern about safety and security. These factors did not greatly alter overall tourism volumes, but influenced destination choice, and therefore the size and direction of specific tourism flows.

Exchange rate movements shifted the purchasing power of many source markets and the price competitiveness of multiple destinations. The appreciation of the US dollar, in particular, fuelled outbound demand from the United States. Euro area destinations benefitted from more favourable exchange rates, as did a number of emerging economies with weaker currencies. Drops in prices of oil and other commodities contributed to tourism growth globally, aided by lower prices of transport and increased disposable income in importing countries, although it weakened demand from commodity exporting markets.

Finally, security and geopolitical tensions have redirected travel flows and remain a global challenge. Most noticeably, terrorist actions in different locations around the world such as Belgium, Egypt, France, Tunisia and Turkey had negative effects on tourism. On a positive note, many countries around the world reported double-digit growth, including major destinations like Canada, Japan, Spain and Thailand.

Share of international tourism rises to 7 per cent of world exports

International tourism receipts reached US$1,260 billion in 2015, up 4 per cent in real terms (taking into account exchange rate fluctuations and inflation) from 2014. International passenger transport (rendered to non-residents) generated another US$211 billion in 2015. Total tourism export earnings reached US$1.5 trillion, or US$4 billion a day on average. International tourism represents 7 per cent of the world's exports in goods and services, up from 6 per cent in 2014, as it has grown faster than total world trade (figure II.2.1). International tourism has proven to be more stable and resilient than trade. As an export category, tourism now ranks third after fuels and chemicals, and ahead of food and automotive products (figure II.2.2).

Tourism is an essential component of export diversification and has shown a strong capacity to compensate for weaker export revenues in many commodity and oil exporting countries. For many developing countries, it is an important, if not critical part of the economy, generating a large part of their export revenues and creating much needed employment. Tourism accounts for 10 per cent of world gross product and one in 11 jobs globally.

In order to realize the full potential of revenue generation and job creation through tourism, destinations must continue to create adequate conditions in terms of planning and promotion. Policies should aim to build a healthy business environment, promote travel facilitation and ensure appropriate

(continued)

Box II.2 (*continued*)

Figure II.2.1

Year-on-year real change in international tourism (*BOP Travel & Passenger transport*) **and merchandise trade, 2006–2015**

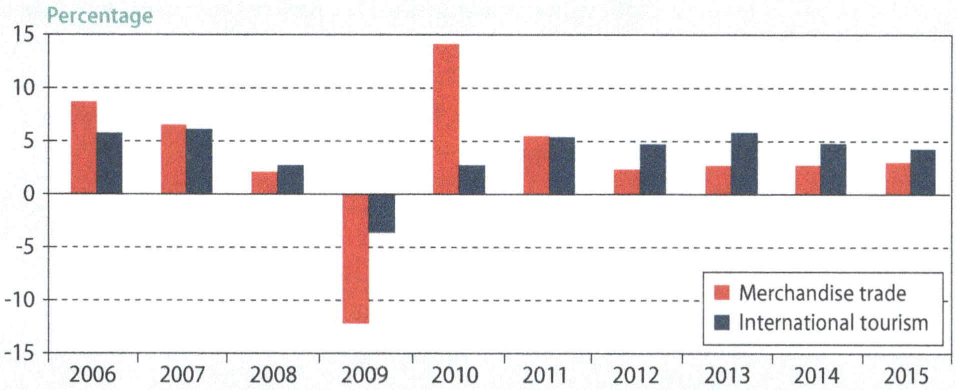

Source: United Nations World Tourism Organization (UNWTO) and World Trade Organization (WTO).

Figure II.2.2

International tourism (*BOP Travel & Passenger transport*) **and exports, world total, 1995–2015**

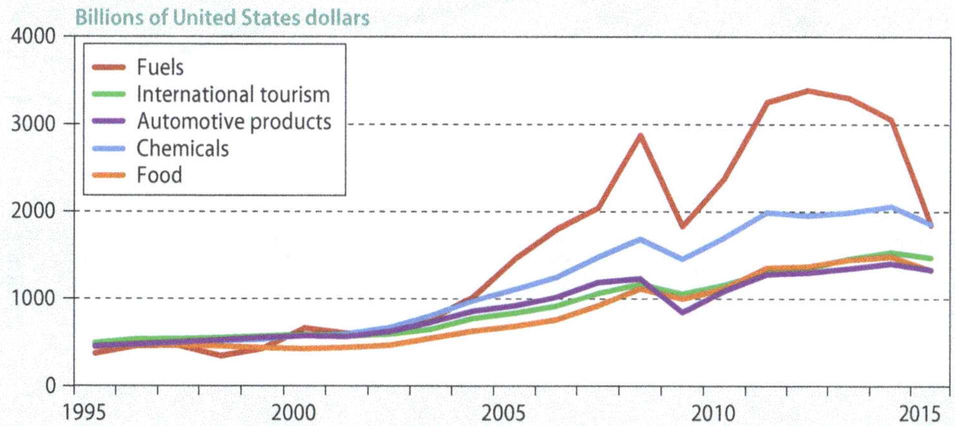

Source: United Nations World Tourism Organization (UNWTO) and World Trade Organization (WTO).

infrastructure to accommodate growth, including the development of roads, railways and airports. Air connectivity is particularly important, especially for remote island states which depend on tourism and trade. Policies must also strive for the adoption of sustainable production and consumption patterns, to enhance environmental and social outcomes, as well as improve economic performance.

International Year of Sustainable Tourism for Development (IY2017)

The importance of tourism for economic development around the world is well reflected in the designation of 2017 as the International Year of Sustainable Tourism for Development[a] by the United Nations General Assembly at its 70th session. The International Year resolution states that tourism can make a significant contribution to the three dimensions of sustainable development — economic, social and environmental — and can create decent jobs and generate trade through its close links to other sectors. IY2017 aims to support a change in policies, business practices and consumer behaviour towards a more sustainable tourism sector in the context of the SDGs.[b] Tourism is featured as targets within three specific SDGs (8, 12 and 14), which focus on sustainable and inclusive economic growth, job creation and sustainable consumption and production. In many developing and least developed countries, tourism is the most viable, effective and sustainable option for development and poverty alleviation.

a See Roadmap and other information on the International Year of Sustainable Tourism for Development at: http://www2.unwto.org/.tourism4development2017.

b More information on the Sustainable Development Goals (SDGs) at: http://icr.unwto.org/content/tourism-and-sdgs.

Authors: John Kester, Michel Julian and Javier Ruescas (UNWTO)

Trends in commodity prices

Commodity prices rose in 2016

The UNCTAD non-oil nominal commodity price index has been trending upwards since the beginning of 2016 (figure II.8). It stood at 204.0 points in September 2016, compared to 181.8 points in January 2016, which constitutes a 12.2 per cent increase. On a year-on-year basis, commodity prices had increased by 5.8 per cent from September 2015. Overall, commodity prices remain substantially lower than at the peaks of the boom period. In February 2011, the index was at 329.5 points, implying that its value in September 2016 was still 38.2 per cent lower than its peak.

Figure II.8

UNCTAD non-oil Commodity Price Index, January 2010–September 2016

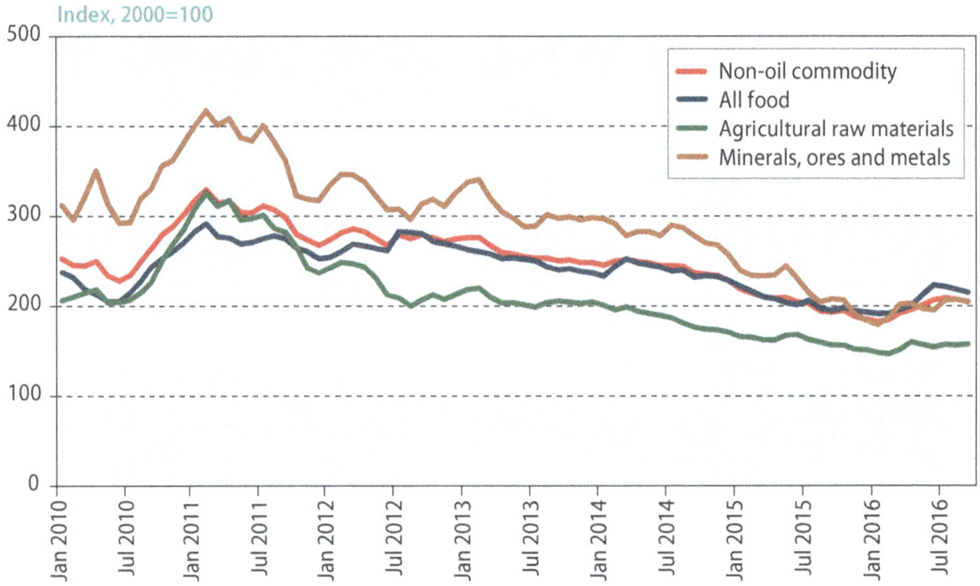

Source: UNCTADstat.

Supply side factors have underpinned higher commodity prices

Supply cuts and output uncertainties, especially for metals and agricultural commodities, pushed up commodity prices during 2016. For agricultural commodities, El Niño-related adverse weather conditions caused output shortfalls for commodities such as palm oil, rice and coffee. Mineral, ore and metal supply has been constricted by production suspension, for example, with nickel mines in the Philippines, copper mines in the Democratic Republic of the Congo and Zambia and zinc mines in Australia and Peru. A partial reversal of the United States dollar appreciation and rising oil prices also supported gains in commodities prices during the first two quarters of 2016.

Food prices showed the steepest increase

Among the subcategories of the UNCTAD non-oil nominal commodity price index, minerals, ores and metals prices showed the steepest increase from January to September 2016, at 14.5 per cent, followed by food at 12.2 per cent. The upward price trend for agricultural raw materials was more subdued at 6.4 per cent. Prices of almost all major commodities increased, albeit from a relatively low base. Notable exceptions were wheat and tea, which experienced significant price drops, as well as cocoa beans, cottonseed oil and maize, for which prices mildly decreased (figure II.9).

Figure II.9
Percentage change of the price index of selected commodities between January and July 2016

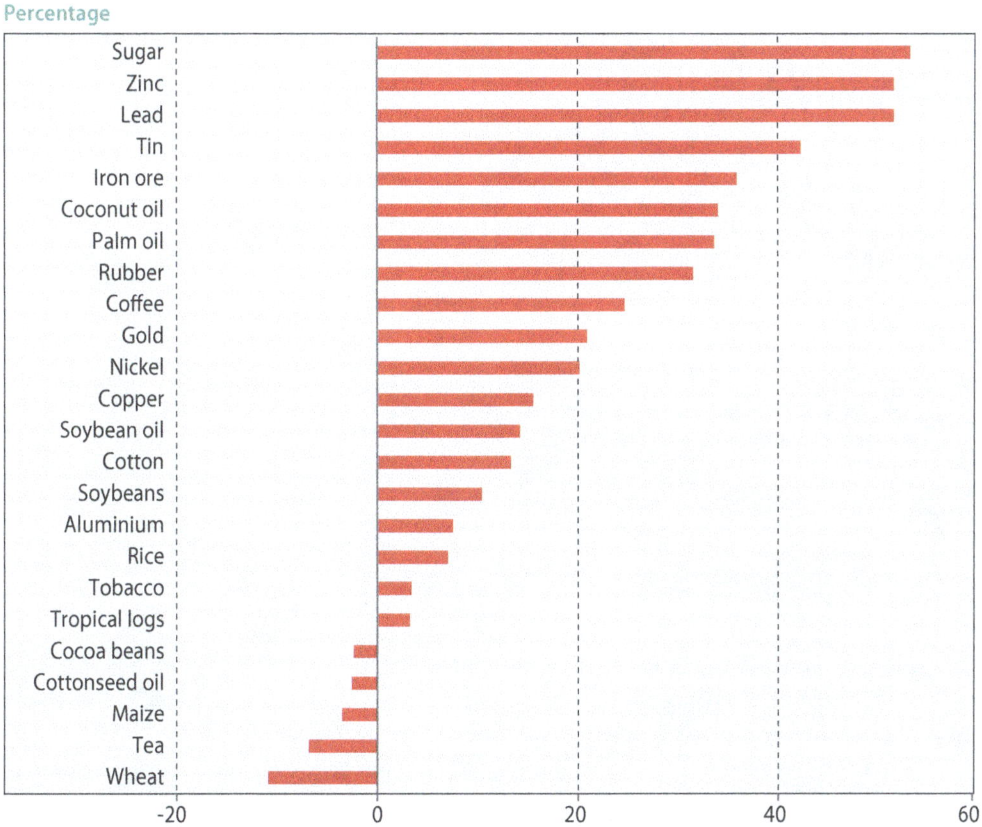

Source: UNCTADstat.

In the outlook, large price swings are unlikely, given slack supply capacities

Going forward, large swings in commodity prices seem unlikely. Supply conditions could ease for some commodities. For instance, Indonesian ferronickel exports to China are picking up and replacing some of the shortfalls in nickel ore supply from the Philippines. Also, copper from new mines in Peru has started to reach the market, counterweighing supply constrictions elsewhere. For other commodities, output remains uncertain. For example, the supply deficit of sugar is forecast to increase. Overall, commodity prices are likely to increase moderately in 2017.

Food and agricultural commodities

Agricultural commodity prices have trended upwards

In agricultural food markets, prices generally trended upwards over the first nine months of 2016 (figure II.10). Vegetable oilseeds and oils showed the steepest increase among the three components of the UNCTAD All Food Index, gaining 22.7 per cent, closely followed by food commodities at 10.9 per cent; the price of tropical beverages rose by 11.6 per cent, with the increase owing largely to coffee.

Sugar registered the steepest price increase due to low inventories

Sugar (*Caribbean ports*) registered the biggest price gains — at 53.2 per cent from January to September 2016. In September 2016, the FOB price of sugar at Caribbean ports reached its highest level since July 2012 at US¢ 21.5 per lb. This price spike was mainly

Figure II.10
Price indices of food and agricultural commodity groups, January 2010–September 2016

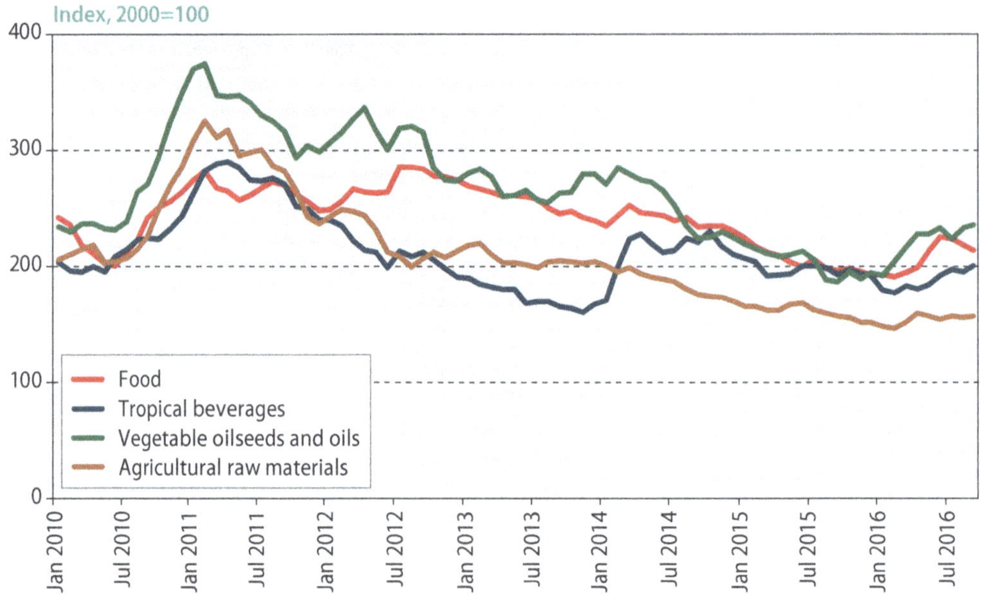

Source: UNCTADstat.

due to low inventories triggered by a growing production-demand gap, which is expected to further widen after falling output forecasts for Brazil, India and Thailand. Hence, the upward trend in sugar prices is likely to continue in the near future.

Thai rice has seen a major price increase of 26.9 per cent over the first three quarters of 2016 amid production losses due to droughts in India, Thailand and Viet Nam caused by El Niño. In August and September, the rice price plummeted amid projections of gains in world rice production in the 2016/17 season, which could end the price hike in the second half of 2017.

Maize (*Yellow Maize No. 3*) registered a slight price decrease of 3.6 per cent between January and September 2016. With forecasts showing global output to rise in 2016/17, including a record harvest in the United States, price hikes are not likely in 2017.

Two major exceptions to the higher trend of food commodity prices were wheat and tea. The price of wheat (*Hard Red Winter No.2*) reached $190 per ton in September 2016, its lowest level since June 2010 and second lowest level in a decade. Large harvests in the main producing countries — Canada, the United States and the Russian Federation — are continuing to exert downward pressure on the price of wheat. The price of Kenyan tea declined throughout the first quarter of 2016 based on strong supply and weak demand, reaching a low of US¢ 238 per kg in April 2016, but then made gains, reaching US¢ 298 per kg in September 2016. Prices are expected to remain fairly stable.

The UNCTAD Vegetable Oilseeds and Oils Price Index stood at 236 points in September 2016, up 22.7 per cent since the beginning of 2016 and up 26.4 per cent since September 2015. Almost all individual oilseeds and oils had trended upwards by September 2016. Shortfalls in production of oilseeds such as soybeans in South America and palm oil in South-East Asia due to adverse weather conditions caused by El Niño mainly drove this trend. Tentative forecasts for the 2016/17 growing season show supply will continue to fall short of demand, continuing to push up prices of oilseeds and vegetable oils into 2017.

The first three quarters of 2016 showed mixed results for tropical beverages. While the price of tea dropped considerably, the price of cocoa beans decreased by just 2.4 per cent. It peaked in June 2016 amid a weakening pound sterling and reports of subdued production. Triggered by positive production forecasts for the 2016/17 season, the price of cocoa continued its slide, which looks set to continue. The price of coffee (*ICO composite indicator price*) showed a steep uptick of 24.6 per cent. This was fuelled by droughts in Brazil and a strong Brazilian real. Looking forward, rising world demand combined with uncertainty about key producers' output may continue to exert upward pressure on coffee prices.

With the exception of jute, linseed oil and sisal, prices of all agricultural raw materials increased from January to September 2016. From January to September 2016, the price of rubber (*RSS 3*) rose sharply by 31.6 per cent, driven by an export quota scheme set in force in March 2016 by major producers such as Indonesia, Malaysia and Thailand. However, the September 2016 price was still 74.4 per cent lower than the peak price in February 2011.

Cotton prices (*Cotlook A Index*) also trended upwards, increasing by 13.3 per cent over the first three quarters of 2016. For the 2016/17 season, world production is forecast to increase slightly faster than demand. In addition, the Chinese government started to auction off some of its large cotton stockpiles in May 2016, which could push down global prices by reducing Chinese demand for imported cotton. Overall, a further increase of the cotton price in 2017 does not seem likely.

Minerals, metals and ores

Supply cuts and uncertainties drove up prices of minerals, ores and metals

In January 2016, the UNCTAD Minerals, Ores and Metals Price Index reached its lowest level since February 2009 at 178 points, which was also the second lowest level in more than a decade. From January 2016 onwards, the index trended upwards, reaching 204.3 points in September (figure II.11). Price increases were mainly driven by supply cuts and uncertainties.

Figure II.11

Price indices of selected minerals, ores and metals, January 2010–September 2016

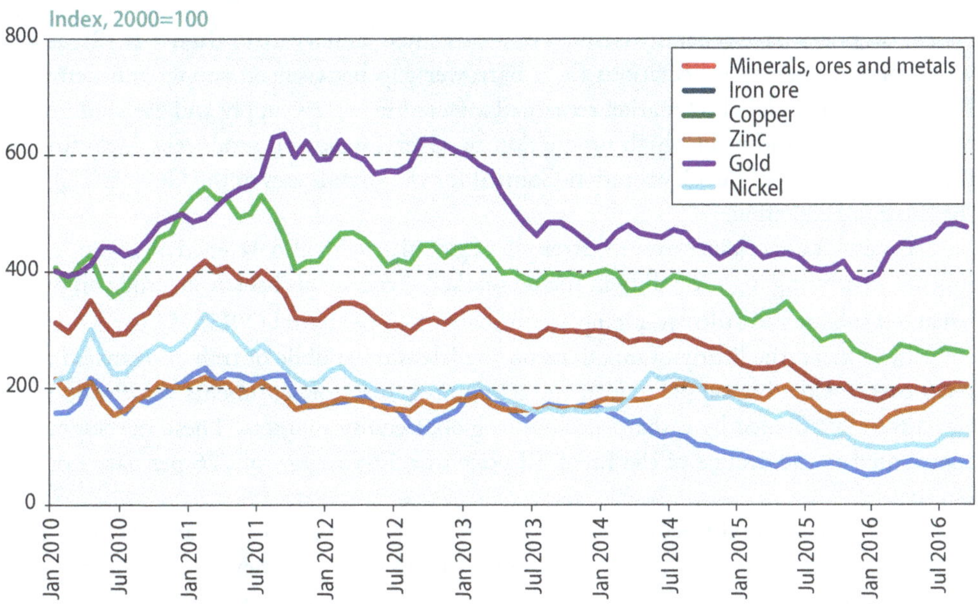

Source: UNCTADstat.

The London Metal Exchange (LME) price of nickel increased by 20.1 per cent between January and September 2016, up 2.9 per cent on a year-on-year basis. Mine shutdowns in the Philippines due to environmental concerns were a key driver. The market outlook depends largely on the extent to which the shortfall in Philippine nickel exports, in particular to China, could be replaced by other sources. Early signs indicate that ferronickel exports from Indonesia are growing, which suggest that nickel supply conditions could ease in 2017.

The iron ore prices at the port of Tianjin climbed 35.8 per cent from a very low basis of $42 per dry metric ton at the beginning of the year. In September 2016, the price of iron ore averaged $57 per dry metric ton, which was still down 68.3 per cent from the peak in February 2011. Expectations of substantive low-cost supply reaching the market in the second half of 2016 and early 2017 pose a significant downside risk to the price of iron ore in the near future.

Copper registered the weakest price increase among metals

Copper's price rise was the weakest in 2016, registering an increase of 5.6 per cent between January and September 2016. In September, the LME price of copper stood at $4,706 per metric ton, less than half of its peak value in February 2011. With estimates showing supply for refined copper growing faster than demand due to expanded operations in existing mines and new mine production (such as in Peru), the outlook for recovery remains subdued.

The LME price of zinc showed a particularly sharp increase of 51.6 per cent during the first three quarters of 2016. The main drivers were supply cuts by major zinc producers. For instance, Glencore closed zinc mines in Australia and Peru, reducing its zinc output by 30.6 per cent in the first half of 2016. Mine closures and supply cuts look set to continue to put upward pressure on the zinc price.

Investment demand drove gold prices higher

The gold price increased by 20.8 per cent from January to September 2016 and by 17.9 per cent on a year-on-year basis. The low-yield environment and macroeconomic uncertainties seem to be the main drivers of increased investment demand for gold (box II.3).

Oil prices

Oil prices have increased but remain affected by excess supply

Global oil prices have generally trended upwards since January 2016 (figure II.12), as developments supported expectations for a narrower gap between oil supply and demand. Nevertheless, the global oil market remained affected by excess supply and elevated inventories in 2016, amid record-high production by several major oil producers, including in the member States of the Cooperation Council for the Arab States of the Gulf (GCC) and the Russian Federation.

Persistent uncertainty over the strength of global growth also weighed on investor sentiments, generating high volatility in the oil market. Against this backdrop, crude oil prices remained subdued in 2016, averaging an estimated $43 per barrel (2015: $52 per barrel).

In January, the lifting of sanctions on the Islamic Republic of Iran exacerbated concerns over a widening supply glut in the oil market. Investor sentiments worldwide were also adversely affected by a sharp decline in global equity markets. These developments contributed to the decline of the Brent oil price to a 12-year low of $26 per barrel on 20 January.

The decline in oil prices reversed as large supply disruptions in Canada, Libya and Nigeria tightened global oversupply conditions. In addition, persistently low oil prices continued to restrain profits and output of the higher cost oil producers. In the United States,

Box II.3

Recent trends and the future of the gold market

Gold is a special commodity. It serves a wide variety of uses including as a store of value, raw material for jewellery and industrial applications and as a conductor in electronic devices.[a] Gold is also an important asset class for investors and a component of central banks' reserve holdings. There is a close correlation between gold prices and changes in macroeconomic and geopolitical conditions. In this regard, an analysis of the gold investment market is particularly relevant, given the current environment of heightened uncertainty about the future of the world economy and near-zero and negative rates of return on alternative assets.

Investment was the largest component of gold demand in the first half of 2016 and has been one of the key determinants of gold prices over the past decade. While jewellery has accounted for 56.4 per cent of net cumulative gold demand in 2006-2015, volatility of investment demand, particularly through gold-backed exchange-traded funds (ETFs), was more than twice that of demand for jewellery.

ETFs and physical gold attract different types of investors. For example, in 2013, demand for bars and coins reached its peak of 1,705 tonnes, while ETFs recorded an unprecedented net outflow of 916 tonnes (figure II.3.1). This suggests that to a large extent, investors in ETFs are driven by strategic motives, introducing more volatility in the gold market than physical gold holders who tend to purchase gold with a longer-term perspective. The largest gold ETFs now hold more gold than major central banks. For instance, industry leader SPDR Gold Shares has more than $40 billion worth of assets under management; they hold more gold than the Bank of Japan, the Reserve Bank of India or the European Central Bank (ECB). This seems to illustrate the commodities financialization hypothesis, which is defined as the expanding role of financial motives, markets, actors and institutions in the development of commodity prices.

After a steady decline from the historic peak of $1,772 per troy ounce in September 2011 to $1,068 per troy ounce in December 2015,[b] the price of gold increased by 21.9 per cent between January and July 2016.[c] Two factors seem to have stimulated demand for investment and thus strengthened the price of gold — uncertainty and low interest rates.

Uncertainty pushes economic agents to buy gold as a safe haven product. For example, the spot price of gold increased by 7.5 per cent within two weeks following the vote by the United Kingdom to leave the European Union ("Brexit") on 23 June 2016. Also, from the day that Lehman Brothers announced that it would file for Chapter 11 bankruptcy protection on 15 September 2008, triggering a global economic crisis, the price of gold increased by 15.1 per cent in two weeks' time.

a See also UNCTAD (2016f).
b Data from UNCTADStat database.
c Calculation based on data from the London Bullion Market Association (LBMA).

Figure II.3.1

Gold investment demand, 2006–mid-2016

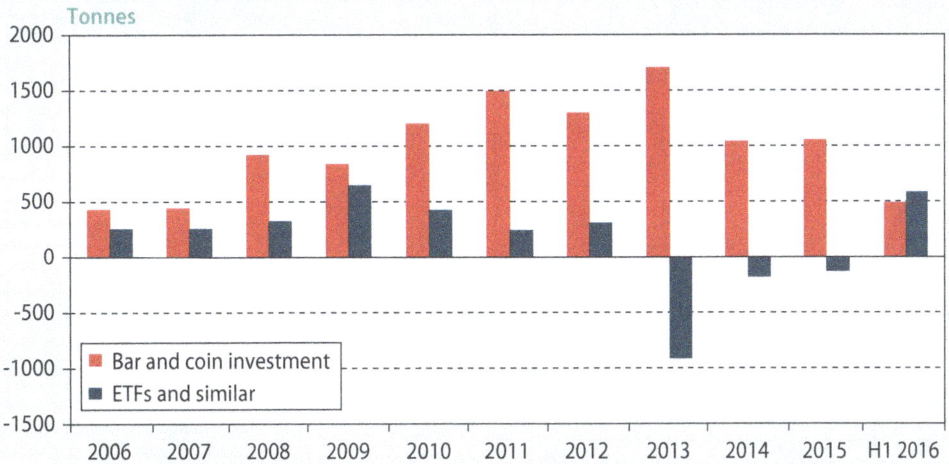

Source: World Gold Council (2016).

(continued)

Box II.3 (*continued*)

Low interest rates increase the attractiveness of gold by decreasing the opportunity costs of holding it, suggesting a negative correlation between rates of return on alternative assets and the price of gold. For instance, the coefficient of correlation between monthly gold prices and 10-year United States government bond yields from January 2005 to July 2016 is -0.83.[d] In the first quarter of 2016, policy rates have been cut to zero and below zero by the ECB and the Bank of Japan, respectively. This reinforced the low-yield environment in major economies and could be a factor contributing to the current increase in the price of gold.

The medium-term outlook for the gold market strongly depends on expectations regarding the development of investment demand. In this context, a rise of the policy rate by the United States Federal Reserve Board is likely to have a moderating effect on gold investments and prices. Also, a further strengthening of the United States dollar against major currencies could weigh on the gold price. On the upside, policy rates in Japan, the euro area and the United Kingdom are expected to remain negative or near zero at least in the near future. The uncertainty created by the Brexit vote will continue to exert influence and drive risk-adverse capital towards gold. Furthermore, central bank demand for gold has been substantial over the past five years, with the Central Bank of the Russian Federation and the People's Bank of China being the largest net buyers in 2016 amid a push towards reserve asset diversification. This trend is expected to continue and support gold prices. Finally, if continued expansionary monetary policies in major economies raise inflation expectations, this would also put upward pressure on the gold price. Overall, the price of gold is expected to keep rising in 2016 and 2017.

d Calculation based on data from US Federal Reserve Bank of St. Louis and LBMA.

Authors: Stefan Csordas, Samuel K. Gayi and Janvier D. Nkurunziza

Figure II.12
Oil price and major events, October 2015–November 2016

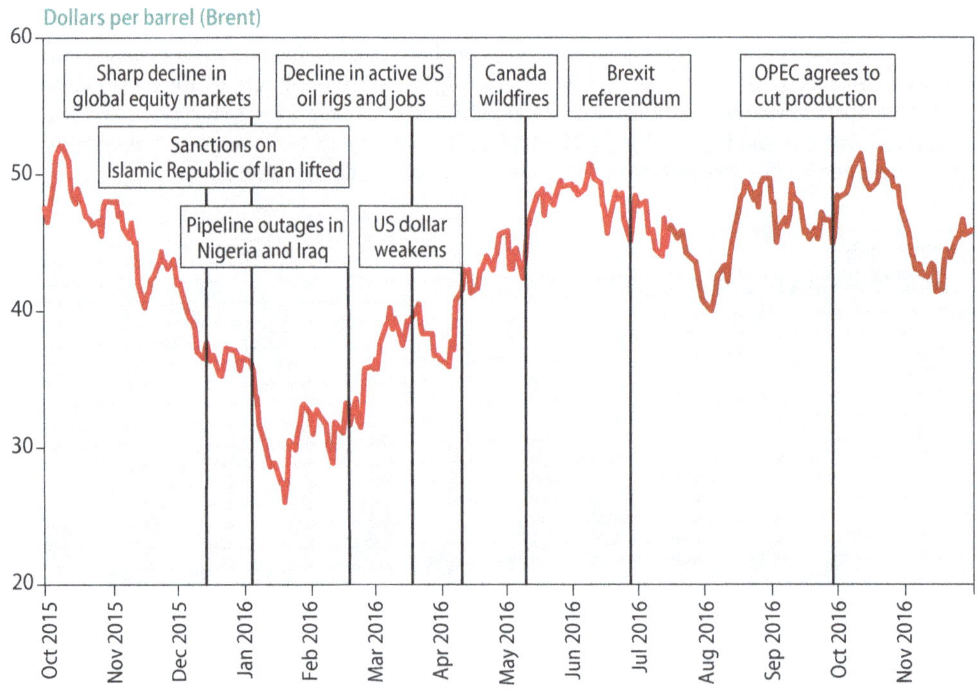

Source: U.S. Energy Information Administration, CEIC Data.

crude oil production declined amid a falling number of active oil rigs and further cutbacks in shale investment.

Oil demand expanded, but at a slower pace

Meanwhile, global oil demand continued to grow in 2016. The pace of growth, however, was slower than in 2015 as the positive boost from low oil prices to consumption growth waned. Oil demand was driven mainly by robust consumption in the large emerging economies, particularly China and India. Amid a continued moderate expansion of economic activity, oil demand in Europe and the United States also improved during the year. Consequently, in May, oil prices surpassed $50 per barrel for the first time since November 2015.

Oil prices edged up towards the end of November, following an agreement by the Organization of the Petroleum Exporting Countries (OPEC) producers to cut oil production for the first time since the global financial crisis. The move by OPEC to bolster oil prices marks a reversal in its strategy of defending market share since the collapse of crude oil prices in 2014. Indeed, total supply from OPEC producers continued to expand at a strong pace in 2016, contributing to persistent global oversupply concerns during the year. Notably, output of the low-cost producers such as Kuwait, Saudi Arabia, and the United Arab Emirates reached record highs in 2016 while the Islamic Republic of Iran's production rose rapidly to pre-sanction levels.

Oil supply growth will slow due to production cuts and lower investment

Looking ahead, oil supply growth is expected to slow as OPEC producers move to cut production and non-OPEC supply continues to decline. In addition, the fall in new investments in the oil and gas industry will potentially constrain the pace in global oil output going forward. Of note, the International Energy Agency reported that global energy investment contracted at an annual pace of 8 per cent in 2015, mainly due to lower upstream oil and gas investment.

Oil demand will strengthen in line with global economic growth

Oil demand is expected to continue strengthening in line with the projected improvement in global growth. Growth in oil demand will remain supported mainly by the United States and the large emerging economies, particularly China and India. Nevertheless, China's ongoing economic rebalancing efforts will constrain its oil consumption growth while its accumulation of strategic oil reserves is expected to moderate as storage capacity is filled.

Given these dynamics, crude oil prices are assumed to recover modestly to an average of $52 per barrel in 2017 and increase further to $61 per barrel in 2018.

There are several downside risks to this outlook. Global growth which is weaker than expected, especially a potentially sharp slowdown in the emerging economies, could weigh on oil demand and prices.

More resilient supply by high-cost producer countries, such as the United States, would place further downward pressure on oil prices. Global oil prices remain vulnerable to shifts in investor sentiments, amid high economic and policy uncertainty. Heightened investor risk aversion resulting in a strengthening of the United States dollar will lead to a further decline in crude oil prices, given the strong inverse relationship between the two variables (figure II.13).

There are also upside risks to the oil prices. A larger-than-expected production cut by OPEC countries would boost sentiment and support oil prices. An escalation of security threats or internal conflicts such as in the Middle East and Western Africa could result in significant and prolonged supply disruptions, placing upward pressure on oil prices. Nevertheless, given that higher oil prices will incentivize more production, particularly in the shale industry, there will be a ceiling on the magnitude of oil price increases.

Figure II.13
Crude oil prices and the US dollar, January 2000–October 2016

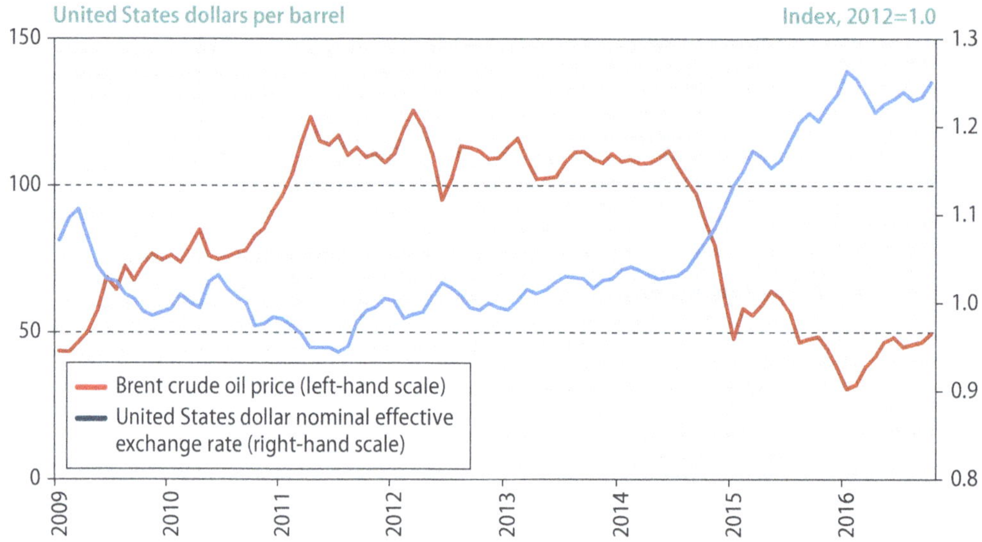

Source: UN/DESA estimates of nominal effective exchange rate, measured against a weighted average of 175 trading partners; Brent crude price from U.S. Energy Information Administration.

Trade policy developments

Multilateral trade negotiations

The 2030 Agenda for Sustainable Development requires a revitalized global partnership for the implementation of the SDGs, including in the area of trade

International trade and foreign investment have been mutually supportive, contributing to the transformation of many developing economies and, with the support of a coherent and appropriate policy mix, to lifting more than one billion people out of extreme poverty (UNCTAD, 2016g). Global trade is identified by the Addis Ababa Action Agenda as an important engine for inclusive economic growth, sustainable development and poverty reduction, and the multilateral trading system is the primary channel for its promotion (UNCTAD, 2016g). The 2030 Agenda requires a revitalized global partnership for the implementation of the SDGs, including in the area of trade. In this regard, as called for under target 17.10 in SDG 17, a universal, rules-based, open, non-discriminatory and equitable multilateral trading system continues to be the cornerstone of such partnership.

A favourable national and international environment must be promoted through coherent and sustainable policies in support of growth, industrial development, infrastructure, employment and enabling structural change. The fourteenth session of the quadrennial ministerial meeting of UNCTAD, held in July 2016 in Nairobi, was the first United Nations Ministerial Conference after the launch of the 2030 Agenda. It strove for a global consensus on major lines of action which seek to attain the SDGs through trade. This included acknowledging the vital role of reinvigorating the multilateral trading system with a stronger development focus as well as the interdependence of trade, finance, investment, technology and development (UNCTAD, 2016h).

The slowdown in trade makes support for the multilateral trading system even more important

The current slowdown in trade flows and the uneven gains — both among and within countries — call for reinforced support to international trade and to the multilateral trading system. Multilateral rules and disciplines reduce trade barriers and discrimination, supported by the dispute settlement mechanism of the WTO, which is a unique judicial body ensuring automaticity in panel proceedings and remedial action in case of non-compliance. This effective enforcement system has been increasingly used as countries seek to resolve trade disputes through judicial mechanisms in a context of slow pace of the multilateral hard-rule making. Since 1995 and as of June 2016, it has received 507 requests for consultations, handling disputes covering over $1 trillion of trade flows. The effectiveness and legitimacy of the system are confirmed by its use by WTO members seeking to resolve disputes in regional trade agreements.

Overall, non-negotiating functions of the multilateral trading system are central to transparency, predictability and stability of international trade. Furthermore, universality has been pursued by accession processes, with WTO membership reaching 164 with the accession packages of Afghanistan and Liberia being adopted at the tenth Ministerial Conference of the WTO in Nairobi (MC10). Since 1995 and as of July 2016, 36 countries acceded to the WTO, including nine LDCs. These factors allow the multilateral trading system to keep its legitimacy as a global public good, fundamental for sustainable development.

The stalled progress in multilateral trade negotiations under the Doha Round is having a greater effect on the centrality of the multilateral trading system. Originally, negotiations were intended to conclude in 2004 but, even with a work programme to conclude the Doha Round approved in the ninth WTO Ministerial Conference (MC9) in December 2013 in Bali, WTO members could not agree on the way forward. While some countries reaffirm the Doha Development Agenda and the Declaration and Decisions from Doha, other members support new approaches to advance negotiations and liberalization.

When the Doha Round was launched in 2001, it aimed to prioritize attention to implementation difficulties of developing countries and special and differential treatment to address imbalances from the outcomes of the Uruguay Round. Meaningful progress in the Doha Round is relevant to revitalize the global partnership for sustainable development. It is directly related to achieving several goals and targets, most notably target 17.10 of SDG 17 to promote a universal, rules-based, open, non-discriminatory and equitable multilateral trading system under the WTO, including through the conclusion of negotiations under its Doha Development Agenda.

The Doha Round covers a broad range of the market access and rules agenda, in addition to the two built-in agendas of agriculture and services, under a single undertaking. Considering the lack of agreement on how to move forward, some WTO members argue that the Doha Round should be replaced with a new agenda. Developed countries called for differentiation of developing countries according to their share in global trade, claiming lack of reciprocity in negotiations from emerging economies. Developing countries in general wish to continue negotiations on key issues under the existing structure and special and differential treatment, and argue that the Doha Round can only be terminated by consensus — since it was launched by consensus.

Several countries have pursued their trade interests through plurilateral and regional negotiations

In this context, several countries have pursued their trade interests through plurilateral and regional negotiations. This shift is also motivated by the changing nature of trade, spurred by GVCs as well as the rising significance of trade in services and, in particular, ICT services-enabled trade. With already reduced tariffs, this boosts the relevance of regulatory measures in reducing trade costs and addressing trade barriers through regulatory convergence. These alternative plurilateral and regional approaches can be more effective in this regard and have allowed delving into new issues such as regulatory harmonization, investment, competition, and state-owned enterprises.

Efforts to invigorate the multilateral trading system and its negotiations should consider that the broad agenda under the single undertaking did not facilitate inter-sectoral trade-offs as it was expected when the Doha Round was adopted. If prioritization is necessary, special attention should be given to a core development agenda, including a built-in one of agriculture and services, to align the multilateral trading system with the 2030 Agenda for Sustainable Development, including the SDGs.

In addition, multilateral hard-rule making — focused on commitments — could be complemented with soft-rule making initiatives with the participation of all stakeholders, focusing on consensus building. This would address several members' caution in making legally binding commitments as called for in hard-rule making. Promoting consensus on several trade issues and developing best practices, guidelines and lessons learned could facilitate hard-rule making by enabling better understanding, and building national capacity to formulate the required measures. Such an approach, reflected in the UNCTAD mandate, should complement and support efforts to make hard rules and achieve broader multilateralism (UNCTAD, 2016i).

Plurilateral negotiations

The mix of hard-rule commitments and soft-rule non-binding principles can be achieved by plurilateral negotiations

The mix of hard-rule commitments and soft-rule non-binding principles can be achieved by plurilateral negotiations whose flexibility allows pursuing liberalization at a faster pace. Still, plurilateral initiatives can be seen as diverting the focus away from multilateral negotiations. In any case, plurilateral efforts need to ensure inclusiveness, transparency, and flexibility for developing countries in line with the novel form of flexibility adopted in the Trade Facilitation Agreement. Capacity-building support was also critical to facilitate the engagement of developing countries in these negotiations (UNCTAD, 2016i).

The Information Technology Agreement (ITA) is plurilateral, involving 53 participants, but is applied on a most-favoured nation (MFN) basis, which means that tariff reductions will be extended to all WTO members.

The agreement covers a list of more than 200 information and technology products, valued at $1.3 trillion and representing 10 per cent of global merchandise trade and 90 per cent of global trade in these products. Products covered by the ITA expansion include new generation multi-component integrated circuits, touch screens, medical and Global Positioning System (GPS) navigation equipment.

About 65 per cent of the tariff lines were to be fully eliminated by July 2016 and most of the remaining tariffs are to be phased out until 2019. Most importantly, the ITA is expected to contribute to further expanding the digital economy (United Nations, 2016c).

The environmental goods agreement involves 17 participants and it covers more than 50 products and almost 80 per cent of global trade of these products (UNCTAD, 2016j). It intends to allow the addition of new products and services linked to environmental goods. This agreement envisages eliminating tariffs in the covered products and to be extended to all WTO members through MFN basis. The environmental goods agreement can be crucial in fostering environmental technologies.

Plurilateral negotiations for a Trade in Services Agreement (TISA) are continuing

Plurilateral negotiations for a TISA are ongoing among 23 participants, mostly high-income and upper-middle-income countries, which account for around 70 per cent of global services trade. The agreement would seek ambitious services liberalization, addressing behind the border measures and holding the potential to strongly impact regulatory frameworks. However, major developing countries are not participating, which impedes a critical mass that would be necessary for the multilateralization of the agreement. TISA could therefore become a preferential services agreement not extended to all WTO members.

Regional trade agreements

Regional trade agreements have become more important in the international trading system

Regional trade agreements (RTAs) have increased their importance in the international trading system because they can more effectively address behind-the-border and overall regulatory measures stemming from the changing nature of trade. The WTO was notified of 635 RTAs as of July 2016, of which 423 were in force.[2] This trend was accentuated by mega-RTAs that aim to achieve a duty-free and other barriers-free environment and address regulatory diversity through coherence and convergence.

The African Continental Free Trade Area (CFTA) is a large scale RTA in a South-South context that aims to boost intraregional trade, including through deepened regional regulatory cooperation. Negotiations were launched in June 2015 and are expected to be concluded in 2017, covering both goods and services. They are building on progress achieved by Regional Economic Commissions (RECs), including the Tripartite Free Trade Agreement among the Common Market for Eastern and Southern Africa (COMESA), East African Community (EAC) and the Southern African Development Community (SADC). CFTA-related efforts recognise the importance of setting the adequate level of ambition, considering the asymmetric level of integration in different RECs and the multiplicity of sub-regional and inter-sub-regional integration processes (United Nations, 2016c; UNCTAD, 2015c).

The negotiations of the Trans-Pacific Partnership (TPP) were concluded in October 2015, potentially creating a market of 800 million people and $28 trillion among Australia, Brunei Darussalam, Canada, Chile, Japan, Malaysia, Mexico, New Zealand, Peru, Singapore, the United States and Viet Nam. Within its comprehensive 30 chapters, it covers goods and services trade, investment, e-commerce, intellectual property, government procurement, competition, labour protection, environment, regulatory coherence, SMEs and state-owned enterprises. It sets a high-standard template seeking regulatory harmonization.

The "WTO-plus-plus" nature of mega-RTAs would imply that developing countries exporting to those countries would need to accept the higher regional standards. Not only will countries in the agreement encounter adjustment costs derived from upward harmonization, but other countries will be subject to additional costs of higher regulatory standards spread, for example, by neighbouring countries which are part of some regional integration scheme. The bulk of gains from the TPP, with a market covering 40 per cent of global GDP, is expected from regulatory harmonization and mutual recognition.

Trade diversion remains a major concern

Still, although some members of mega-RTAs could have gains, non-members, and even some members that already have preferential access, may lose due to trade diversion. Because of the diversion, the annual gains from a Doha Round outcome would far exceed the global benefits of mega-RTAs, including the TPP, the Regional Comprehensive Economic Partnership (RCEP) and the Trans-Atlantic Trade and Investment Partnership Agreement (TTIP). In spite of its higher potential global benefits, the Doha Round would be adversely affected by mega-RTAs as they reduce incentives for multilateralism and may create a "two-tiered" and fragmented trading system.

2 WTO website, 2016-10-07.

Trade and least developed countries

The Istanbul Programme of Action defined the target of doubling the share of LDCs' exports in global exports by 2020

Recognising the demanding situation of LDCs, the Fourth United Nations Conference on the Least Developed Countries adopted in 2011 in Istanbul the Programme of Action for the Least Developed Countries for the Decade 2011-2020 to overcome the structural challenges LDCs face in order to eradicate poverty, achieve internationally agreed development goals and enable graduation from the LDC category. Trade's major role in ensuring sustainable economic development was acknowledged. The Conference established the goal of increasing the share of LDCs in global trade through broadening their export base (box II.4). In particular, the Istanbul Programme of Action defined the target of doubling LDCs' global exports by 2020.

In this regard, the Istanbul Programme of Action called for LDCs, with support from their development partners, to address supply-side constraints by enhancing productive capacities and reducing constraints on the private sector, as well as building and diversifying their export base. It also called for favourable market access conditions for all products originating in LDCs, including through the reduction or elimination of arbitrary or unjustified non-tariff barriers and other trade-distorting measures.

Specific mentions were made of a supportive and responsive international trade and finance architecture, and of regional cooperation, including through regional trade integration and other arrangements. These could facilitate LDCs' development and beneficial integration into the world economy by increasing the size of markets, improving their competitiveness and enhancing regional connectivity (United Nations, 2011).

In May 2016, the Istanbul Programme of Action went through a comprehensive high-level midterm review of its implementation, which underlined the importance of trade and investment as major drivers of economic growth, employment generation and structural transformation. Notwithstanding, it was recognised that many LDCs continue to face multiple challenges, including stagnant trade flows, and that swift actions were necessary to realize the Istanbul Programme of Action and the 2030 Agenda promise of leaving no one behind.

It was noted that market access for products of LDCs has seen improvement in some developing countries, but LDCs' exports remain highly concentrated in a few primary products vulnerable to commodity price volatility and to exogenous economic and environmental shocks (United Nations, General Assembly, 2016a).

The share of LDCs' exports in global merchandise decreased from 1.1 per cent in 2010 to 0.9 per cent in 2015, while the share of services exports from LDCs in world services increased from 0.6 per cent in 2010 to 0.8 per cent in 2015. The level of merchandise exports is far behind the objective of doubling shares of global exports by 2020, while services exports are closer to this target.

Emphasis was placed on the key role of a universal, rules-based, open, non-discriminatory and equitable multilateral trading system in promoting export diversification, trade and economic growth. In this regard, importance was given to accelerating accession of engaged LDCs and to reducing trade barriers to LDCs by, for example, meeting the commitments of the Agreement on Sanitary and Phytosanitary Measures and the Agreement on Technical Barriers to Trade.

The agricultural sector in LDCs continues to be affected by trade restrictions and distortions in world agricultural markets and public stockholding in a manner that adversely affects food security. Countries were also urged to make use of WTO ministerial decisions on Duty Free and Quota Free (DFQF) market access for LDCs and on preferential rules of origin for those countries, as well as aid for trade, also in the context of the extension of the Enhanced Integrated Framework for Trade-related Technical Assistance to LDCs.

LDCs were also encouraged to use existing trade and investment support mechanisms, including programmes from international organizations.

The WTO Ministerial decisions adopted at MC10 are non-binding guidelines to encourage preferential origin-related criteria for LDCs. This included the promotion of the use of a low-threshold level for ad valorem percentage criteria, allowing the use of non-originating materials for 75 per cent of the product's value. It also included the encouragement of the use of simple change in tariff heading or subheading rules and the use of the single-transformation rule for apparels. Also of central importance, it called for more user-friendly document requirements and customs procedures.

The WTO Ministerial decisions adopted at MC10 are non-binding guidelines to encourage preferential origin-related criteria for LDCs

MC10 also extended the validity period of the waiver allowing for preferential treatment for services and services providers of LDCs until 31 December 2030, compensating for the four years that have elapsed without concrete results since the waiver was adopted in 2011. It calls for increased efforts to notify commercially meaningful preferences. LDCs have expressed concern about the commercial value of preferences and non-market access, as the development impact of the waiver depends on the content of the preference and on the capacity of LDCs to take advantage of such preferences.

The way forward

The way forward in realizing the development potential of international trade requires addressing several challenges. The first relates to trade liberalization, as the progress in reducing tariffs, the rise of trade associated with GVCs, the increasing service-orientation of economies and ICT services shift the focus of trade policy to behind-the-border regulatory measures.

The second challenge concerns the new issues being proposed for the negotiating agenda of the WTO, including topics ranging from the environment to public health. The third challenge is the need to mix hard rule making approaches with supportive and complementary soft rule making efforts. Finally, the fourth challenge is the growing prevalence of RTAs, particularly mega-RTAs, which have a significant impact on the multilateral trading system owing to their size, number and novelty (UNCTAD, 2016i).

Overall, the development effects of RTAs need to be continuously monitored and assessed. Action must be taken to support the multilateral trading system, ensuring that regional efforts complement, rather than substitute, an enabling environment for trade and development centred in multilateralism and are aligned with the SDGs.

Box II.4

G20 policies and LDCs' economic integration

Promoting the economic integration of least developed countries (LDCs) into the global economy has been the objective of many multilateral declarations and has been more recently reiterated in the SDGs.

Specifically SDG 17, related to strengthening the means of implementation and revitalizing the global partnership for sustainable development, aims to "increase significantly the exports of developing countries, in particular with a view to doubling the least developed countries' share of global exports by 2020" (Target 17.11) and to "realize timely implementation of duty-free and quota-free market access on a lasting basis for all least developed countries" (Target 17.12).

While LDCs represent around 12 per cent of the world's population, they contribute only about one per cent of global exports. Moreover, LDCs' exports are largely concentrated in commodities. Their export-to-GDP ratio is significantly below the average of developing countries and has been on a clear downward trend since 2011, partially driven by the fall in commodity prices. The G20 generally recognize LDCs' trade constraints and provide LDC exporters with preferential market access and technical cooperation programs to increase competitiveness. The G20 have made progress towards allowing duty-free quota-free market access for LDCs and affirmed their commitment to assist developing countries in complying with standards and regulations.

Many G20 members, including some of the G20 developing countries such as China and India, provide tariff preferences to LDCs on a non-reciprocal basis. Although most of the preferential schemes are generous, in many sectors of importance for LDCs, such as agriculture, textiles and apparel, tariffs remain substantial and tariff peaks (particularly high rates on specific products) are prominent.

While tariffs are just one of the burdens to LDCs' exports, there are also a large and increasing set of regulations and requirements which are generally referred to as non-tariff measures (NTMs). NTMs pose a particular challenge for LDCs in two respects. First, NTMs tend to be more prevalent in products that are typically exported by LDCs, such as agriculture, textiles and apparel. Second, NTMs can have a potentially distortionary effect on trade, as the compliance with NTMs depends on technical know-how, production facilities, and an infrastructural base which many LDCs lack, leading to negative effects on their export competitiveness (Nicita and Seiermann, 2016).

Preferential tariff schemes are important, but will not be sufficient to meet the ambitious SDG target of doubling LDCs' export share by 2020. They need to be complemented by policies which help LDCs comply with NTMs. At the aggregate level, allowing for tariff-free market access for LDCs is likely to boost LDC exports to G20 by almost $10 billion, equivalent to an increase in LDCs' total exports of almost 5 per cent. Eliminating the distortionary trade effects of NTMs would increase LDC exports to G20 countries by about $23 billion, equivalent to about a 10 per cent increase. Together, LDCs would increase their exports by about 15 per cent.

The impact differs across product categories, LDCs and G20 countries. The largest effects would be concentrated in the textile and apparel sectors (figure II.4.1), as well as in some of the agricultural categories, in particular vegetable products. Consequently, LDCs which tend to export such products (e.g. Asian LDCs and some of the African agricultural exporters) would benefit more than natural resource exporters.

Heterogeneous results across G20 countries depend largely on the size of their economy but also on the existing tariff concessions, their regulatory framework and import composition. For the EU, which already sets most tariffs at zero for LDCs, a significant 6 per cent increase of LDC exports would be obtained by assisting developing countries in complying with the EU's regulatory framework. The United States must enlarge its preferential tariff schemes, as the effects of tariffs and NTMs are roughly equal. Results dwindle in improving LDCs' access to the Chinese market, because existing LDC exports to China are highly concentrated in natural resources, which face zero or very low tariffs and few NTMs. With regard to other G20 members, LDCs would benefit from both enhancing the preferential schemes and increasing the ability of LDC exporters to comply with NTMs (figure II.4.2).

(*continued*)

Box II.4 *(continued)*

Fundamentally critical is whether the policy options identified in this study are feasible to implement. Enlarging preferential tariff schemes to cover all LDC exports is straightforward, but reducing the distortionary trade effects of NTMs on LDCs requires a more complex approach. Many NTMs serve important and legitimate domestic public policy objectives in G20 countries.

G20 countries should facilitate LDCs' integration into the global economy by helping them comply with NTMs through regulatory frameworks that prevent discrimination, encourage transparency and provide technical assistance to minimize LDCs' cost of compliance.

Authors: Alessandro Nicita and Julia Seiermann, drawing on a recent study by Nicita and Seiermann (2016).

Figure II.4.1

Impact of duty free access and elimination of negative effect of NTMs on LDC exports to G20 countries, by product

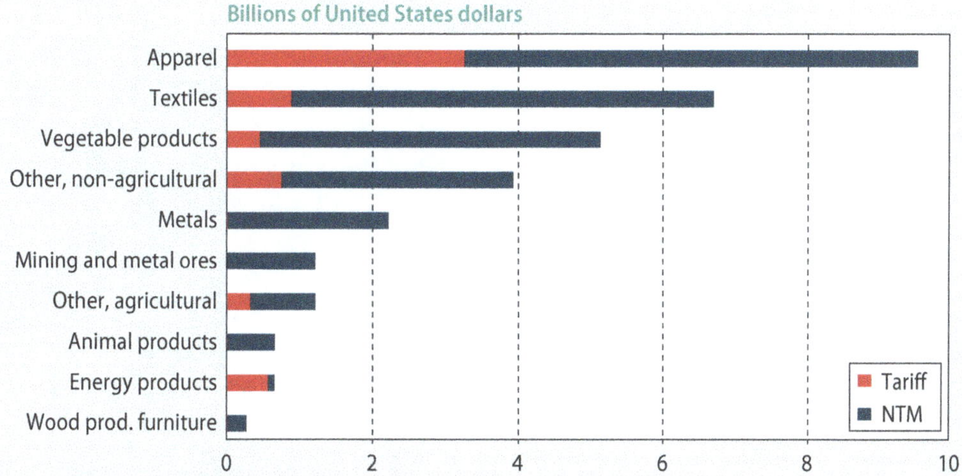

Source: Nicita and Seiermann (2016).

Figure II.4.2

Impact of duty free access and elimination of negative effect of NTMs on LDCs total exports, by G20 country

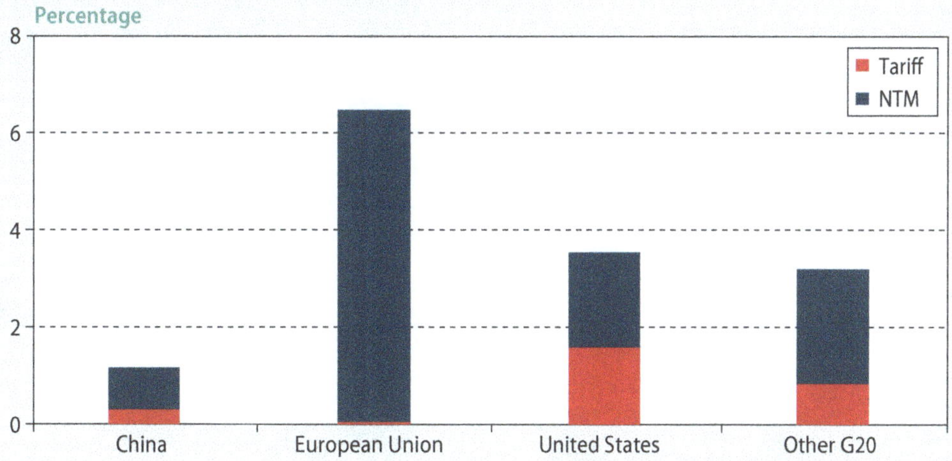

Source: Nicita and Seiermann (2016).

Chapter III

Finance for sustainable development

Closing the investment gap to achieve the Sustainable Development Goals (SDGs) by 2030 requires the mobilization of significant financial resources. Estimates of the financing needs for public and private investments vary, but are invariably large (United Nations, 2014). As noted in chapter 1, addressing the shortfall in productivity growth in the least developed countries (LDCs) alone will require investment in these countries to rise at an annual average rate of at least 11 per cent through 2030. This significantly exceeds the rate of investment growth between 2010 and 2015, which averaged 8.9 per cent annually. At the same time, the global environment, including the weak economy, low trade growth, soft commodity prices, volatile international capital flows, and the increase of geopolitical risks make raising long-term investment and increasing capital formation particularly challenging.

At the Third International Conference on Financing for Development in July 2015 in Addis Ababa, Member States of the United Nations agreed that both private sources of finance (including financial and direct investment) and public resources (including domestic and international) are necessary to achieve sustainable development and the SDGs. Public and private resources should not be seen as substitutes, as they have different investment objectives. For example, despite growing pockets of socially conscious and/or impact investors, most investors of private capital remain driven by a profit motive, and will under-invest in public goals when the expected financial return underperforms compared to other opportunities on a risk-adjusted basis.

Public goods, such as combating climate change, are generally not sufficiently incorporated into risk-return analyses by private investors, requiring policy intervention, such as carbon pricing or strengthened regulations. Investment in sustainable development is further challenged as many investors evaluate risk and return over a short-term horizon. This myopia leads to not only herd behaviour and volatility, but also failure to incorporate long-term risks, such as those associated with climate change, in investment decisions.

This short-term investment perspective is reflected in the behaviour of international capital flows, particularly commercial bank lending and portfolio flows from institutional investors. While there is much discussion on rising risk aversion and increasing volatility of capital, the data shows that, for the countries analysed, volatility has not increased compared to earlier decades and is still lower than that in past crisis periods (see the section on the analysis of volatility).

International capital inflows remain subject to volatility and net flows to developing countries are projected to remain negative at least through 2017

Rather, international capital inflows remain subject to periodic episodes of high volatility as in the past, often triggered by global systemic risks. Nonetheless, the section on the trends in private resources for sustainable development shows that total net capital flows to developing countries and transition economies, which turned negative in 2014, are estimated to remain negative at least through 2017. This represents the longest multi-year reversal of flows since the United Nations began monitoring them in 1990, although divergence between countries and regions is significant, with some large emerging market countries experiencing increasingly large outflows and others registering inflows.

Achieving the SDGs will require policies and regulatory frameworks that incentivize changes in investment patterns to better align investment with sustainable development. Despite the challenging global economy, public and private actions can effect change. Though still somewhat limited, there are ongoing efforts within the private sector to improve reporting and better align investment with sustainable development. Changes in public policies and regulatory frameworks can help mainstream these efforts, while also reducing excessive capital market volatility. Public policies are thus the lynchpin of financing for sustainable development.

International public finance is a critical complement to domestic revenue mobilization, which remains insufficient to meet public investment needs

Changes in public policies and regulatory frameworks have to be accompanied by increases in and more effective use of public finance. Official development assistance (ODA) and other international public finance is a critical complement to domestic revenue mobilization. As described in detail in the section on trends in public resources flows, both concessional and non-concessional international public financial flows to developing countries rose in 2015, albeit modestly. In this context, multilateral development banks (MDBs) have taken initial steps to optimise their balance sheets and expand lending, as well as to better align their investments with the SDGs. Building on these efforts, development banks, both national and multilateral, are well-placed to contribute to the mobilization of additional resources, in particular with the provision of long-term capital for sustainable infrastructure investments.

Trends in net resource transfers and international reserves

For many years, developing countries as a whole have experienced negative net resource transfers, as shown in figure III.1, meaning that capital has flowed from developing to developed countries. Such resource transfers consist of the net flow of funds to a country, including capital flows, capital servicing, income and current transfers (i.e. grants and other transfers, including ODA), as well as the net change in a country's official international reserves.[1] In 2016, net transfers from developing countries are estimated to have totalled close to $500 billion, slightly more than 2015 levels, but significantly below their peak of $800 billion in 2008 at the time the global financial crisis erupted.

East and South Asia continue to experience significant negative net resource transfers, but transfers have turned positive in most other regions

The aggregate numbers, however, mask significant differences across regions and countries. While East and South Asia continues to experience significant negative transfers, driven in large part by China, net resource transfers have turned positive in most other regions, albeit at low levels. LDCs, where the need for resource transfers is the greatest, continue to see only a small positive net transfer of resources.

The trends in the flow of net resources in large part reflect the build-up of international foreign exchange reserves, which are generally recycled back into high quality foreign assets, such as United States Treasury bills, and are thus included in the calculation of net resource transfers. In the first quarter of 2016, 64 per cent of official reported reserves were held in assets denominated in US dollars, up from 61 per cent in 2014 (IMF, 2016d). Overall, developing countries' foreign exchange reserves fell to $7.5 trillion in 2015, down from $8.2 trillion in 2014, with further reductions estimated in 2016.

1 For a full definition of net transfer of resources, please see Box IV.1 of United Nations (1990) and Annex III of United Nations (1986).

As shown in figure III.2, as a share of world gross product (WGP), total reserves globally fell to 14.6 per cent in 2015, or $10.76 trillion. This marks the first aggregate fall in nominal reserve levels since 1982 and the first fall relative to WGP since 1992. The reversal of reserve accumulation mirrored the trends in capital flows. As capital inflows turned to outflows, many developing countries, particularly China, allowed reserves to decline to help stabilise exchange rates.

Figure III.1
Net transfer of resources to developing economies and economies in transition, 2004–2016

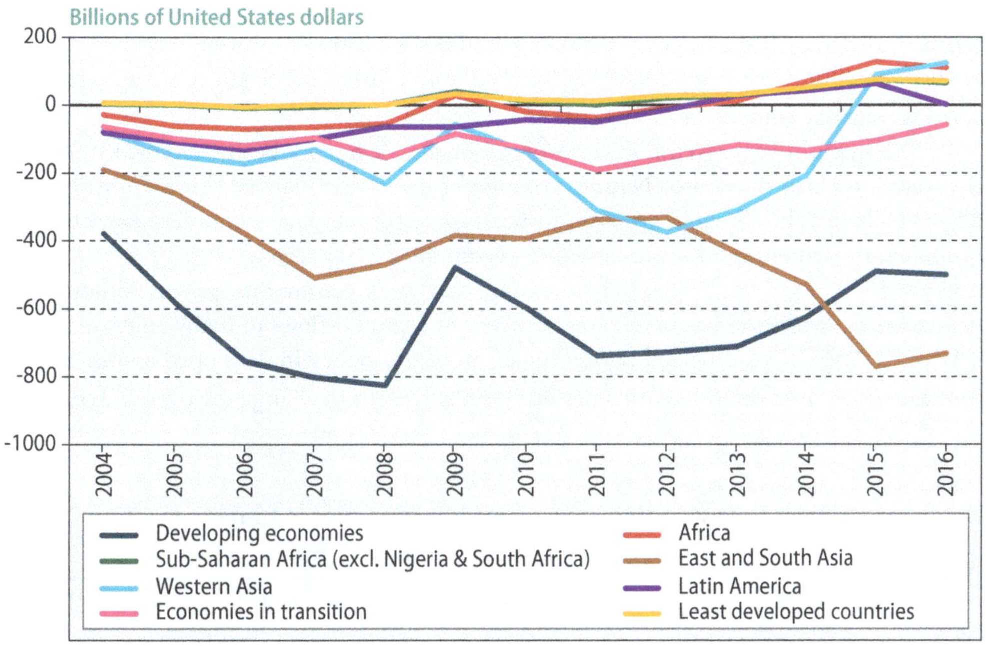

Source: UN/DESA, based on IMF (2016a) and World Bank (2016b).
Note: Data for 2016 is partly estimated.

Figure III.2
Foreign exchange reserves as a percentage of world gross product, 1990–2015

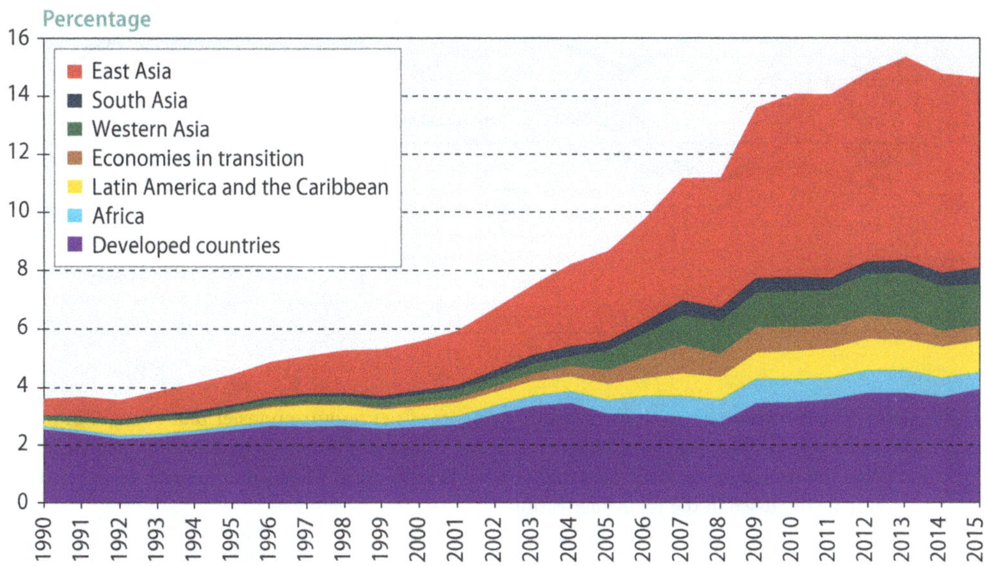

Source: UN/DESA, based on IMF (2016d).
Note: Excludes the value of gold held as official reserves.

Trends in private resources for sustainable development

Net financial outflows from developing countries underscore the challenges of financing long-term sustainable development through international capital flows

Table III.1 and figure III.3 show the breakdown of recent trends in net financial flows to developing countries by type of flow, along with changes in international reserves.[2] As shown, both total net financial flows and changes in international reserves turned negative in 2015, underscoring the challenges associated with financing long-term sustainable development through international capital flows.

For 2016, net financial outflows from developing countries and economies in transition are estimated at $456 billion, with further outflows expected in 2017. This estimate nonetheless represents an improvement from outflows of $543 billion in 2015. While most forms of financial flows to developing and transition economies initially rebounded following the 2008 crisis, they peaked at $615 billion in 2010 and began to slow thereafter, turning negative from 2014.

Such a multi-year reversal in flows on a global scale has not been seen since 1990, the first year for which the United Nations compiled data on net financial flows. Contributing factors include a slowdown in growth prospects in key developing economies, expectations of monetary tightening in some developed economies, after several years of near-zero or negative interest rates and quantitative easing, and weak commodity prices. Although in the course of 2016 there has been some recovery in capital inflows to many emerging markets amid slower-than-expected tightening of monetary policy in developed countries and increases in commodity prices, this has not been sufficient to change the overall dynamic.

Figure III.3
Net financial flows to developing countries and economies in transition, 2006–2016

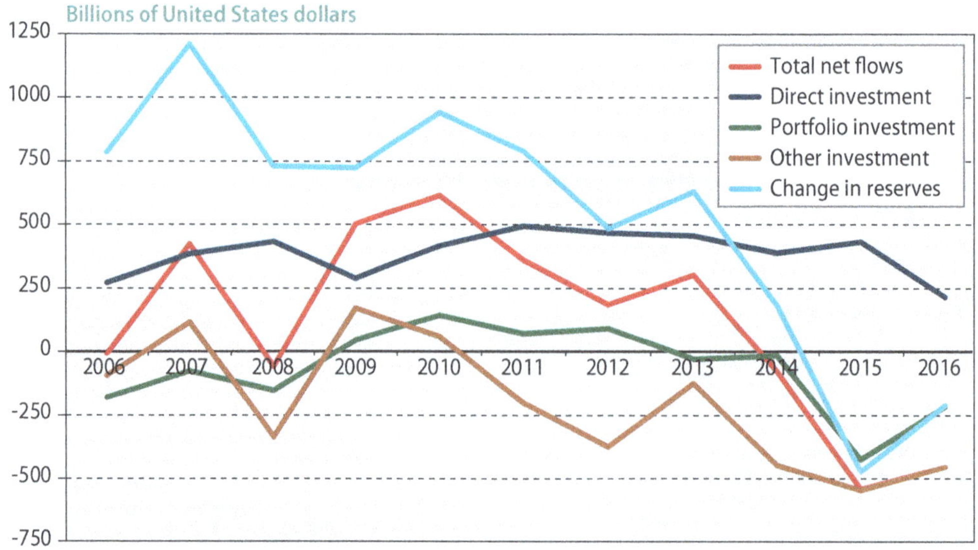

Source: Table III.1 of this publication.
Note: A positive value means inflow of capital and increase in reserves.

2 These datasets represent the capital account elements of net resource transfer plus changes in international reserves. Some additional elements of net resource transfer, such as income (e.g. retained earnings transferred out of countries) and current transfers (e.g. ODA) that are part of the current account are discussed in the following sections.

Table III.1

Net financial flows to developing countries and economies in transition, 2007–2016

	2007	2008	2009	2010	2011	2012	2013	2014	2015	2016[a]
Developing countries										
Total net flows	308.20	51.12	513.08	637.50	433.80	213.85	365.53	44.10	-446.21	-430.76
Direct investment	345.87	375.38	265.98	401.20	473.65	434.69	457.54	402.83	431.25	209.21
Portfolio investment[b]	-74.74	-117.19	38.20	128.12	86.57	93.16	-14.57	6.47	-412.93	-218.14
Other investment[c]	37.08	-207.07	208.90	108.17	-126.41	-314.00	-77.45	-365.20	-464.53	-421.83
Change in reserves[d]	-1038.05	-749.62	-709.10	-878.78	-752.15	-471.82	-667.71	-313.03	435.42	215.77
Africa										
Total net flows	36.22	38.17	58.28	21.44	32.46	55.65	77.37	82.68	82.05	81.86
Direct investment	41.12	57.98	44.45	47.28	41.39	41.83	35.20	38.96	39.60	36.40
Portfolio investment[b]	9.81	-26.00	-1.28	9.05	12.83	21.42	20.23	17.90	9.15	0.61
Other investment[c]	-14.71	6.19	15.11	-34.89	-21.76	-7.60	21.93	25.82	33.30	44.84
Change in reserves[d]	-63.38	-57.10	8.87	-17.05	-26.33	-13.66	-4.16	9.23	31.29	27.74
East and South Asia										
Total net flows	110.06	-34.46	357.63	382.30	273.29	44.80	206.09	-142.53	-677.56	-666.17
Direct investment	160.71	157.57	94.68	202.75	260.99	217.34	270.17	196.28	244.32	27.89
Portfolio investment[b]	-52.48	-43.20	40.87	29.96	23.85	-0.06	-83.27	-8.39	-383.50	-240.31
Other investment[c]	1.83	-148.83	222.08	149.59	-11.55	-172.48	19.20	-330.42	-538.39	-453.75
Change in reserves[d]	-676.96	-512.21	-670.52	-682.22	-505.23	-224.85	-513.26	-264.20	241.88	108.67
West Asia										
Total net flows	42.88	-35.61	11.51	19.64	-109.53	-107.77	-130.38	-156.16	-33.40	40.14
Direct investment	48.10	57.66	54.62	39.69	24.20	25.36	7.82	26.55	13.43	13.00
Portfolio investment[b]	-75.43	-54.13	-26.75	-17.75	-57.29	-23.48	-58.52	-120.68	-98.93	-25.67
Other investment[c]	70.22	-39.14	-16.36	-2.31	-76.44	-109.64	-79.68	-62.03	52.10	52.81
Change in reserves[d]	-167.14	-138.81	7.01	-89.09	-110.17	-173.77	-143.95	-20.13	129.55	74.77
Latin America and the Caribbean										
Total net flows	119.04	83.02	85.67	214.11	237.57	221.16	212.45	260.10	182.72	113.41
Direct investment	95.94	102.17	72.24	111.48	147.06	150.17	144.35	141.04	133.90	131.91
Portfolio investment[b]	43.36	6.14	25.36	106.86	107.18	95.28	106.99	117.64	60.36	47.23
Other investment[c]	-20.26	-25.29	-11.93	-4.23	-16.67	-24.28	-38.89	1.42	-11.54	-65.73
Change in reserves[d]	-130.58	-41.50	-54.47	-90.42	-110.42	-59.54	-6.33	-37.94	32.69	4.59
Economies in transition										
Total net flows	112.00	-111.30	-12.53	-22.05	-72.96	-31.31	-63.41	-121.77	-97.47	-25.21
Direct investment	36.29	55.40	22.03	12.89	21.02	30.64	0.24	-15.45	-0.67	6.45
Portfolio investment[b]	-2.68	-36.02	5.93	14.12	-15.84	-1.31	-15.20	-22.64	-11.77	1.21
Other investment[c]	78.39	-130.68	-40.49	-49.06	-78.14	-60.64	-48.45	-83.68	-85.03	-32.87
Change in reserves[d]	-171.39	19.91	-14.19	-60.32	-34.72	-11.12	40.52	132.25	38.10	-3.85

Source: UN/DESA, based on IMF (2016a).

Note: The composition of developing countries above is based on the country classification located in the statistical annex, which differs from the classification used in the IMF World Economic Outlook.

a Preliminary estimates.

b Including portfolio debt and equity investment.

c Including short and long-term bank lending.

d Negative values denote increases in official reserves.

Nonetheless, compared to previous episodes of financial crises in emerging markets, high levels of international reserves and greater exchange-rate flexibility in many developing economies have provided a cushion in coping with the reversal in capital flows. The volatility of capital flows, while still high compared to the period before capital account liberalization, is below the volatility associated with earlier episodes in many countries (see the section on the analysis of volatility). It is unclear, however, whether all developing countries will be able to continue to smoothly manage such volatility, given their current rate of drawdown in international reserves and the potential for greater capital withdrawal when monetary policy normalizes in developed countries.

Specific national economic and political circumstances affect the cross-country distribution of these flows. East and South Asia drove the overall trend due to continued large outflows of portfolio and other investment, and growing net outflows of direct investment. While economies in transition also experienced net capital outflows, characterized both by low levels of direct investment and continued deleveraging, all other regions are estimated to have experienced positive net flows in 2016. The Africa region has had relatively stable total net inflows over the past three years, at about $82 billion annually. Direct investment remained more or less constant, albeit at relatively low levels. Portfolio investment collapsed to net zero, but was offset by an increase in other investments, such as cross-border bank loans. West Asia and Latin America and the Caribbean also experienced positive inflows in 2016, though at a low level compared to the first half of the decade.

While table III.1 is based on net flows (inflows net of outflows), gross capital flows, by all indications, have increased in size, both nominally and as a proportion of GDP. The growing magnitude of both gross inflows and outflows reflects in part growing South-South flows (including outward foreign direct investment, as discussed below), as well as institutional developments such as the emergence of pension funds and sovereign wealth funds (SWFs) in some countries (IMF, 2016e).

Table III.1 shows that across regions, portfolio investments and other investments (mostly bank loans and currency/deposits, trade credits, and other equity) have been the largest source of outflows, as well as the most volatile. As shown in table III.1, foreign direct investment (FDI), which has generally tended to be relatively more stable than other flows, is estimated to have fallen significantly in net terms in 2016.

Foreign direct investment

FDI to developing countries fell to an estimated $209 billion in 2016, from $431 billion in 2015. In spite of this, and as indicated in table III.1 and figure III.3, FDI has tended to be relatively more stable and longer-term than the other types of cross-border private finance, such as bank lending and portfolio flows. When FDI is invested in sustainable development-enhancing sectors, such as resilient infrastructure, it can help to further sustainable development and implementation of the SDGs. While FDI flows to developing countries have been on an upward trend since 2000 (when they amounted to around $149 billion), they peaked at $474 billion in 2011 and have registered lower levels in subsequent years. They have in general been suppressed by the fragility of the global economy, weak growth in emerging economies, and low commodity prices. The sharp fall in 2016 is largely driven by FDI trends in China, with mainland China projected to record a net outflow of FDI of about $48 billion. At the same time, inward FDI in China has slowed in response to the lower Chinese growth trajectory and lower global trade growth. Over the medium term, an expected pick-up in economic activity around the world should lead to higher levels of global FDI flows.

There are concerns regarding the concentration and development impact of FDI

There are concerns, however, regarding the concentration and development impact of many forms of FDI. The large majority of FDI to developing countries continues to be channelled to Asia and Latin America. Developing Asia remained the largest FDI recipient region in the world in 2015 and will likely continue to attract large inflows, despite estimates of a net decline in 2016. During the past year, falling commodity prices have depressed foreign investment in natural-resource-based economies in sub-Saharan Africa and South America, limiting FDI flows to those regions (UNCTAD, 2016b).

Compared to their 2012 peak, 2015 net FDI flows were down nearly 11 per cent in Latin America and the Caribbean, but FDI inflows have stabilized at between 3.5 per cent and 3.7 per cent of GDP in the region. FDI to LDCs as a group increased in 2015 to $35 billion on a gross basis, or 5 per cent of gross FDI to developing countries. This upturn was largely due to investment in one country, Angola, over three-quarters of which were loans provided by foreign parent firms to their Angolan affiliates. FDI to LDCs is estimated to decline in 2016 due to falling commodity prices leading to sluggish investment, along with cancellation of projects in a number of countries (UNCTAD, 2016b).

The Addis Ababa Action Agenda (AAAA) emphasized the importance of the quality of FDI, along with quantity, in supporting sustainable development. Current FDI patterns do not appear to be fully aligned with sustainable development. Greenfield investment tends to have a greater impact on jobs and development than other forms of FDI, but an increase in global FDI projected for 2016 is principally driven by a surge in cross-border mergers and acquisitions, which hit an all-time high in 2014. At the same time, FDI to LDCs and small island developing States (SIDS) remains concentrated in extractive industries; the number of investments in the natural resource sector in LDCs more than doubled in 2015 to reach a three-year high, while announced greenfield projects fell by 6 per cent (UNCTAD, 2016b).

Developing economies have become important sources of investments in the LDCs

In gross terms, FDI flows to developing economies amounted to $765 billion in 2015, representing an increase of 9 per cent over the previous year, while outward investment from some developing and transition economies has been limited by weakening aggregate demand and declining commodity prices, accompanied by depreciating national currencies. Nonetheless, from a longer-term perspective, developing economies have become important sources of investments in LDCs, landlocked developing countries and SIDS (UNCTAD, 2016b).

Other investment, including bank lending

In gross terms, international bank claims (cross-border bank claims plus local claims in foreign currencies) are amongst the largest form of international capital flows, with trillions of dollars moving across borders. Total gross international bank claims totalled $31.6 trillion in 2016, with cross-border bank credit to emerging market economies of $3.2 trillion (BIS, 2016a). On a net basis, the "other investment" category (which includes bank claims) represents the largest capital outflow from developing countries, at $465 billion in 2015 and an estimated $422 billion in 2016. The impact of this was greatest in China, where cross-border lending to residents of mainland China dropped $305 billion from its mid-2014 peak (BIS, 2016b).

Cross-border bank lending has been subdued in recent years as a number of international banks — particularly from Europe — continue to face deleveraging pressures. Figures released by the Bank for International Settlements (BIS) show a decline in global cross-border bank claims since 2008, with a peak-to-trough drop of 26.2 per cent from the first quarter of 2008 until end-2015. As illustrated in figure III.4, in contrast to total cross-border claims, bank credit to developing economies increased by over 72 per cent from early 2009 to mid-2014, at which point it also began a downward trend (despite a small increase in the second quarter of 2016).[3]

There is some concern that the Basel capital adequacy rules for banks might, by raising the cost of long-term and riskier lending, have the effect of reducing the availability of long-term financing, with a particularly negative impact on investment in developing countries as well as on riskier investments such as some clean technologies. While it is difficult to calculate the impact of the regulations because the counterfactual is not known, figure III.4 does show that long-term lending to developing countries has been stagnant since the crisis, with annual growth remaining low or at zero for most years since 2008.

The growth of international bank credit has been fuelled by short term loans

The declining share of long-term claims further shows that the growth of bank credit has been fuelled by short-term loans. Indeed, volatility of total flows to developing countries has been almost entirely due to shifts in short-term lending. The lack of growth in long-term commercial bank flows to developing and transition economies is of particular concern for sustainable development since they have historically played an important role in financing longer-term infrastructure projects in these countries.

Portfolio flows

Portfolio flows to developing countries have turned negative in recent years

Given the drop in bank lending, institutional investors have been viewed as a potential source of financing for sustainable development. Indeed, institutional investors manage assets of between $75 and $85 trillion. However, similar to bank lending, portfolio flows (which are driven by institutional investors) to developing countries have turned negative in recent years. Developing countries and economies in transition experienced net outflows of $425 billion in 2015 and estimated outflows of $217 billion in 2016. Declines have been strongest in East and South Asia, particularly reflecting large capital outflows from China.

Chinese domestic actors have sought overseas assets as China has slowly liberalized outward investment, while foreign investors have withdrawn capital due to downgraded growth expectations. This follows several years of robust inflows to developing countries and transition economies following the financial crisis of 2008, as portfolio investors in developed countries searched for higher yields in the context of low interest rates in developed countries.

There is a risk that capital flows into emerging market debt securities could go into reverse if interest rates in the developed economies rise

While a large part of the volatility in portfolio flows has been witnessed in equity markets, emerging market bonds have also experienced turbulence. Over the past couple of years, there have been concerns regarding a trend of increasing levels of borrowing through international debt securities by companies in emerging economies, as discussed below.

International bond issuance recovered sharply in developing countries after the global financial crisis, in contrast to bank loans, which have remained subdued. As a result,

3 Debt securities are covered in multiple categories of the balance of payments. Foreign investment in domestically issued debt is covered under portfolio flows below. External sovereign debt is covered in the section on debt and debt sustainability. External debt issued by emerging market and developing country corporations is covered in Box III.1.

Figure III.4
International claims of BIS reporting banks vis-à-vis developing countries, 2000 Q1–2016 Q2

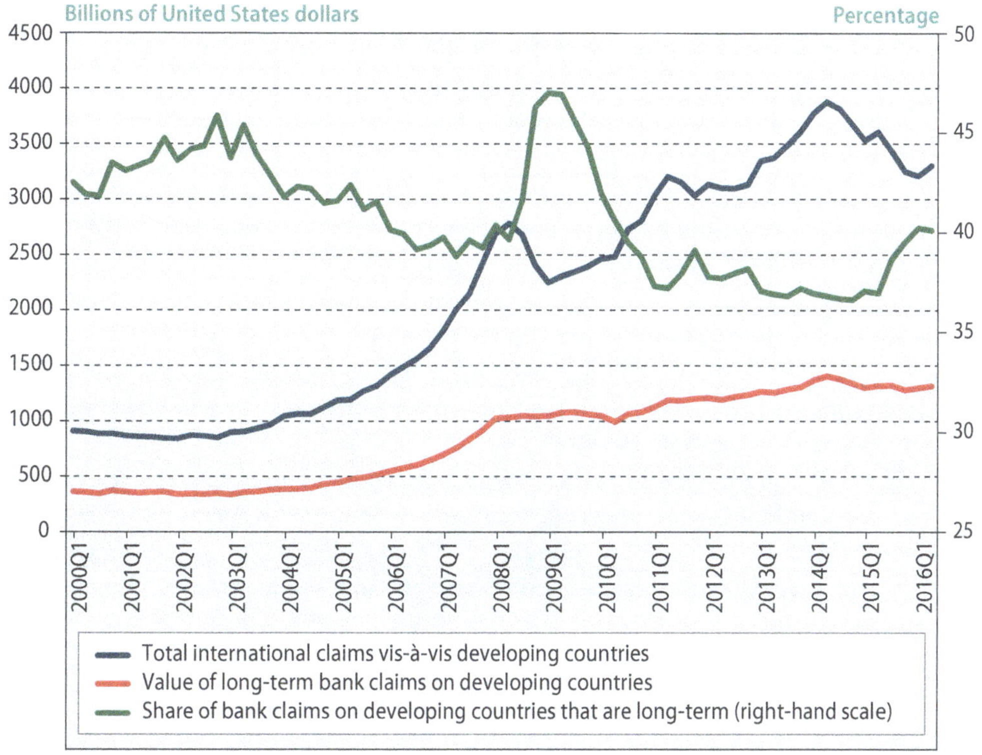

Source: UN/DESA, based on data from the BIS.
Note: International claims of BIS reporting banks include cross-border claims of foreign banks in all currencies plus local claims of foreign banks in foreign currency, long-term corresponds to maturities of one year or greater.

in a number of emerging economies, dollar bonds have become an increasingly important source of debt finance vis-à-vis dollar bank loans. Moreover, international debt issuers from emerging economies that have traditionally relied mostly on the United States dollar as a funding currency have also been increasing their net issuance in euros (see Box III.1). There is a risk that these flows could go into reverse if interest rates in the developed economies rise (BIS, 2016a).

Sudden surges or exits associated with portfolio flows can undermine sustainable development rather than support it

The high volatility of portfolio flows is indicative of short-term investment horizons of institutional investors. The impact of the sudden surges or exits associated with these flows can undermine sustainable development rather than support it, as was seen in past financial crises in Asia, the Russian Federation and Latin America (Muchhala, 2007; Dasgupta and others, 2001; De Paula and Alves, 2000). Despite institutional investors' promise to contribute to sustainable development, due to the short-term nature of capital flows, portfolio flows cannot currently be regarded as part of sustainable finance.

Analysis of volatility

As illustrated in figure III.3, portfolio flows and cross-border bank lending to developing countries have undergone bouts of turbulence. It is important to distinguish between gross and net cross-border capital flows, and to disaggregate the actions by different type of investors, as they may have different motivations (Broner and others, 2013; Lane and Milesi-Ferretti, 2001 and 2007; Forbes and Warnock, 2012). Conventional studies that look at cross-country regressions on the impact of capital flows tend to use quarterly or annual data, often on a net basis (Ariyoshi and others, 2000; Broner and others, 2013). Rapid movements in capital can be masked, as sudden surges (withdrawals) in some months may be netted out by a slowdown (return of inflows) in the next month. To examine the volatility trends, analysis was conducted on five developing countries' capital flows for which monthly disaggregated data was available going back at least 12 years.

Figure III.5 shows the gross volume of different types of capital and financial market investment for five countries as a proportion of GDP, broken down by portfolio and other investment (primarily bank lending) and separated by domestic and international investors. In four of the countries, the volume of portfolio investment by non-residents is larger than the volumes by domestic investors, with the notable exception of Chile, where a relatively large private pension system means that investments by residents account for a larger component of capital flows. On the other hand, cross-border flows in the other investment category (largely bank lending) tend to have larger activity by resident actors, although in some countries, such as Poland, non-resident activity outweighs resident activity in this category, as it does in portfolio flows.

There are persistent spikes of volatility in capital flows at certain times and in certain countries

Figure III.6 shows volatility of portfolio investment and other investment, as measured by the conditional, time-weighted standard deviation,[4] disaggregated by residents and non-residents, for four of these countries. The data available through 2015 shows that volatility levels, including through the periods of expectations of monetary policy normali-

Figure III.5
Volume of portfolio and other investment flows, selected countries and years

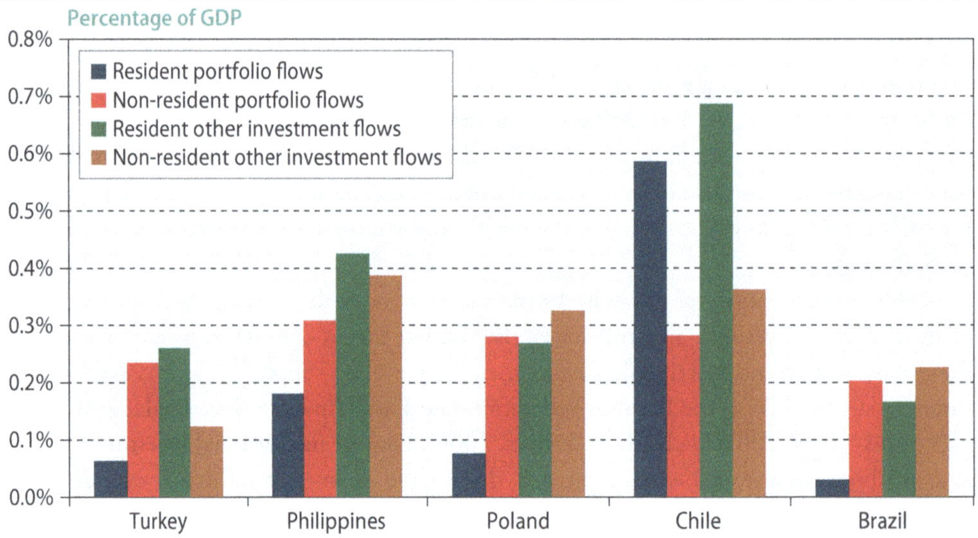

Source: UN/DESA calculations based on official national data.
Note: The figure shows the magnitude of average gross movements of capital. The average was calculated using the absolute value of each month's flows divided by the GDP of the year in which that flow occurred. Data through December 2015 and starting from: 1992 (Turkey), 1995 (Brazil), 1997 (Poland), 1999 (Philippines) and 2003 (Chile).

4 Use of standard deviation as a measure for volatility of capital flows is problematic because of illiquid markets, non-random behaviour by market actors, and heteroscedasticity – meaning the exhibition of non-uniform behaviour over time. These volatility estimates were generated using a database of monthly disaggregated capital flow data from national official sources. Instead of traditional standard deviations, an autoregressive model was specified and uses both values of past variances and the observations themselves to model the variance at a particular point in time. The generalized autoregressive conditionally heteroscedastic (GARCH) model uses both the lagged squared residual and the lagged conditional variance to estimate a time-weighted conditional standard deviation (Bollerslev, 1986).

Figure III.6
Volatility of capital flows, selected countries and years

Conditional time-weighted standard deviation

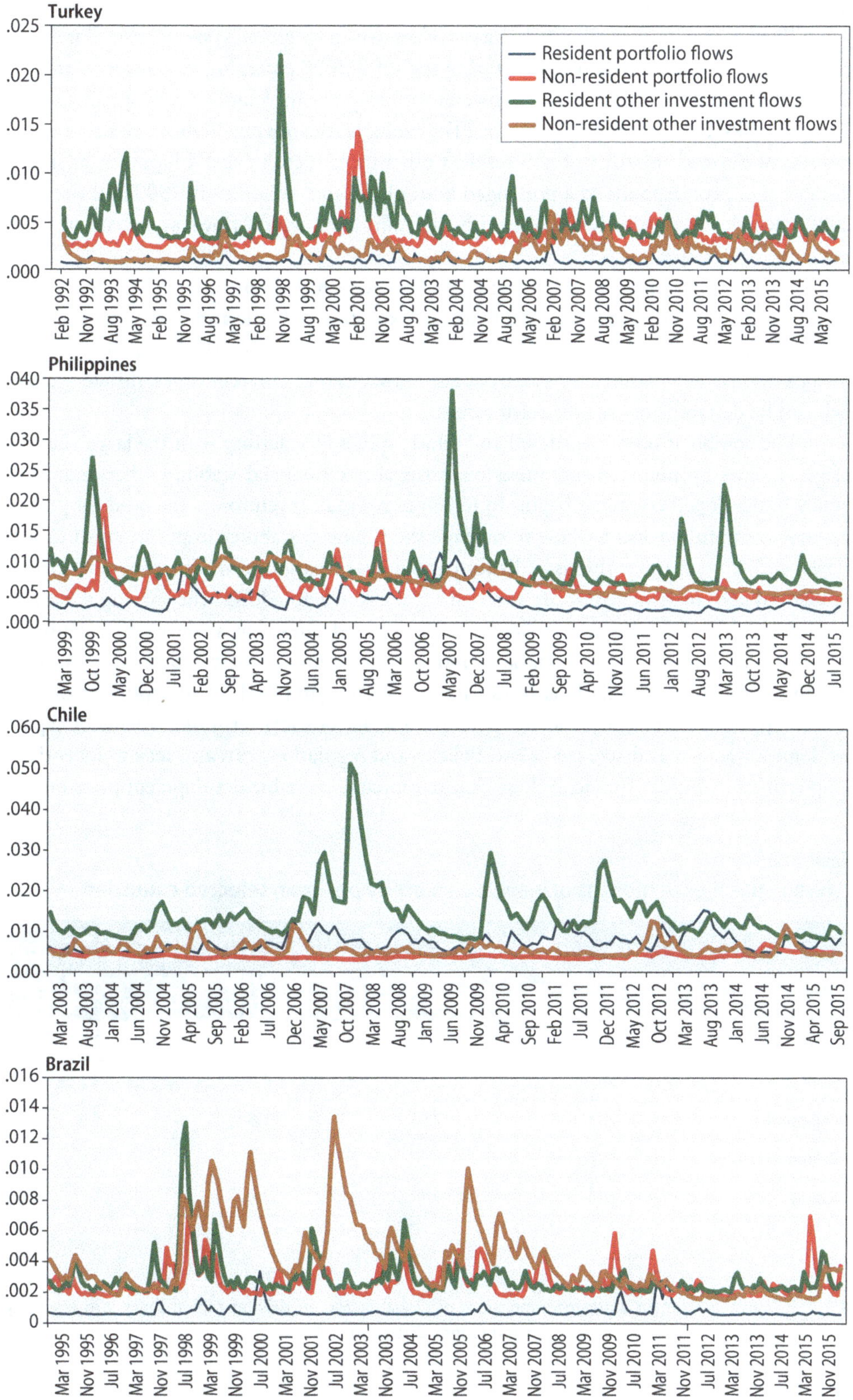

Source: UN/DESA, based on data from national official sources.

Note: the activities of non-residents are recorded in the balance of payments as an incurrence of liabilities, and an increase in liabilities relates to an inflow of capital; the activities of residents are recorded in the balance of payments as an acquisition of assets, and an increase in assets relates to an outflow of capital.

sation in the United States in 2014 and 2015, have remained low, and not reached the peaks seen at times of domestic financial crises in the past. While there is no discernible trend toward increasing volatility over time, there are persistent high volatility spikes at certain times and in certain countries.

The charts also show that volatility is often driven by global systemic risk. For example, volatility spiked across countries during the 1998-2000 emerging market crises and the 2007-2008 global financial crisis.[5] However, other spikes in volatility correspond to idiosyncratic risks, based on domestic factors. For example, the notably high average number of months of elevated volatility of non-resident other investment in the Philippines, as shown in table III.2, corresponds to a prolonged bout of elevated volatility in 1999 and the early 2000s, which has diminished along with the volume of capital flows as a share of GDP since the 2008 crisis.

In the countries analysed, foreign investors tend to exhibit more volatile behaviour than domestic investors in most cases (with the exception of Chile and Turkey for portfolio investment, and Poland for other investment), as shown in table III.2, which quantifies periods of elevated volatility. The analysis also shows that at different times, different channels can be destabilising to a different extent.

Continued and erratic spikes in volatility and the large volumes of gross capital flows by non-residents raise concerns about financial stability

The combination of continued and erratic spikes in volatility with the large volumes of gross flows by non-residents raises concerns about financial stability when monetary policy in developed countries begins to return to normal. It reinforces the need for policymakers to carefully consider how to manage the financial stability implications of capital flows, and, among other things, calls for careful coordination of macroeconomic, macroprudential and, in some instances, more direct measures, to address the varying dynamics motivating different categories of investors. It also indicates that as developing countries build deeper domestic capital markets and an institutional investor base, they need to design capital market regulations and structures, keeping in mind the susceptibility of markets to episodes of volatility and the potential impact of short-term movements of capital by domestic actors, as discussed below. Policies and regulations can also seek to incentivise long-term cross-border financial flows that reinforce sustainable development priorities.

Table III.2

Average number of months of elevated volatility per year, selected countries

	Residents		Non-residents	
Countries	Portfolio investment	Other investment	Portfolio investment	Other investment
Brazil	1.9	2.3	3.2	3.5
Chile	4.7	3.1	4.0	3.7
Philippines	3.2	2.9	3.6	5.9
Poland	1.7	4.2	4.0	3.9
Turkey	3.5	3.1	2.8	4.5

Source: UN/DESA, based on data from official national sources.
Note: A month is defined as having elevated volatility when the estimation of the conditional time-weighted standard deviation is larger than an ordinary standard deviation.

5 Research has shown a greater importance of global factors in driving capital flows into emerging economies over time (Eichengreen and Gupta, 2016 and 2015).

Incentives to align institutional investment with sustainable development

Institutional investors have been looked to as a potential source of financing for sustainable development, both because of the size of assets under their management, and because of the long-term liabilities of some investors, which should enable the longer-term investment necessary for sustainable development. Around $78 trillion of the total $115 trillion in institutional investor assets at the end 2014 is held by "primary" institutional investors, such as pension funds, insurance companies, and sovereign wealth funds (SWFs), with long-duration liabilities (TheCityUK, 2015).

The incentives in capital markets are not well-aligned with long-term investment or with sustainable development

A reallocation of a small percentage of institutional investor assets, say 3 to 5 per cent, towards long-term investment in sustainable development could have an enormous impact. Yet, a shift of even this relatively small percentage will be extremely challenging. Indeed, it is unlikely to happen without a significant shift in behaviour, necessitating changes in both private actions and public policies. This is because the incentives in capital markets are not well-aligned with long-term investment or with sustainable development.

To date, investment by institutional investors in long-term illiquid assets necessary for sustainable development has been limited — in both developed and developing countries. For instance, direct investment in infrastructure globally represents less than 3 per cent of pension fund assets, with even lower allocations to infrastructure in developing countries and low-carbon infrastructure (Della Croce, 2012). This low level of investment reflects the duality of illiquidity of assets on the one hand and a short-term investment horizon of institutional investors on the other, as manifested in the volatility of international portfolio flows to developing countries, as well as in volatility in developed-country capital markets. In the United States, for example, the average holding period for stocks fell from about eight years in the 1960s to approximately six months in 2010 (Kleintop, 2012).

To analyse the impediments to long-term investment, we must understand the incentives of investors in capital markets

In this regard, the AAAA includes a commitment by Member States of the United Nations to "endeavour to design policies, including capital market regulations where appropriate, that promote incentives along the investment chain that are aligned with long-term performance and sustainability indicators, and that reduce excess volatility." While there has been significant research on impediments to investment at the country level, including regulatory uncertainty and weak governance, imperfect information and other market failures, there is less research on impediments on the investor side. In this regard, an understanding of the incentives across the full range of players in capital markets, particularly for long-term investing, is crucial.

For the purpose of financing long-term sustainable development, long-term investment should meet two criteria: the investor's time horizon should be sufficiently long to finance long-duration assets of say, 10 to 20 years, and the investor should be *able* to hold a position through economic cycles and downside events. In other words, long-term investors should have the willingness not only to buy long-term illiquid assets, but also the ability to hold these assets for a full holding period, irrespective of market pressures. For example, managers that invested in long-duration illiquid assets funded by short-term liabilities prior to the global economic and financial crisis were forced to sell these assets when liquidity became scarce and debt refinancing became difficult. This was seen in the fields of renewable energy and biofuels.

While investment in renewable energy grew by 85 per cent in 2007, it fell by 42 per cent during the crisis. When investment and financing dried up, many companies were forced to exit the market and/or file for bankruptcy (IEA, 2009). Investors' inability to maintain illiquid positions through the crisis had severe implications for investments in sustainable development as well as for the real economy.

Indeed, for investors able to hold long-term positions, buying and holding illiquid assets should be a profitable strategy. Short-term investors that need liquidity are often willing to pay a higher price for liquid assets; hence long-term investors can buy cheaper illiquid assets, and earn the higher return, or the "liquidity premium". In essence, they can arbitrage the short-term nature of markets, buying illiquid assets when the liquidity premium is high, and selling them when it is low. They would also play a stabilizing role in the market because they act counter-cyclically to liquidity cycles.

Figure III.7 shows the three-month "Libor-OIS" spread from 2007 to 2008. The Overnight Index Swap (OIS) rate is the rate for unsecured overnight lending between banks, while the London Interbank Offered Rate (Libor) represents term lending between banks. The spread between the two rates is thought to indicate the additional liquidity risk premium associated with taking on longer-term, less liquid lending (Thorton, 2009).

Prior to the financial crisis, the three-month Libor-OIS spread was around 9 basis points (Kwan, 2009), making long-term assets particularly expensive (and implying that investors are not being paid to take long-term liquidity risk). During the crisis, the spread peaked at an all-time high of approximately 400 basis points in October 2008. Some long-term investors, particularly some sovereign wealth funds, were able to take advantage of this spike by buying cheap assets, especially in the financial sector.

Such long-term investments would match these investors' longer-term liability structures. Pension funds, which hold around $34 trillion in assets, distribute around 40 per cent of their assets within 10 years, and 60 per cent within 20 years, so that, to match liabilities, they could hold 60 per cent of their assets in long-duration instruments. Similarly, life insurers distribute about 60 per cent of their assets to beneficiaries within 10 years, and 40 per cent within 20 years (TheCityUK, 2013a and 2013b; World Economic Forum, 2011).

Sustainable or green investments, in theory, should be attractive to long-term funds from an asset-liability perspective

Infrastructure investment should be particularly attractive to these investors because of its low risk and stable real return profile, which also matches pension funds' "real" liabilities (in that many funds pay pensioners a return over inflation). Sustainable or green invest-

Figure III.7
Yield spreads of USD Libor (*3-month*) over OIS rates, 2007–2008

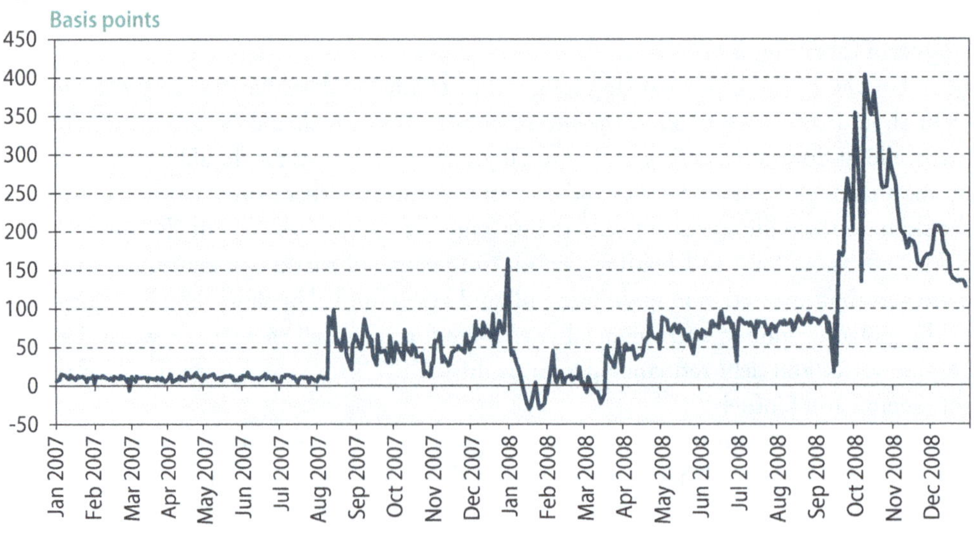

Source: UN/DESA calculations based on Federal Reserve Bank of New York (2016) and Federal Reserve Bank of St. Louis (2016).

ments, in theory, should be attractive to long-term funds from an asset-liability perspective, since the risks associated with climate change can be seen as a potential liability in the long run (Bolton and others, 2010).

Nonetheless, and despite their ability to arbitrage short-termism, most primary intermediaries have traditionally held relatively liquid portfolios. The largest pension markets hold 76 per cent of their portfolios in liquid assets (Willis Towers Watson, 2016). The majority of insurance assets are liquid securities, with 70 per cent in bonds and 10 per cent in equities in the United States (National Association of Insurance Commissioners, 2011), and 90 per cent in bonds, and 7 per cent in equities in Europe (Deutsche Bank, 2011). Many SWFs hold the bulk of their funds in liquid financial assets in the mature economies, with less than 5 per cent in direct investments (UNCTAD, 2013b). Since the financial crisis, however, an important trend has been a substantial increase in institutional investor allocation to less liquid alternative investments, particularly by pension funds. Allocations to alternative asset classes increased from around 5 per cent in 1995 to around 19 per cent in 2012 in the largest pension markets (Towers Watson, 2013) and around 7 per cent overall (Prosser, 2013).

The interests of intermediary funds are not necessarily well-aligned with either institutional investors' interests or with public goals

However, much of this increase is being outsourced to secondary financial intermediaries, such as private equity firms and hedge funds. Those intermediary funds, many of which were designed for high net worth individuals willing to take high risks, are not necessarily well-aligned with either the interest of the investors, or with public goals. In particular, many have shorter-term liabilities and/or incorporate a greater degree of short-term incentives in compensation, neither of which is conducive to long-term sustainable investment.

The fee structure (of a 2 per cent management fee and 20 per cent performance fee) is characterized by asymmetric returns — managers have a potential upside monetary gain but no downside penalty when losses are realized. This asymmetry provides strong incentives for managers to increase risk and leverage in order to boost short-term returns.[6]

Hedge funds are often highly leveraged, with quarterly, semi-annual, or annual redemptions, and are not well-suited for long-term investment. Private equity funds are longer-term, and typically feature a maturity of ten years with two optional one-year extensions. However, the private equity investment approach is generally built around an "exit strategy", based on buying risky assets, transforming them, and selling them to investors who might have been unwilling or unable to take the initial high risks. While this can play an important role in financing the economy, it is not clear that these are appropriate as long-term investment vehicles, especially given the relatively low risk tolerance of pension funds and other primary intermediaries. Infrastructure funds are a case in point. While infrastructure investment in developed countries is generally more stable and less correlated with market indices than private equity, infrastructure funds are less stable and are, in fact, correlated with market indices (Bitsch and others, 2010). This is partially attributable to the effect of the exit strategy, which links returns on the fund to the exit price, making the returns susceptible to market sentiment.

Other institutional factors can also have an impact. First, the structure of the firm affects incentives. For example, in the case of a publicly traded insurance company, shareholders may have a much shorter time horizon than policyholders and may encourage man-

6 This issue is mitigated to an extent for private equity funds, which only receive performance fees on realized gains, once an asset has been sold. Nonetheless, managers can still earn performance fees by selling profitable assets, even when all other assets in the fund are at an unrealized loss.

agers to shift the portfolio towards a shorter horizon. Second, both long-term and riskier investments will have losses in the short-term. If trustees, senior managers, or in the case of public pension funds and SWFs, politicians, do not have appetite for short-term losses it will be difficult for managers to maintain longer-term positions. Third, the high mobility of portfolio managers between firms may represent a further disincentive to long-term investing, as managers can earn a high bonus, and then move to another firm before the "tail-risk" has materialized.

For instance, the average tenure of a chief investment officer of a public pension plan is four years, with even shorter periods for more junior staff (World Economic Forum, 2011). Finally, firm culture can affect investment strategies, including how fiduciary responsibilities and non-financial impacts are viewed and taken into account in performance evaluations of individual managers.

In addition, many managers lack in-house expertise in certain sectors, such as infrastructure and new technologies. Facing increased pressure to reduce costs, public funds are sometimes unable to pay salaries and bonuses that compete with other areas of finance. While this has benefits from the perspective of incentives as discussed above, it makes it difficult to attract the best talent and build expertise, especially in new areas. As a result many primary intermediaries are increasing their exposure to alternatives by investing through external managers.

Regulations and accounting standards can reduce the appetite for long-term investment

Regulations and accounting standards can reduce the appetite for long-term investment. In the insurance sector, Solvency II in the European Union includes new capital adequacy and risk management requirements, which impose higher costs for riskier holdings, based on maturity and credit rating, thus penalizing both long-term investment and investment in riskier assets. The new requirements include the need for equities to be backed by reserves of 30-40 per cent, which has further strengthened the trend, started after the crisis, of insurers reducing exposure to equities.

Mark-to-market accounting also impacts investors' ability to hold positions over the long term. Mark-to-market accounting values assets based on daily market prices in the open market. While this reflects the most up-to-date valuations, it also incorporates short-term market fluctuations into portfolio asset values. This can be particularly problematic for illiquid assets that only trade infrequently, as daily price fluctuations often do not reflect the intrinsic value of the assets. Managers whose incentives are linked to the value of assets under management and their returns are often incentivized to readjust their portfolios based on these short-term movements.

Many pension funds are subject to minimum funding, accounting and other requirements. While these rules are important for ensuring solvency, combined with mark-to-market accounting, they can inhibit long-term investment. For example, during the crisis, some pension funds breached their funding ratios due to a collapse in prices.

The decline in prices was largely due to the liquidity crisis, and not due to the solvency of the underlying assets, and many asset prices later rebounded. Nonetheless, some pension funds had to reduce risk to meet ratios, forcing some to sell, and inhibiting others from buying cheap long-term assets during the crisis.

Aligning financing flows with sustainable development can be done through various policies

In addition to the long-term horizon of investments, the AAAA notes that financing flows need to be aligned with sustainable development. This can be done through various policy mixes, including pricing externalities, blended finance and guarantees and leveraging private investment through public intermediaries such as development banks.

Box III.1

Emerging markets' corporate debt

Recent years have been marked by growing concerns about financial fragility in emerging economies and, in particular, about fast rising corporate debt in these economies. According to the BIS, the debt of non-financial corporations in emerging and large developing economies[a] more than tripled from $7.6 trillion at the end of 2008 to $24.5 trillion in the first quarter of 2016, reaching just over 100 per cent of GDP on average.

This rapid increase of corporate debt in emerging economies has taken place against a background of highly volatile international capital flows. Between 2009 and mid-2014, these economies faced a deluge of financial inflows and cheap credit through bank loans and bonds, driven largely by low interest rate policies and extensive asset purchasing programmes (quantitative easing) in major advanced economies. With yields on financial assets in the main financial centres dramatically lowered through these policies, investors adjusted their portfolios to include more "high-risk high-yield" assets in emerging markets, widely considered, at the time, to have "decoupled" from troubled developed economies and capable of delivering self-sustained high growth.

However, by mid-2014, net capital flows to these economies turned sharply negative (Table III.1). As a consequence, emerging market corporations now face substantial excess capacities and rising debt service costs (see figure III.1.1). Debt service-to-income ratios (DSRs) are generally considered a reliable early warning indicator of banking crisis originated from non-performing loans, with high DSRs also usually affecting consumption and investment negatively. While available data for DSRs is calculated for private non-financial sectors, including corporations and households, it is clear that rising household debt for now poses a problem primarily in some East and South-East Asian economies, with the bulk of rising DSRs attributable to rising corporate indebtedness. With the exception of South Africa and the advanced economies, the DSR not only is higher now in emerging economies compared to levels prior to the global financial crisis, but the trend is overwhelmingly rising.

Most worryingly, evidence is emerging that the increase in emerging and large developing countries' corporate debt has not been used to finance productive activities, but has instead been channelled mostly into very few sectors with an, at best, ambiguous impact on long-term productivity and trans-

Figure III.1.1

Debt service-to-income ratio of the private non-financial sector, selected countries and years

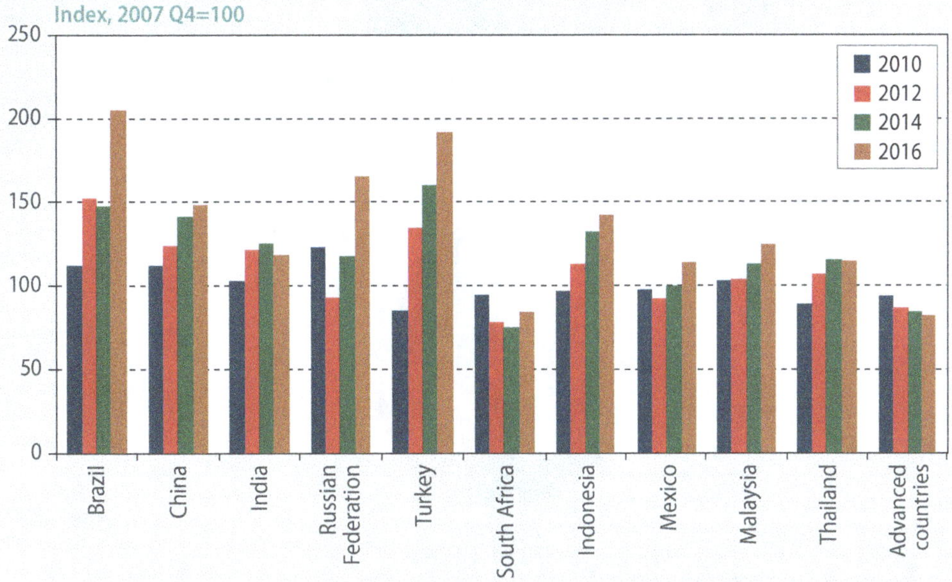

a Data refers to Argentina, Brazil, China, Chile, Hong Kong SAR, India, Indonesia, Malaysia, Mexico, Republic of Korea, Russian Federation, Singapore, South Africa, Thailand and Turkey.

Source: UNCTAD secretariat, based on BIS debt service ratios statistics.

Note: Figures are for March of each year. Advanced economies include France, Germany, Japan, the United Kingdom and the United States.

(continued)

Box III.1 (*continued*)

formational investment. As can be seen from figure III.1.2, a large proportion of corporate debt in these countries was incurred by companies operating in utilities, (residential) construction, real estate, mobile communications and mining.

This use of debt-financing is indicative of a growing financialization trend in emerging-market corporations (UNCTAD, 2016a), emphasising short-term speculative over longer-term productive profit and investment strategies.

Regional patterns of corporate indebtedness, and of its sources, have varied. While in Brazil, India and Mexico, the ratio of corporate debt to GDP has increased steadily over the past two decades, other major developing economies, in particular in East and South-East Asia, have experienced a more recent but steep increase in this ratio, following a period of decline. Similarly, domestic bank lending has been more prevalent in East and South-East Asia, whereas bond financing in international financial markets and cross-border bank lending have played a larger role in Latin American economies.

Spiralling corporate indebtedness in China has attracted the most attention more recently, reaching 170 per cent of GDP by mid-2016, according to the BIS.[b] With state-owned enterprises (SOEs) being the largest borrowers and the bulk of corporate debt being held domestically, concerns focus on the growing role of China's sprawling shadow banking sector. Based on data released recently by the China Government Securities Depository Trust & Clearing Company, the nominal value of wealth management products amounted to 35 per cent of GDP in mid-2016, amidst falling aggregate profits of SOEs (from 6.5 per cent of GDP in 2007 to 3.4 per cent in 2015) (Yao and others, 2016), and growing excess capacities.

b The IMF has put this figure slightly lower, at 145% of GDP for 2016 Q1 (Lipton, 2016).

Authors: Division on Globalization and Development Strategies (DGDS), UNCTAD

Figure III.1.2
Sectoral contribution to the increase in nominal value of total debt and capital stock, 2010–2014

Percentage

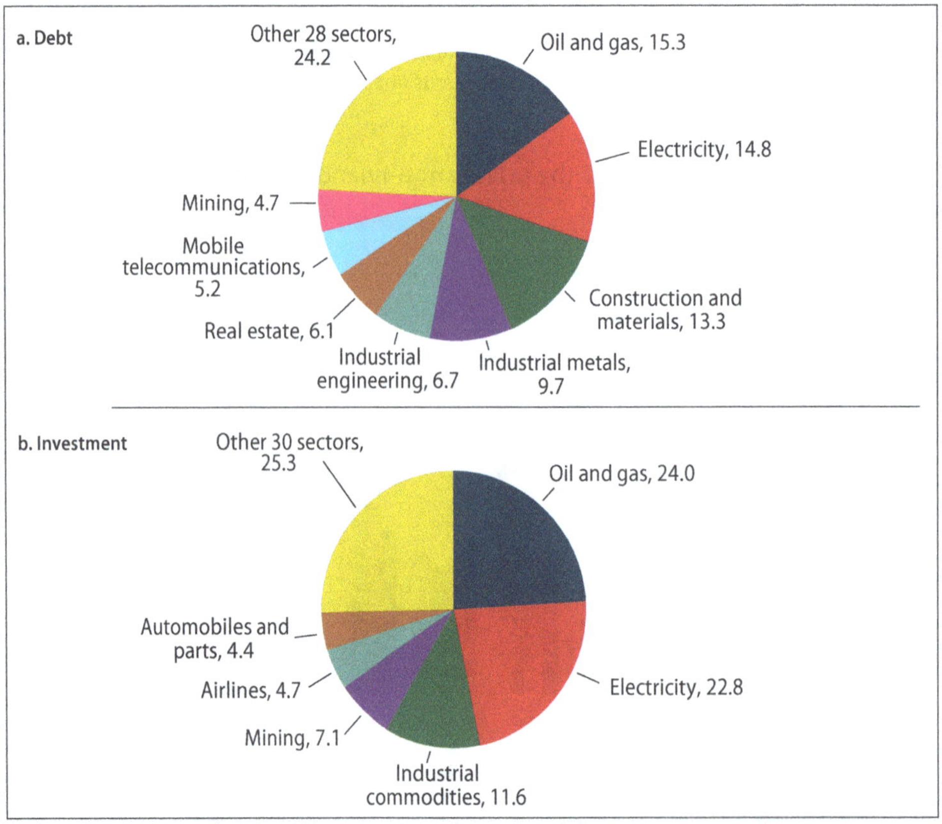

Source: UNCTAD secretariat, calculations, based on Thomson Reuters Worldscope database.

Note: The figure shows aggregate data for Argentina, Brazil, China, Chile, India, Indonesia, Malaysia, Mexico, Republic of Korea, Russian Federation, South Africa, Thailand and Turkey. Nominal value is in United States dollars.

It can also be included in the financial governance architecture. For example, the Central Bank of Brazil focuses on socio-environmental risk management flows as part of its core functions as a prudential bank regulator; the Bangladesh Bank supports rural enterprises and green finance; and the Bank of England has a prudential review of climate risks for the United Kingdom's insurance sector based on a connection between its core prudential duties and the United Kingdom Climate Change Act (for example, see UNEP, 2016 and 2015).

Trends in public resource flows

Public sources of financing are indispensable to making progress in key areas of sustainable development. It is primarily the public sector that addresses unmet social needs of the population, takes action to relieve poverty, finances health care and education for all, and provides funding for infrastructure investments and basic research. In most countries, these tasks are overwhelmingly funded through public domestic resource mobilization.

In addition, from a broader perspective, public spending can be employed to promote equity and stability in a country, which are widely considered to be among the core functions of the state. Therefore, domestic resource mobilization to finance their provision is also important for the state's legitimacy.

At the same time, developing countries and LDCs, land locked developing countries, SIDS and conflict-affected countries in particular — also rely on ODA and other external sources to finance public expenditure. In the LDCs for example, concessional public finance represents over 70 per cent of all external financing available to close the savings gap (OECD, 2014).

International public financial flows remain insufficient to fill the financing gap for public investments in sustainable development

As noted in the AAAA, international public finance complements efforts by developing countries to raise such resources domestically. In addition, international public finance has an important role to play in financing global public goods. The provision of international public finance, including ODA from Members of the OECD Development Assistance Committee (DAC) and lending by MDBs, has increased between 2014 and 2015 (see the section on the provision of international public finance), continuing a rising trend since the turn of the millennium.

In addition, the provision of international public finance from developing countries — in the form of South-South cooperation and more recently through the establishment of two new development banks — has risen commensurate with rapid growth in developing countries. Despite this expansion, international public financial flows remain insufficient to fill the financing gap for public investments in sustainable development, particularly in developing countries with limited ability to increase domestic resource mobilization (see the section on cross-border aid flows). Partly in response to this shortfall, and partly due to the favourable financing conditions, developing countries have also increased borrowing from capital markets. Sovereign bond issuances in particular have increased significantly, raising concerns over debt sustainability (see the section on debt and debt sustainability).

Provision of international public finance

ODA from Members of the OECD DAC amounted to $131.6 billion in 2015, representing an increase of 6.9 per cent in constant prices and exchange rates ("real terms") over 2014. Additional spending on refugees reported as ODA accounts for a major share of this increase. Stripping out funds spent on refugees, 2015 aid increased by 1.7 per cent in real terms from 2014. This continues a long-term rising trend in ODA, which has increased by 83 per cent in real terms since the adoption of the Millennium Declaration in 2000.

However, at 0.3 per cent of gross national income (GNI) of OECD DAC members, ODA falls short of the commitment by many developed countries to provide ODA equivalent to 0.7 per cent of GNI. Only six countries — Denmark (0.85 per cent), Luxembourg (0.93 per cent), the Netherlands (0.76 per cent), Norway (1.05 per cent), Sweden (1.4 per cent) and the United Kingdom (0.71 per cent) — met or exceeded the United Nations target of providing ODA equivalent to 0.7 per cent of GNI in 2015 (OECD, 2016a).

Spending plans through 2019 suggests that ODA flows to LDCs will continue to rise, reversing the earlier decline

Preliminary figures by the OECD indicate that ODA to LDCs increased in 2015 for the first time in several years. Bilateral aid to LDCs rose by 4 per cent in real terms in 2015 from the previous year, amounting to $25 billion. This represents a reversal of the earlier trend of falling ODA to LDCs. In 2014, the latest year for which comprehensive data is available, total ODA from DAC members to LDCs was $41 billion or 0.09 per cent of GNI, significantly below the UN targets of 0.15-0.20 per cent.

Denmark, Finland, Luxembourg, Norway, Sweden and the United Kingdom provided ODA to LDCs in excess of 0.2 per cent of their GNI, while Belgium and Ireland provided between 0.15 and 0.2 per cent (OECD, 2016a). The 2015 data will reflect the recent rise in ODA to LDCs, and the OECD survey of donor spending plans through 2019 (OECD, 2016b) suggests that ODA flows to LDCs will continue to rise.

Donors who report their aid to the DAC also report other official flows (OOF) toward ODA-eligible countries — these include flows that do not meet the concessionality criteria of ODA, such as non-concessional lending by bilateral providers and multilateral development banks, and export credits. Net disbursements of total official flows (ODA and OOF), including from a number of countries that are not members of the DAC but report their transactions to the OECD, amounted to $183 billion in 2014 for all developing countries. In LDCs, OOF and non-concessional lending in particular play a much smaller role (figures III.8 and III.9).

MDBs' disbursements increased only marginally in 2015

Other official flows contain lending by MDBs disbursed to developing countries. The AAAA recognizes the significant potential of MDBs to provide stable, long-term finance for sustainable development investments. Overall, MDBs' disbursements increased only marginally in 2015. The World Bank's International Bank for Reconstruction and Development (IBRD) commitments rose sharply to $23.5 billion in 2015 over 2014 (World Bank, 2016c).

At the same time, the International Finance Corporation (IFC), the private sector arm of the World Bank Group, saw a decline in lending to $10.5 billion. Commitments by the World Bank's concessional lending arm, the International Development Association (IDA), which relies on donor contributions to provide concessional credits and grants to low-income countries, have grown in nominal terms over the past five years, but did experience a decline from 2014 to 2015 (World Bank, 2016c). The last IDA replenishment, agreed in 2013, saw an increase in pledges of 5 per cent in nominal terms over the sixteenth replenishment round in 2010, but growth was broadly flat in real terms (IDA, 2014).

Figure III.10 displays recent trends in MDB lending for the African Development Bank (AfDB), Asian Development Bank (ADB), European Bank for Reconstruction and Development (EBRD), Inter-American Development Bank (IDB), Inter-American Investment Corporation (IIC), International Bank for Reconstruction and Development (IBRD), and International Finance Corporation (IFC). The New Development Bank (NDB) and

Figure III.8
Net disbursements of ODA, CPA and OOF to developing countries by all donors, 2000–2014

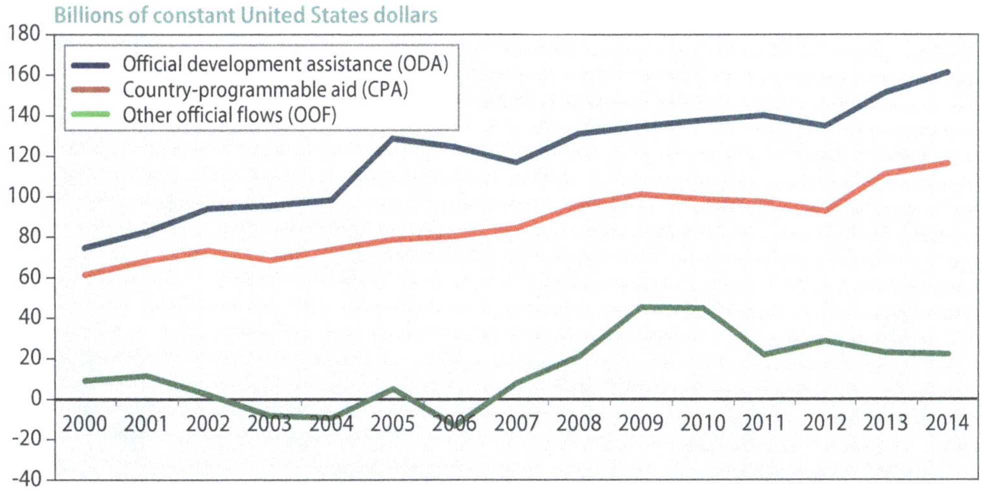

Source: UN/DESA based on data from OECD.

Figure III.9
Net disbursements of ODA, CPA and OOF to LDCs by all donors, 2000–2014

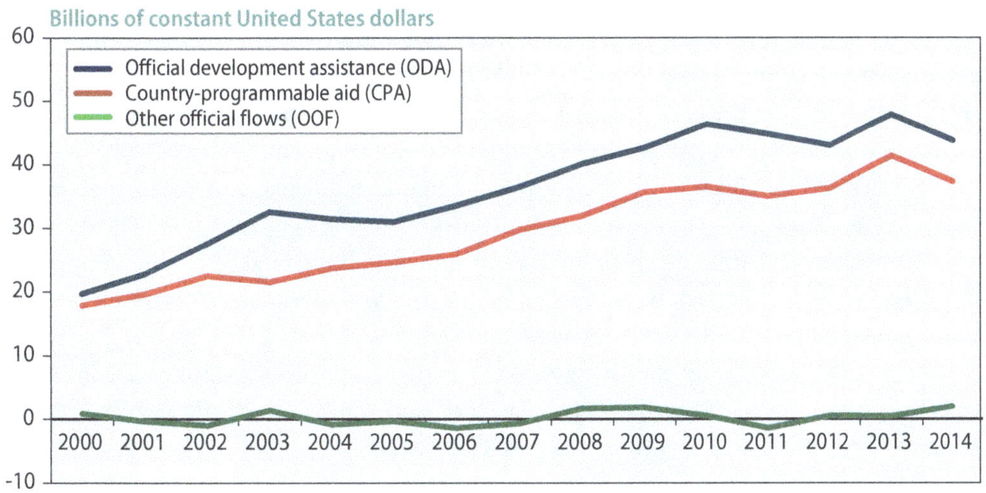

Source: UN/DESA based on data from OECD.

Asian Infrastructure Investment Bank (AIIB) are not included in the diagram, as they did not approve any lending in 2015.[7]

Annual commitments of non-grant subsidized finance from the seven MDBs reached $74.1 billion in 2015, with disbursements at $57.3 billion, and a total exposure of $377.4 billion. Lending disbursement volumes are only growing marginally and new commitments have declined. Total exposure of all banks increased by 3 per cent (figure III.10).

7 Concessional lending classified as ODA is also excluded. Lending from MDBs to developing countries can be divided into concessional or non-concessional. The status of concessionality is achieved either through imposing interest rates below market rates or by introducing grace periods, or a combination of these two. The largest concessional lenders are the World Bank Group through IDA, EIB, AfDB (partly through African Development Fund), and ADB (through Asian Development Fund).

Figure III.10
Multilateral development bank financing, 2000–2015

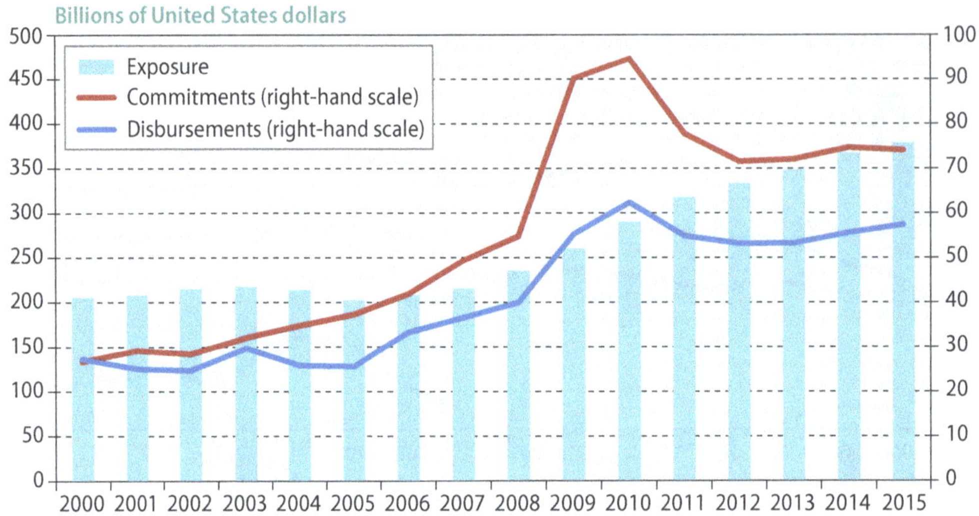

Source: UN/DESA calculations based on annual reports from MDBs.
Note: Includes non-grant subsidised finance from ADB, AfDB, EBRD, IADB, IIC, IBRD and IFC.

The AAAA stresses that MDBs should make optimal use of their resources and balance sheets, and should update and develop their policies in support of the 2030 Agenda. Most MDBs are leveraged at close to their operational limits and there is an ongoing discussion about their capacity to increase lending. The MDBs presented action plans on balance sheet optimization to the G20 group of countries in July 2016, highlighting their work on increased capital efficiency, exposure exchanges, reforms to concessional lending windows, risk transfer and mobilization for non-sovereign-guaranteed loans, and net income measures (MDBs, 2016).

Development banks also operate at the regional, sub-regional and national level. A global survey of development banks carried out by the World Bank in 2012, which defined development banks as at least 30 percent state-owned, and with a legal mandate to reach socioeconomic goals, found that they were the main source of long-term credit in many emerging market economies. They also played an active role in strategic sectors in some advanced economies (de Luna-Martinez and Vicente, 2012).

Figure III.11 shows a sample of some of these banks, including the main multinational regional banks. The regional development banks show a similar trend to the multilateral banks, with lending growing marginally or even declining. The main exceptions are the ADB, which increased its lending by 20 per cent in 2015, and the Development Bank of Southern Africa (DBSA), which increased lending by more than 35 per cent in 2015. National and sub-regional development banks in Latin America and the Caribbean also exhibited stabilizing levels of commitments and disbursements, with the exception of the Brazilian Development Bank (BNDES). BNDES scaled back its lending activities following economic recession and a change of government in Brazil.

Beyond the OECD DAC members, provision of international public finance has also increased from providers of South-South cooperation. While comprehensive data are not available, DESA estimates that concessional South-South cooperation may have exceeded \$20 billion in 2013 and may have further increased in 2014, owing to a scale-up by Saudi

Figure III.11

Annual disbursement of selected regional and national development banks, 2000–2015

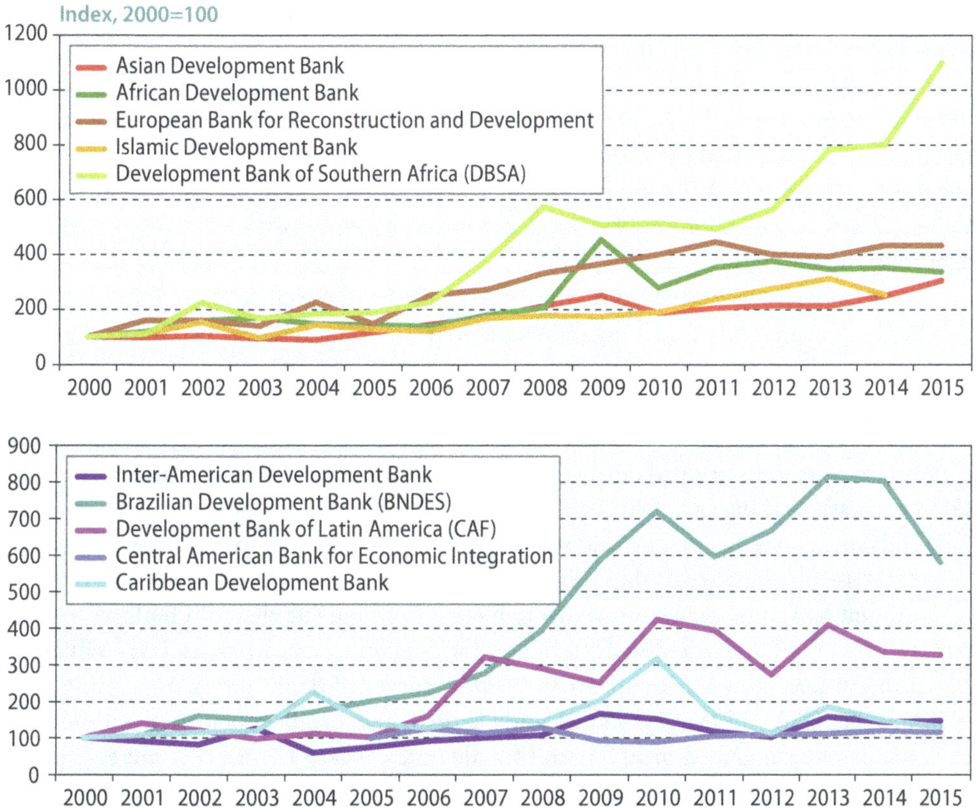

Source: UN/DESA, based on data from annual reports from relevant organisations.

Arabia.[8] The OECD, which estimates "ODA-like" flows from countries that are not members of the DAC, arrived at a comparable figure of $23.5 billion in 2013 (OECD, 2015b).[9] Both NDB and AIIB also initiated their first lending and held their first annual meetings in 2016. The NDB approved over $800 million in investments in the first half of 2016, while the AIIB approved over $500 million for four projects in the same period.

Cross-border aid flows

From a recipient perspective, a major concern is which flows are available for investments, and to what extent international public financial flows are earmarked for specific sectors and global priorities.

Overall, ODA plays a vastly more important role in quantitative terms in LDCs as compared to developing countries as a whole. ODA disbursements amounted to 5 per cent of recipient GNI on average in LDCs in 2014, compared to 0.6 per cent in all developing

8 The estimates include concessional loans and grants as well as debt relief and technical cooperation provided within the South for development purposes (United Nations, Economic and Social Council, 2016).

9 The OECD figure refers to gross flows, including flows from countries that report to the DAC and estimates from published national sources for countries that do not (such as Brazil, China and India).

countries, and 0.1 per cent in upper middle-income countries (figure III.12). ODA's share of recipient GNI has declined across these country groups in the last 15 years however, due to their growth performance.

Total ODA figures also overstate the amount available for country-level spending. Items such as debt relief, administrative costs, in-donor refugee costs or humanitarian and food aid either do not give rise to financial flows into developing countries or are not predictable and programmable by the recipient country. The measure of country-programmable aid (CPA), tracked by the OECD DAC, accounts only for aid that reaches developing countries and is available for country-level or regional programming. In contrast to total ODA, CPA does not include aid for refugees or administrative costs in donor countries nor debt relief, humanitarian aid or food aid.

In-donor refugee costs rose to 9.1 per cent of ODA in 2015, though ODA increased even when stripping out aid related to refugees

The global refugee crisis has further underlined the importance of decomposing ODA into its components and of tracking CPA separately. In-donor refugee costs jumped in 2015 because of the large numbers of refugees arriving in DAC countries after fleeing instability and insecurity in their home countries. As a percentage of the total, these costs rose from 4.8 percent of ODA in 2014 to 9.1 per cent in 2015. In five DAC countries, ODA fell once the refugee costs were stripped out. At the same time, other countries saw large increases in ODA even after taking out their increases in ODA related to refugees. In total, stripping out funds spent on refugees, 2015 aid still increased by 1.7 per cent in real terms from 2014.

The rise in refugee costs thus did not significantly cut into development programmes, with around half of donor countries using money from outside their aid budgets to cover refugee costs. CPA amounted to $116 billion for developing countries, and $37 billion for LDCs in 2014, as shown in figure III.13. A DAC survey of donor forward spending plans indicates that CPA will increase significantly in 2016 and stabilize thereafter, with increases particularly pronounced in LDCs and fragile states, where a 6 per cent increase in real terms is expected (OECD, 2016a).

Gross sovereign borrowing by developing countries exceeds gross aid and other financing

Developing countries have increasingly looked at other sources of financing for public investments, owing to increased access to international financial markets. Gross sovereign borrowing by developing countries from international private sources, mainly bond issuances, amounted to $225 billion in 2014. This significantly exceeds gross CPA and gross OOF (including bilateral and multilateral non-concessional lending) (figure III.13). Access

Figure III.12
ODA disbursements as percentage of recipient GNI, selected years

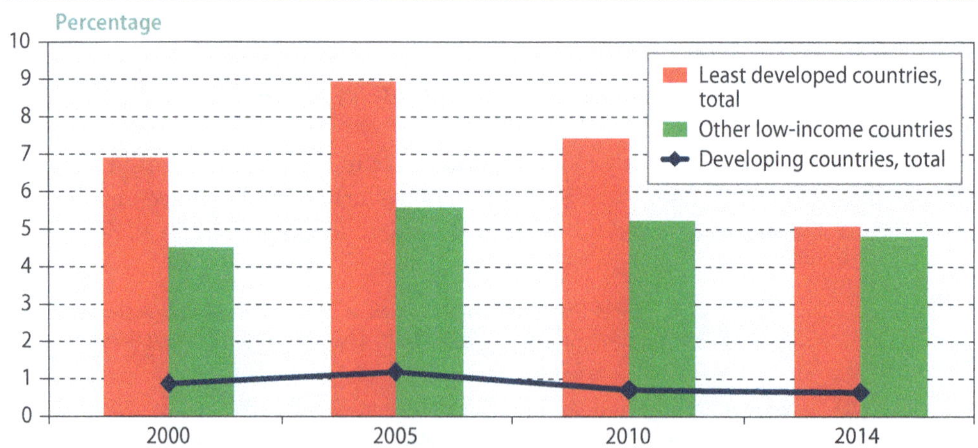

Source: UN/DESA, based on data from OECD.

by LDCs to markets is much more limited. Gross sovereign borrowing from capital markets is concentrated in a small number of LDCs (primarily Angola, as well as Ethiopia, Mozambique, Senegal, Tanzania and Zambia) and remains only a fraction of official concessional financing (World Bank, 2016d).

In order to paint a more complete picture of international financing sources available for public investments in sustainable development, efforts are underway to comprehensively monitor all relevant financing sources. The Inter-agency Task Force on Financing for Development is mandated to monitor all international public financing flows in its reporting on the commitments related to action area II.C of the AAAA on International Development Cooperation and related Financing for Development outcomes. The OECD DAC has also initiated discussions on Total Official Support for Sustainable Development (TOSSD), which would measure all officially supported resource flows that support sustainable development in developing countries.

The Inter-agency Task Force on Financing for Development monitoring will thus cover most of the same areas under discussion in TOSSD. However, while TOSSD proposes to add up all relevant financing flows from both OECD DAC countries and other providers into one metric (e.g. concessional finance including ODA, and non-concessional lending, as well as possibly private finance mobilized by public interventions), the Task Force has not agreed on which, if any, elements should be added up to a composite total, due to their different qualities, characteristics and development impacts.

Accounting for the quality of financing flows is a major challenge

In any such exercise, accounting for the quality of financing flows is a major challenge. For example, private investment leveraged with public funds does not necessarily have the same developmental impact as public finance. Even within such private finance, the development impact of leveraging private investments from foreign companies is likely to differ from the development impact of leveraging funds from domestic companies, as the latter generally have a greater impact on domestic employment and resource mobilization.

Similarly, short-term government borrowing at high cost (e.g. on international markets) differs in its budgetary implications from long-term concessional loans from multilateral sources. These differences are even larger across different types of financing flows. There are concerns about the implicit incentives associated with more comprehensive measures of development finance, which could, for example, encourage the use of instruments to leverage large amounts of private finance at the expense of grant finance. One solution that the Task Force is exploring is to create a measurement framework that presents different international public financing flows separately but in a harmonized and comparable manner.

Domestic public resource mobilization

Tax revenues are orders of magnitude greater than ODA or development bank lending as a financing source for public investment

In general, developing countries have increased their tax revenue over the last 15 years. While generating consistent, comparable revenue data and measuring revenue as a percentage of GDP is a complex undertaking,[10] the overall trends in domestic resource mobiliza-

10 For example, there are changes in and uneven implementation of the system of national accounts, discontinuities in time series, differences between federal and non-federal systems, differences between budgetary and other central government information, and different measures of GDP as reported by different institutions. These challenges create difficulties in aggregation, as well as in measuring trends over time. In addition, the methodology used for aggregation will often depend on the expected use of the data set. For example, the treatment of revenue from natural resource extraction varies across data sets, partially reflecting the different purposes for which they were designed.

Figure III.13
Official flows and sovereign borrowing for developing countries and LDCs, 2014

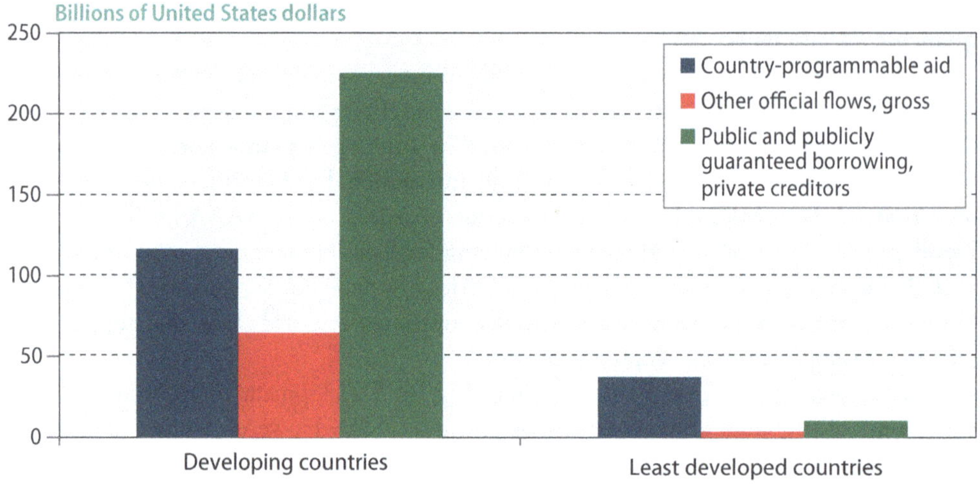

Source: UN/DESA, based on data from OECD and World Bank International Debt Statistics.

tion indicate that median tax revenue excluding social contributions as a proportion of GDP has generally gone up in most categories of countries over the past 25 years (figure III.14).

The largest increases in median revenues were seen in LDCs, economies in transition and countries in Latin America and the Caribbean. For 2013, the most recent year with available data, developing countries raised about $4.7 trillion (figure III.15). Tax revenue has been increasing more quickly than other types of finance. While the distribution of this revenue is highly variable (table III.3), the data indicate that, in aggregate, tax revenues are orders of magnitude greater than ODA or development bank lending as a financing source for public investment, as would be expected. However, in LDCs, ODA and other types of flows are comparable in scale to aggregate tax revenue, as shown in figure III.16.

Nonetheless, in many countries domestic resource mobilization remains insufficient to meet sustainable development needs (United Nations, 2014). The AAAA recognizes that the foremost driver of domestic resource mobilization is economic growth, supported by sound policies and an enabling environment at all levels. It also notes the need to strengthen tax administration, implement policies to generate additional resources and combat corruption in all its forms.

There are many possibilities for governments to improve tax administration and tax collection, including by enhancing efficiency, digitization, and stronger enforcement. In a globalized world, there are also limits as to what countries can do on their own through domestic policies. The AAAA thus also calls for strengthening international tax cooperation including combating tax avoidance and evasion. At the same time, it stresses the importance of combating illicit financial flows.

Some UN regional economic commissions, including the Economic Commission for Latin America and the Caribbean (ECLAC) and the Economic Commission for Africa (UNECA), have estimated the trade mis-invoicing component of illicit financial flows, finding them to be significant (ECLAC, 2016a; UNECA, 2015). In the AAAA, Governments committed to making sure that all companies, including multinationals, pay taxes to the Governments of the countries where economic activity occurs and value is created, in accordance with national and international laws and policies.

Concerns remain over the ability of developing countries to benefit from changes to international tax norms

While some Member States are pursuing implementation of new international tax norms agreed at the OECD in 2015, there remain concerns about the comprehensiveness

Figure III.14

Median tax revenue as a share of GDP by various country groupings, 1991–2013

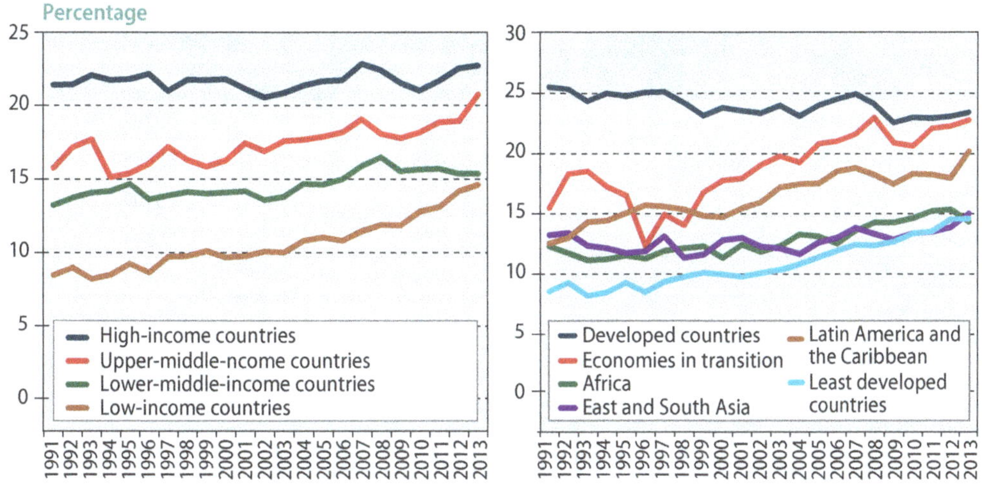

Source: UN/DESA calculations, based on Prichard and others (2014).

Note: Tax revenue excludes social contributions. In the left panel, the World Bank's income classification for 2016 is used. In the right panel, country classification is based on UN conventions, with Western Asia excluded due to lack of data.

Figure III.15

Aggregate global tax revenue, 2000–2013

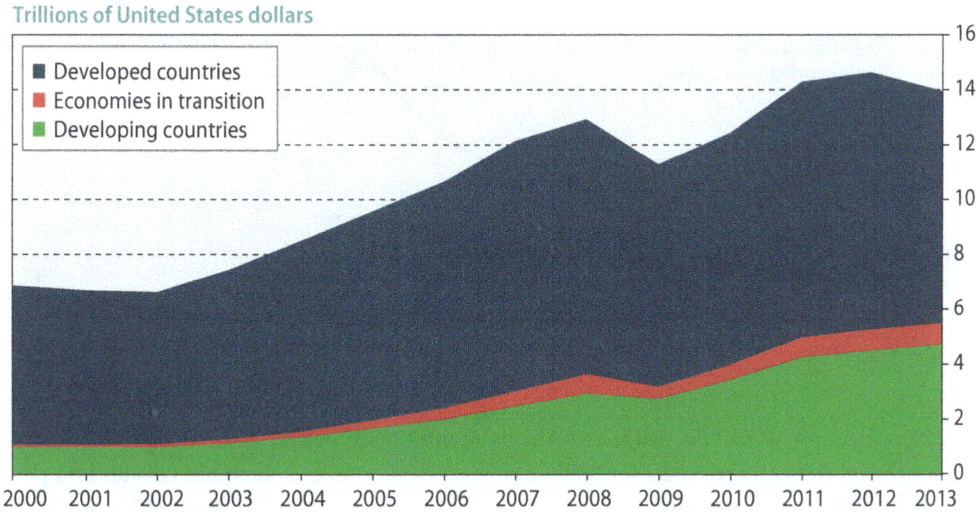

Source: UN/DESA, based on IMF (2015, 2016d).

Note: Estimates of nominal tax revenue in current prices and dollars, not adjusted for inflation.

of implementation and the ability of developing countries to benefit from the changes (United Nations, 2016a). Exchange of tax information related to financial accounts and country-by-country reports from multinational enterprises are being pursued through multilateral instruments. Developing countries may be disadvantaged in gaining access even if they sign the instruments. Further consideration is being given to the exchange of beneficial ownership information among tax authorities, but no standard or multilateral accord has yet been developed.

Debt and debt sustainability

Debt financing is an important source of financing for sustainable development investments, both by public and private actors. Global gross debt reached a record $152 trillion,

Table III.3
Tax revenue by region, 2013

United States dollars

Region	Per capita taxation (average)	Gross taxation receipts (billions)
Economies in transition	$2,610	$789
Latin America and the Caribbean	$2,095	$1,265
Western Asia	$1,378	$300
East Asia	$1,158	$2,364
Africa	$393	$423
South Asia	$202	$359
Least developed countries	$129	$111

Source: UN/DESA, based on IMF (2015) and United Nations (2015).

Figure III.16
Finance for LDC governments, 2000–2013

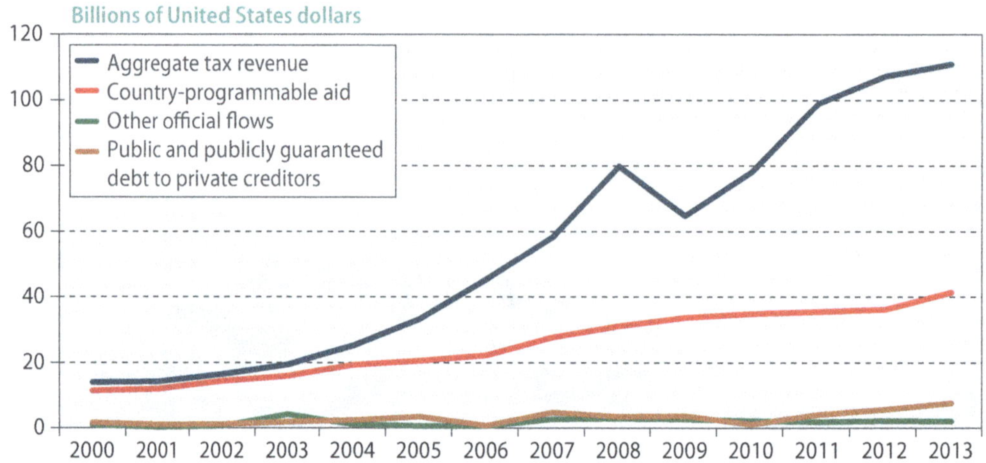

Source: UN/DESA, based on data from OECD, IMF (2015, 2016a) and World Bank (2016e).
Note: The figures are in current prices, not adjusted for inflation. Nominal tax revenue does not include royalties or social contributions. Country-programmable aid is a proxy for ODA that arrives in countries, thus excluding in-donor refugee costs and other domestic expenditure by the donor.

or 225 per cent of WGP, in 2015, two-thirds of which are liabilities by the private sector. Such debt levels can carry risks for economic growth prospects and financial stability, particularly in developed and some emerging market economies (IMF, 2016c). The challenge will be to take advantage of fiscal space where it exists in developed and developing economies to finance necessary public investments, and to minimize the impact of private sector deleveraging on growth, while also ensuring that investments financed out of additional borrowing are productive and contribute to sustainable development.

The global debt build-up was primarily driven by the credit boom and household and corporate borrowing in developed countries prior to the global economic and financial crisis. Public debt ratios barely increased in developed countries and decreased in developing countries over the period 2000 to 2008. However, public debt increased significantly following the crisis, in both developed and developing economies, while progress on private sector deleveraging in developed countries has been uneven.

Low-income countries experienced a pronounced increase in their external debt in 2015

Developing countries' external debt is estimated to be 26 percent of GDP in 2015, representing only a very modest increase over previous years (figure III.17). External-debt-to-GDP ratios in developing countries declined significantly in the first decade of the new

Figure III.17
External debt of developing countries, 2000–2015

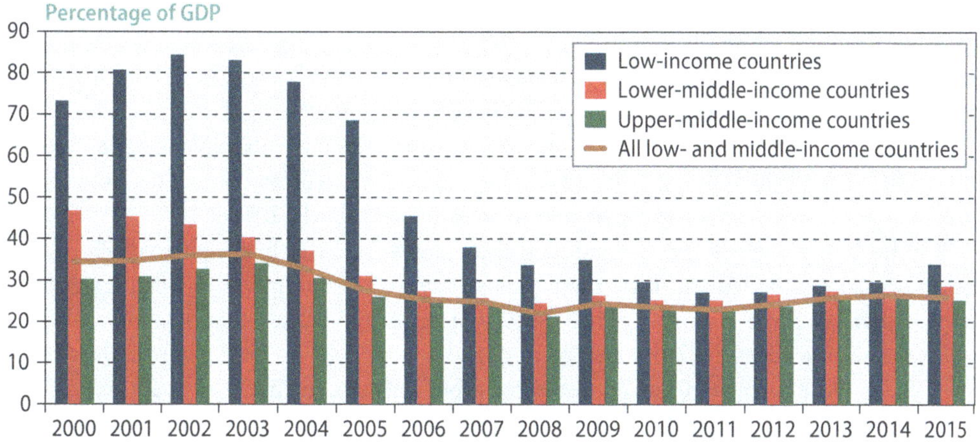

Source: UN/DESA, based on IMF (2016a).
Note: Countries are classified according to World Bank's income group classification for the year 2015.

millennium, in particular thanks to high GDP growth and debt relief, but have started to rise modestly since then. This recent rise is more pronounced in low-income countries, which saw an increase in their external debt from 31 per cent of GDP in 2014 to 35 per cent in 2015. While the overall debt situation of developing countries remains relatively benign, risks to debt sustainability persist for a number of small states, and also arise from changes in the debt composition and increased borrowing from capital markets.

Three low-income countries are currently considered to be in debt distress by the IMF and the World Bank, and an additional 17 countries are at high risk of debt distress, as compared to 13 countries in April 2015.[11] The sharp fall in commodity prices and the slowdown in economic growth have forced a number of countries to seek financial assistance from the IMF and the World Bank in recent months. In addition, there are also a number of lower middle-income countries that are Small States[12] — often hampered by limited economic activity and a small tax base — with very high debt-to-GDP ratios. Exposure to climate change and natural disasters further exacerbates their sovereign debt challenges.

In terms of the composition of external debt, developing countries have increasingly been able to tap financial markets and borrow from private creditors. In terms of public financing, the share of external public and publicly guaranteed debt owed to private creditors increased from 41 per cent in 2000 to 62 per cent in 2015 (United Nations, General Assembly, 2016b).

However, in 2015, bond issuances by low- and middle-income countries fell by 7 per cent from 2014 globally, due to declines in Central Asia, Europe and Latin America. In sub-Saharan Africa,[13] sovereign bond issuance increased significantly in recent years, with total bond issuances increasing from $1 billion in 2011 to $6.2 billion in 2014. Issuances

11 See List of LIC DSAs for PRGT-Eligible Countries As of October 01, 2016, available from https://www.imf.org/external/Pubs/ft/dsa/DSAlist.pdf.

12 "Small States" as defined by the Commonwealth Secretariat is a group of sovereign countries with a population of 1.5 million people or less, plus a number of larger countries (Botswana, Jamaica, Lesotho, Namibia and Papua New Guinea) that share certain characteristics.

13 Excluding South Africa.

remained at steady volumes in 2015, but at higher costs due to more difficult market conditions and concerns over growth prospects (World Bank, 2016e).

In parallel to greater sovereign borrowing from capital markets, external borrowing by the private sector in developing countries also increased significantly. While private external debt remains concentrated in a small number of more advanced developing countries (notably, there was a surge in corporate debt in some emerging market economies, see Box III.1), private sector borrowers in low-income countries were also able to raise external financing — with the share of private non-guaranteed debt in total external debt increasing from 0.6 per cent in 2005 to 6.8 per cent in 2014 (World Bank, 2016e).

In middle-income countries, the share of short-term debt in total external debt has risen

The increase in private external debt coincided with a rise in the share of short-term debt in total external debt. This trend was steady and pronounced in both lower- and upper-middle-income countries, since 2000 and up until recent years, leading to higher rollover risk. However, in 2015, the share of short-term debt in total external debt of all low- and middle-income countries decreased from 33 per cent in 2014 to 28 per cent in 2015 (figure III.18).

Figure III.18
External short-term debt as a share of total external debt, 2000–2015

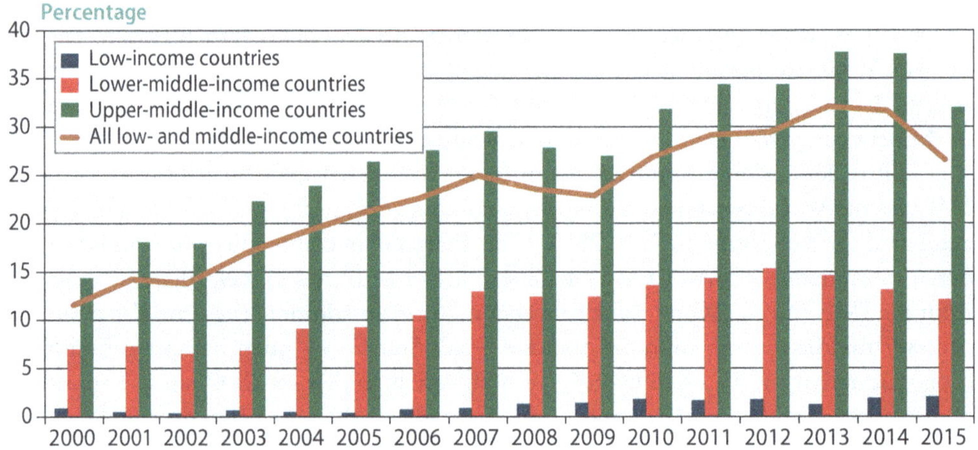

Source: UN/DESA, based on IMF (2016a).
Note: Countries are classified according to World Bank's income group classification for the year 2015.

Conclusions

There is a need to revamp the international financial system to align it with sustainable development

The above analysis underscores the difficulties in ensuring sufficient financing for sustainable development, given the current economic environment and global financial system. Private cross-border flows are largely short-term oriented, as reflected in the volatility of international capital flows, which is not conducive for the long-term investment needed for sustainable development. A complete revamping of the international financial system is necessary, which is aimed at better aligning private sector incentives with sustainable development, while also making greater use of public entities, such as development banks. Such public entities are particularly important for investments that have a public good character but are not sufficiently competitive in terms of risk-adjusted returns when compared with other investments.

In the AAAA, Member States of the United Nations agreed to a range of commitments and actions across these issues. Monitoring progress in these areas is part of the Financing for Development follow-up process. In many of these areas, there are no ready-made policy solutions applicable across different country or regional contexts. The Inter-agency Task Force on Financing for Development has set up a series of work streams to explore policy options.

Current streams include work on illicit financial flows, measures of official support for sustainable development, and aligning capital market incentives with sustainable development. In each of these areas, the Task Force will explore new ideas and new mechanisms to promote the alignment of all financing flows with sustainable development, and to further implementation of the 2030 Agenda and achievement of the SDGs.

Chapter IV

Regional developments and outlook

Developed economies

Developed economies are expected to see a slight increase in economic growth from 1.5 per cent in 2016 to 1.7 per cent in 2017 and 1.8 per cent in 2018, driven by relatively strong private consumption. Improvement in employment and subdued inflation continue to support households' purchasing power. At the same time, accommodative monetary policy stances will support economic activity, especially in Europe and Japan, although the limitations of unconventional monetary policy measures increasingly illustrate the need for a broader policy approach to create a more dynamic growth trajectory.

This is especially relevant in view of the continued drag on growth stemming from a number of factors. Investment remains weak, as commodity-related sectors continue to face pressure from generally low prices; in addition, businesses are confronted with major uncertainties related to the future direction of policy in the United States of America, the looming exit of the United Kingdom of Great Britain and Northern Ireland from the European Union (EU) and various geopolitical crises. Relatively high unemployment, including among youth, in numerous developed countries not only hampers economic growth, but also represents a major policy challenge as it threatens to increase structural unemployment, which in turn makes integration into the labour market increasingly difficult and costly.

In the monetary policy area, the United States Federal Reserve (Fed) is expected to continue to gradually raise interest rates, resulting in a widening divergence in interest rates relative to Europe and Japan. Inflation in the developed economies will pick up to 1.6 per cent in 2017 and 2.0 per cent in 2018, although some of this increase is less an indication of solid demand than the consequence of a base effect caused by the previous sharp fall in commodity prices.

North America: inventory destocking restricted growth in the United States in 2016

The United States economy is estimated to have expanded at a modest pace of 1.5 per cent in 2016. This growth momentum was considerably weaker than had been anticipated when the Fed raised interest rates in December 2015 — the first rise since rates were reduced to near zero levels at the height of the global financial crisis in December 2008. The sharper-than-expected deterioration in growth from the last quarter of 2015 to mid-2016 primarily reflected a steep downward adjustment in non-farm inventories and a contraction in private non-residential investment, especially in oil-related sectors (figure IV.1). As the temporary impact of inventory destocking eases, more solid growth of 1.9 per cent is expected in 2017. With the change in Administration in January 2017, however, there is considerable uncertainty regarding the future direction of policy in the United States — including monetary, fiscal, trade, immigration, environmental and foreign policy prospects. This uncertainty is expected to have restrained investment in the short run. The potentially far-reaching spillover effects on both domestic and global economic prospects have increased the margin of uncertainty around the baseline forecasts for the United States and many other economies.

Uncertainty regarding trade policy may delay investment decisions by Canadian exporting firms

Canada, which exports roughly three-quarters of its goods and services to the United States, is highly sensitive to economic conditions across the border. The outcome of elections in the United States has heightened uncertainty in Canada, especially for exporting firms that would be impacted if the United States were to introduce any changes to existing trade agreements. This heightened uncertainty is expected to delay a recovery in investment in Canada. Real non-residential investment in Canada dropped by 10 per cent in 2015 and by a similar magnitude in the first half of 2016 (figure IV.2), largely driven by cutbacks in extraction and oil-related sectors.

Figure IV.1
Contribution to GDP growth in the United States, 2014Q1–2016Q3

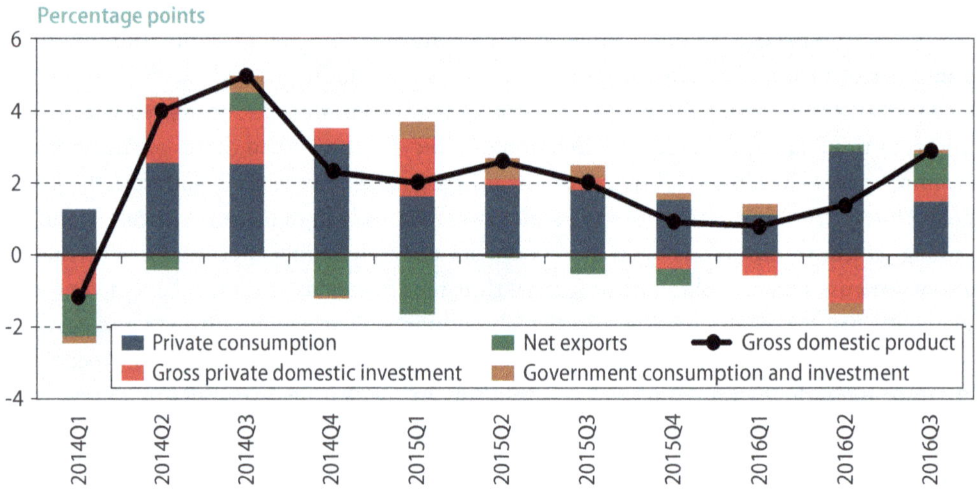

Source: US Bureau of Economic Analysis.

The persistent weakness of investment in both the United States and Canada is symptomatic of the broader global trend that continues to hamper productivity growth. Labour productivity in the United States, measured as output per hour in the non-farm business sector, rose by less than 1 per cent in 2015 and declined at an annual rate of 0.6 per cent in the first half of 2016. Given the protracted period of weak investment in the United States and other large developed economies, as discussed in chapter I, a substantial rebound in productivity growth is not anticipated in the forecasting period. This will continue to restrain short-term growth prospects.

Consumer spending in North America remains firm

Household consumption has been the sustaining force behind otherwise lackluster gross domestic product (GDP) growth in North America. Private consumption is estimated to have expanded by 2.5 per cent in the United States in 2016, and is projected to grow by 2.0 per cent in 2017, supported by the low level of unemployment and rising household incomes. Since October 2015, unemployment in the United States has fluctuated within

Figure IV.2
Oil price, investment and exchange rate in Canada, 2013Q1–2016Q2

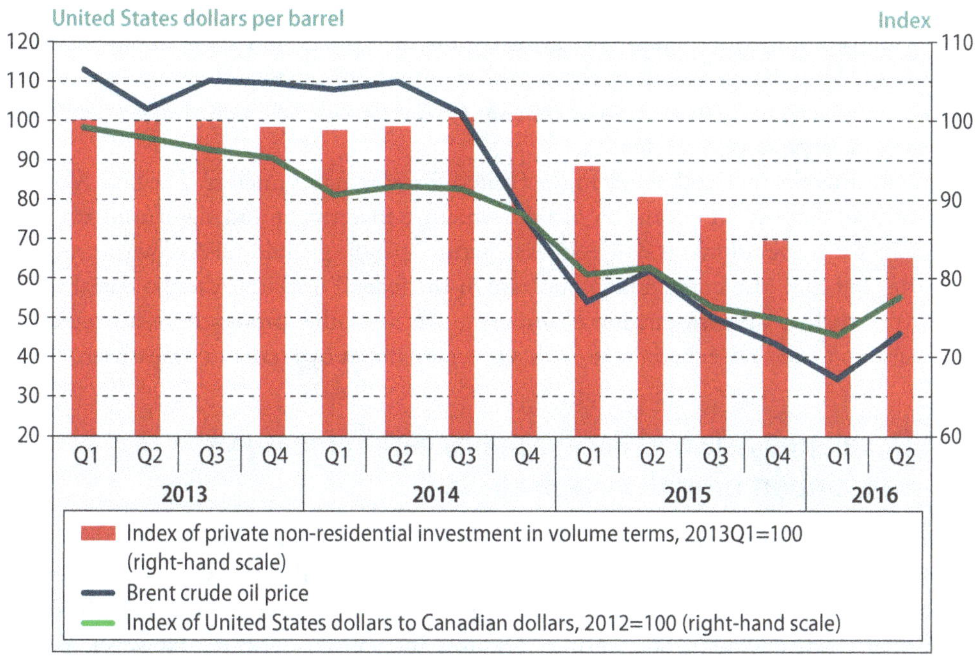

Source: UN/DESA, based on data from Statistics Canada and IMF International Financial Statistics.

the range of 4.7-5.0 per cent, which is the "central tendency" of the Fed's estimates of its longer-run level.

In Canada, household consumption has also held up relatively well, despite a sharp deterioration in terms of trade and loss of export revenue. Private consumption is expected to grow by 2.1 per cent per annum in 2016-2017. The unemployment rate, at 7.0 per cent, remains in line with its average level in 2014. Unemployment is expected to average 7.1 per cent in 2017 and 6.9 per cent in 2018.

The United States dollar has appreciated by 20 per cent against the Canadian dollar since 2014

Given the deterioration in short-term economic prospects and concerns related to various global uncertainties, the Fed held interest rates unchanged throughout most of 2016. The postponement of expected interest rate rises in the United States eased some of the upward pressure on the United States dollar, and supported a recovery of capital flows to developing countries, from investors seeking higher rates of return. Nonetheless, over the last two years, the United States dollar has appreciated considerably against all major currencies, including by roughly 20 per cent against the euro and the Canadian dollar. The sharp depreciation of the Canadian dollar illustrates the close correlation between the oil price and this bilateral rate (figure IV.2).

Inflation is expected to meet or exceed central bank targets in 2017

The Bank of Canada has kept monetary policy unchanged since July 2015, and considers inflation on track to reach its 2 per cent target in 2017. Inflation in the United States has remained below the Fed's medium-term objective of 2 per cent, but has edged up towards the inflation target as the impact of both the decline in the oil price and the rise in the exchange rate recedes. As the contribution of the oil price to inflation becomes positive, consumer price inflation is expected to rise to 2.3 per cent in 2017 and 2.4 per cent in 2018.

Expansionary fiscal policy will lift growth in Canada in 2017

In the budget of March 2016, the Canadian Government set out an ambitious plan of fiscal expansion focused on investment in basic infrastructure. This marked a departure from the previous Government's policy priority of achieving a balanced budget, and singled

Canada out as one of the few developed economies to introduce a more expansive fiscal stance. While the shift in policy will allow the general government deficit to deteriorate towards 3 per cent of GDP in 2016-2017, it will offer support to the flagging economy.

Coupled with the modest revival in commodity prices and some competitiveness gains from the exchange rate depreciation, GDP growth in Canada is forecast to accelerate from 1.2 per cent in 2016 to 2.4 per cent in 2017, although heightened uncertainty will prevent a more pronounced rebound.

A rise in infrastructure spending could accelerate growth in the United States in 2018

The direction of fiscal policy in the United States remains unclear. The new Administration may propose an expansion of infrastructure investment and significant tax cuts, especially for corporations. A rise in infrastructure spending could raise growth prospects for 2018, but may also entail a large increase in the federal deficit. Other potential policy initiatives, such as the introduction of import tariffs and other protective measures, could raise inflation and slow economic growth, especially if met by retaliatory measures.

Developed Asia and Pacific: policy easing measures will support growth in Japan in 2017

GDP growth in Japan is projected to improve modestly to 0.9 per cent in 2017 and 2018, from an estimated 0.5 per cent in 2016. Growth is expected to be supported by rising household consumption and higher government investment, which will benefit from the additional fiscal and monetary easing measures introduced in 2016. However, private non-residential investment and exports both declined in the first half of 2016, and the economy remains restrained by the strong exchange rate, which is one of the forces that has pushed the economy back into deflation.

Low unemployment and rising real wages support household demand in Japan

Labour market conditions in Japan have strengthened, and the unemployment rate is expected to continue to hover at about 3 per cent in 2017-2018. In May 2016, the ratio of active job openings to job seekers rose to its highest level in 25 years. While wage pressures remain relatively muted despite the Government's efforts to accelerate pay rises, nominal employee wages have continued to edge upwards. As consumer price inflation has been stagnant or negative since March 2016 (figure IV.3), this has allowed real wages to register more substantial gains.

Figure IV.3
Inflation in Japan, January 2010–August 2016 *(year-on-year)*

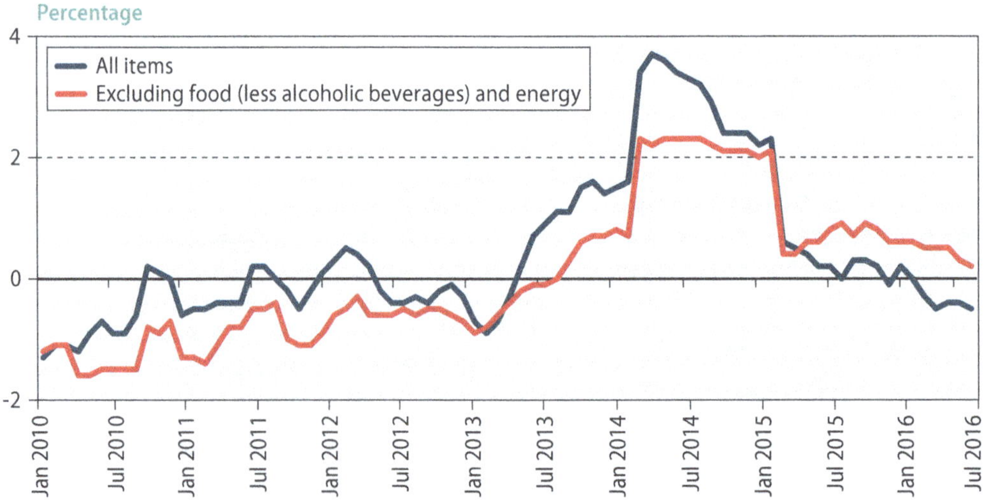

Source: Statistics Bureau of Ministry of Internal Affairs and Communication, Japan.

Nationwide consumer price inflation in Japan is estimated to have averaged -0.1 per cent in 2016 and is projected at 0.6 per cent in 2017, and will remain below the central bank's target of 2 per cent in 2018. The significant drag on the overall price level arising from low oil prices — with energy prices reducing the overall consumer price by 1 percentage point in June 2016 — will dissipate towards the end of the year. Nevertheless, the strong yen and weak wage growth will continue to exert downward pressure on inflation.

Deflationary pressures ease, but inflation will remain below the Bank of Japan's target

In reaction to the stalled progress towards achieving the target of 2 per cent inflation, the Bank of Japan (BoJ) announced a new set of unconventional monetary policy measures aimed at boosting inflation and reviving growth. The BoJ's new monetary policy strategy consists of two components. The first is a "quantitative and qualitative monetary easing with yield curve control" framework to anchor 10-year Japanese Government Bond yields at around 0 per cent. The second component is an explicit commitment to increase the monetary base until inflation overshoots the 2 per cent target. Both of these policy strategies are intended to complement the existing quantitative and qualitative easing measures of the BoJ and the negative interest rate of -0.1 per cent applied since January 2016 on a portion of banks' current account balances held at the BoJ.

The BoJ's introduction of its new monetary policy framework came after the Japanese Government announced increased spending in the fiscal year 2016 supplementary budget and introduced a new fiscal stimulus package in August 2016, including 4.6 trillion yen additional spending for the current fiscal year and the postponement of the consumption tax increase planned for April 2017 to October 2019. The stimulus package amounts to 28.1 trillion yen, making it the third-largest ever implemented. It is expected to give a strong boost to government investment spending in 2017, which is forecast to contribute roughly 0.4 percentage points to GDP growth.

Housing investment has been supported by the BoJ's negative interest rate policy

The rise in government investment in Japan will partially compensate for the persistently weak private sector non-residential investment, as export-oriented firms remain under pressure from the strong yen and sharp slowdown in global trade. Service industries have also been affected by the currency appreciation. While international visitor numbers continue to increase steadily, their direct expenditure in Japan has started to decline.

Residential investment, on the other hand, has rebounded. Housing starts have been supported by Japan's negative interest rates, which have allowed home-loan rates to fall to an all-time low. With monetary policy expected to remain accommodative for the foreseeable future, the housing sector is expected to strengthen further.

Longer-term prospects in Japan remain challenging

While the introduction of additional fiscal and monetary easing measures will offer some support to growth in the short term, there is considerable uncertainty regarding the Japanese economy's longer-term growth prospects. Deflation is well-entrenched in expectations, and may persist despite the commitment of the BoJ to an easier monetary stance. The evolution of wages over the next few years will be crucial in this context.

In addition, Japan faces some imposing policy challenges, which include addressing the large overhang of government debt amid a lower rate of potential growth. While the slowdown in potential growth is largely driven by demographic developments, it also reflects the slower rate of productivity growth, which may prove persistent.

Australian exports remained strong in 2016

Australia's economy expanded at an estimated pace of 2.8 per cent in 2016, benefiting from the modest recovery in commodity prices during the year, as well as monetary and fiscal stimulus measures. In contrast to global trends, export volumes from Australia remained strong in 2016, expanding by more than 7 per cent in the first half of the year. However, export growth is expected to decelerate in 2017, reflecting the broad weakness of world trade and continuing rebalancing in China. Import volume growth is expected to improve compared to 2016, resulting in a deteriorating contribution of net trade to growth, and restraining GDP growth to 1.9 per cent in 2017. Growth is expected to pick up somewhat in 2018, on the back of a recovery in fixed investment, following two years of cutbacks in mining investment.

Tax cuts will support business investment in Australia in 2017

Australia has also introduced some fiscal easing measures, including new tax cuts for small and medium-sized businesses, which have been introduced in an effort to stem the decline in private sector investment. While government debt still remains low compared to other developed economies, it is expected to reach over 40 per cent of GDP in 2017, which marks a 10 percentage point rise compared to only four years ago. This reflects the country's continued vulnerability to swings in commodity prices.

Europe: economic activity in Europe will remain subdued

Economic activity in Europe will remain subdued, with growth expected to stay at 1.8 per cent in the EU for the period from 2016 to 2018. This implies a downward revision compared to the previous forecast, primarily due to the expected negative impact from the "Brexit". On the upside, domestic demand will continue to support growth, as low inflation rates and lower unemployment in some countries bolster private consumption, while the expansive monetary policy stance supports business investment.

At the same time, a number of factors will continue to prevent a more vibrant economic revival across the region. These include the major uncertainty stemming from the Brexit, which has already dented business investment in some key sectors both in the United Kingdom and its major European trading partners. In addition, structural issues such as a need for labour market reforms impede the development of small and medium-sized companies in several countries. Linked to this, unemployment still remains high in several countries, with negative effects on overall growth. High public and private debt levels constrain investment in some countries and lingering balance sheet problems in the banking sector put a drag on the proper functioning of the banking system. A number of risk factors could affect this baseline forecast, notably further negative fallout from the Brexit, more severe problems in the banking sector, a recurrence of the debt crisis in Greece and policy uncertainties related to forthcoming elections in numerous countries including France, Germany and the Netherlands in 2017.

The external sector has remained solid, but Brexit entails significant uncertainty

The external sector has weathered the restrained global economic growth environment so far better than expected, largely owing to more solid intra-European trade. The Brexit and political instability in Turkey have so far had only a limited negative impact on export demand. In the outlook period, this trend of robust export demand will remain intact, as solid private consumption will underpin intra-European trade and some economies will benefit from a competitive euro exchange rate.

However, the economic weakness in Brazil and the Russian Federation and the slowdown in China remain a drag on exports. Linked to this, depressed levels of investment in commodity sectors, notably oil, continue to pose a challenge for exporters of investment goods such as plants and machinery. A major uncertainty will be further developments in the wake of the Brexit. The pound sterling has depreciated sharply (figure IV.4), benefiting exporters but also showing the high level of risk moving forward. For many companies that have invested in the United Kingdom, access to the single EU market has been a major business advantage, but the Brexit has upended the institutional framework for business decisions.

While the United Kingdom has not yet given formal notice of leaving the EU, any such move would require a fundamental rearrangement of the economic relations. A pronounced interest on the United Kingdom side is to remove or at least limit the free movement of EU workers, while at the same time maintaining free access to the single EU market. However, various EU countries have already made clear that free access to the EU market does not come without any obligations in return and that adherence to the free movement of labour remains a core principle of the EU. Consequently, should the United Kingdom start the formal process of exiting from the EU, contentious negotiations would lie ahead with significant uncertainty for businesses, which in turn could lead to a more pronounced decrease in investment levels.

Figure IV.4

Major developed market currencies' exchange rate against the United States dollar, January 2016–October 2016

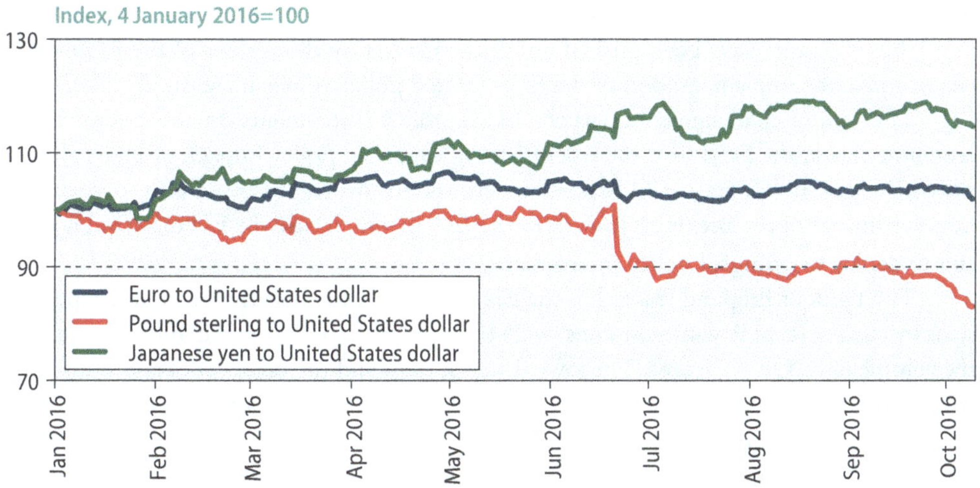

Source: JPMorgan Markets.

Despite an improvement in labour markets, unemployment remains high in several countries

The employment situation has been improving for the region as a whole, with unemployment in the EU standing at 8.5 per cent and in the euro area at 10.0 per cent in September 2016. However, this overall picture encompasses significant national variations. Greece and Spain continue to register the highest unemployment rates in the region, at 23.2 per cent and 19.3 per cent, respectively, followed by several countries including France, Italy and Portugal that also experience double-digit unemployment rates. Youth unemployment rates are particularly high, averaging over 18 per cent in the EU as a whole. In some countries, this partly reflects barriers that restrict labour market access for young people in certain professions. Relatively high tax burdens and inefficient and complicated administrative procedures in some countries also make it difficult for small and medium-size firms to expand capacities and discourage the creation of new enterprises.

By contrast, other countries are experiencing relatively low unemployment rates, notably Germany, the United Kingdom and Hungary with 4.2 per cent, 5.0 per cent and 5.1 per cent, respectively. Driving factors in these cases include internationally competitive economic sectors, more flexible labour markets and, as in the case of Germany, a more diversified vocational training system that provides a solid basis for promoting youth employment. For several countries, a major challenge will lie in integrating a large number of refugees into the labour market.

Monetary policy continues to play a major role relative to fiscal policy and structural reforms

Given the continued tightening stance of fiscal policy in most countries, which is partly related to the high levels of public debt, and only hesitant structural reforms, monetary policy continues to play a disproportionate role. The European Central Bank (ECB) maintains an extremely accommodative monetary policy stance that comprises three elements: policy interest rates at or below zero, quantitative easing (QE) in the form of asset purchases of 80 billion euros per month; and targeted longer-term refinancing operations (TLTROs) intended to move banks to lend more money.

Despite these policy actions, inflation remains significantly below the ECB's policy target of below but close to 2 per cent, raising questions regarding the effectiveness of monetary policy and its adequacy given the nature of the region's economic challenges.

The ECB faces challenges in implementing its policies and in addressing any additional shock

Under its current policy stance, the ECB is facing two major challenges in the near-term in its policy-making process. The first challenge concerns the ECB's policy operations; the amount of asset purchases by the ECB has already led to a significant reduction and shortage in available assets that satisfy the purchase criteria of the ECB. In addition, commercial participants have been pushed out of the market by the actions of the ECB. Both factors make the implementation of the ECB's stated policy stance increasingly difficult.

The second challenge concerns the ECB's policy instruments; in the case of a new economic shock, the ECB runs the risk of having a reduced policy impact, given its already extremely loose policy stance. One possible scenario in this regard could be a more drastic negative impact of the Brexit on growth in the EU, in which case the EU may find it difficult to deploy meaningful policy instruments.

The Bank of England reacted to the Brexit vote by loosening its policy stance

The Bank of England reacted to the Brexit vote and the negative economic repercussions by cutting its policy interest rates by 25 basis points to 0.25 per cent and by increasing the volume of its QE measures. The lower interest rates and the prospect of additional cuts will put further pressure on the pound, creating the risk of a significant increase in inflation through higher import prices.

The negative growth impact from fiscal consolidation is diminishing, but elevated debt levels remain a risk

Fiscal policy in the region maintains a tightening stance overall, given institutional requirements such as the excessive-deficit mechanism of the EU and because of political preferences. However, the negative impact from fiscal consolidation on growth is diminishing. Some countries, such as Austria and Germany, will have to increase fiscal spending in view of the large number of refugees and the challenge of integrating them into their societies and labour markets.

Moreover, big parts of the major fiscal adjustments that were initiated across the region in the aftermath of the financial crisis have been completed. This is illustrated by the significant improvements in fiscal balances in various countries in the region, notably Greece, Iceland, Ireland and Lithuania. Despite these improvements, relatively high public debt levels remain a challenge and risk factor. The currently low level of interest rates helps in sustaining these debt levels, but higher financing costs, especially if they occur suddenly in the form of a financial shock, may have severe negative effects on national fiscal budgets.

In the United Kingdom, the Brexit will put pressure on fiscal policy

In the United Kingdom, the decision to leave the EU has major implications for fiscal policy. Instead of a significant budget surplus by 2019 as envisaged some time ago, the country is now expected to face a further increase in its budget deficit, which stood at 4.3

per cent in 2015. As the British economy is projected to experience a significant slowdown, tax revenues will likely suffer, while spending requirements will increase, given the dislocations and adjustment needs caused by leaving the EU.

Growth in the EU member States from Eastern Europe and the Baltics region moderated in 2016

In the EU member States from Eastern Europe and the Baltics region, economic growth remains on a higher trajectory than in the EU-15 as the countries continue to catch up through capital accumulation and productivity growth. In 2016, the pace of economic expansion slowed slightly to 3 per cent, following the robust investment cycle of 2014-2015 that was driven by the expedited absorption of the 2007-2013 EU funds.

Credit availability in the region is improving thanks to the continuing accommodative policy of the ECB and the ultra-low policy rates in the countries with flexible currencies (the Czech Republic, Hungary, Poland and Romania). The impact of fiscal policy on growth is largely expansionary, as public spending is increasing in real terms (most noticeably in Poland), benefiting from higher tax intake and exceptionally low financing costs.

In the first half of 2016, Romania recorded the highest growth in Europe at 5 per cent. In Central Europe, the automotive industry, which is well integrated into the EU-15 production chain, saw a strong performance, while attracting further foreign direct investment (FDI) flows. The Baltic States, which are more exposed to trade with the Russian Federation than other countries in the group, exhibit a more modest growth pattern.

Foreign-exchange-denominated consumer loans remain a contentious issue

On the policy front, foreign-exchange-denominated (Swiss franc and the euro) consumer loans remain a major problem. Prior to the global economic crisis of 2008-2009, a large number of households in Eastern Europe had taken such loans, benefiting from low interest rates and expecting a steady appreciation of the domestic currencies, but the situation reversed after the crisis. In Poland and Romania, the resolution of this problem has become a contentious issue as the suggested and implemented solutions shift the burden to the banking sector.

The baseline forecast projects robust growth in 2017-2018

In the outlook period, the EU member States from Eastern Europe and the Baltics region are expected to see average growth of about 3 per cent. The full impact of the Brexit on the region has yet to be assessed, but the economies are likely to be affected by more modest EU funding. The weaker pound is already weighing on the value of remittances they receive. The possible return of migrant workers from the United Kingdom may increase labour market tensions in a number of countries, but could also alleviate the serious demographic pressures in the Baltic States and emerging labour shortages in parts of Eastern Europe and facilitate business start-ups.

Economies in transition

Following a 2.8 per cent contraction in 2015, the aggregate GDP of the Commonwealth of Independent States (CIS) and South-Eastern Europe contracted further by an estimated 0.2 per cent in 2016. Economic activity is expected to recover in 2017 and 2018, with aggregate GDP expanding at 1.4 per cent and 2.0 per cent, respectively. The economies of the CIS have entered a period of tentative stabilization. While output continued to decline in several countries in 2016, the aggregate indicators of the region started to show some improvement. The contraction in GDP in 2016 was much milder than in 2015, and a return to a low growth trajectory is expected for 2017. In South-Eastern Europe, economic growth accelerated further, largely owing to the strength of domestic factors.

The economic outlook is subject to downside risks, especially in the case of the CIS. Since commodity prices are expected to remain fairly low, the region's economies will need to find new drivers of growth. Geopolitical tensions in the region, along with a number of structural constraints, continue to limit countries' ability to reduce dependence on primary commodities and low-tech exports. South-Eastern Europe, in turn, remains heavily dependent on the EU and vulnerable to a possible intensification of the refugee crisis or deterioration in global financing conditions.

The Commonwealth of Independent States: tentative recovery amid persistent uncertainty

Following the severe terms-of-trade shock of 2014/15 and the consequent economic contraction in most of the CIS energy exporters (figure IV.5), the region's economies have entered a period of tentative stabilization. Economic activity in parts of the CIS continued to decline in 2016, but at a much reduced pace. As a result of the more moderate contraction in the Russian Federation and the return to sluggish growth in Ukraine, the aggregate indicators of the region improved. Some Central Asian economies, such as Tajikistan and Uzbekistan, continued to register strong growth. The aggregate GDP of the CIS is estimated to have fallen by 0.3 per cent in 2016, following a decline of 3 per cent in 2015. In 2017, the region is expected to return to growth, but amid continued fragilities the expansion will be muted, projected at 1.4 per cent. Growth is forecast to pick up to 2.0 per cent in 2018. Still depressed commodity prices and persistent geopolitical tensions, along with structural constraints, such as an outdated capital stock, deindustrialization in Ukraine, demographic pressures in the European part of the CIS, inadequate energy generation in Central Asia and the challenging business conditions, will continue to generate an inauspicious growth environment and the region's larger economies are expected to remain on a low-growth trajectory.

Figure IV.5
Oil price and the terms of trade of selected CIS energy exporters, 2010–2017

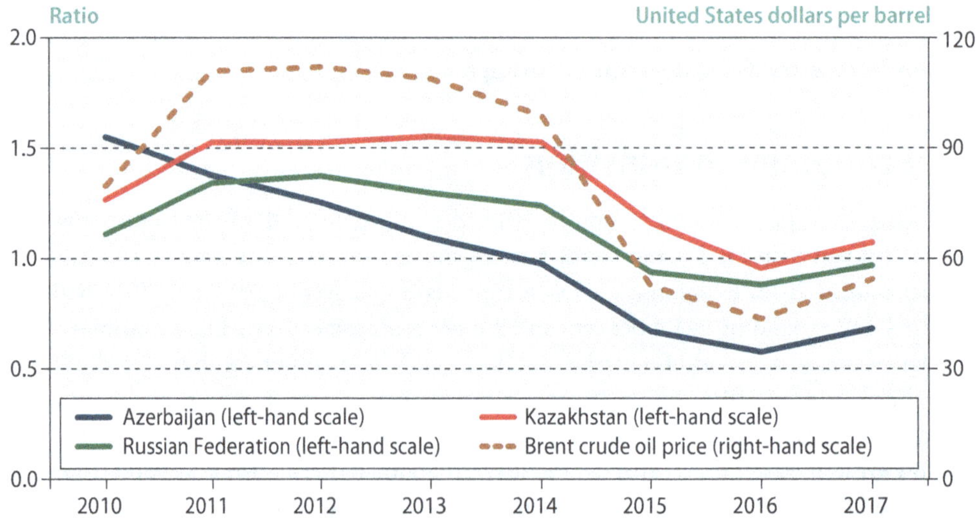

Source: UN/DESA, based on data from Project LINK. Figures for 2016 are partially estimated and figures for 2017 are forecast.

Note: The terms of trade are calculated as the ratio of the unit value of exports to the unit value of imports.

On the positive side, stronger links with China, in particular, within the framework of the "Belt and Road" initiative,[1] will contribute to an upgrade of the Central Asian infrastructure grid and have positive spillover effects. Thanks to continuing robust capital accumulation, growth in Central Asia will exceed the CIS average.

Domestic demand remains subdued

Domestic demand, both consumption and investment, remained very weak in the CIS amid stagnating or declining real wages, poor access to credit and high uncertainty. The continuing international sanctions against the Russian Federation, which limit access to capital markets, weigh on business sentiment and investment prospects. Investment weakened significantly in most countries in 2016, with especially large falls in Azerbaijan, Belarus and the Republic of Moldova, while recovering mildly in Ukraine after three years of precipitous contraction (figure IV.6).

Figure IV.6

Annual change in gross fixed investment in selected CIS economies, 2012–2016

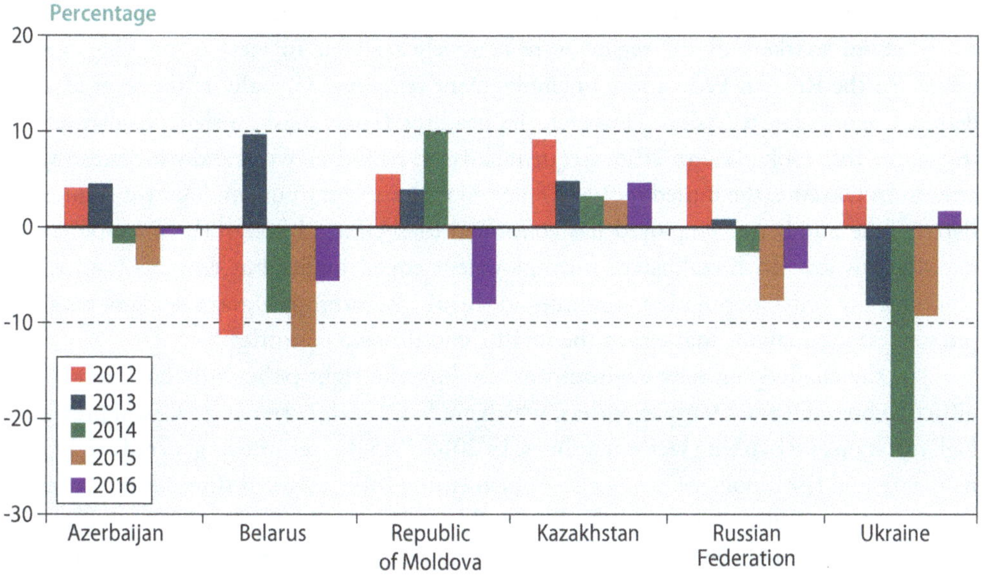

Source: UN/DESA, based on data from Project LINK and National Statistical Offices. Figures for 2016 are partially estimated.

Net external demand was partly able to offset these negative trends. The ongoing fiscal adjustment in energy-exporting countries added to contractionary forces. Falling remittances from the Russian Federation, which are estimated to have further declined in 2016 despite the recovery of the rouble, have depressed incomes in the region's small energy-importing countries. On the positive side, import-substitution policies and a weaker currency in the Russian Federation have supported the performance of certain sectors, namely the agriculture and the chemical industries.

In 2015, Ukraine signed the Deep and Comprehensive Free Trade Area (DCFTA) agreement with the EU, which entered into force in January 2016. In response, the Russian Federation suspended its free trade agreement with Ukraine. This has led to a further col-

1 The initiative of jointly building the Silk Road Economic Belt and the 21st Century Maritime Silk Road was launched in 2013 by China.

lapse in bilateral trade. A similar agreement with the EU for Georgia (not a CIS member) and the Republic of Moldova came into force in July 2016. This leads to further fragmentation of trade in the CIS area. Armenia, Belarus, Kazakhstan, Kyrgyzstan and the Russian Federation are members of the Eurasian Economic Union (EEU) — a free trade area and a customs union aiming at free movement of production factors (including labour) and policy harmonization.

Inflation declines further amid more stable currencies and subdued demand

Inflation subsided throughout the CIS in 2016, as the impact of past currency depreciations wore off, exchange rates stabilized and aggregate demand remained subdued. Strong harvests in the Russian Federation and Ukraine contributed to disinflation. In Ukraine, inflation declined sharply from over 48 per cent in 2015 to single digits in mid-2016 as base year effects wore out; the forthcoming utility price increases and possible currency depreciation will sustain inflationary pressure. In Belarus, despite a large increase in regulated tariffs in early 2016, inflation stabilized but remains high relative to other countries. In several small countries, including Armenia, Kyrgyzstan and the Republic of Moldova, price growth remained subdued. On average, a further slowdown in inflation is projected for 2017-2018.

Labour market shows resilience, but headline figures may be misleading

Labour markets in the region were relatively resilient in view of ongoing output trends. In the Russian Federation, unemployment remained virtually at the level of 2015 despite the ongoing recession. However, the headline figure masks a sharp adjustment of real wages that took place in 2015, frequent shifts to part-time work and widespread wage arrears. In Ukraine, the muted recovery failed to make a dent in unemployment figures. In Belarus, the number of employed has continued to decline, although the unemployment rate remains low. In Kazakhstan, unemployment edged higher but remains low, as the economically active population continues to shrink. Returning migrant workers have put pressure on local labour markets in the small Central Asian countries.

Conditions for economic policymaking are challenging

In the challenging new environment, finding the right policy mix has presented a difficult choice for the energy exporters, which are faced with currency and fiscal pressures, high inflation and banking sector fragilities. In 2014-2015, Governments generally tightened monetary and fiscal policies, while also implementing some targeted stimulus measures.

Monetary policy has been loosened, with some exceptions

Monetary policy was generally loosened throughout the CIS in 2016, against the backdrop of slowing inflation. However, in the larger countries, interest rates remain relatively high. While the shift towards inflation-targeting (following the introduction of free-floating regimes in some countries) facilitates adjustment to external shocks, it has also created new challenges, limiting the room for monetary easing. Persistent concerns over exchange rate stability and inflation limit the scope for countercyclical monetary policy. In the Russian Federation, the policy rate was cut by a total of 100 basis points in 2016; as inflation still far exceeds the official target, further rate cuts are likely to be cautious. By contrast, the Republic of Moldova cut rates rapidly as inflation declined sharply. In Armenia and Kazakhstan, despite ongoing disinflationary trends and continued cuts, rates remain high. Monetary policy was tightened in Azerbaijan and Tajikistan, where the currencies came under severe pressure as a result of lower oil revenues and falling remittance inflows, respectively. Some CIS countries have put in place tight restrictions on the foreign exchange operations of businesses and households and cross-border transactions.

Fiscal adjustment adds to contractionary forces

On the fiscal policy front, even in those CIS energy producers that entered the downturn with significant fiscal buffers, consolidation measures were required to maintain stability of public finances and slow down the depletion of accumulated reserve funds.

In the Russian Federation, public wages remained frozen and benefits were indexed below the inflation rate. Spending in the 2017-2019 budget is likely to decline in real terms. On the positive side, public debt remains low and the country was able to issue a sovereign Eurobond in 2016 despite non-cooperation of foreign banks. Fiscal spending has also been tightened in Azerbaijan.

In Kazakhstan, the adjustment, including the reduction of lending activities by the oil fund, has been accompanied by fiscal reforms to boost non-oil income. To compensate for the budgetary shortfall, as well as to attract FDI and to revitalize growth, partial privatization of state-owned assets is planned in several countries. In the energy-importers, fiscal policy remains largely neutral or slightly expansionary, although the weaker remittance inflows from the Russian Federation exerted pressure on import tariff and indirect tax revenues through weak private consumption. Large public debt is limiting fiscal options in Kyrgyzstan. The banking sector may remain a source of continued fiscal outlays in some countries.

The aggregate current account surplus narrowed

External balances deteriorated in most CIS countries. The region's aggregate current account surplus shrank sharply, driven by trends in the Russian Federation. The contraction of exports in 2016 exceeded the observed fall in imports. The region's terms of trade continued to deteriorate, albeit at a much reduced pace and an improvement is expected in 2017-2018 (figure IV.5).

In the Russian Federation, imports have started to pick up while exports remain subdued. The resulting pressure on the balance of payment was offset by a reduction in capital outflows (box IV.1). A major external adjustment has taken place in recent years in Ukraine as a consequence of the currency depreciation. In the small Central Asian countries, current account deficits remain very large. After plummeting in 2015, remittances have continued to fall, albeit at a reduced pace. There are signs of recovery in remittances in Kyrgyzstan, perhaps linked to the country's membership in the EEU.

Fragilities and downside risks persist

The economic outlook is facing continued downside risks as the recovery of commodity prices is expected to be limited and the region's economies will need to search for new drivers of growth. The ability to overcome the dependence on primary commodities and low-tech exports is constrained by inadequate access to modern technology and limited resources for investment. Currency depreciations have, in part, been harmful and their full consequences have yet to be seen. On the other hand, weaker currencies have provided opportunities for economic diversification, but the supply response will be limited by sluggish domestic and external demand, credit rationing, and subdued investment. The banking system remains fragile, although concerns about financial stability have receded. Geopolitical risks are undermining confidence and business sentiment in the region. For the smaller CIS economies, diversification of their export markets remains an important challenge.

Box IV.1

The "de-offshorisation" of the Russian economy

The Russian economy has experienced large fluctuations in private capital flows over the last decade, driven by external and domestic developments. Prior to the 2008 global financial crisis, both capital inflows and outflows (net acquisition of Russian assets by foreigners and net investments by Russians abroad) grew steadily (figure IV.1.1), with the net balance registering a strong positive value in 2006-2007 (an annual average of 5.2 per cent of GDP). The 2008 crisis brought a sudden stop in capital inflows, while the appetite of Russian residents for foreign assets only gradually diminished. This resulted in large net outflows since 2008 despite some recovery in inflows in the post-crisis period. A specific model of exporting capital and afterwards borrowing overseas prevailed. In 2008, net private capital outflows from the Russian Federation were over $130 billion, while in 2014 the amount exceeded $150 billion.

Figure IV.1.1

Net private capital flows in the Russian Federation, rolling four quarters, 2001Q1-2016Q2

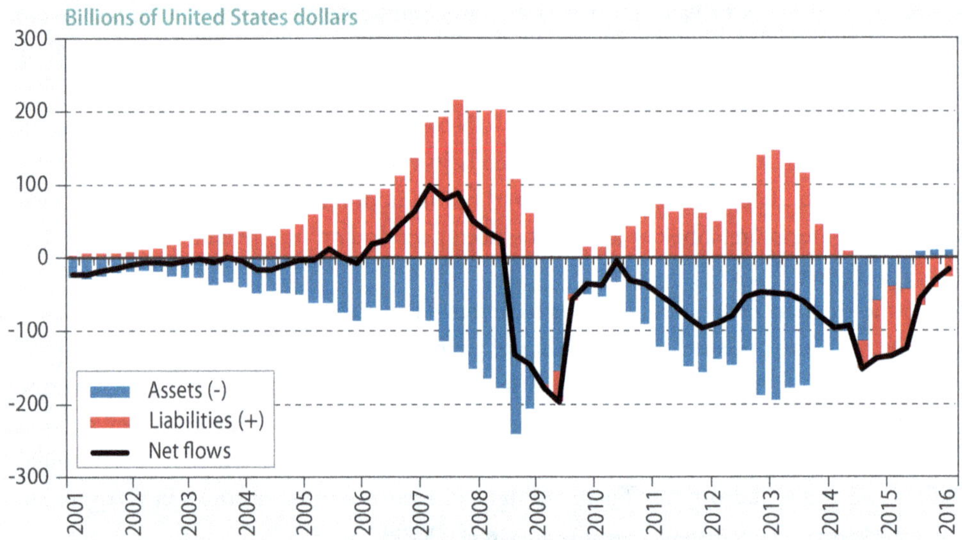

Source: Central Bank of the Russian Federation.
Note: Increases in assets appear with a negative sign, increases in liabilities have a positive sign.

Some of those capital flows reflected de-facto transactions between Russian companies. The share of net inward FDI from the jurisdictions where "round-tripping" investment is more likely to originate reached more than 50 per cent of the total in 2014.

Partially as a result of those developments, the period of high oil prices between 2011 and 2014 was accompanied by a shrinking current account surplus (figure IV.1.2), both in United States dollar terms and as a share of GDP, which is generally not typical for an oil-exporting country. The current account surplus was accompanied by large net private capital inflows and concealed a high deficit on investment income (including that derived from "round-tripping" investments, where interest was paid on the borrowed funds or profit was repatriated back to the offshore locations that acted as a source for FDI).

In 2014, both private capital inflows and outflows fell drastically, amid the collapse in global oil prices and the imposition of international sanctions, which curtailed access to capital markets (figure IV.1.3). Net acquisition of Russian assets by foreigners turned negative in the third quarter of 2014 as investors pulled out of the Russian economy.

Russian companies reduced their debt, which was refinanced only partly, while other sources of financing also dried up. Given increased difficulties in raising external finance, the Russian private sector, particularly banks, drew down on earlier accumulated foreign assets. Consequently, net private capital flows (increases in assets minus increases in liabilities) have been declining sharply since late 2015. The

(continued)

Box IV.1 (*continued*)

Figure IV.1.2
Oil price and current account balance of the Russian Federation, 2000–2015

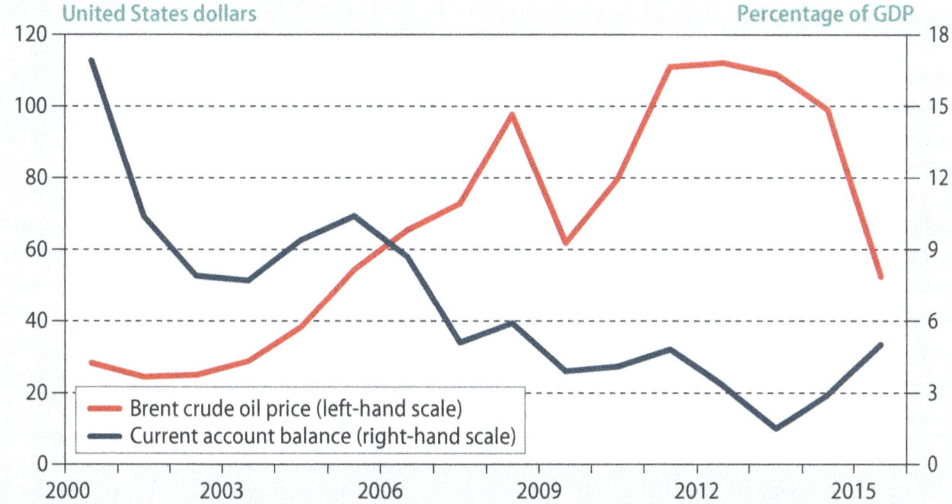

Source: International Monetary Fund and Central Bank of the Russian Federation.

typical strong correlation between foreign inflows and outflows of Russian money has now been broken for some time.

The deterioration in the terms of trade since 2014 has taken place together with a widening of the current account surplus. This is partly explained by the weaker rouble and contraction in imports; however, the reduction of the investment income deficit in 2014-2015 accounts for most of the observed increase in the current account surplus. In 2016, a smaller current account surplus was accompanied by much lower net private capital outflows.

The initiatives to "de-offshorise" the Russian economy and the measures to reduce shadow capital transactions have also played an important role in reducing outflows, resulting in lower dependency on external financing. The Central Bank of the Russian Federation provides estimates of fictitious transac-

Figure IV.1.3
Net incurrence of liabilities by Russian residents, by investment category, 2008–2015

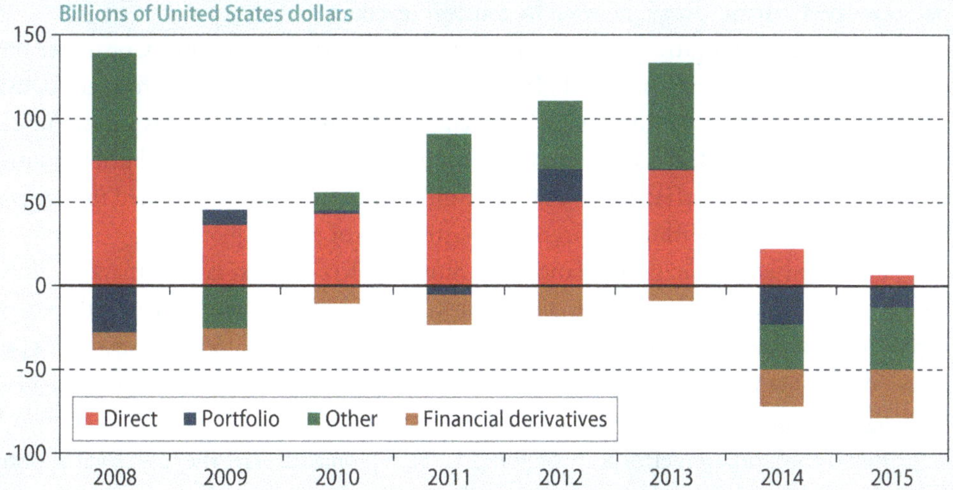

Source: Central Bank of the Russian Federation.

(continued)

Box IV.1 (*continued*)

tions to transfer funds abroad. These irregular transactions have been traditionally quite high, reaching about 10 per cent of exports in 2008. They have been on a declining trend since then, dropping sharply since late 2013, and are now less than 1 per cent. Tighter banking sector rules have also reduced the outflow of illicit capital.

The ongoing deleveraging process has contributed to a reduction in total foreign debt by around 30 per cent between the end of 2013 and the first half of 2016. Exchange rate depreciation amplified the decline (approximately one quarter of this stock was initially rouble-denominated). However, the reduction of liabilities has slowed down in recent quarters, as debt refinancing ratios improved, in particular in the non-financial sector, with liabilities increasing again in the second quarter of 2016.

Regardless of the continuation of international sanctions, the accumulation of assets abroad is unlikely to take place at the same pace as in the past. As a result, lower liabilities will reduce the traditional but volatile deficit of the investment income balance. Debt refinancing ratios have improved, but the persistence of difficulties in accessing external finance will continue to spur the search for domestic alternatives. Thus the "de-offshoring" trend of the Russian economy is expected to continue.

Authors: José Palacín (UN/ECE) and Grigor Agabekian (UN/DESA)

South-Eastern Europe: economic growth accelerates

Economic activity in South-Eastern Europe gained further strength in 2016, driven by the strong pick-up in Serbia, the region's largest economy. The improved performance reflects largely domestic factors. However, there are marked differences across the region, with some countries, in particular the former Yugoslav Republic of Macedonia, losing momentum.

The region's GDP growth is projected to strengthen from an estimated 2.6 per cent in 2016 to 3.1 per cent in 2017 and 3.3 per cent in 2018. However, average growth will remain weaker than in the pre-crisis period, when it was accompanied by heavy private and public borrowing.

Domestic demand drives the expansion

Investment has been a main driver of growth in the region. Albania, Bosnia and Herzegovina and Serbia have seen large public investments in infrastructure. Improved labour market dynamics have boosted private consumption, following years of moderation. In some countries, in particular Albania and Serbia, domestic demand was supported by higher growth. By contrast, net external demand contributed negatively to growth in most economies in the region, with the exception of Serbia and, notably, Montenegro, where the external sector performance was supported by tourism revenues.

Low inflation persists

Despite stronger growth, inflationary pressures remained very low. Consumer price inflation was negative in Bosnia and Herzegovina, and close to zero in the former Yugoslav Republic of Macedonia. While domestic demand has strengthened, there is still significant slack in the labour market. The external environment with low oil and food prices contributes to persistently low inflation. In 2017, consumer price inflation is projected to accelerate to 1.7 per cent, in line with the expected strengthening of energy prices.

Labour market conditions improve

Sustained economic growth and, in a number of countries, labour market reforms have resulted in rapid job creation. Despite recent progress, unemployment still remains high, exceeding the pre-2008 crisis levels, with the exception of the former Yugoslav Republic of Macedonia and Montenegro. Long-term and youth unemployment are particularly high, aggravating social problems.

Fiscal consolidation advances

Fiscal consolidation efforts are ongoing as the region addresses the high level of public debt. The results of these efforts have so far been mixed. Albania, Bosnia and Herzegovina and Serbia have made some progress; other countries have seen further deterioration.

Financing of infrastructure remains a significant source of outlays in the former Yugoslav Republic of Macedonia and Montenegro.

Large external imbalances remain

With the notable exception of Serbia, the current account deficit widened in almost all countries; in Albania (where low oil prices continued to weigh on the value of exports) and Montenegro, the deficit-to-GDP ratios reached double-digit figures. Growing foreign investment in the region translates into large profit repatriation. At the same time, remittance inflows are on a declining trend as the ties between emigrant workers and their countries of origin continue to weaken. FDI remains the main source of financing for the current account deficits.

Improved prospects are accompanied by lingering uncertainties

The region remains closely linked with the EU, which will continue to influence economic prospects. A possible intensification of the refugee crisis would have negative implications, as it may result in disrupting trade flows. The region still remains highly dependent on external financing. In the aftermath of the Brexit vote, there is a risk that funding from the EU may diminish if the United Kingdom eventually exits the EU. In addition, the weaker pound sterling associated with the increased uncertainty will continue to weigh on the value of remittances received by the region.

Developing economies

Growth in developing economies slowed to a meagre 3.6 per cent in 2016, the slowest pace of expansion since the global financial crisis. The causes for this subdued performance are numerous, ranging from international factors such as lower commodity prices, weak global trade and persistent uncertainties in the world economy, to domestic vulnerabilities, reduced macroeconomic policy space and, in some cases, political instability. Several large economies in Latin America and the Caribbean suffered contractions in 2016, while growth in Africa and Western Asia slowed markedly.

In contrast, most economies in East Asia and South Asia, led by China and India, saw robust growth driven by strong expansion of domestic demand. Going forward, average growth in developing economies is expected to pick up to 4.4 per cent in 2017 and 4.7 per cent in 2018 on the back of a moderate recovery in Africa, Latin America and the Caribbean and Western Asia. A pick-up in demand from developed economies will likely support stronger export growth. Higher commodity prices will somewhat alleviate fiscal and external pressures in commodity-exporting countries. While the room for more expansionary monetary and fiscal policies is generally limited, it varies considerably by region and country.

Africa: growth expected to recover at a moderate pace

Following a sharp growth deceleration in 2016, growth in Africa is expected to recover at a moderate pace going forward. Regional GDP is projected to expand by 3.2 per cent in 2017 and 3.8 per cent in 2018, up from an estimated 1.7 per cent in 2016. The aggregate growth figures, however, mask a marked divergence in the growth prospects of the different African subregions (figure IV.7) and economies.

The anticipated upward trend in global oil and non-oil commodity prices for the next two years will, to a certain extent, ease fiscal and external pressures for the commodity exporters. Nevertheless, given that global commodity prices are expected to remain well below pre-2014 levels, a strong growth rebound in the highly commodity-dependent coun-

Figure IV.7
Average annual GDP growth in Africa, by subregion, 2001–2018

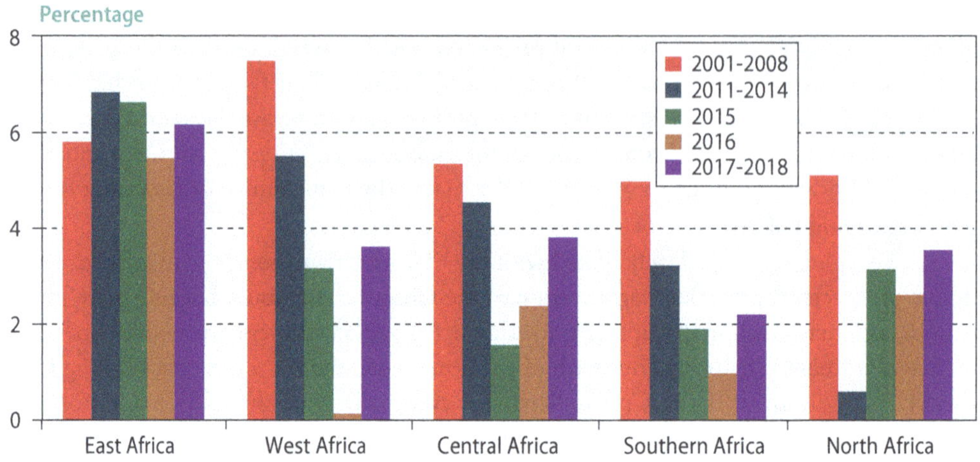

Source: UN/DESA, based on United Nations Statistics Division National Accounts Main Aggregates Database.
Note: Excluding the global financial crisis in 2009 and 2010, for periods of more than one year, growth numbers refer to the arithmetic mean. Figures for 2016 are partly estimated. Figures for 2017 and 2018 are forecasts.

tries, including Algeria, Angola and Nigeria, appears unlikely. In contrast, the growth outlook is more favourable for countries in the East African Community, including Ethiopia, Kenya and the United Republic of Tanzania, as well as the Western African economies of Côte d'Ivoire, Ghana and Senegal. Growth in these economies will continue to be driven by robust private consumption and the continued implementation and completion of large infrastructure projects.

Low commodity prices contributed to a significant growth slowdown

Buffeted by strong external and domestic headwinds, growth in Africa experienced a significant slowdown in 2016. For the highly commodity-dependent economies in the region, persistently low commodity prices weighed on economic activity. Modest global growth and fragile investor sentiments worldwide also contributed to weaker external demand for the region. These global headwinds were compounded by an increasingly challenging domestic climate in several African countries, including unfavourable weather conditions, higher political and policy uncertainty and an escalation of security concerns.

Africa as a whole is expected to have expanded by a modest 1.7 per cent in 2016, marking one of the slowest rates of expansion in more than two decades. The economic picture, however, was one of multi-speed growth. While growth in the oil-exporting and mineral-rich countries weakened, there were bright spots in the region as several economies, including Côte d'Ivoire, Kenya and Senegal, continued to grow at a strong pace. Amid a more favourable business climate, ongoing infrastructure development and improved macroeconomic management, growth in these economies was driven by resilient private consumption and investment activity.

Rapid expansion of domestic markets and strong infrastructure spending drive East Africa's growth

Following robust growth of 5.5 per cent in 2016, East Africa is positioned to remain the fastest growing African subregion in 2017 and 2018. Growth is projected to accelerate to about 6 per cent in both years, reflecting the subregion's favourable macroeconomic fundamentals. Growth in Ethiopia, Kenya, Rwanda and the United Republic of Tanzania in the next two years will remain driven by the rapid expansion of domestic markets and strong infrastructure spending, particularly in the energy and transport sectors. In the subregion's net oil importers such as Kenya and Rwanda, economic activity will continue to benefit from low inflationary pressures, amid a sluggish recovery in oil prices. In addition, the adverse effect of prolonged droughts that dampened 2016 growth in countries such as

Ethiopia and Uganda is expected to dissipate in 2017. A potential escalation of social unrest in Ethiopia may however weigh on the short-term growth outlook.

Modest growth rebound in West Africa as oil prices recover

Growth in West Africa is expected to rebound modestly to 3.1 per cent in 2017, as the projected increase in oil prices eases severe fiscal and external pressures in Nigeria. In 2016, the subregion's aggregate GDP virtually stagnated, growing only by 0.1 per cent due to a contraction in the Nigerian economy. Nigeria's growth was adversely affected by declining oil revenues, amid low oil prices and disruptions to oil production. Heightened financial market volatility and an escalation of security issues also affected investment flows. In contrast, the growth outlook for Côte d'Ivoire, Ghana and Senegal remains strong, underpinned by ongoing large infrastructure investments and progress on structural policies to improve the domestic business climate. In Guinea and Liberia, growth in 2017 is expected to strengthen further given the diminishing impact of the Ebola outbreak on economic activity.

Growth in North Africa is contingent on improved security situation

Growth in North Africa is projected to increase to 3.5 per cent in 2017, contingent on a gradual improvement in the security situation. In 2016, growth in the subregion slowed to 2.6 per cent. Security threats and social unrest weighed on investor sentiments and adversely affected the subregion's vital tourism industry, particularly in Egypt and Tunisia. In Egypt, the sharp decline in tourism revenues contributed to a severe foreign currency shortage. This prompted the Central Bank of Egypt to devalue the Egyptian pound by more than 30 per cent against the United States dollar and announce a free-float of the currency. The Libyan economy also continued to face significant political challenges and unrest, with spillover effects to its neighbouring countries. Given its high dependence on crude oil revenues, Algeria's growth slowed in 2016. Growth in the Algerian economy is expected to remain subdued in 2017 as planned cuts to government spending offset the boost from higher oil prices. Going forward, greater stability in the subregion will support a rebound in exports and a recovery in tourist arrivals.

Southern Africa's growth is projected to pick up as commodity prices increase and drought effects dissipate

The growth outlook for Southern Africa is relatively subdued, with economic activity projected to improve modestly to 1.8 per cent in 2017 and 2.6 per cent in 2018. In 2016, growth in the subregion slowed to 1.0 per cent, as severe droughts adversely affected growth in several countries, including Botswana, Lesotho, Malawi, Namibia and South Africa. In South Africa, growth is projected to improve going forward as the agriculture and mining sectors recover while inflationary pressures subside. However, renewed global financial market volatility may dampen investor sentiments in the short term. Domestically, higher political uncertainty may also weigh on investment in South Africa. Meanwhile, an improvement in oil revenues will support a modest recovery in Angola.

Central Africa's growth is expected to improve even as political uncertainty persists

In the Central Africa subregion, growth is expected to strengthen from 2.4 per cent in 2016 to 3.4 per cent in 2017 and improve further to 4.2 per cent in 2018. The recovery in oil prices will revive export revenues and growth, particularly in Congo, Equatorial Guinea and Gabon. However, ongoing domestic political unrest in the Central African Republic and Gabon will restrain economic activity in these economies. In Cameroon, the diminishing impact of lower oil revenues and continued strong public investment in infrastructure will support growth going forward.

Low commodity prices have resulted in a deterioration of fiscal positions in Africa

External shocks compounded by adverse domestic developments have collectively contributed to rising vulnerabilities in many African countries. The prolonged low commodity price environment has intensified fiscal pressures in the region, particularly for the oil and metal exporters, as evidenced in the considerable widening of fiscal deficits in these economies (figure IV.8).

Figure IV.8
Fiscal deficits of selected oil and metal-exporting African economies, 2003–2007 vs. 2016

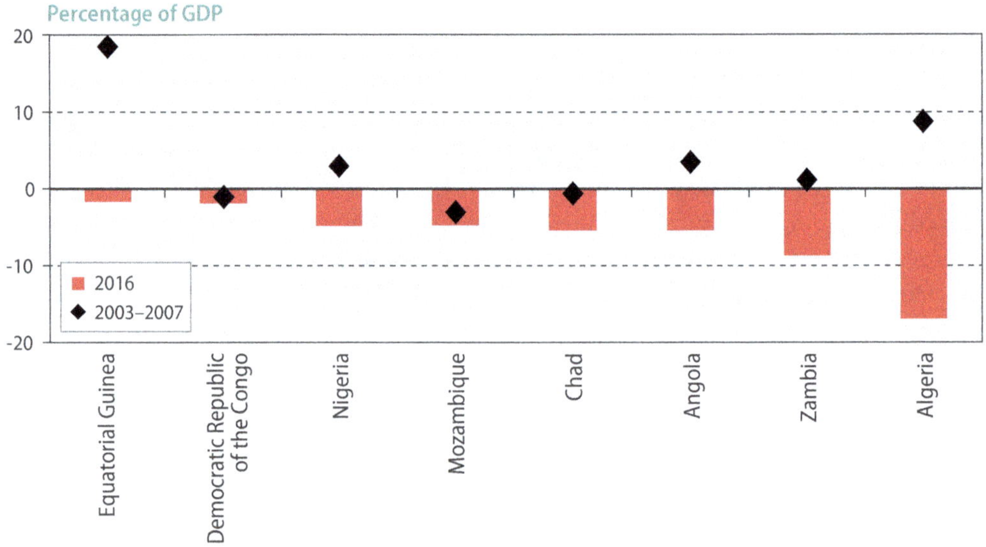

Source: UN/DESA; International Monetary Fund (2016a).
Note: Figures for 2016 are estimates.

For a few countries, the rapid deterioration in public finances has prompted Governments to introduce measures to preserve fiscal sustainability. Large oil exporters, including Algeria and Angola announced significant cuts to budget plans, while Nigeria removed fuel subsidies. In addition, countries such as Nigeria and Zambia sought financial assistance from international organisations to alleviate growing budget shortfalls.

Against a backdrop of high capital flow volatility and declining international reserves, exchange rates of commodity-dependent countries faced downward pressure in 2016. Reflecting the collapse in export income and rising concerns over fiscal sustainability, the domestic currencies of Angola, Mozambique and Zambia depreciated significantly during the year. For South Africa, global financial market volatility, domestic political uncertainty and concerns over the risk of a sovereign rating downgrade contributed to a further weakening of the rand. Faced with severe foreign currency shortages, Nigeria removed its currency peg to the United States dollar in June. The Nigerian naira subsequently depreciated sharply, losing more than 40 per cent of its value over just a few months.

Growth and inflation dynamics vary considerably across the region

Across the African region, growth and inflation dynamics varied considerably in 2016 (figure IV.9). The weakening of domestic currencies fuelled inflationary pressures, particularly in the less diversified economies.

The adverse impact of drought conditions on agricultural production and rising electricity tariffs also exerted upward pressure on consumer prices. Inflation accelerated to multi-year highs in Angola, Mozambique and Nigeria, with domestic prices growing at double-digit rates during the year. For Nigeria, the removal of fuel subsidies resulted in a sharp increase in retail petrol prices, exacerbating inflationary pressures.

Amid rising consumer prices and production costs, several central banks increased key policy rates in 2016. Looking ahead, as high inflationary pressures are expected to persist for these economies, monetary policy stances will remain tight. Given the weakening growth momentum, however, the increase in domestic borrowing costs will likely further constrain private consumption and investment activity, reflecting a rising dilemma

Figure IV.9
GDP growth and inflation in selected African economies, 2016

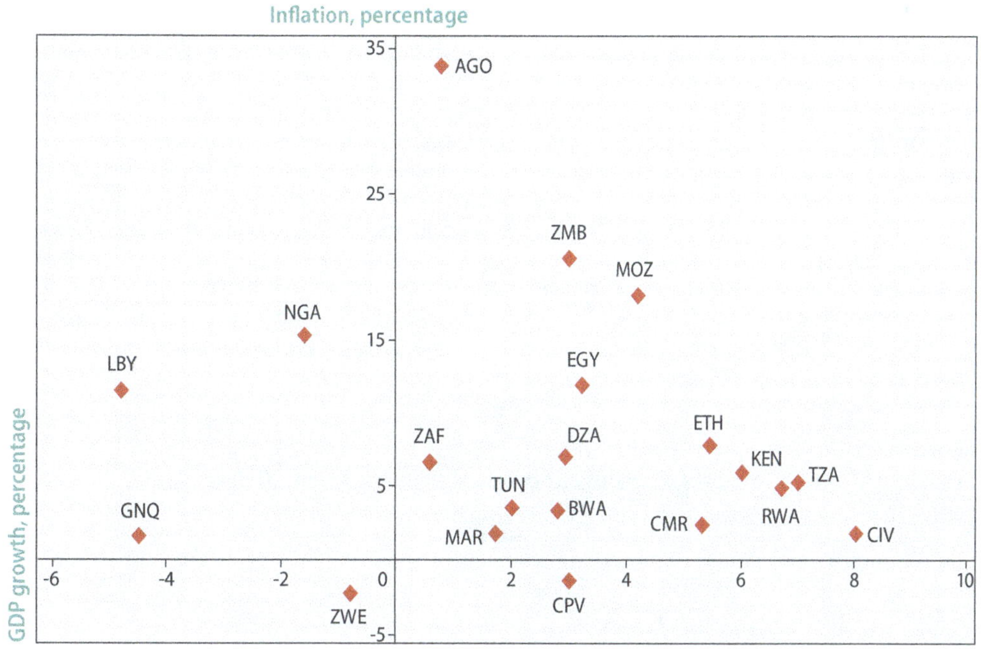

Source: UN/DESA estimates, based on data from National Statistical Offices and Central Banks.
Note: See Table J in the Statistical Annex for definitions of country codes.

in the conduct of monetary policy in these economies. In contrast, inflation in the net oil importers in the region stabilised or declined in 2016, with inflationary pressures expected to remain subdued going forward. In a few of these countries, such as Botswana, Kenya and Morocco, central banks reduced policy rates during the year, reflecting the availability of policy space.

The growth outlook for Africa faces high domestic and external risks

Several risks and challenges remain to the growth outlook for the African region. On the external front, a reversal of the recent upward trend in global oil prices would result in further growth deterioration in oil-exporting countries. A sharper-than-expected growth moderation in China would weigh on the region's commodity exports (box IV.2). In addition, the uncertainties associated with the coming process of Brexit, with deterioration in the growth outlook for the United Kingdom and Europe, would pose a risk to the trade performance of countries such as Kenya and South Africa, given the importance of Europe as a major export destination.

Domestically, an escalation of security concerns, particularly in the Central, North and West African subregions could deter foreign investment and severely disrupt economic activity. Growing political unrest such as in Burundi, the Democratic Republic of the Congo, Gabon and Zimbabwe could also impact growth. For the highly agriculture-dependent economies such as Ethiopia and Malawi, growth will remain susceptible to weather-related shocks.

Importantly, the growth outlook for Africa is contingent on the ability of countries to mitigate the impact of external risks while containing domestic vulnerabilities. Although debt levels in Africa are still relatively low, the sharp widening of fiscal deficits has contributed to rising concerns over the pace of debt accumulation in the region. In particular, tighter international financial conditions and further weakening of domestic currencies could lead to higher borrowing costs, given the structure of Africa's external debt that

Box IV.2

The impact of China's economic slowdown on Africa

The Chinese economy has been on a moderating growth path since 2010. Ongoing structural reform measures to rebalance growth have resulted in slower investment, particularly in the industrial sectors with excess capacity. China's economic transition from investment to consumption-led growth will contribute to more robust and more sustainable growth prospects going forward. Nevertheless, the Chinese economy is projected to expand at a pace well below the double-digit growth rates experienced in the past decades. Given China's significant influence on global growth and trade developments, the slowdown in China's economic growth and changing demand composition have important implications for the rest of the world, including Africa.

China's economic rebalancing is affecting the growth outlook for the African economies through three key transmission channels. The first and most important channel is the trade channel. Slowing growth in China has been accompanied by deceleration in its overall import volume growth in recent years (figure IV.2.1).

Figure IV.2.1

Growth of China's imports of goods and services in constant 2010 prices, 1996–2016 *(year-on-year)*

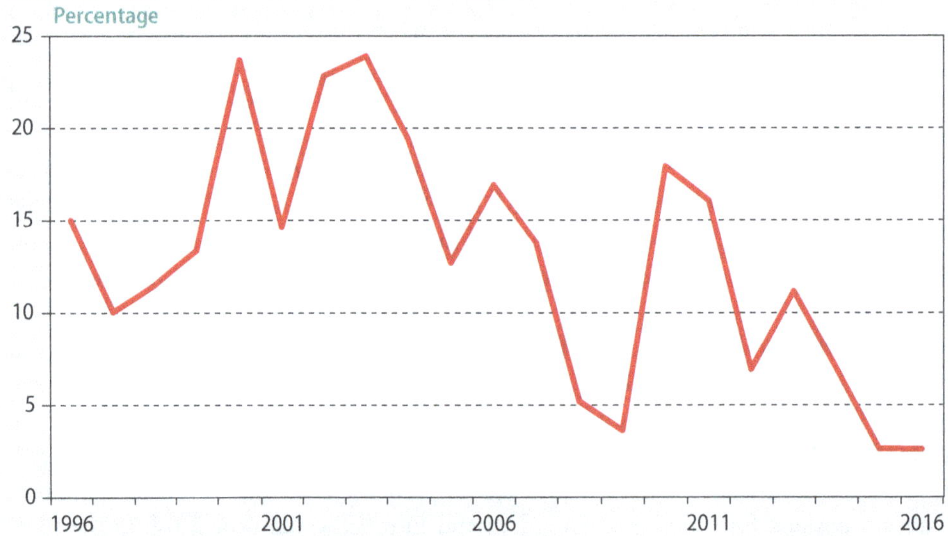

Source: UN/DESA, based on national data.
Note: Figure for 2016 is estimated.

In the last decade, the value of China's imports from Africa has risen more than 20-fold, reaching a peak of $116 billion in 2013 (figure IV.2.2). The rapid expansion in trade activity between China and the African economies was largely fuelled by China's trade liberalisation measures as well as its rapid growth in demand for natural resources and primary commodities. Amid the collapse in global commodity prices, the value of China's imports from Africa has contracted since 2013, falling by almost 50 per cent to $69 billion in 2015.

While this to a certain extent reflects the large decline in commodity prices, it is also indicative of weaker Chinese demand, given that China's import volume growth has also slowed. The sharp decline in trade value is also associated with a fall in income for the African economies, with adverse effects on both the public and private sectors.

The impact of China's slowdown will vary from country to country. For several economies, including Angola, Congo, Mauritania, South Africa and Zambia, weaker Chinese demand significantly affects their trade outlook, given that China is the largest export destination for these economies, representing

(continued)

Box IV.2 (*continued*)

Figure IV.2.2
China's imports from Africa, 1995–2015

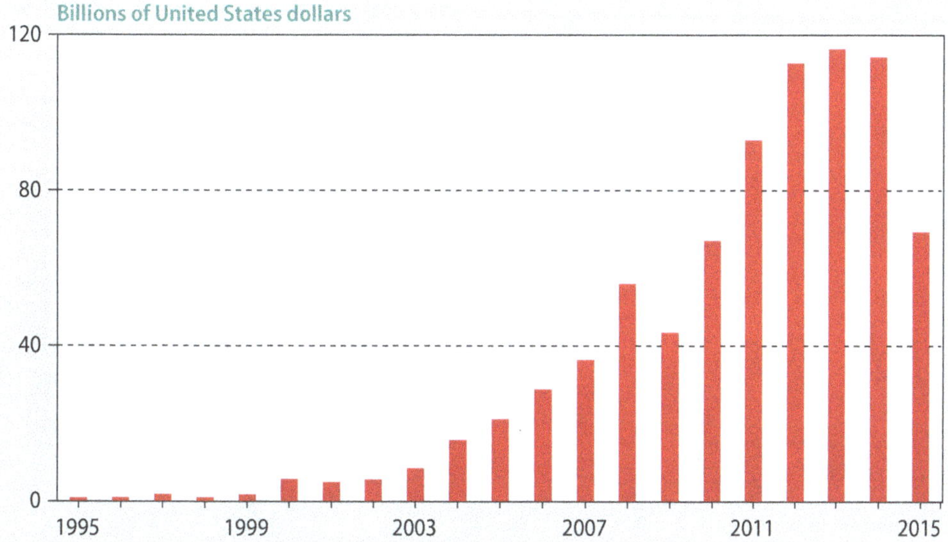

Source: UN Comtrade.

between 8 and 44 per cent of total exports. In addition, China's shift away from imports of investment-related goods will lower its demand for raw materials and intermediate inputs for the industrial sector. This will have a disproportionately large negative impact on the African economies given that about 90 per cent of Africa's total exports to China are composed of primary commodities, in particular mineral fuel and oils (64 per cent), ores (14 per cent) and copper (6 per cent).

China's slower growth is also exerting downward pressure on global commodity prices, indirectly affecting the growth performance of the African economies. China constitutes around 50 per cent of total global consumption for several base metals, including aluminium, copper, nickel and zinc. Weaker Chinese demand for these commodities will dampen global prices, weighing on income of the metal exporters in Africa. For example, copper and copper-related products constitute 57 per cent and 78 per cent of total exports in the Democratic Republic of the Congo and Zambia, respectively. In Madagascar, nickel accounts for 23 per cent of total exports, while in Mozambique, aluminium represents 34 per cent of total exports.

Through the investment channel, slower growth in China may weigh on the capacity of Chinese firms to engage in overseas direct investment activity, including in Africa. While the stock of Chinese foreign direct investment in Africa is still relatively small, it has been growing at a rapid pace. Data from The China-Africa Research Initiative (CARI) at the Johns Hopkins University School of Advanced International Studies (SAIS) showed that China's stock of FDI into Africa has grown from $0.3 billion in 2003 to $32 billion in 2014, with investments mainly concentrated in the extractive industries.

Finally, through the financing channel, slower growth in China may lead to a decline in loans, aid and grants that are extended to African countries, potentially affecting financing for development, including much-needed infrastructure. According to SAIS—CARI, the Chinese Government, banks and contractors extended a total of $86.3 billion between 2000 and 2014 to African Governments and state-owned enterprises, with Angola, Ethiopia, Kenya and Sudan among the largest recipients of these loans. Data from the research institute also revealed that between 2000 and 2013, loans to African Governments and state-owned enterprises increased from $0.13 billion to $17 billion. In 2014, however, the value of loans declined to $16.7 billion (figure IV.2.3).

Amid declining commodity-related revenue and rising domestic vulnerabilities, the slower growth in China is adding to the strong headwinds already faced by African economies. In this environment, African economies have to adapt to the rapidly changing global economic and trade landscape.

(*continued*)

Box IV.2 (*continued*)

Figure IV.2.3
Chinese loans to Africa, 2000–2014

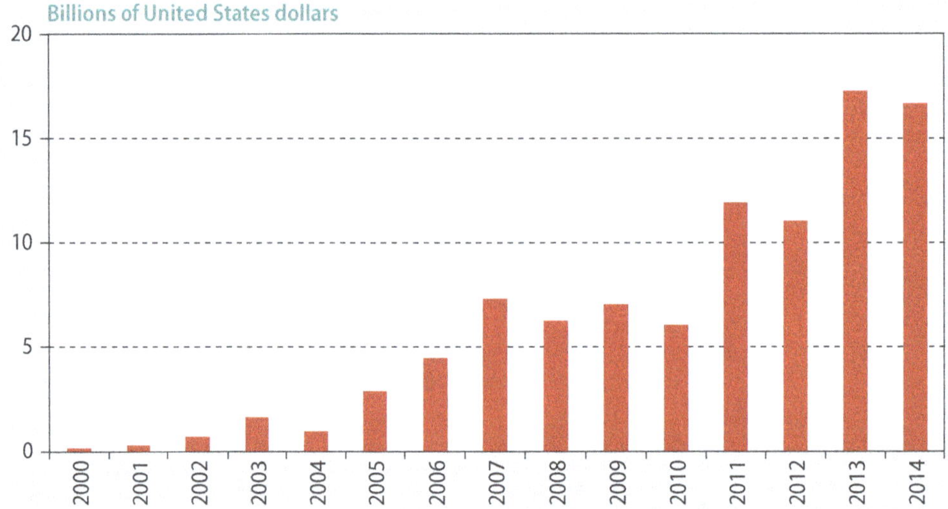

Source: Johns Hopkins School of Advanced International Studies – China-Africa Research Institute (SAIS –CARI) dataset. Available from http://www.sais-cari.org/data-chinese-loans-and-aid-to-africa.

Note: Chinese loans refer to loans by the Chinese Government, banks and contractors to African Governments and state-owned enterprises.

China's growing middle class represents an opportunity for other economies to tap into its large domestic market and rising demand for consumption goods. To leverage this opportunity, African economies need not only diversify their export product structures, but also prioritize policy measures to enhance productivity growth and competitiveness in order to move up the value chain.

Authors: Yesuf Awel (UN/ECA), Hopestone Chavula (UN/ECA) and Poh Lynn Ng (UN/DESA)

is largely denoted in foreign currency, with relatively short maturities and in some cases, floating interest rates.

For many African economies, growth prospects going forward are dependent on the effectiveness of policy measures taken in adjusting to lower commodity prices. Amid increased pressure for fiscal consolidation, there is a risk that countries will resort to cutting expenditure on critical infrastructure such as in the areas of energy, transport and healthcare. This could lead to a worsening of existing structural bottlenecks and constrain productivity growth, undermining medium-term growth prospects and sustainable development.

African economies need to advance structural reforms to boost growth prospects

Amid declining monetary and fiscal policy space, African economies will need to make substantial progress on reform measures in order to address domestic structural weaknesses. For the highly commodity-dependent economies, there is an urgent need to accelerate economic diversification and rebuild policy buffers in order to enhance resilience to external shocks. In addition, double-digit unemployment rates in many African economies, including Algeria, Egypt, South Africa and Tunisia significantly undermine progress towards sustainable and inclusive growth. In this respect, policy initiatives to promote FDI in high value-added industries can help to create better quality jobs in the economy. Ongoing initiatives to foster closer regional economic integration, such as the Northern Corridor Integration Projects (NCIP) framework will not only improve connectivity and lower the cost of doing business between countries, but will also generate positive spillovers to growth and employment.

East Asia: domestic demand continues to drive positive near-term outlook amid weak export performance

Growth in East Asia is estimated to have moderated slightly to 5.5 per cent in 2016, from 5.7 per cent in 2015 (figure IV.10), with a marginal pick up to 5.6 per cent projected for both 2017 and 2018. Domestic demand, in particular private consumption and public investment, remained the key driver of regional growth. However, the region continued to experience exceptionally weak export growth in 2016, contributing to the underperformance of several larger economies. The prolonged sluggish performance of the external sector has had negative spillover effects on consumer sentiments, which is weighing on household spending in several economies in the region. Inflation remains generally subdued, largely as a result of low energy and food prices. There are however encouraging signs of the region emerging from the two-year stretch of producer-price deflation. This could have a positive impact on corporate profits and investment.

China's output growth stabilizes

China's growth figures for the first three quarters of 2016 have somewhat alleviated near-term concerns over a drastic output slowdown. The Chinese economy is estimated to have grown by 6.6 per cent in 2016, which is 0.2 percentage points above the forecast in WESP 2016 (United Nations, 2016a). Growth has been supported by robust private consumption, as reflected in stable retail sales growth throughout the year. Growth of fixed investment, particularly infrastructure investment, also provided solid support to overall growth.

A notable development is that fixed investment has been predominately driven by state-owned enterprises. Private investment decelerated due to overcapacity in several industrial sectors, sluggish market demand, and higher corporate financing costs. While industrial profits have seen some overall recovery, there are also rising defaults on corporate debt. The Chinese economy is expected to grow by 6.5 per cent in both 2017 and 2018, supported by favourable domestic demand and accommodative fiscal measures, including off-budget fiscal support through policy banks and public-private partnerships. Neverthe-

Figure IV.10

Contributions to real GDP growth in East Asia and selected economies, 2015–2017

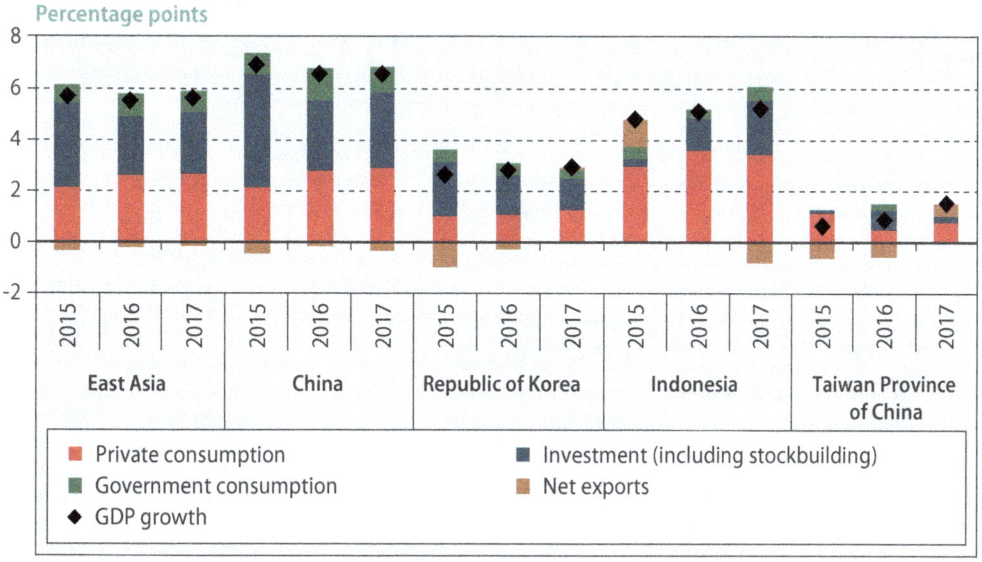

Source: UN/DESA, based on United Nations Statistics Division National Accounts Main Aggregates Database.

Note: Figures for 2015 and 2016 are partially estimated and figures for 2017 are forecast.

less, the implications of China's ongoing economic rebalancing will inevitably be felt by the region in the medium and long-run through trade (including commodity prices) and financial channels, albeit to a varied extent across countries.

Domestic demand growth in the Republic of Korea is restrained by weak employment and corporate restructuring

The Republic of Korea's growth is estimated to have improved moderately from 2.6 per cent in 2015 to 2.8 per cent in 2016. Domestic demand remains relatively robust, with construction investment being a main growth driver. Construction investment is expected to maintain its favourable momentum in 2017. Export growth has remained sluggish owing to low global investment and weaker external competitiveness. Looking ahead, the Republic of Korea is projected to grow by 2.8 per cent to 2.9 per cent annually during 2017-2018, supported by the continued expansion of domestic demand. Economic activity will, however, be weighed down by weak employment growth and corporate restructuring of distressed firms that are facing rising insolvency risks.

Output growth in Indonesia, the Philippines and Thailand accelerated

Among the larger Association of Southeast Asian Nations (ASEAN) economies, output growth in Indonesia, the Philippines and Thailand is estimated to have accelerated in 2016, driven by stronger domestic demand. Indonesia is expected to grow by 5.1 per cent to 5.3 per cent annually during 2016-2018, up from 4.8 per cent in 2015. Private consumption has benefited from lower inflation, which also allowed the Central Bank of Indonesia to make multiple rate cuts. Policy measures, such as higher minimum wages and an increase in the tax-free threshold, were also introduced to support household incomes. Meanwhile, the Philippines is estimated to have grown by 6.3 per cent in 2016, up from 5.9 per cent in 2015, and is expected to expand by 6.0 per cent to 6.1 per cent annually during 2017-2018. Household spending grew at a strong pace, underpinned by favourable employment conditions, larger remittance inflows, higher public sector salaries and an increase in government spending, particularly preceding the general election in May 2016. In Thailand, the economy is estimated to grow at an annual pace of 3.1 per cent to 3.4 per cent between 2016 and 2018, up from 2.8 per cent in 2015. Both public consumption and investment rose considerably, as a result of an increase in public sector salaries, higher social transfers and the implementation of large-scale infrastructure projects. The transition related to the royal succession could lead to some temporary slowdown of economic activities, but the impacts are not expected to be significant. In contrast, growth in Malaysia is estimated to have moderated to 4.4 per cent in 2016 from 5 per cent in 2015. The slowdown is a result of subdued domestic demand and worsening net exports. In particular, consumer spending — the main growth driver in recent years — was held back by less robust job markets and households' adjustment to the higher cost of living, especially since the introduction of the goods and services tax in 2015.

Growth in Singapore is also expected to have decelerated to 1.7 per cent in 2016, down from 2.0 per cent in 2015, due to subdued externally-oriented service sectors and manufacturing production. Growth is projected to improve to 2.4 per cent to 2.6 per cent in 2017 and 2018, supported by a modest recovery in global and regional trade.

Hong Kong SAR and Taiwan Province of China saw the slowest growth among larger economies

Hong Kong Special Administrative Region (SAR) of China and Taiwan Province of China are estimated to have experienced the slowest growth among the larger economies in the region in 2016, growing by 1.4 per cent and 0.9 per cent, respectively. In Hong Kong SAR, prolonged weakness in the external sector and recent asset market corrections undermined business sentiments. Private consumption remains a key growth driver, but retail sector performance was mixed amid a continued slowdown in tourism. In Taiwan Province of China, private investment continued its previous weak trend in 2016 and household consumption growth was dampened by weak or even negative real wage growth during the year. Growth in both economies is expected to recover in 2017 and 2018, conditional on improvements in external demand conditions.

Domestic credit growth has not increased significantly despite loose monetary policy

Policy rates across major economies in the region approached or reached historic low levels in 2016. With few exceptions, there remains some — albeit limited — room for further rate cuts, especially given the overall low inflationary environment. However, concerns regarding large capital outflows have weighed on central banks' rate-cut decisions, as the region saw the greatest annual net capital outflow on record in 2015. High levels of household and corporate debt — and possibly narrowing banks' profit margins — have also factored into central banks' decisions. The effectiveness of monetary easing also appears to be waning as domestic credit growth has not increased significantly despite the overall loose monetary stance across the region.

Financial markets in the region were broadly stable in 2016

As domestic credit growth did not see much acceleration, regional financial markets were broadly stable in 2016. The Renminbi's exchange rate against the United States dollar and its effective exchange rate depreciated consistently during 2016, with the former reaching the lowest level since 2010. For most of the other major currencies in the region, the effective exchange rate experienced less volatility in 2016 than in 2015.

Room for more active fiscal intervention exists...

With many economies facing relatively limited room for furthering monetary easing, the fiscal stance in East Asia has been mostly expansionary and countercyclical to support growth. Overall fiscal balances worsened in 2015 across the region and this trend is projected to continue going forward, resulting in higher public debt. Nevertheless, given the still relatively low public debt levels (figure IV.11), economies in the region could engage in more active fiscal intervention, particularly in the areas of infrastructure and social spending, which would support the region's long-term potential growth.

Figure IV.11
Public debt and short-term fiscal spending multipliers of selected economies in East Asia (*2007 vs. 2015*)

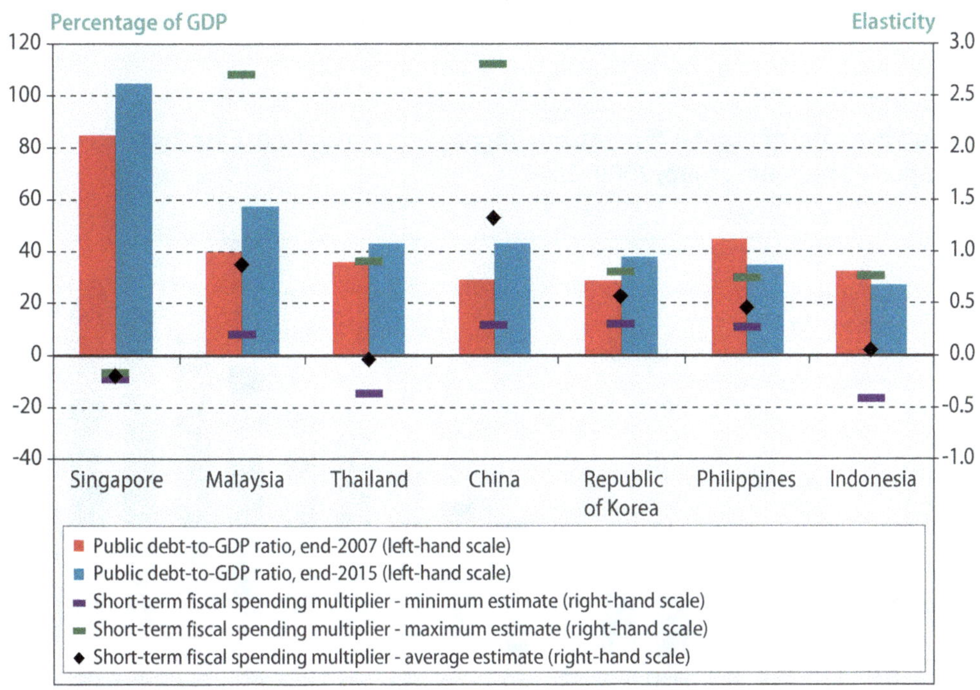

Source: IMF Fiscal Monitor October 2016 and existing literature on estimates of Asian economies' fiscal multipliers.

Note: Estimates of fiscal multipliers are obtained from a number of studies published during 2006-2013. Short-term multipliers for most studies refer to first-year multipliers in non-recession times. Tax multipliers are not covered in this chart. The range of estimates presented here is intended to be indicative, rather than exhaustive, and estimates are not strictly comparable.

...but effectiveness of fiscal spending in supporting output growth varies across the region

Existing estimates of fiscal multipliers show that the effectiveness of fiscal spending varies significantly across economies in the region (figure IV.11). In particular, fiscal multipliers of a few smaller, open economies are estimated to be possibly negative, which could be a reflection of country-specific characteristics, the phase of economic cycle, the choice of fiscal instruments and the targeted area of fiscal spending. In view of this, economies would have to identify the most effective means of fiscal intervention to maximize its positive impact on growth.

Trade growth has been exceptionally weak in East Asia

East Asia has until recently been the engine for global trade. However, trade in the region has been exceptionally weak in 2015 and 2016, weighed down by a slowdown in the developed economies and major economies in the region. Structural factors such as economic rebalancing in China are also at play, with the country's import composition expected to gradually shift away from intermediate goods and capital goods, which currently account for over 70 per cent of the region's exports to China. Even though tariff rates have fallen significantly for over a decade, non-tariff measures on goods appear to be on the rise (figure IV.12). While cumulative non-tariff measures imposed on East Asia experienced a steady increase between 2000 and 2015, the pace appears to have accelerated during the post-crisis period. These barriers may have partly contributed to the weak export performance in recent years. Growth in the value of services exports of the region has been declining since 2010 and became negative in 2015 and early 2016, even as global services trade has been gaining relative importance during the same period. This may be a cause for concern considering that the average share of value added by services in total exports is over 55 per cent for the region's top five trading economies (China, Republic of Korea, Hong Kong SAR, Taiwan Province of China and Singapore).

Relatively optimistic regional outlook is clouded by considerable uncertainties

While the economic outlook is relatively more optimistic for East Asia compared to most of the other developing regions, risks for the region remain tilted to the downside. Factors that could drive faster economic growth in 2017, such as stronger demand in developed economies, higher global commodity prices and rising infrastructure investment are subject to considerable uncertainty. High and rising corporate and household debt in several economies in the region, including China, pose downside risks to growth. If not

Figure IV.12

Cumulative total of non-tariff measures imposed on goods from East Asia, by imposing regional group, 2000–2016

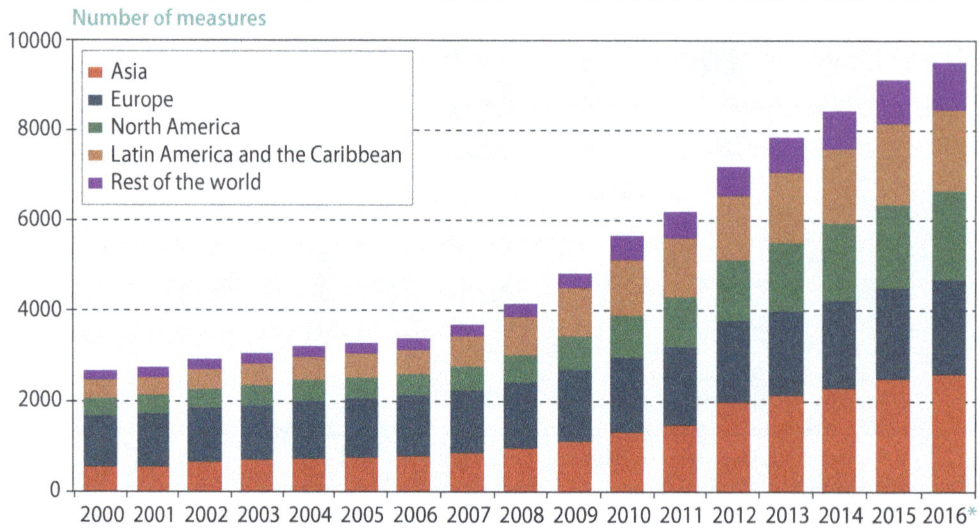

Source: WTO Integrated Trade Intelligence Portal.

Note: East Asia here covers 22 of the major trading economies in the region, excluding Japan. Data shows the end-of-year number for each year. Data for 2016 covers the period to 30 September 2016.

adequately addressed, this could further add to Governments' contingent liabilities, curbing engagement in supportive fiscal measures.

South Asia: positive economic outlook supported by robust private consumption

South Asia is the fastest-growing developing region and its economic outlook remains largely positive, benefiting from robust private consumption, a modest pickup in investment and the continuing implementation of domestic reforms. Macroeconomic policies have also played a positive role: monetary policy continues to provide support to economic activity, while the fiscal policy stance remains moderately tight but with some degrees of flexibility. Against this backdrop, regional GDP growth is expected to remain robust, reaching 6.9 per cent in 2017 and 2018, following 6.7 per cent in 2016 (figure IV.13). However, the relative weakness of investment demand in some countries underscores the need for continuous reform efforts. After slowing to a multiyear-low of 6.2 per cent in 2016, regional inflation is expected to remain relatively low and stable. Overall, the positive economic outlook will likely enable further progress in labour market indicators, albeit gradual and moderate, and a reduction in poverty in the coming years.

Despite vigorous growth, private investment remains subdued in several economies

The favourable outlook is contingent on the continuing strength of private consumption, which has recently been pushed up by accommodative monetary policies and other stimulus measures such as public salary increases in Bangladesh, India and Nepal. However, recent signs of stagnation in remittance flows could negatively affect this trend in some countries, such as Bangladesh, Nepal and Pakistan. Meanwhile, investment demand continues to display an anaemic performance. The transmission mechanism from monetary policy remains weak, and corporates with stressed balance sheets are channelling cash flows towards deleveraging rather than to expansion projects. Against this backdrop, public investments in infrastructure have been critical to avoid a further deterioration in investment demand, notably in India. In the outlook period, a key challenge in this regard

Figure IV.13
GDP growth for selected countries in South Asia, 2012–2018

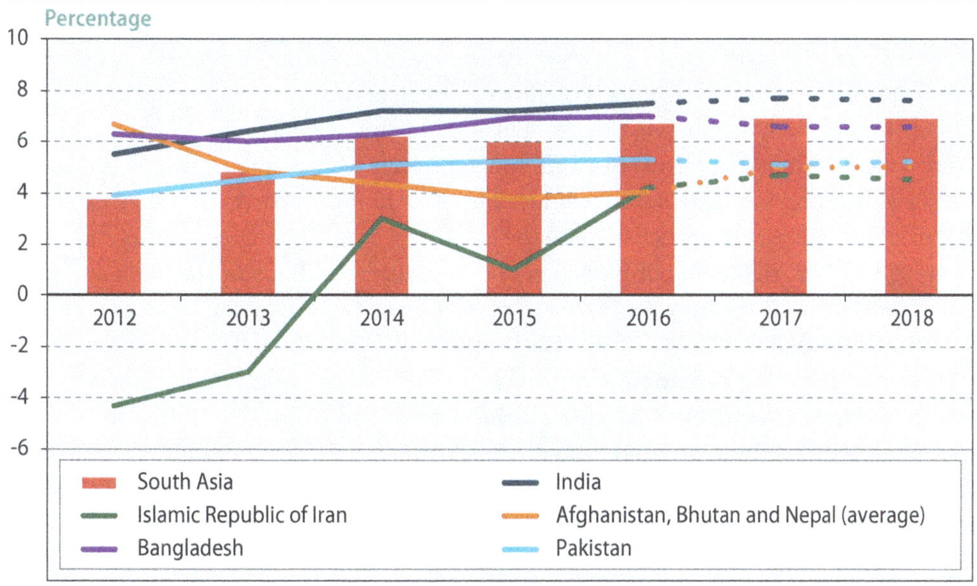

Source: UN/DESA, based on United Nations Statistics Division National Accounts Main Aggregates Database.
Note: GDP growth rates are adjusted to calendar year. Figures for 2016 are partially estimated. Figures for 2017 and 2018 are forecast.

is to generate a crowding-in of private investment. This is particularly important given the large infrastructure and energy deficits, which remain a major structural barrier to a more inclusive and sustained growth across the region. Meanwhile, exports remain constrained in many countries owing to subdued global growth and trade flows, uncompetitive real exchange rates in smaller economies, and structural impediments to increase production.

Economic activity in India is further benefiting from domestic reforms

Among the largest countries, India has positioned itself as the most dynamic emerging economy. India's economy is projected to expand by 7.7 per cent and 7.6 per cent in 2017 and 2018, respectively, benefiting from strong private consumption. Investment demand is expected to slightly pick up, helped by monetary easing, government efforts towards infrastructure investments and public-private partnerships, and the implementation of domestic reforms such as the introduction of the Goods and Services Tax (GST) Bill. This reform constitutes a major change by establishing a new uniform tax rate, and it should promote investment in the medium term through lower transaction and logistic costs and efficiency gains. Importantly, an effective GST implementation also requires adequate capacity building of the tax administration. Nevertheless, low capacity utilization and stressed balance sheets of banks and businesses will prevent a strong investment revival in the short term.

The outlook for the Islamic Republic of Iran is strengthening visibly. This can be attributed to the strong expansion of oil production and exports (international sanctions were lifted by early 2016), lower inflation, increasing business confidence, and a surge in foreign investments. GDP growth is estimated to have accelerated to 4.3 per cent in 2016, with an expected further pickup to 4.7 per cent and 4.4 per cent in 2017 and 2018, respectively.

In Pakistan, economic growth is also projected to remain robust, above 5.0 per cent. Economic activity will be driven by strong consumption, a supportive monetary policy stance and rising investment and infrastructure projects boosted by the China-Pakistan Economic Corridor. Against this backdrop, youth unemployment is expected to slightly decline in the near term. Among smaller economies, the outlook for Sri Lanka's economy has recently improved after serious balance of payments and debt turbulences in early 2016. Economic activity will, however, likely remain constrained by fiscal consolidation measures and a tight monetary stance implemented to contain external risks.

Accommodative monetary policies are expected to continue in the near term

Amid relatively low inflationary pressures, monetary policies in South Asia are moderately accommodative. The supportive monetary stance is expected to continue in the near term, with potential further easing in India, the Islamic Republic of Iran and Pakistan. However, credit growth remains below trend in several countries, especially in industrial and infrastructure sectors in India. Fragilities in the banking sector and stressed balanced sheets of corporates remain important challenges for some economies. For instance, the Government of India committed to a $3.7 billion package to recapitalize state-owned banks, and various regulations have been introduced in order to reduce banks' financial exposures and to encourage private participation in the banking sector. Although countries should try to avoid a sudden tightening of monetary and liquidity conditions in the outlook period, policy measures will critically depend on the evolution of external factors, such as oil prices.

Despite high deficits, fiscal policy shows some flexibility in several countries…

Most South Asian Governments have announced relatively tight fiscal stances. However, during the implementation, Governments have tended to provide more support for their economies, responding to large development needs and political pressures. In India, in spite of a strong emphasis on rural areas and infrastructure investments on the expenditure side, fiscal policy has largely followed a cautious approach and the budget deficit is expected to further decline gradually. For 2016/17, the deficit is projected to reach 3.5 per cent of GDP and is on track to meet the medium-term target of 3.0 per cent of GDP.

In Bangladesh and Pakistan, fiscal policy is gradually becoming more expansionary, and thus deficits are expected to remain elevated. In Sri Lanka, the fiscal deficit is relatively high and the efforts to reduce it are tilted to the revenue side, as the country has one of the lowest tax-to-GDP ratios in the world. Sri Lanka recently received a three-year Extended Fund Facility (EFF) of $1.5 billion from the International Monetary Fund (IMF) to support the reform agenda.

...but raising tax-to-GDP ratios remains a key challenge across the region

Against this backdrop, fiscal deficits are expected to remain elevated in most economies, and recent large increases in wages and other benefits in the public sector are likely to further reduce fiscal space. From a medium-term perspective, key fiscal challenges for the region are to improve tax revenues and to promote a supportive environment for the private sector, which together can enhance the capacity to implement counter-cyclical policies.

In fact, most economies are constrained by very low tax-to-GDP ratios in comparison to other developing regions and high debt-to-GDP ratios (figure IV.14). Despite increasing efforts to strengthen tax revenues and the efficiency of the whole tax system, significant delays and problems remain. For instance, high levels of informality represent a major challenge to the implementation and potential benefits of tax reforms across the region.

Domestic reforms should prioritize productivity growth

Despite the favourable outlook, South Asian economies face several downside risks. On the domestic front, the reform agenda could experience setbacks in some countries, while political instabilities might dampen investment prospects. Structural reforms in labour markets, financial sectors, public finances and competition are crucial to increase productivity growth across the region. Heightened regional geopolitical tensions could also weigh on the outlook. For example, intra-regional trade facilitation and integration projects could experience delays and obstacles, while large infrastructure investments to improve connectivity may face institutional uncertainty. On the external front, potential renewed episodes of high financial volatility, including a sudden surge in external borrowing costs and large capital outflows, could significantly increase the difficulties to roll over debt, especially in countries with relatively low financial buffers and high debt denominated in United States dollars.

Figure IV.14
Tax revenues in South Asia and world regions, latest available year

Percentage of GDP

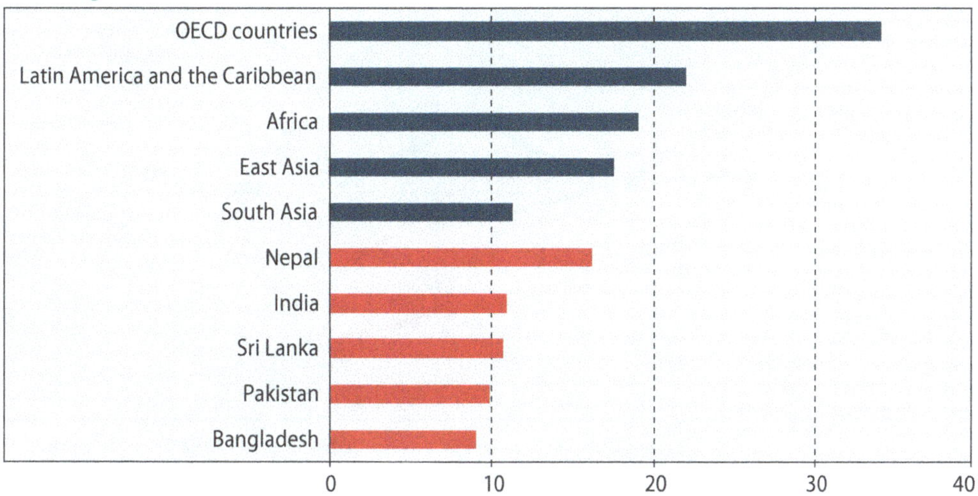

Source: UN/DESA, based on data from IMF Government Finance Statistics and OECD.

Note: Figures for Nepal, Pakistan and Sri Lanka are for FY2014; and figures for Bangladesh and India are for FY2013.

Western Asia: subdued growth and continuing macroeconomic adjustments

The economic outlook for Western Asia remains weak and turbulent amid macroeconomic adjustments in oil-dependent economies, ongoing conflicts and long-lasting geopolitical concerns. Regional GDP growth declined from 2.7 per cent in 2015 to an estimated 2.1 per cent in 2016, mainly due to deteriorating economic conditions in the countries of the Cooperation Council for the Arab States of the Gulf (GCC). In these economies, lower oil prices have seriously affected investment and government budgets, prompting Governments to undertake major reforms towards fiscal consolidation. While non-oil exporting economies exhibited a more heterogeneous outlook, military conflicts and geopolitical tensions continue to curb investment and restrain economic activity (box IV.3). Going forward, regional GDP growth is expected to remain subdued in 2017, but is likely to improve more visibly in 2018 as international oil prices and domestic demand recover. Average economic growth in the region is expected to reach 2.5 per cent in 2017 and 3.0 per cent in 2018. GCC countries have been experiencing a noticeable growth slowdown, with average GDP growth declining from 3.2 per cent in 2015 to 2.0 per cent in 2016 (figure IV.15).

The weakening of economic activity was especially pronounced in Oman, Saudi Arabia and the United Arab Emirates. Saudi Arabia is estimated to have grown by a meagre 1.1 per cent in 2016 — its slowest growth rate since the global financial crisis — as economic activity was dragged down by fiscal austerity, tumbling investment and a severe contraction in non-oil sectors. In 2017, investment and overall economic activity in the GCC countries are expected to remain largely subdued, amid slower growth in bank lending, increasing dependence of Governments on debt financing and rising interest rates in line with the Fed's tightening path. Alongside fiscal consolidation, these challenging conditions are likely to constrain and delay the recovery. As a result, GDP growth in GCC countries is projected to grow at a modest pace of 2.2 per cent and 2.8 per cent in 2017 and 2018, respectively.

Figure IV.15
GDP growth for selected countries in Western Asia, 2012–2018

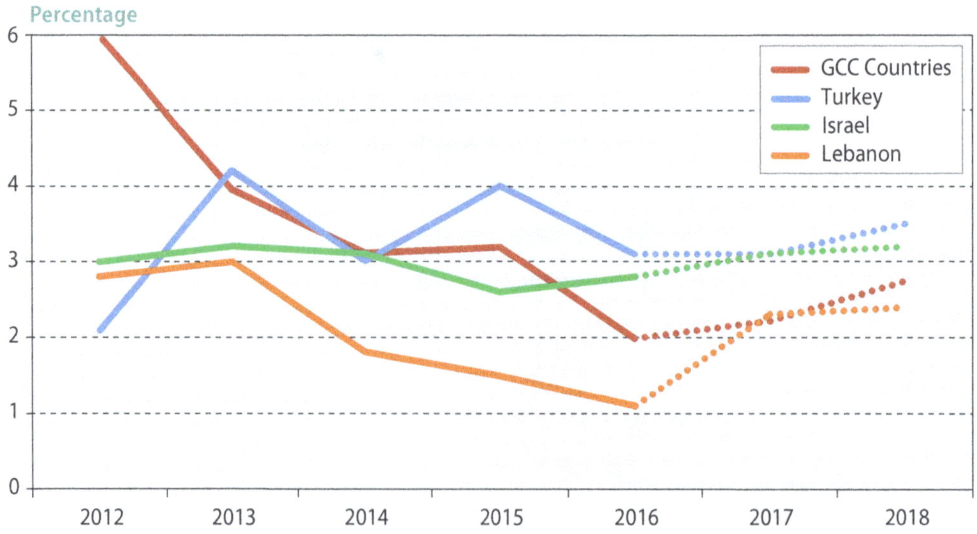

Source: UN/DESA, based on United Nations Statistics Division National Accounts Main Aggregates Database.
Note: Figures for 2016 are partially estimated. Figures for 2017 and 2018 are forecast.

Among the more diversified economies, Turkey is projected to continue growing at a moderate pace, expanding by 3.1 per cent in 2017 and 3.5 per cent in 2018, supported by resilient domestic demand. Nevertheless, the Turkish economy faces considerable headwinds arising from pressures on fiscal and monetary policy stances, as well as security and political concerns. Likewise, Israel's economy is expected to continue on a moderate growth trend, with GDP expanding above 3.0 per cent per annum in the outlook period, underpinned by relatively robust domestic demand.

Conflicts and geopolitical concerns continue to restrain economic activity in several countries

Despite recent improvements in the terms of trade, weak economic conditions have prevailed in Jordan and Lebanon as the impact of the Syrian crisis became more widespread. In countries experiencing military conflicts such as Iraq, the Syrian Arab Republic and Yemen, the economy is in a perilous state. The economies of the Syrian Arab Republic and Yemen are estimated to have contracted further in 2016, due to the intensification of armed conflicts and severe foreign exchange constraints.

Meanwhile, Iraq is expected to continue experiencing positive growth, but this will be entirely driven by the expansion of oil production. So far, Iraq has shown little progress on the appropriate use of oil rents to promote non-oil productive sectors and the diversification of its economic structure.

High youth unemployment remains a key labour market challenge

Labour markets have deteriorated in both the GCC countries and the more diversified economies of the region. Unemployment rates have risen, while job creation has been hampered by the growth slowdown, particularly in the GCC countries. Consequently, several countries are implementing labour market reforms to adjust to the more challenging economic conditions. Some labour market reforms in Bahrain, Oman, and Saudi Arabia have been mainly aimed at prioritizing national workers. These measures are likely to affect the dominance of expatriate workers in the service sector. In Saudi Arabia, a slight decline in youth unemployment of national workers has recently been observed. Kuwait, Qatar and the United Arab Emirates have undertaken reforms to increase labour market flexibility, including measures to ease the mobility of foreign workers.

In addition, non-economic factors continue to hamper labour markets across the region. Conflicts have caused large-scale unemployment in Iraq, the Syrian Arab Republic and Yemen, with some negative spillover effects to the labour markets of Jordan, Lebanon and Turkey. Overall, the labour market situation in the region is not expected to improve significantly in the near term; structural unemployment is expected to remain high, particularly among the youth, amid a widespread lack of decent work.

Relatively high inflation constrains Turkey's monetary policy space

The inflation outlook remains tame in most economies, given subdued domestic demand and the relatively low level of commodity prices. In the GCC countries, inflation is expected to remain low and stable, below 4.0 per cent, following the trend of previous years. In contrast, inflation in Turkey has remained relatively high, well above the official target of 5.0 per cent, as the lira continued to depreciate, offsetting the effect of lower commodity prices. In the outlook period, inflation in Turkey is expected to remain relatively high, limiting space for monetary policy to support growth. Inflationary pressures in the Syrian Arab Republic and Yemen will also remain elevated, due to the significant shortages of goods, the depreciation of domestic currencies and the monetization of fiscal budgets.

Monetary policy is gradually tightening in GCC countries

A gradual tightening of monetary policy stances has been observed across the region. This trend is expected to continue following the expected increase in the Fed funds rate. Furthermore, liquidity conditions have deteriorated in most GCC countries throughout 2016, and borrowing costs have risen visibly. In August, the interbank interest rate in Saudi Arabia reached the highest level since the financial crisis. Credit growth has also decelerat-

Box IV.3

The impact of unrest and conflict in the Arab region

The collective political changes and movements that began across the Arab region in 2011 have had significant economic, social and institutional impacts over the course of the past five years. Furthermore, the region is still undergoing strong political turbulence, replete with uncertainty, insecurity and, in some cases, conflict. Many of these conflicts, in the Syrian Arab Republic and also in Yemen, have witnessed an increasing intensity in terms of violence, deaths, forced migration and displacement and the destruction of economic capital, with significant spillover effects on neighbours across the region. Economic literature has demonstrated the long-term economic impact of conflict. For instance, Gates and others (2010) note that conflict can not only knock a country off its growth path, but also prevent the country from returning to its previous growth trajectory long after the conflict ends. Similarly, Collier and others (2003) emphasize that conflicts reduce both the rate of growth and the level of GDP.

In order to examine the lasting economic impact of conflict on the countries of the Arab region, the Economic and Social Commission for Western Asia (ESCWA, 2016) compares pre-crisis projections made in 2010 by the IMF and national Governments for a number of macroeconomic variables — namely GDP and fiscal balance — with observations as of end-2015 (figure IV.3.1 and figure IV.3.2). Countries are classified in two groups: those engaged in ongoing conflict since 2011 (Libya, the Syrian Arab Republic and Yemen) and countries affected by spillover effects of conflicts (Egypt, Jordan, Lebanon and Tunisia). Together these two groups constitute "countries in and affected by conflicts".

Figure IV.3.1

Level of GDP: countries in and affected by conflicts, 2010–2015

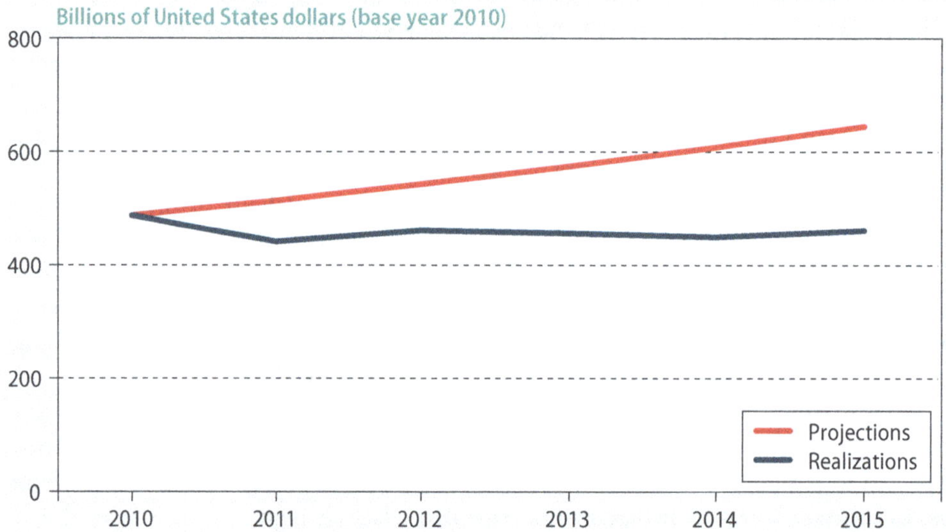

Source: ESCWA, based on IMF Article IV consultations (2008-2014).

Note: Countries engaged in conflict since 2011: Libya, the Syrian Arab Republic and Yemen; countries affected by conflicts: Egypt, Jordan, Lebanon and Tunisia.

The aggregate results from this analysis indicate that as compared with pre-crisis projections, countries in and affected by conflict have lost a cumulative $613.8 billion in foregone GDP since 2010, representing 6 per cent of the Arab region's GDP. More specifically, Libya and the Syrian Arab Republic witnessed the greatest cumulative losses, at $227 billion and $169 billion, respectively. The main channels are the lower production activities and trade, weak investment as a result of large uncertainties plaguing the political and business environments, the flight of human capital and the significant destruction of physical capital. At the country level, some specific challenges are, for instance, the stoppage of energy exports and the damage to the agricultural sector in Yemen; the capital flight and subsequent pressure

(continued)

Box IV.3 (*continued*)

Figure IV.3.2
Fiscal balance: countries in and affected by conflicts, 2011–2015

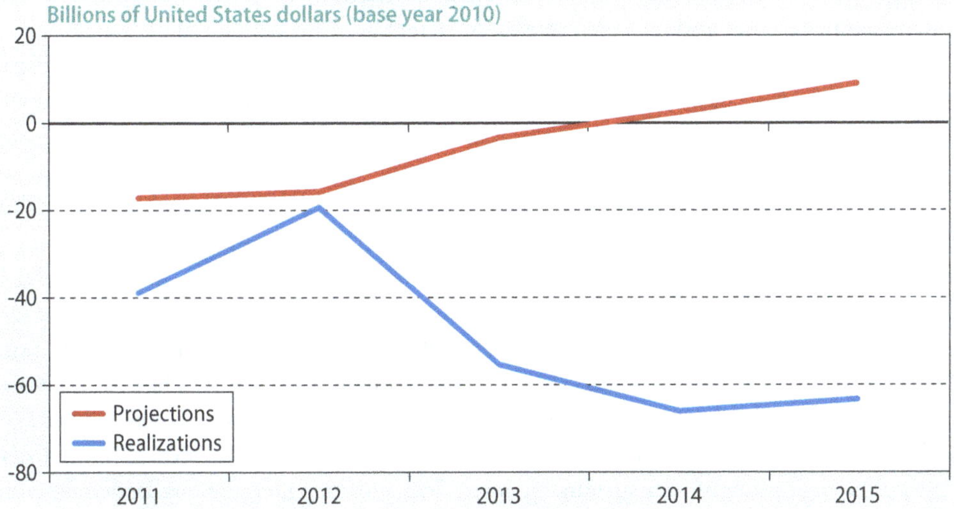

Source: ESCWA, based on IMF Article IV consultations (2008-2014).
Note: Countries engaged in conflict since 2011: Libya, the Syrian Arab Republic and Yemen; countries affected by conflicts: Egypt, Jordan, Lebanon and Tunisia.

on the balance-of-payments in Egypt; falling oil revenues, weaker domestic demand and exodus of foreign labour in Libya; and insufficient financial resources to host refugees in Jordan and Lebanon.

The fiscal accounts have also been severely affected. In particular, the cumulative fiscal deficit for countries in and affected by conflicts is $218 billion larger than was previously projected. The fiscal balance had been projected to achieve a 1.1 per cent surplus in terms of nominal GDP in 2015, but actually registered a deficit of 11.7 per cent of GDP. Budget difficulties arise for a number of reasons, including the need for higher spending to mitigate the effects of conflicts on security and to provide services for vulnerable and displaced populations. Tax revenues declined due to uncertainties, and a poor business climate also came into play.

The negative economic impact has been compounded by a large-scale displacement of the population in Iraq, Libya, the Syrian Arab Republic and Yemen. Matching skills and production facilities became immensely difficult due to the dislocation of talented workers and the destruction of factories and infrastructure. In short, the labour market ceased functioning, negatively impacting the level and growth of productivity of economic sectors and activities that have managed to survive. Thus, in addition to the humanitarian sufferings of individual refugees and the internally displaced population, the productive sector has severely suffered from labour market disruptions.

Besides these direct impacts, conflicts have halted progress across the Arab world in pursuing regional integration, such as implementing the Greater Arab Free Trade Agreement, breaking ground and completing regional infrastructure for transport, water, electricity, oil and gas through various multilateral and bilateral initiatives within the region. However, regional integration does represent a policy option for strengthening cross-country ties and helping to prevent future conflicts and economic disruptions. Regional trade is in fact increasingly important for countries in conflict such as the Syrian Arab Republic, where informal cross-border trade with its immediate neighbours fills in for falling trade with other partners.

Plans for post-conflict reconstruction have been formulated, such as the National Agenda for the Future of the Syrian Arab Republic. This plan encompasses $183.5 billion in public investments, which is equal to the sum of cumulative capital loss during the conflict and the investments intended under the pre-conflict national growth plan. A key aspect of the plan is to boost economic growth through multiplier effects and to crowd-in large private investments. Given the destruction and disruptions experienced across the region, bridging the enormous financing gap for reconstruction will certainly require a combination of different sources: Official Development Assistance (ODA) from donors and external partners, private and public financial resources and surpluses from the Arab region.

Author: John Robert Sloan (UN/ESCWA)

ed, particularly in Oman, Saudi Arabia and the United Arab Emirates. As GCC economies are projected to follow the Fed's interest rate decisions, given their pegs to the United States dollar, monetary authorities may introduce different measures to boost liquidity, including changes in reserve requirements. Most of these economies continue to benefit from large international reserves and, despite increasing current account deficits, there are no signs of severe external constraints. Saudi Arabia's foreign reserves stood in the first half of 2016 at the equivalent of 29 months of imports of goods and services. Countries with lower reserve levels, such as the United Arab Emirates, have already seen improvements in their current accounts.

Despite higher fiscal deficits, public debt in GCC countries remains sustainable

Against a backdrop of lower oil prices, the GCC countries are currently undertaking fiscal consolidation. Several policy measures have been introduced in order to address the rising deficits, including spending and subsidy cuts, tax increases and new issuances of debt. Notably, capital expenditures have been less affected, illustrating the priority given to large infrastructure projects. With respect to new debt issuance, Saudi Arabia recently raised $17.5 billion, the largest-ever bond sale made by an emerging economy. The introduction of a regional value-added tax and privatization plans in some economies are also on the agenda. Despite these efforts, fiscal deficits have widened in most GCC countries (figure IV.16), but public debt remains at a sustainable level. Policymakers face the challenge of striking a balance between the use of sovereign wealth funds, the level and composition of further expenditure cuts and the introduction of direct and indirect taxes to increase non-oil fiscal revenues. In Turkey, fiscal policy is expected to remain tight, in order to maintain public debt levels and contain renewed pressures on the current account. The fiscal situation in Iraq, the Syrian Arab Republic and Yemen has further worsened owing to fragile revenues, increasing expenditures and over-reliance on debt financing.

Progress towards the SDGs is severely affected by armed conflicts

There are a number of risks to the regional outlook. The expansion of armed conflicts and the escalation of geopolitical tensions will worsen the already severe impact on the short and medium-term economic and development prospects, hindering progress towards the Sustainable Development Goals (SDGs). A potential sharp decline in oil prices will serious-

Figure IV.16

Fiscal deficits in GCC countries, 2013–2016

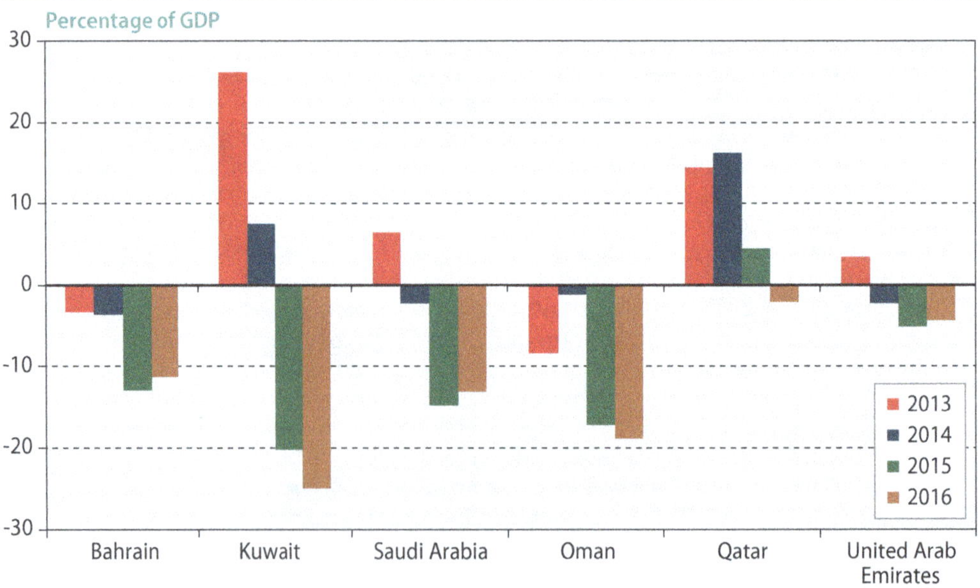

Source: UN/DESA and UN/ESCWA.
Note: Figures for 2016 are estimates.

ly affect the economic situation in the oil-exporting economies. The regional outlook will also be affected by external developments. For instance, higher interest rates in the United States might lead to tighter global credit conditions, making it even more difficult to revive investment demand in the GCC countries.

Latin America and the Caribbean: a return to positive growth is projected for 2017

After contracting for two consecutive years, the economy of Latin America and the Caribbean is expected to return to positive growth in 2017. The region's aggregate GDP is projected to increase by 1.3 per cent in 2017 and by 2.1 per cent in 2018, following an estimated decline of 1.0 per cent in 2016. While the region continues to face significant internal and external headwinds, economic growth is forecast to gradually pick up in most countries. South America is expected to see a modest cyclical recovery from the severe downturn of 2015 and 2016, with Argentina and Brazil, the subregion's two largest economies, set to emerge from recession. Several factors are likely to support this recovery, including a strengthening of external demand, an increase in international commodity prices, a decline in political uncertainty, and some monetary easing amid lower inflation. Average growth in South America will, however, remain fairly weak, weighed down by a rise in unemployment and ongoing fiscal consolidation (box IV.4).

The economic situation and prospects in Mexico and Central America and the Caribbean are generally more favourable as most countries depend less on commodity exports. However, growth projections for both subregions have been downgraded from earlier forecasts in the face of weaker-than-expected activity in the United States, persistent structural constraints (including high debt and unemployment, low productivity growth, and weak institutional capacity) and limited macroeconomic policy space.

The region continues to face significant external risks

The outlook for Latin America and the Caribbean is subject to significant downside risks. These include a sharper-than-expected deceleration in China, the adoption of protectionist measures by the new Administration in the United States and renewed financial market turbulences. The latter could, for example, be triggered by a faster-than-expected pace of interest rate hikes in the United States. A rebound in commodity prices and unexpectedly strong demand from developed economies, in particular the United States, present upside risks for many countries.

Subdued medium-term outlook could hamper progress towards the SDGs

The subdued medium-term outlook for Latin America and the Caribbean poses a threat to the social achievements of the past decade and could significantly complicate the region's path towards the realization of the SDGs. These challenges underscore the importance of reorienting macroeconomic and other policies, with a view to promote investment in physical and human capital and strengthen the innovative capacities across the region.

Several South American economies experienced contractions in 2016

In the face of ongoing global uncertainty and a slump in domestic demand, South America's GDP contracted for a second consecutive year in 2016. After declining by 1.9 per cent in 2015, the subregion's output is estimated to have fallen by 2.3 per cent in 2016 amid recessions in Argentina, Brazil, Ecuador and the Bolivarian Republic of Venezuela, and slow growth in Chile and Colombia. Brazil has witnessed the deepest recession on record during the past two years. The cumulative decline in Brazil's economic output since late 2014 exceeds 8 per cent as severe macroeconomic imbalances and a political crisis led to a sharp contraction of domestic demand. The Venezuelan economy faces an even deeper crisis amid large financing needs, shortages of basic goods, and spiralling inflation. GDP is estimated to have fallen by about 8 per cent in 2016, bringing the cumulative output contraction since 2013 to almost 20 per cent. Among the few bright spots in the sub-

Box IV.4

Fiscal challenges in Latin America and the Caribbean

Fiscal positions in Latin America and the Caribbean diverged in 2015 and 2016. In the South American countries, fiscal deficits increased as reductions in public expenditures were more than offset by declines in revenues amid faltering economic growth and plummeting commodity-related revenues. In contrast, in Central America and parts of the Caribbean, including the Dominican Republic, fiscal deficits declined moderately from 2014 to 2016 owing to reduced government outlays and slightly higher revenues. Public debt levels have generally been on the rise, especially in South American countries.

A key concern arising from fiscal consolidation measures that were introduced in 2015 and 2016 has been their impact on public investment. Capital expenditures at the central government level were down by 0.5 percentage points of GDP in 2015 from a year ago, with some countries registering large reductions (figure IV.4.1). The marked declines in the Plurinational State of Bolivia and Ecuador were largely the result of significantly lower hydrocarbon-related revenues, which in previous years had boosted public investment levels to historic levels. Preliminary data for 2016 suggests that lower commodity-related revenues have also weighed on public investment in several other countries, including Colombia and Peru.

Figures IV.4.1

Change in central government capital expenditures in Latin America and the Caribbean, 2014–2015 (*year-on-year*)

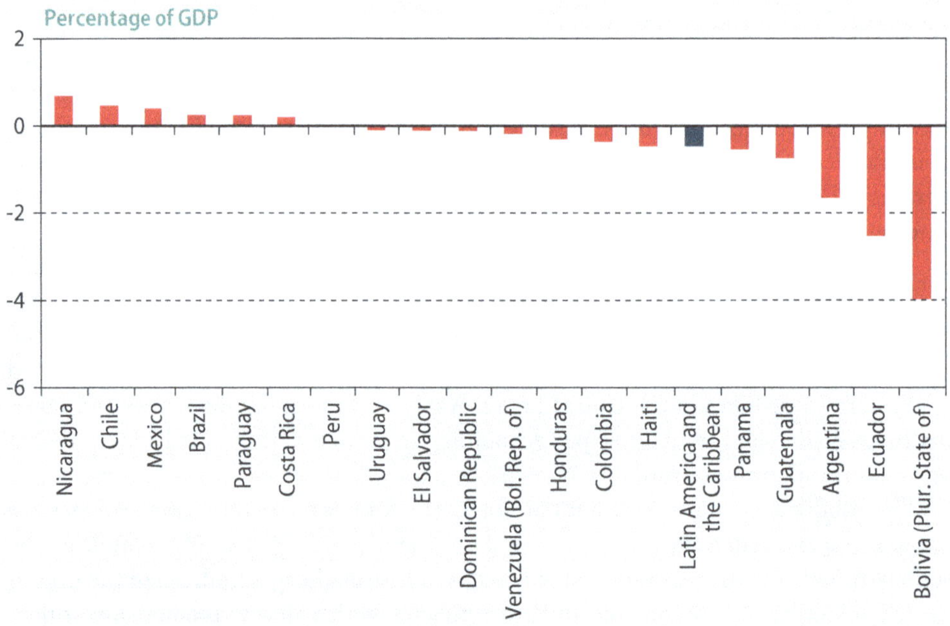

Source: UN/ECLAC, based on official national data.

Declining public investment is of particular concern given its already modest level in Latin America and the Caribbean, relative to GDP (figure IV.4.2). This is especially true for the region's largest economies, where capital expenditures are generally well below the regional average. Despite modest gains in 2015, Brazil and Mexico continued to rank among the region's countries with the lowest levels of public capital expenditures as a proportion of GDP. Persistently low levels of public investment, particularly in much-needed infrastructure and human capital development poses a risk to the medium-term and long-term potential growth of the Latin American economies. Austerity measures that involve deep capital expenditure cuts therefore threaten to undermine future fiscal sustainability by creating a vicious cycle: investment cuts engender lower growth, which in turn leads to greater reduction in public expenditures (ECLAC, 2016b).

In the context of a new "normal" of relatively slow economic growth, breaking the aforementioned vicious cycle and raising public investment to levels that are more in line with the commitments

(*continued*)

Figure IV.4.2

Central government capital expenditures in Latin America and the Caribbean, 2014–2015

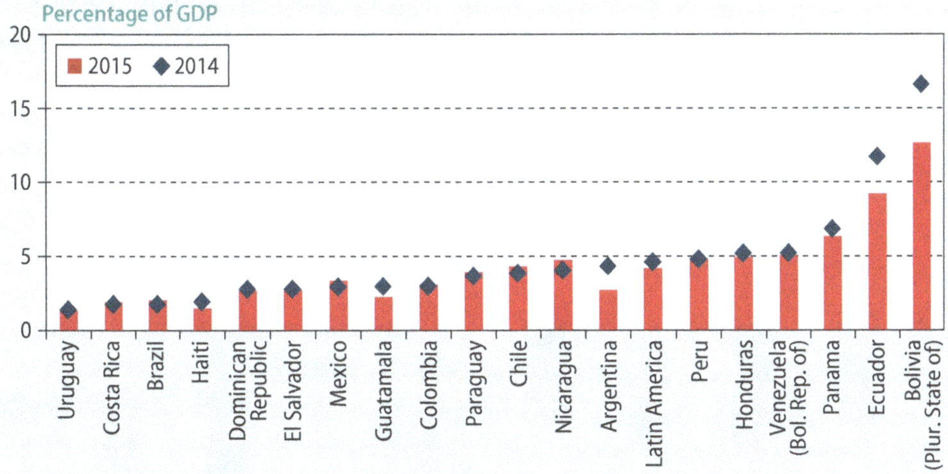

Box IV.4 *(continued)*

Source: ECLAC (2016a).

embodied in the 2030 Agenda for Sustainable Development will require Latin America and the Caribbean countries to boost their tax revenues. Over the past decade, the region has made significant progress in increasing tax revenues, although in several countries, overall tax revenues remain below 20 per cent of GDP. Direct taxation remains very low when compared with other countries at a similar level of development. This is due to a number of factors, including structural deficiencies, such as low marginal tax rates and tax bases that have been hollowed out by exceptionally generous tax breaks, and harmful tax competition, among others. In addition, elevated tax evasion plays a pernicious role.

While tax evasion is not unique to Latin America and the Caribbean, it is particularly rampant in the region's largely informal economies and deprives national Governments of significant revenues that could be used to finance public investment and services. Latin American and the Caribbean countries on average collect only about 50 per cent of the revenues that their personal and corporate income tax systems should theoretically generate (ECLAC, 2016b). Evasion of the personal income tax ranges from 33 per cent in Peru to 70 per cent in Guatemala. Likewise, corporate tax evasion is estimated to span a range from 27 per cent in Brazil to over 60 per cent in Costa Rica, Ecuador and Guatemala. In 2015, it is estimated that the revenues foregone due to the evasion of these two taxes accounted for $220 billion, or 4.3 per cent of the region's GDP.

In this context, there has been growing understanding in recent years of the role that multinational enterprises and high net-worth individuals play in eroding the region's tax revenues. ECLAC (2016a) estimated that between 2004 and 2013, trade price manipulation resulted in a gross outflow of capital on the order of $765 billion. These illicit financial flows were found to be highly concentrated in products associated with global value chains, highlighting the potentially significant role of transfer pricing between associated enterprises in artificially reducing taxable income. Latin America and the Caribbean high net-worth individuals have also made extensive use of offshore finance to reduce their tax payments to their governments.

While estimates of the share of the region's wealth held abroad differ, Chile's recent partial tax amnesty for undeclared wealth abroad is an indication that this value is substantial. By the end of 2015, 7,832 declarations had been filed with the country's tax authority, registering approximately $20 billion in assets abroad and resulting in a tax payment of $1.5 billion.

Taken together, the evasion of personal and corporate income taxes as well as value-added taxes, have cost the region's Governments an estimated $340 billion in potential revenues in 2015 (ECLAC, 2016a). To put that number into context, total central government capital expenditures — including public investment in fixed capital and capital transfers — in Latin America and the Caribbean amounted to $154 billion in the same year. Closing the revenue gaps associated with tax evasion and avoidance would provide an important sustainable revenue stream for financing investments associated with the 2030 Agenda for Sustainable Development. While in past decades, tax reforms have favoured indirect taxes, such as value-added and commodity taxes, making progress towards the Sustainable Development Goals demands a strengthening of direct taxes, especially those on income and wealth.

Author: Economic Development Division of UN/ECLAC

region are the Plurinational State of Bolivia and Peru, which defied the regional downturn, largely owing to strong private and government consumption.

The slump in investment in South America continued in 2016

A closer examination of the expenditure components across South America reveals broad-based weakness, underscoring the challenges for the subregion going forward (figure IV.17). In most countries, fixed capital formation fell sharply in both 2015 and 2016 (figure IV.18), mainly due to a downturn in investment in the extractive industries and lower

Figure IV.17
Contributions to real GDP growth in Latin America and the Caribbean subregions, 2015–2017

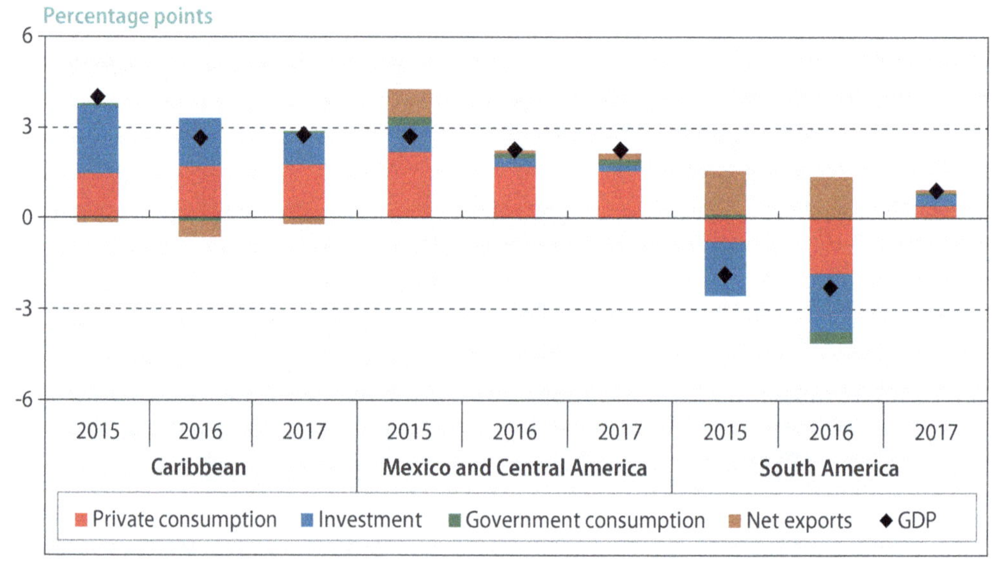

Source: UN/DESA, based on United Nations Statistics Division National Accounts Main Aggregates Database.
Note: Inventories and residual components are excluded, so individual components do not sum up to GDP growth. Figures for 2015 and 2016 are partially estimated. Figures for 2017 are forecast.

Figure IV.18
Changes in gross fixed capital formation in Latin America, 2012Q1–2016Q1 (*year-on-year*)

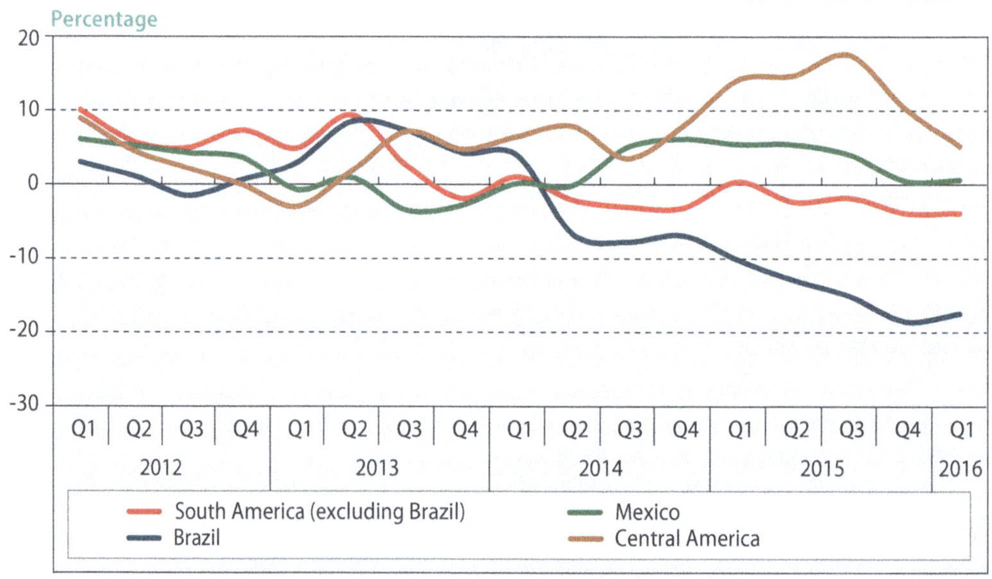

Source: UN/ECLAC, based on official figures.

Figure IV.19
General government primary balance in selected Latin American economies, 2011–2016

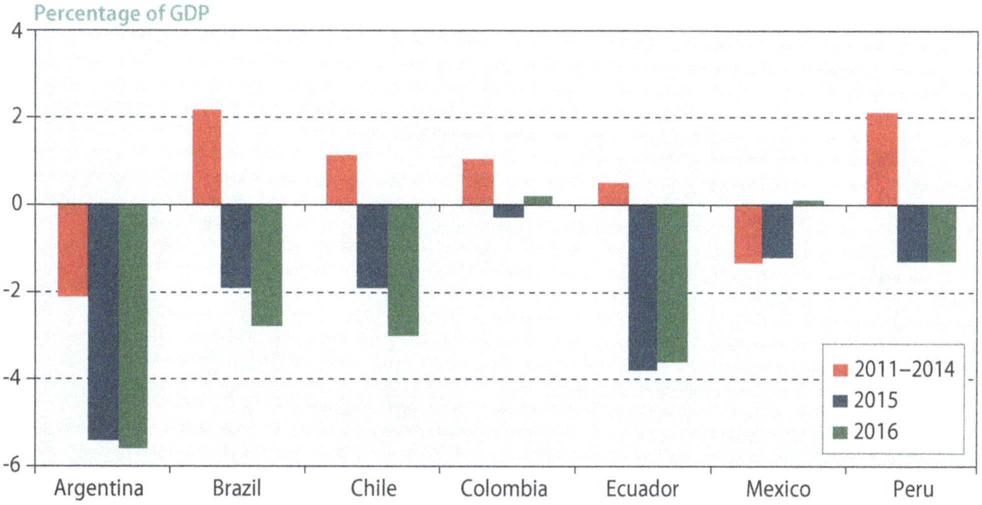

Source: UN/DESA, based on data from IMF Fiscal Monitor October 2016.

public investment. Tight monetary policies, elevated corporate debt levels as well as weak business and consumer sentiments have also weighed on investment activity in the region.

Regional unemployment has risen notably amid deterioration in South America's labour markets

In addition, South America's labour markets, which had shown some resilience in the early stages of the economic downturn, deteriorated considerably in 2016. Brazil's unemployment rate reached 11.8 per cent in the third quarter of 2016, up from 6.5 per cent in late 2014. Argentina, Chile, Colombia and Ecuador also registered increases in unemployment. Although unemployment declined in Mexico and most Central American and Caribbean countries, the average urban unemployment rate in the region rose sharply from 7.6 per cent in the first half of 2015 to 9.2 per cent in the first half of 2016. In the face of rising unemployment, elevated inflation and restrictive credit conditions, household consumption in South America weakened notably. Brazil suffered a particularly severe contraction in private consumption of about 5 per cent in 2016.

Fiscal tightening has compounded the slump in private demand

Since the commodity super cycle has come to an end, government budgets across Latin America have been under significant pressure, with primary deficits rising rapidly (figure IV.19). To offset declining revenues, several Governments, particularly in South America, implemented fiscal tightening measures in 2016, compounding the slump in private demand (figure IV.17).

Given the large decline in domestic demand — both private and public —, only a positive contribution from net trade prevented an even sharper downturn. Supported by more competitive national currencies, following large depreciations in 2013-15 (figure IV.20), exports showed some modest growth over the past year, whereas imports declined — in some cases steeply. In Brazil, for example, real exports of goods and services grew by an estimated 6 per cent in 2016, while real imports fell by about 10 per cent.

South America is expected to see a mild recovery

Looking ahead, South America is projected to see a mild — largely cyclical — recovery in 2017 and 2018. While economic activity has generally remained weak in 2016, some positive signs — both on the domestic and the external front — have started to emerge. In several countries, including Brazil and Colombia, consumer and business confidence have shown improvements. At the same time, net capital inflows and asset prices, including

Figure IV.20
Real effective exchange rates of selected economies in Latin America, January 2012–September 2016

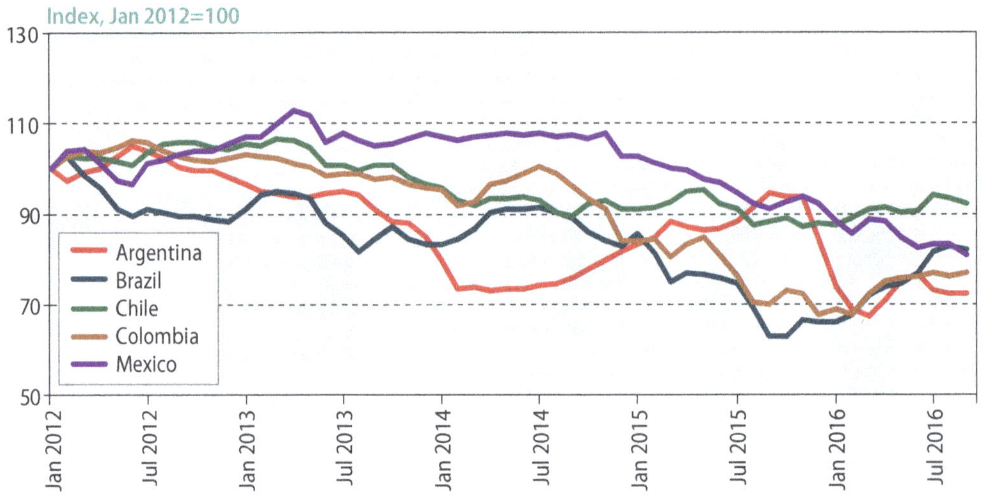

Source: UN/DESA, based on data from the Bank for International Settlements.
Note: A reduction in the index value reflects a real effective depreciation of the currency.

domestic currencies, have recovered, following the slump in 2015. These positive trends reflect firmer commodity prices and a search for yield among international investors. At the same time, inflation has started to moderate in almost all South American countries owing to stronger domestic currencies, a diminishing impact of El Niño and the lack of demand pressures. With inflationary pressures in South America declining, average consumer price inflation in Latin America and the Caribbean is projected to slow from 9.2 per cent in 2016 to 6.1 per cent in 2017 (excluding the Bolivarian Republic of Venezuela).

Some monetary easing in South America is expected

Given lower inflationary pressures and more stable financial market conditions, the monetary tightening cycle in South America appears to be mostly over and some easing is projected for 2017 and 2018. In Argentina, the benchmark policy rate has already been lowered from 38 per cent in April 2016 to 26.75 per cent in early November. Brazil's central bank cut its main policy rate in October for the first time in four years to 14 per cent. In both countries, further easing is expected over the outlook period. A key question for South America, and in particular the recession-hit economies of Argentina and Brazil, is whether the positive trends on the monetary side (i.e. lower inflation and lower interest rates) can offset the negative impact on domestic demand associated with fiscal consolidation and rising unemployment. In most South American countries, fiscal policy will remain contractionary during the forecast period, but the adjustment is expected to be gradual in order to avoid strong downward pressure on aggregate demand. In some cases, notably Argentina and Brazil, a more credible and stringent fiscal policy, including forward guidance, could help support business confidence and investment.

Overall, the baseline forecast predicts a return to positive growth in Argentina and Brazil in 2017. The recovery is, however, expected to be relatively shallow, especially in Brazil, which continues to face macroeconomic imbalances (including high stocks of public and private debt) and major policy challenges such as reforming the pension system. The Bolivarian Republic of Venezuela is projected to remain in recession until at least 2017. Although growth in most other economies, including Chile and Colombia, is expected to gradually strengthen on the back of a recovery in domestic demand, the medium-term outlook remains clouded by long-standing structural weaknesses, including a strong dependence on commodities and low productivity growth.

Mexico's growth is projected to remain weak amid significant uncertainty

Average growth in Mexico and Central America is projected to remain subdued in the forecast period. The subregion's GDP is projected to grow by 2.3 per cent in 2017 and 2.2 per cent in 2018, following estimated growth of 2.3 per cent in 2016. The slow growth trajectory primarily reflects a weak performance of the Mexican economy. Amid low oil prices, sluggish industrial production in the United States and tight monetary and fiscal policy, Mexico's GDP is estimated to have grown by only 2 per cent in 2016. The outcome of the elections in the United States has further complicated the short to medium-term outlook for Mexico's economy, raising the uncertainty around the baseline forecasts. Since nearly 80 per cent of Mexico's exports are destined for the United States, any protectionist trade measures by the new Administration in the United States would have a severe impact on growth. Remittance inflows could also take a hit if the new Administration were to introduce a tax on outward remittance flows.

Outcome of election in the United States has reinforced downward pressure on the peso

Increasing concerns over the outlook for Mexico's economy reinforced downward pressure on the peso, causing a sharp decline in the aftermath of the election in the United States. The peso's weakness could further drive up inflation, which has increased steadily since mid-2016, exceeding the central inflation target level of 3 per cent in October. The combination of a weaker peso, rising inflation and a subdued growth outlook poses a major challenge for Mexico's central bank. After raising interest rates considerably over the past year, further tightening is expected for 2017. Given a high degree of macroeconomic uncertainty and tight fiscal and monetary policy, investment growth is projected to further slow during the outlook period. As a result, GDP growth in Mexico is forecast to remain subdued at about 2 per cent in 2017 and 2018 amid a still negative output gap.

Prospects vary widely across Central American and Caribbean economies

In Central America and the Caribbean, the economic situation and prospects vary widely across countries. Strong domestic demand continues to boost economic activity in Costa Rica, the Dominican Republic, Nicaragua and Panama. To varying degrees, these countries are benefiting from buoyant public investment (particularly in infrastructure), robust private consumption (supported by remittance inflows), and dynamic tourism industries. During the forecast period, they will remain among the region's fastest-growing countries, with annual growth projected to exceed 4 per cent.

In contrast, Cuba, Haiti and Jamaica recorded weak growth in 2016. Cuba's economy has suffered from reduced support from the Bolivarian Republic of Venezuela and low prices for major export goods, including petroleum and nickel. Economic activity in Haiti and Jamaica was adversely affected by drought conditions as well as structural obstacles, including institutional weaknesses, tight fiscal budgets and high unemployment and underemployment. Suriname and Trinidad and Tobago experienced significant contractions of GDP in 2016 as both countries suffered the consequences of the sharp drop in energy prices. All of these countries are projected to see a mild pickup in growth during the forecast period. Nevertheless, deep-rooted structural impediments and high vulnerability to external developments will continue to cloud their growth prospects.

Statistical annex

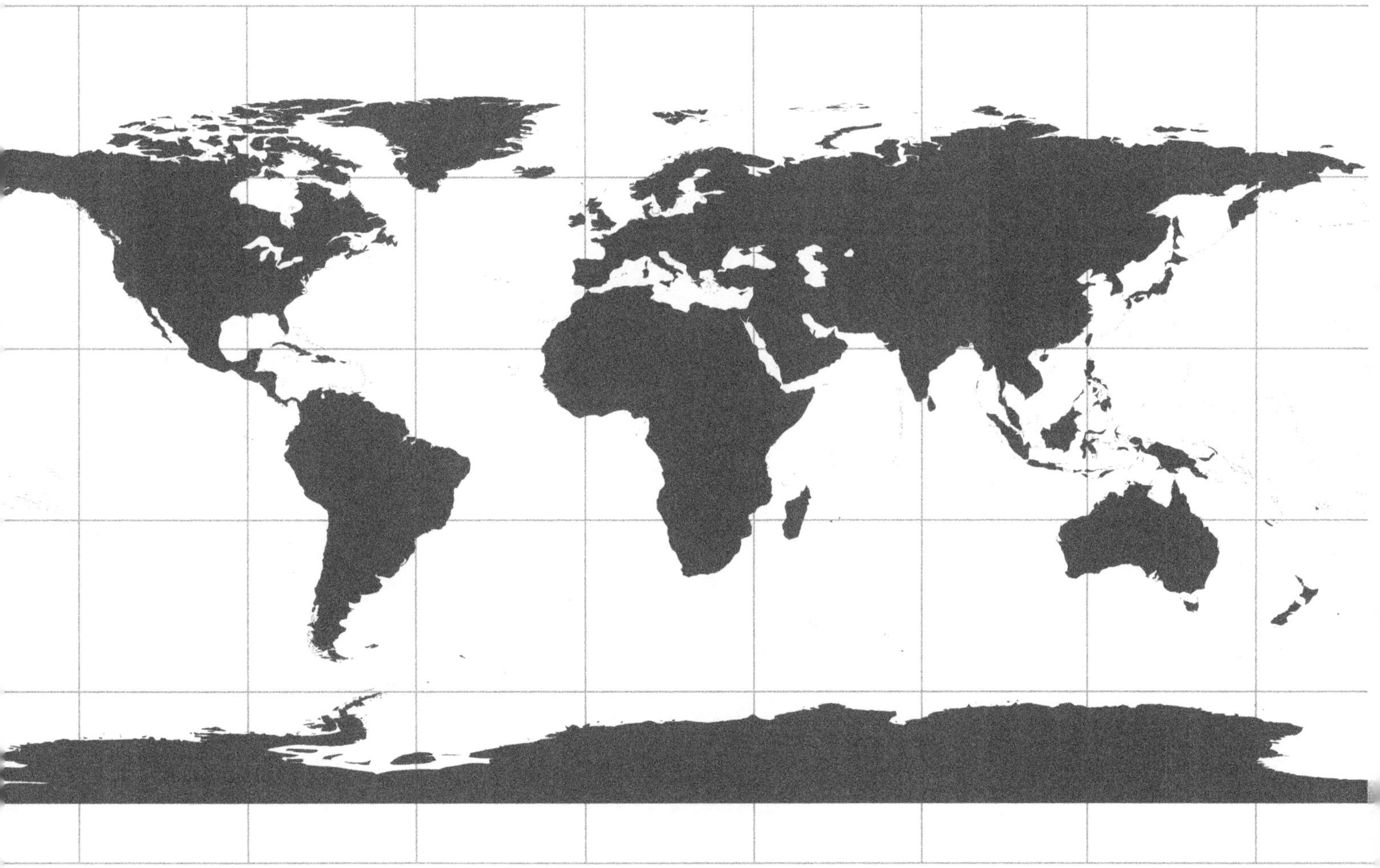

Country classifications

Data sources, country classifications and aggregation methodology

The statistical annex contains a set of data that the *World Economic Situation and Prospects* (*WESP*) employs to delineate trends in various dimensions of the world economy.

Data sources

The annex was prepared by the Development Policy and Analysis Division (DPAD) of the Department of Economic and Social Affairs of the United Nations Secretariat (UN/DESA). It is based on information obtained from the Statistics Division and the Population Division of UN/DESA, as well as from the five United Nations regional commissions, the United Nations Conference on Trade and Development (UNCTAD), the United Nations World Tourism Organisation (UNWTO), the International Monetary Fund (IMF), the World Bank, the Organisation for Economic Co-operation and Development (OECD), and national and private sources. Estimates for the most recent years were made by DPAD in consultation with the regional commissions, UNCTAD, UNWTO and participants in Project LINK, an international collaborative research group for econometric modelling coordinated jointly by DPAD and the University of Toronto. Forecasts for 2017 and 2018 are primarily based on the World Economic Forecasting Model of DPAD, with support from Project LINK.

Data presented in *WESP* may differ from those published by other organizations for a series of reasons, including differences in timing, sample composition and aggregation methods. Historical data may differ from those in previous editions of *WESP* because of updating and changes in the availability of data for individual countries.

Country classifications

For analytical purposes, *WESP* classifies all countries of the world into one of three broad categories: developed economies, economies in transition and developing economies. The composition of these groupings, specified in tables A, B and C, is intended to reflect basic economic country conditions. Several countries (in particular the economies in transition) have characteristics that could place them in more than one category; however, for purposes of analysis, the groupings have been made mutually exclusive. Within each broad category, some subgroups are defined based either on geographical location or on ad hoc criteria, such as the subgroup of "major developed economies", which is based on the membership of the Group of Seven. Geographical regions for developing economies are as follows: Africa, East Asia, South Asia, Western Asia, and Latin America and the Caribbean.[1]

1 Names and composition of geographical areas follow those specified in the statistical paper entitled "Standard country or area codes for statistical use" (ST/ESA/STAT/SER.M/49/Rev. 4).

In parts of the analysis, a distinction is made between fuel exporters and fuel importers from among the economies in transition and the developing countries. An economy is classified as a fuel exporter if the share of fuel exports in its total merchandise exports is greater than 20 per cent and the level of fuel exports is at least 20 per cent higher than that of the country's fuel imports (table D). This criterion is drawn from the share of fuel exports in the total value of world merchandise trade. Fuels include coal, oil and natural gas.

For other parts of the analysis, countries have been classified by their level of development as measured by per capita gross national income (GNI). Accordingly, countries have been grouped as high-income, upper middle income, lower middle income and low-income (table E). To maintain compatibility with similar classifications used elsewhere, the threshold levels of GNI per capita are those established by the World Bank. Countries with less than $1,025 GNI per capita are classified as low-income countries, those with between $1,026 and $4,035 as lower middle income countries, those with between $4,036 and $12,475 as upper middle income countries, and those with incomes of more than $12, 475 as high-income countries. GNI per capita in dollar terms is estimated using the World Bank Atlas method,[2] and the classification in table E is based on data for 2015.

The list of the least developed countries (LDCs) is decided upon by the United Nations Economic and Social Council and, ultimately, by the General Assembly, on the basis of recommendations made by the Committee for Development Policy. The basic criteria for inclusion require that certain thresholds be met with regard to per capita GNI, a human assets index and an economic vulnerability index.[3] As at 30 November 2016, there were 48 LDCs (table F).

WESP also makes reference to the group of heavily indebted poor countries (HIPCs), which are considered by the World Bank and IMF as part of their debt-relief initiative (the Enhanced HIPC Initiative).[4] In September 2016, there were 39 HIPCs (see table G).

Aggregation methodology

Aggregate data are either sums or weighted averages of individual country data. Unless otherwise indicated, multi-year averages of growth rates are expressed as compound annual percentage rates of change. The convention followed is to omit the base year in a multi-year growth rate. For example, the 10-year average growth rate for the decade of the 2000s would be identified as the average annual growth rate for the period from 2001 to 2010.

WESP utilizes exchange-rate conversions of national data in order to aggregate output of individual countries into regional and global totals. The growth of output in each group of countries is calculated from the sum of gross domestic product (GDP) of individual countries measured at 2010 prices and exchange rates. Data for GDP in 2010 in national currencies were converted into dollars (with selected adjustments) and extended forwards and backwards in time using changes in real GDP for each country. This method supplies a reasonable set of aggregate growth rates for a period of about 15 years, centred on 2010.

2 See http://data.worldbank.org/about/country-classifications.

3 *Handbook on the Least Developed Country Category: Inclusion, Graduation and Special Support Measures* (United Nations publication, Sales No. E.07.II.A.9). Available from http://www.un.org/esa/analysis/devplan/cdppublications/2008cdphandbook.pdf.

4 IMF, Debt Relief Under the Heavily Indebted Poor Countries (HIPC) Initiative Available from http://www.imf.org/external/np/exr/facts/pdf/hipc.pdf

The exchange-rate based method differs from the one mainly applied by the IMF and the World Bank for their estimates of world and regional economic growth, which is based on purchasing power parity (PPP) weights. Over the past two decades, the growth of world gross product (WGP) on the basis of the exchange-rate based approach has been below that based on PPP weights. This is because developing countries, in the aggregate, have seen significantly higher economic growth than the rest of the world in the 1990s and 2000s and the share in WGP of these countries is larger under PPP measurements than under market exchange rates.

Table A
Developed economies

North America	Europe: European Union	Europe: Other Europe	Major developed economies (G7)
Canada	**EU-15**	Iceland	Canada
United States	Austria[a]	Norway	Japan
	Belgium[a]	Switzerland	France
	Denmark		Germany
	Finland[a]		Italy
	France[a]		United Kingdom
	Germany[a]		United States
	Greece[a]		
	Ireland[a]		
	Italy[a]		
	Luxembourg[a]		
	Netherlands[a]		
	Portugal[a]		
	Spain[a]		
	Sweden		
	United Kingdom		
Developed Asia and Pacific	**EU-13[b]**		
Australia	Bulgaria		
Japan	Croatia		
New Zealand	Cyprus[a]		
	Czech Republic		
	Estonia[a]		
	Hungary		
	Latvia[a]		
	Lithuania[a]		
	Malta[a]		
	Poland		
	Romania		
	Slovakia[a]		
	Slovenia[a]		

a Member of Euro area.
b Used in reference to the 13 countries that joined the EU since 2004.

Table B
Economies in transition

South-Eastern Europe	Commonwealth of Independent States and Georgia[a]	
Albania	Armenia	Republic of Moldova
Bosnia and Herzegovina	Azerbaijan	Russian Federation
Montenegro	Belarus	Tajikistan
Serbia	Georgia[a]	Turkmenistan
The former Yugoslav Republic of Macedonia	Kazakhstan	Ukraine[b]
	Kyrgyzstan	Uzbekistan

a Georgia officially left the Commonwealth of Independent States on 18 August 2009. However, its performance is discussed in the context of this group of countries for reasons of geographic proximity and similarities in economic structure.
b Starting in 2010, data for the Ukraine excludes the temporarily occupied territory of the Autonomous Republic of Crimea and Sevastopol.

Table C
Developing economies by region[a]

Africa

North Africa

- Algeria
- Egypt
- Libya
- Mauritania
- Morocco
- Sudan
- Tunisia

Central Africa

- Cameroon
- Central African Republic
- Chad
- Congo
- Equatorial Guinea
- Gabon
- Sao Tome and Prinicipe

East Africa

- Burundi
- Comoros
- Democratic Republic of the Congo
- Djibouti
- Eritrea
- Ethiopia
- Kenya
- Madagascar
- Rwanda
- Somalia
- Uganda
- United Republic of Tanzania

Southern Africa

- Angola
- Botswana
- Lesotho
- Malawi
- Mauritius
- Mozambique
- Namibia
- South Africa
- Swaziland
- Zambia
- Zimbabwe

West Africa

- Benin
- Burkina Faso
- Cabo Verde
- Côte d'Ivoire
- Gambia (Islamic Republic of the)
- Ghana
- Guinea
- Guinea-Bissau
- Liberia
- Mali
- Niger
- Nigeria
- Senegal
- Sierra Leone
- Togo

Asia

East Asia[b]

- Brunei Darussalam
- Cambodia
- China
- Fiji
- Hong Kong SAR[c]
- Indonesia
- Kiribati
- Lao People's Democratic Republic
- Malaysia
- Mongolia
- Myanmar
- Papua New Guinea
- Philippines
- Republic of Korea
- Samoa
- Singapore
- Solomon Islands
- Taiwan Province of China
- Thailand
- Timor-Leste
- Vanuatu
- Viet Nam

South Asia

- Afghanistan
- Bangladesh
- Bhutan
- India
- Iran (Islamic Republic of)
- Maldives
- Nepal
- Pakistan
- Sri Lanka

Western Asia

- Bahrain
- Iraq
- Israel
- Jordan
- Kuwait
- Lebanon
- Oman
- Qatar
- Saudi Arabia
- Syrian Arab Republic
- Turkey
- United Arab Emirates
- Yemen

Latin America and the Caribbean

Caribbean

- Bahamas
- Barbados
- Cuba
- Dominican Republic
- Guyana
- Haiti
- Jamaica
- Trinidad and Tobago

Mexico and Central America

- Belize
- Costa Rica
- El Salvador
- Guatemala
- Honduras
- Mexico
- Nicaragua
- Panama

South America

- Argentina
- Bolivia (Plurinational State of)
- Brazil
- Chile
- Colombia
- Ecuador
- Paraguay
- Peru
- Suriname
- Uruguay
- Venezuela (Bolivarian Republic of)

a Economies systematically monitored by the Global Economic Monitoring Unit of DPAD.

b Throughout the report the term 'East Asia' is used in reference to this set of developing countries, and excludes Japan.

c Special Administrative Region of China.

Table D
Fuel-exporting countries

Economies in transition	Developing countries				
	Latin America and the Caribbean	Africa	East Asia	South Asia	Western Asia
Azerbaijan	Bolivia (Plurinational State of)	Algeria	Brunei Darussalam	Iran (Islamic Republic of)	Bahrain
Kazakhstan	Colombia	Angola	Indonesia		Iraq
Russian Federation	Ecuador	Cameroon	Viet Nam		Kuwait
Turkmenistan	Trinidad and Tobago	Chad			Oman
Uzbekistan	Venezuela (Bolivarian Republic of)	Congo			Qatar
		Côte d'Ivoire			Saudi Arabia
		Egypt			United Arab Emirates
		Equatorial Guinea			Yemen
		Gabon			
		Libya			
		Nigeria			
		Sudan			

Table E

Economies by per capita GNI in September 2016[a]

High-income

- Australia
- Austria
- Bahamas
- Bahrain
- Barbados
- Belgium
- Brunei Darussalam
- Canada
- Chile
- Croatia
- Cyprus
- Czech Republic
- Denmark
- Estonia
- Finland
- France
- Germany
- Greece
- Hong Kong SAR[d]
- Hungary
- Iceland
- Ireland
- Israel
- Italy
- Japan
- Kuwait
- Latvia
- Lithuania
- Luxembourg
- Malta
- Netherlands
- New Zealand
- Norway
- Oman
- Poland
- Portugal
- Qatar
- Republic of Korea
- Saudi Arabia
- Singapore
- Slovak Republic
- Slovenia
- Spain
- Sweden
- Switzerland
- Taiwan Province of China
- Trinidad and Tobago
- United Arab Emirates
- United Kingdom
- United States
- Uruguay

Upper middle income

- Albania
- Algeria
- Angola
- Argentina[b]
- Azerbaijan
- Belarus
- Belize
- Bosnia and Herzegovina
- Botswana
- Brazil
- Bulgaria
- China
- Colombia
- Costa Rica
- Cuba
- Dominican Republic
- Ecuador
- Equatorial Guinea[b]
- Fiji
- Gabon
- Georgia[c]
- Guyana[c]
- Iran (Islamic Republic of)
- Iraq
- Jamaica
- Jordan
- Kazakhstan
- Lebanon
- Libya
- Malaysia
- Maldives
- Mauritius
- Mexico
- Montenegro
- Namibia
- Panama
- Paraguay
- Peru
- Romania
- Russian Federation[b]
- Serbia
- South Africa
- Suriname
- Thailand
- The former Yugoslav Republc of Macedonia
- Turkey
- Turkmenistan
- Venezuela (Bolivarian Republic of)[b]

Lower middle income

- Armenia
- Bangladesh
- Bhutan
- Bolivia (Plurinational State of)
- Cambodia
- Cameroon
- Cabo Verde
- Congo
- Côte d'Ivoire
- Djibouti
- Egypt
- El Salvador
- Ghana
- Guatemala
- Honduras
- India
- Indonesia
- Kenya
- Kiribati
- Kyrgyz Republic
- Lao People's Democratic Republic
- Lesotho
- Mauritania
- Mongolia
- Morocco
- Myanmar
- Nicaragua
- Nigeria
- Pakistan
- Papua New Guinea
- Philippines
- Republic of Moldova
- Samoa
- São Tomé and Principe
- Solomon Islands
- Sri Lanka
- Sudan
- Swaziland
- Syrian Arab Republic
- Tajikistan
- Timor-Leste
- Tunisia[b]
- Ukraine
- Uzbekistan
- Vanuatu
- Viet Nam
- Yemen
- Zambia

Low-income

- Afghanistan
- Benin
- Burkina Faso
- Burundi
- Central African Republic
- Chad
- Comoros
- Democratic Republic of the Congo
- Eritrea
- Ethiopia
- Gambia
- Guinea
- Guinea-Bissau
- Haiti
- Liberia
- Madagascar
- Malawi
- Mali
- Mozambique
- Nepal
- Niger
- Rwanda
- Senegal[b]
- Sierra Leone
- Somalia
- Togo
- Uganda
- United Republic of Tanzania
- Zimbabwe

a Economies systematically monitored for the World Economic Situation and Prospects report and included in the United Nations' global economic forecast.

b Indicates the country has been shifted downward by one category from previous year's classification.

c Indicates the country has been shifted upward by one category from previous year's classification.

d Special Administrative Region of China.

Table F

Least developed countries *(as of November 2016)*

Africa		East Asia	South Asia	Western Asia	Latin America and the Caribbean
Angola	Madagascar	Cambodia	Afghanistan	Yemen	Haiti
Benin	Malawi	Kiribati	Bangladesh		
Burkina Faso	Mali	Lao People's Democratic Republic	Bhutan		
Burundi	Mauritania	Myanmar	Nepal		
Central African Republic	Mozambique	Solomon Islands			
Chad	Niger	Timor Leste			
Comoros	Rwanda	Tuvalu[a]			
Democratic Republic of the Congo	Sao Tome and Principe	Vanuatu			
Djibouti	Senegal				
Equatorial Guinea	Sierra Leone				
Eritrea	Somalia				
Ethiopia	South Sudan[a]				
Gambia	Sudan				
Guinea	Togo				
Guinea-Bissau	Uganda				
Lesotho	United Republic of Tanzania				
Liberia	Zambia				

a Not included in the WESP discussion because of insufficient data.

Table G

Heavily indebted poor countries *(as of September 2016)*

Post-completion point HIPCs[a]		Pre-decision point HIPCs[b]
Afghanistan	Haiti	Eritrea
Benin	Honduras	Somalia
Bolivia	Liberia	Sudan
Burkina Faso	Madagascar	
Burundi	Malawi	
Cameroon	Mali	
Central African Republic	Mauritania	
Chad	Mozambique	
Comoros	Nicaragua	
Congo	Niger	
Côte D'Ivoire	Rwanda	
Democratic Republic of the Congo	São Tomé and Principe	
Ethiopia	Senega	
Gambia	Sierra Leone	
Ghana	Togo	
Guinea	Uganda	
Guinea-Bissau	United Republic of Tanzania	
Guyana	Zambia	

a Countries that have qualified for irrevocable debt relief under the HIPC Initiative.

b Countries that are potentially eligible and may wish to avail themselves of the HIPC Initiative or the Multilateral Debt Relief Initiative (MDRI).

Table H
Small island developing States

United Nations members		Non-UN members/Associate members of the Regional Commissions
Antigua and Barbuda	Marshall Islands	American Samoa
Bahamas	Mauritius	Anguilla
Bahrain	Nauru	Aruba
Barbados	Palau	Bermuda
Belize	Papua New Guinea	British Virgin Islands
Cabo Verde	Saint Kitts and Nevis	Cayman Islands
Comoros	Saint Lucia	Commonwealth of Northern Marianas
Cuba	Saint Vincent and the Grenadines	Cook Islands
Dominica	Samoa	Curaçao
Dominican Republic	São Tomé and Príncipe	French Polynesia
Federated States of Micronesia	Seychelles	Guadeloupe
Fiji	Singapore	Guam
Grenada	Solomon Islands	Martinique
Guinea-Bissau	Suriname	Montserrat
Guyana	Timor-Leste	New Caledonia
Haiti	Tonga	Niue
Jamaica	Trinidad and Tobago	Puerto Rico
Kiribati	Tuvalu	Turks and Caicos Islands
Maldives	Vanuatu	U.S. Virgin Islands

Table I
Landlocked developing countries

Landlocked developing countries		
Afghanistan	Kyrgystan	South Sudan
Armenia	Lao People's Democratic Republic	Swaziland
Azerbaijan	Lesotho	Tajikistan
Bhutan	Malawi	The former Yugoslav Republic of Macedonia
Bolivia (Plurinational State of)	Mali	Turkmenistan
Botswana	Mongolia	Uganda
Burkina Faso	Nepal	Uzbekistan
Burundi	Niger	Zambia
Central African Republic	Paraguay	Zimbabwe
Chad	Republic of Moldova	
Ethiopia	Rwanda	
Kazakhstan		

Table J
International Organization for Standardization Country Codes

ISO Code	Country
AFG	Afghanistan
AGO	Angola
ALB	Albania
AND	Andorra
ARE	United Arab Emirates
ARG	Argentina
ARM	Armenia
ATG	Antigua and Barbuda
AUS	Australia
AUT	Austria
AZE	Azerbaijan
BDI	Burundi
BEL	Belgium
BEN	Benin
BFA	Burkina Faso
BGD	Bangladesh
BGR	Bulgaria
BHR	Bahrain
BHS	Bahamas
BIH	Bosnia and Herzegovina
BLR	Belarus
BLZ	Belize
BOL	Bolivia (Plurinational State of)
BRA	Brazil
BRB	Barbados
BRN	Brunei Darussalam
BTN	Bhutan
BWA	Botswana
CAF	Central African Republic
CAN	Canada
CHE	Switzerland
CHL	Chile
CHN	China
CIV	Côte D'Ivoire
CMR	Cameroon
COD	Democratic Republic of the Congo
COG	Congo
COL	Colombia
COM	Comoros
CPV	Cabo Verde
CRI	Costa Rica
CUB	Cuba
CYP	Cyprus
CZE	Czech Republic
DEU	Germany
DJI	Djibouti
DMA	Dominica
DNK	Denmark
DOM	Dominican Republic
DZA	Algeria
ECU	Ecuador
EGY	Egypt
ERI	Eritrea
ESP	Spain
EST	Estonia
ETH	Ethiopia
FIN	Finland
FJI	Fiji
FRA	France
FSM	Micronesia (Federated States of)
GAB	Gabon
GBR	United Kingdom of Great Britain and Northern Ireland
GEO	Georgia
GHA	Ghana
GIN	Guinea
GMB	Gambia
GNB	Guinea Bissau
GNQ	Equatorial Guinea
GRC	Greece
GRD	Grenada
GTM	Guatemala
GUY	Guyana
HND	Honduras
HRV	Croatia
HTI	Haiti
HUN	Hungary
IDN	Indonesia
IND	India
IRL	Ireland
IRN	Iran (Islamic Republic of)
IRQ	Iraq
ISL	Iceland
ISR	Israel
ITA	Italy
JAM	Jamaica
JOR	Jordan
JPN	Japan
KAZ	Kazakhstan
KEN	Kenya
KGZ	Kyrgyzstan
KHM	Cambodia
KIR	Kiribati
KNA	Saint Kitts and Nevis
KOR	Republic of Korea
KWT	Kuwait
LAO	Lao People's Democratic Republic
LBN	Lebanon
LBR	Liberia
LBY	Libya
LCA	Saint Lucia
LIE	Liechtenstein
LKA	Sri Lanka
LSO	Lesotho
LTU	Lithuania
LUX	Luxembourg
LVA	Latvia
MAR	Morocco
MCO	Monaco
MDA	Republic of Moldova
MDG	Madagascar
MDV	Maldives
MEX	Mexico
MHL	Marshall Islands
MKD	The former Yugoslav Republic of Macedonia
MLI	Mali
MLT	Malta
MMR	Myanmar
MNE	Montenegro
MNG	Mongolia
MOZ	Mozambique
MRT	Mauritania
MUS	Mauritius
MWI	Malawi
MYS	Malaysia
NAM	Namibia
NER	Niger
NGA	Nigeria
NIC	Nicaragua
NLD	Netherlands
NOR	Norway
NPL	Nepal
NRU	Nauru
NZL	New Zealand
OMN	Oman
PAK	Pakistan
PAN	Panama
PER	Peru
PHL	Philippines
PLW	Palau
PNG	Papua New Guinea
POL	Poland
PRK	Democratic People's Republic of Korea
PRT	Portugal
PRY	Paraguay
QAT	Qatar
ROU	Romania
RUS	Russian Federation
RWA	Rwanda
SAU	Saudi Arabia
SDN	Sudan
SEN	Senegal
SGP	Singapore
SLB	Solomon Islands
SLE	Sierra Leone
SLV	El Salvador
SMR	San Marino
SOM	Somalia
SRB	Serbia
SSD	South Sudan
STP	Sao Tome and Principe
SUR	Suriname
SVK	Slovakia
SVN	Slovenia
SWE	Sweden
SWZ	Swaziland
SYC	Seychelles
SYR	Syrian Arab Republic
TCD	Chad
TGO	Togo
THA	Thailand
TJK	Tajikistan
TKM	Turkmenistan
TLS	Timor-Leste
TON	Tonga
TTO	Trinidad and Tobago
TUN	Tunisia
TUR	Turkey
TUV	Tuvalu
TZA	United Republic of Tanzania
UGA	Uganda
UKR	Ukraine
URY	Uruguay
USA	United States of America
UZB	Uzbekistan
VCT	Saint Vincent and the Grenadines
VEN	Venezuela (Bolivarian Republic of)
VNM	Viet Nam
VUT	Vanuatu
WSM	Samoa
YEM	Yemen
ZAF	South Africa
ZMB	Zambia
ZWE	Zimbabwe

Annex tables

Table A.1

Developed economies: rates of growth of real GDP, 2008–2018

Annual percentage change

	2008-2015[a]	2008	2009	2010	2011	2012	2013	2014	2015	2016[b]	2017[c]	2018[c]
Developed economies	0.8	0.1	-3.7	2.6	1.5	1.1	1.0	1.7	2.1	1.5	1.7	1.8
United States	1.2	-0.3	-2.8	2.5	1.6	2.2	1.5	2.4	2.6	1.5	1.9	2.0
Canada	1.5	1.0	-2.9	3.1	3.1	1.7	2.2	2.5	1.1	1.2	2.4	2.3
Japan	0.1	-1.0	-5.5	4.7	-0.5	1.7	1.4	-0.1	0.6	0.5	0.9	0.9
Australia	2.5	2.6	1.8	2.3	2.7	3.5	2.0	2.7	2.4	2.8	1.9	2.5
New Zealand	1.8	-0.4	0.3	2.0	1.8	2.8	1.7	3.0	3.0	2.5	2.5	2.4
European Union	0.4	0.5	-4.4	2.1	1.8	-0.5	0.2	1.5	2.2	1.8	1.8	1.8
EU-15	0.3	0.2	-4.4	2.1	1.6	-0.6	0.1	1.4	2.0	1.7	1.6	1.7
Austria	0.6	1.5	-3.8	1.9	2.8	0.8	0.3	0.8	0.8	1.4	1.5	1.4
Belgium	0.7	0.7	-2.3	2.7	1.8	0.2	0.0	1.3	1.4	1.4	1.5	1.5
Denmark	-0.2	-0.7	-5.1	1.6	1.2	-0.1	-0.2	1.3	1.0	1.6	1.9	1.9
Finland	-0.6	0.7	-8.3	3.0	2.6	-1.4	-0.8	-0.7	0.2	0.9	1.2	1.3
France	0.5	0.2	-2.9	2.0	2.1	0.2	0.6	0.7	1.2	1.3	1.6	1.6
Germany	0.8	1.1	-5.6	4.1	3.7	0.4	0.3	1.6	1.5	1.8	1.8	1.7
Greece	-3.7	-0.3	-4.3	-5.5	-9.1	-7.3	-3.2	0.7	-0.3	-0.3	1.7	2.0
Ireland	3.6	-2.2	-5.6	0.4	2.6	0.2	1.4	8.5	26.3	3.9	3.1	2.9
Italy	-1.1	-1.1	-5.5	1.7	0.6	-2.8	-1.7	-0.3	0.6	0.9	1.2	1.3
Luxembourg	1.7	-0.8	-5.4	5.7	2.6	-0.8	4.3	4.1	4.9	2.6	3.0	2.8
Netherlands	0.3	1.7	-3.8	1.4	1.7	-1.1	-0.5	1.4	2.0	1.6	1.8	2.0
Portugal	-0.7	0.2	-3.0	1.9	-1.8	-4.0	-1.1	0.9	1.5	1.4	1.4	1.3
Spain	-0.4	1.1	-3.6	0.0	-1.0	-2.6	-1.7	1.4	3.2	2.7	2.3	2.3
Sweden	1.2	-0.6	-5.2	6.0	2.7	-0.3	1.2	2.3	4.1	3.1	2.5	2.3
United Kingdom	0.9	-0.5	-4.2	1.5	2.0	1.2	2.2	3.1	2.2	2.0	1.1	1.3
EU-13	1.6	3.7	-3.7	2.0	3.1	0.5	1.2	2.8	3.6	3.0	3.2	3.3
Bulgaria	1.2	5.6	-4.2	0.1	1.6	0.2	1.3	1.5	3.6	2.9	2.9	3.0
Croatia	-1.2	2.1	-7.4	-1.7	-0.3	-2.2	-1.1	-0.4	1.6	2.6	2.6	2.7
Cyprus	-0.8	3.7	-2.0	1.4	0.4	-2.4	-5.9	-2.5	1.6	1.6	1.7	1.8
Czech Republic	1.0	2.7	-4.8	2.3	2.0	-0.9	-0.5	2.7	4.6	2.8	2.8	2.4
Estonia	-0.1	-5.4	-14.7	2.5	7.6	5.2	1.6	2.9	1.4	1.5	2.3	2.6
Hungary	0.4	0.8	-6.6	0.7	1.8	-1.7	1.9	3.7	2.9	2.0	2.6	2.5
Latvia	-0.6	-3.6	-14.3	-3.8	6.2	4.0	3.0	2.4	2.7	1.5	2.6	2.9
Lithuania	0.7	2.6	-14.8	1.6	6.0	3.8	3.5	3.1	1.6	2.0	2.5	3.2
Malta	2.8	3.3	-2.5	3.5	1.9	2.9	4.1	3.5	6.2	3.2	2.8	2.8
Poland	3.1	3.9	2.6	3.7	5.0	1.6	1.3	3.3	3.9	3.0	3.4	3.8
Romania	1.5	8.5	-7.1	-0.8	1.1	0.6	3.5	3.1	3.8	5.1	4.2	3.8
Slovakia	2.1	5.7	-5.5	5.1	2.8	1.5	1.4	2.5	3.8	3.5	3.5	3.9
Slovenia	-0.2	3.3	-7.8	1.2	0.6	-2.7	-1.1	2.9	2.3	2.5	2.5	2.5
Other Europe	1.2	1.5	-2.0	1.9	1.5	1.8	1.5	2.1	1.2	1.0	1.5	1.8
Iceland	0.7	1.5	-4.7	-3.6	2.0	1.2	3.9	1.8	4.0	3.2	2.9	2.7
Norway	1.0	0.4	-1.6	0.6	1.0	2.7	1.0	2.2	1.6	0.9	1.6	1.9
Switzerland	1.3	2.3	-2.1	3.0	1.8	1.1	1.8	2.0	0.8	1.0	1.4	1.7
Memorandum items												
North America	1.2	-0.2	-2.8	2.6	1.8	2.2	1.6	2.4	2.4	1.5	2.0	2.0
Developed Asia and Pacific	0.6	-0.4	-4.1	4.2	0.2	2.1	1.5	0.5	1.0	1.0	1.1	1.3
Europe	0.4	0.6	-4.3	2.1	1.7	-0.3	0.3	1.6	2.1	1.8	1.8	1.8
Major developed economies	0.8	-0.2	-3.8	2.9	1.5	1.4	1.2	1.6	1.8	1.3	1.6	1.7
Euro area	0.2	0.5	-4.5	2.1	1.6	-0.9	-0.3	1.1	1.9	1.6	1.7	1.7

Source: UN/DESA, based on data of the United Nations Statistics Division and individual national sources.

Note: Regional aggregates calculated at 2010 prices and exchange rates.

a Average percentage change.

b Partly estimated.

c Baseline scenario forecasts, based in part on Project LINK and UN/DESA World Economic Forecasting Model.

Table A.2

Economies in transition: rates of growth of real GDP, 2008–2018

Annual percentage change

	2008–2015[a]	2008	2009	2010	2011	2012	2013	2014	2015	2016[b]	2017[c]	2018[c]
Economies in transition	1.4	5.3	-6.6	4.8	4.6	3.4	2.0	0.9	-2.8	-0.2	1.4	2.0
South-Eastern Europe	1.3	5.8	-2.0	1.5	1.7	-0.7	2.4	0.2	2.0	2.6	3.1	3.3
Albania	3.0	7.5	3.4	3.7	2.5	1.4	1.1	2.0	2.6	3.2	3.5	4.4
Bosnia and Herzegovina	1.2	5.5	-2.9	0.8	0.9	-0.9	2.4	1.1	3.2	2.1	2.9	3.0
Montenegro	1.6	6.9	-5.7	2.5	3.2	-2.7	3.5	1.8	3.4	3.2	3.5	3.2
Serbia	0.6	5.4	-3.1	0.6	1.4	-1.0	2.6	-1.8	0.7	2.7	3.0	3.0
The former Yugoslav Republic of Macedonia	2.5	5.5	-0.4	3.4	2.3	-0.5	2.7	3.8	3.7	2.3	3.0	3.5
Commonwealth of Independent States and Georgia[d]	1.4	5.3	-6.8	4.9	4.7	3.5	2.0	1.0	-3.0	-0.3	1.4	2.0
Net fuel exporters	**1.6**	**5.4**	**-6.3**	**4.9**	**4.6**	**3.8**	**2.1**	**1.4**	**-2.6**	**-0.4**	**1.3**	**1.8**
Azerbaijan	4.6	10.8	9.3	5.0	0.1	2.2	5.8	2.8	1.1	-2.9	1.0	1.5
Kazakhstan	4.4	3.3	1.2	7.3	7.3	5.0	6.0	4.3	1.2	0.3	1.4	2.5
Russian Federation	0.9	5.2	-7.8	4.5	4.3	3.5	1.3	0.7	-3.7	-0.8	1.0	1.5
Turkmenistan	10.3	14.7	6.1	9.2	14.7	11.1	10.2	10.3	6.7	6.0	6.1	6.5
Uzbekistan	8.3	9.4	8.1	8.5	8.3	8.2	8.0	8.1	8.0	7.4	6.0	6.4
Net fuel importers	**-0.4**	**4.4**	**-10.5**	**5.0**	**5.5**	**1.3**	**1.2**	**-2.7**	**-6.0**	**0.3**	**2.1**	**3.0**
Armenia	1.9	6.9	-14.1	2.2	4.7	7.2	3.3	3.6	3.0	2.5	2.7	3.0
Belarus	2.9	10.2	0.2	7.7	5.5	1.7	1.0	1.6	-3.8	-2.7	1.5	1.9
Georgia[d]	3.6	2.6	-3.7	6.2	7.2	6.4	3.3	4.6	2.8	2.8	3.0	4.2
Kyrgyzstan	4.3	8.4	2.9	-0.5	6.0	-0.1	10.5	4.3	3.5	0.2	2.3	2.3
Republic of Moldova	3.4	7.8	-6.0	7.1	6.8	-0.7	9.4	4.6	-0.5	1.2	2.5	3.0
Tajikistan	6.0	7.6	4.0	6.5	2.4	7.5	7.4	6.8	6.0	6.4	5.1	4.8
Ukraine[e]	-2.7	2.2	-15.1	4.1	5.4	0.2	0.0	-6.6	-9.9	0.8	1.9	3.2

Source: UN/DESA, based on data of the United Nations Statistics Division and individual national sources.

Note: Regional aggregates calculated at 2010 prices and exchange rates.

a Average percentage change.

b Partly estimated.

c Baseline scenario forecasts, based in part on Project LINK and the UN/DESA World Economic Forecasting Model.

d Georgia officially left the Commonwealth of Independent States on 18 August 2009. However, its performance is discussed in the context of this group of countries for reasons of geographic proximity and similarities in economic structure.

e Starting in 2010, data for the Ukraine excludes the temporarily occupied territory of the Autonomous Republic of Crimea and Sevastopol.

Table A.3
Developing economies: rates of growth of real GDP, 2008–2018

Annual percentage change

	2008–2015[a]	2008	2009	2010	2011	2012	2013	2014	2015	2016[b]	2017[c]	2018[c]
Developing countries[d]	**5.0**	**5.5**	**2.7**	**7.7**	**6.1**	**5.0**	**4.7**	**4.3**	**3.8**	**3.6**	**4.4**	**4.7**
Africa	**3.8**	**5.5**	**3.1**	**5.1**	**1.3**	**6.0**	**2.2**	**3.8**	**3.1**	**1.7**	**3.2**	**3.8**
North Africa	2.2	5.8	3.2	4.0	-5.2	8.6	-3.0	1.8	3.2	2.6	3.5	3.6
Algeria	3.0	2.4	1.6	3.6	2.9	3.4	2.8	3.8	3.9	2.9	2.8	2.7
Egypt[e]	3.7	7.2	4.7	5.1	1.9	2.2	2.1	2.2	4.2	3.4	3.4	3.7
Libya	-12.2	14.6	-0.7	4.3	-61.3	124.7	-52.1	-24.0	-6.4	-4.8	5.5	6.0
Mauritania	3.6	1.1	-1.0	4.8	4.4	6.0	5.7	6.4	1.9	4.3	4.4	3.9
Morocco	4.2	5.9	4.2	3.8	5.2	3.0	4.7	2.4	4.5	1.7	3.9	4.0
Sudan[e]	3.2	2.2	9.5	6.9	-0.3	-2.2	3.3	3.2	3.3	4.2	4.2	4.0
Tunisia	2.2	4.5	3.1	3.0	-1.9	3.9	2.4	2.4	0.8	2.0	3.1	3.3
East Africa	6.6	5.6	4.8	7.9	7.7	5.8	7.1	7.0	6.6	5.5	6.0	6.3
Burundi	12.7	13.6	28.9	15.7	13.4	13.2	19.6	4.7	-4.1	2.0	3.0	5.0
Comoros	4.1	3.8	3.6	-0.7	4.1	4.2	9.5	3.7	4.8	2.2	3.5	3.8
Democratic Republic of the Congo	6.9	6.2	2.9	7.1	6.9	7.1	8.5	9.5	7.0	4.0	4.5	5.2
Djibouti	5.1	5.4	5.0	3.5	4.5	4.8	5.0	6.0	6.5	6.7	6.8	6.8
Eritrea	2.3	-9.8	3.9	2.2	8.7	7.0	1.3	1.7	4.8	3.6	3.2	3.7
Ethiopia	10.5	10.8	8.8	12.6	13.2	8.6	10.6	10.3	9.6	5.4	7.0	7.4
Kenya	4.9	0.2	3.3	8.4	6.1	4.6	5.7	5.3	5.6	6.0	6.1	6.2
Madagascar	2.0	7.1	-4.1	0.4	1.4	3.0	2.3	3.3	3.0	2.6	3.8	4.4
Rwanda	7.5	11.2	6.3	7.3	7.9	8.8	4.7	7.0	6.9	6.7	6.8	6.9
Somalia	2.6	2.6	2.6	2.6	2.6	2.6	2.6	2.6	2.6	3.4	3.7	3.9
Uganda	6.2	10.4	6.9	8.2	5.9	3.2	4.7	4.9	5.5	5.0	5.4	5.8
United Republic of Tanzania	6.4	5.6	5.4	6.4	7.9	5.1	7.3	7.0	7.0	7.0	7.1	6.9
Central Africa	3.8	4.5	3.1	3.7	4.0	5.9	2.6	5.4	1.5	2.4	3.4	4.2
Cameroon	4.3	2.9	1.9	3.3	4.1	4.6	5.6	5.9	5.8	5.3	5.0	5.2
Central African Republic	-3.3	2.6	1.9	3.6	2.0	2.9	-36.0	1.0	4.3	5.1	5.0	5.1
Chad	6.3	1.3	9.1	13.4	-2.4	10.1	7.4	10.4	1.8	1.1	3.4	4.2
Congo	5.2	5.9	7.5	8.7	3.4	3.8	3.3	6.8	2.5	1.6	3.0	3.5
Equatorial Guinea	0.6	17.8	1.3	-8.9	6.5	8.3	-4.1	-0.5	-12.2	-4.5	-2.2	1.5
Gabon	3.7	-3.5	-0.5	6.8	7.1	5.3	5.6	5.0	4.0	3.2	4.2	4.4
Sao Tome and Principe	4.8	8.2	4.0	4.5	4.8	4.6	4.2	4.5	4.0	5.5	5.5	5.5
West Africa	5.6	6.4	6.1	7.3	5.0	5.3	5.8	6.1	3.2	0.1	3.1	4.1
Benin	4.4	4.9	2.3	2.1	3.0	4.6	6.9	6.5	5.2	4.2	4.8	5.3
Burkina Faso	5.5	5.8	3.0	8.4	6.6	6.5	5.8	4.0	4.0	4.6	5.1	5.5
Cabo Verde	2.0	6.7	-1.3	1.5	4.0	1.1	0.8	1.8	1.8	3.0	3.5	3.8
Côte D'Ivoire	5.4	6.5	3.3	2.0	-4.4	10.7	9.2	8.5	8.6	8.0	7.8	7.5
Gambia (Islamic Republic of the)	3.8	5.7	6.4	6.5	-4.3	5.9	4.8	0.9	4.7	2.1	3.4	4.0
Ghana	7.5	9.1	4.8	7.9	14.0	9.3	7.3	4.0	3.9	3.8	6.8	7.5
Guinea	3.0	4.1	-1.5	4.2	5.6	6.6	4.4	1.1	0.1	4.7	4.4	4.6
Guinea Bissau	3.2	3.2	3.4	4.6	8.1	-1.7	3.3	0.2	4.8	3.9	4.0	4.1
Liberia	7.6	15.8	12.3	10.8	5.8	8.2	8.1	0.7	0.0	2.3	3.0	5.0
Mali	9.2	9.5	11.7	10.9	7.7	11.2	7.0	7.8	7.6	4.5	4.6	4.7
Niger	5.8	9.6	-0.7	8.4	2.3	11.8	5.3	7.0	3.6	4.1	4.5	4.8
Nigeria	5.6	6.3	6.9	7.8	4.9	4.3	5.4	6.3	2.7	-1.6	2.0	3.2
Senegal	3.8	3.7	2.4	4.2	1.8	4.4	3.5	4.3	6.5	6.3	6.2	6.6
Sierra Leone	4.2	5.4	3.2	5.3	6.3	15.2	20.7	4.6	-21.5	4.7	5.1	4.8
Togo	4.6	2.4	3.4	4.0	4.9	5.8	5.1	6.1	5.3	5.5	4.7	5.1

Table A.3

Developing economies: rates of growth of real GDP, 2008–2018 *(continued)*

Annual percentage change

	2008–2015[a]	2008	2009	2010	2011	2012	2013	2014	2015	2016[b]	2017[c]	2018[c]
Southern Africa	**3.0**	**4.6**	**0.0**	**4.0**	**3.7**	**3.8**	**3.3**	**2.7**	**1.9**	**1.0**	**1.8**	**2.6**
Angola	5.1	11.2	0.5	4.7	3.5	8.5	5.0	4.8	3.0	0.8	1.8	2.8
Botswana	3.7	6.2	-7.7	8.6	6.0	4.5	9.9	3.2	-0.3	2.8	3.5	4.2
Lesotho	4.6	5.7	3.4	7.9	4.0	5.0	4.6	3.4	2.5	2.2	3.5	4.1
Malawi	4.3	8.3	6.9	4.9	-0.6	6.3	0.0	6.5	2.9	2.4	3.5	4.5
Mauritius	3.8	5.5	3.0	4.1	3.9	3.2	3.2	3.6	3.5	3.6	3.5	3.8
Mozambique	6.9	6.9	6.4	6.7	7.1	7.2	7.1	7.4	6.6	4.2	5.5	6.2
Namibia	4.6	2.6	0.3	6.0	5.1	5.1	5.7	6.3	5.7	2.5	4.6	5.1
South Africa	1.9	3.2	-1.5	3.0	3.3	2.2	2.3	1.6	1.3	0.6	1.3	2.0
Swaziland	2.9	4.4	2.6	1.8	1.9	3.4	4.6	2.7	1.7	0.8	1.8	2.2
Zambia	7.0	7.8	9.2	10.3	6.3	6.7	6.7	5.6	3.6	3.0	4.1	4.6
Zimbabwe	10.6	-4.7	55.5	11.4	11.9	10.6	4.5	3.1	1.5	-0.8	2.5	3.6
Africa - net fuel exporters	**3.6**	**6.3**	**4.1**	**5.3**	**-1.5**	**7.6**	**0.5**	**4.1**	**3.0**	**1.1**	**2.9**	**3.5**
Africa - net fuel importers	**3.9**	**4.5**	**1.8**	**4.8**	**4.8**	**4.1**	**4.3**	**3.6**	**3.2**	**2.5**	**3.5**	**4.0**
East and South Asia	**6.6**	**6.5**	**5.8**	**9.2**	**7.4**	**5.8**	**6.0**	**6.1**	**5.7**	**5.7**	**5.9**	**5.9**
East Asia	**6.8**	**6.9**	**5.8**	**9.5**	**7.6**	**6.4**	**6.3**	**6.1**	**5.7**	**5.5**	**5.6**	**5.6**
Brunei Darussalam	-0.2	-1.9	-1.8	2.6	3.7	0.9	-2.1	-2.3	-0.6	0.4	2.5	3.5
Cambodia	6.1	6.7	0.1	6.0	7.1	7.3	7.5	7.1	7.0	7.0	7.0	7.1
China	8.6	9.6	9.2	10.6	9.5	7.7	7.7	7.3	6.9	6.6	6.5	6.5
Fiji	2.5	1.0	-1.4	3.1	2.8	1.8	4.6	3.8	4.3	2.9	4.0	4.4
Hong Kong SAR[f]	2.6	2.1	-2.5	6.8	4.8	1.7	3.1	2.7	2.4	1.4	2.0	2.2
Indonesia	5.6	6.0	4.6	6.2	6.2	6.0	5.6	5.0	4.8	5.1	5.2	5.3
Kiribati	1.5	-0.8	0.3	-0.9	-0.2	3.4	2.4	3.7	4.2	2.0	2.0	2.1
Lao People's Democratic Republic	7.7	7.8	7.5	8.1	8.0	7.9	8.0	7.6	7.0	7.0	7.5	7.5
Malaysia	4.6	4.8	-1.5	7.4	5.3	5.5	4.7	6.0	5.0	4.4	4.7	4.7
Mongolia	8.0	8.9	-1.3	6.4	17.3	12.3	11.6	7.9	2.3	0.0	2.1	3.9
Myanmar[e]	8.5	10.3	10.6	10.2	5.6	7.3	8.4	8.1	7.5	8.3	8.0	8.0
Papua New Guinea	7.7	6.6	6.1	7.6	11.3	7.7	4.9	8.4	9.0	2.5	3.2	3.2
Philippines	5.3	4.2	1.1	7.6	3.7	6.7	7.1	6.2	5.9	6.3	6.1	6.0
Republic of Korea	3.1	2.8	0.7	6.5	3.7	2.3	2.9	3.3	2.6	2.8	2.9	2.8
Samoa	0.5	-1.0	-4.0	4.4	3.5	-2.3	0.5	1.6	1.7	2.8	1.2	1.8
Singapore	4.4	1.8	-0.6	15.2	6.2	3.7	4.7	3.3	2.0	1.7	2.4	2.6
Solomon Islands	3.9	3.7	0.2	10.6	6.4	2.6	3.0	1.5	3.3	2.4	2.5	3.0
Taiwan Province of China	2.7	0.7	-1.6	10.6	3.8	2.1	2.2	3.9	0.6	0.9	1.5	2.4
Thailand	2.8	1.7	-0.7	7.5	0.8	7.2	2.7	0.8	2.8	3.1	3.4	3.1
Timor-Leste	1.1	10.4	-7.8	-3.3	12.6	5.2	-13.9	4.5	4.3	4.6	5.1	5.6
Vanuatu	2.4	6.5	3.3	1.6	1.2	1.8	2.0	3.6	-0.8	3.3	3.6	3.9
Viet Nam	5.9	5.7	5.4	6.4	6.2	5.2	5.4	6.0	6.7	6.1	6.3	6.5
South Asia	**5.7**	**4.6**	**5.7**	**8.1**	**6.6**	**3.7**	**4.7**	**6.2**	**6.0**	**6.7**	**6.9**	**6.9**
Afghanistan[e]	6.5	2.3	17.2	3.2	8.7	10.9	6.5	2.1	2.0	3.0	3.7	4.3
Bangladesh[e]	6.0	6.0	5.0	5.6	6.5	6.5	6.0	6.1	6.5	7.0	6.8	6.6
Bhutan	6.4	4.7	6.7	11.7	7.9	5.1	2.1	5.5	7.7	6.3	6.5	7.0
India[e]	7.0	3.9	8.5	10.3	6.6	5.1	6.9	7.3	7.3	7.6	7.7	7.6
Iran (Islamic Republic of)[e]	1.1	0.9	2.3	6.6	3.7	-6.6	-1.9	4.3	0.0	4.3	4.7	4.4
Maldives	5.9	12.5	-5.5	7.1	12.6	3.0	8.8	8.5	1.9	4.0	4.3	4.0

Table A.3
Developing economies: rates of growth of real GDP, 2008–2018 *(continued)*

Annual percentage change

	2008–2015[a]	2008	2009	2010	2011	2012	2013	2014	2015	2016[b]	2017[c]	2018[c]
Nepal[e]	4.6	6.1	4.5	4.8	3.4	4.8	4.1	6.0	2.7	2.2	3.8	4.5
Pakistan[e]	3.4	1.7	2.8	1.6	2.7	3.5	4.4	4.7	5.5	5.3	5.2	5.2
Sri Lanka	6.0	6.0	3.5	8.0	8.4	9.1	3.4	4.9	4.8	4.9	5.0	5.2
East and South Asia - net fuel exporters	4.2	4.7	3.7	6.0	5.5	2.5	2.8	4.4	3.8	4.9	5.2	5.2
East and South Asia - net fuel importers	6.8	6.7	6.0	9.6	7.6	6.3	6.4	6.3	5.9	5.8	5.9	5.9
Western Asia	**3.6**	**4.0**	**-1.6**	**6.0**	**7.4**	**4.1**	**3.5**	**2.6**	**2.7**	**2.1**	**2.5**	**3.0**
Net fuel exporters	4.1	6.0	-1.0	4.5	7.9	6.6	3.9	2.8	2.2	1.7	2.2	2.8
Bahrain	3.9	6.2	2.5	4.3	2.0	3.7	5.4	4.4	2.9	2.0	1.8	1.9
Iraq	5.6	6.6	5.8	5.5	10.2	12.6	7.6	-0.6	-2.4	2.4	3.6	3.9
Kuwait	1.5	2.5	-7.1	-2.4	9.6	6.6	1.1	0.5	1.8	2.3	2.6	2.6
Oman	4.4	8.2	6.1	4.8	-1.1	7.1	3.9	2.9	3.5	1.8	2.3	3.1
Qatar	9.8	17.7	12.0	16.7	13.0	6.0	6.3	4.2	3.7	2.7	3.0	3.6
Saudi Arabia	4.2	6.2	-2.1	4.8	10.0	5.4	2.7	3.6	3.4	1.1	1.5	2.3
United Arab Emirates	2.8	3.2	-5.2	1.6	4.9	7.2	4.3	3.1	3.8	2.0	2.1	3.0
Yemen	-3.5	4.0	4.1	5.7	-12.8	2.0	3.2	-0.2	-28.1	-4.0	5.0	4.0
Net fuel importers	3.0	1.8	-2.3	7.8	6.7	1.1	3.1	2.5	3.4	2.7	2.9	3.2
Israel	3.3	3.1	1.3	5.5	5.0	2.9	3.3	3.1	2.6	2.8	3.1	3.2
Jordan	3.6	7.2	5.5	2.3	2.6	2.7	2.8	3.1	2.5	2.4	2.7	2.9
Lebanon	4.6	9.2	10.1	8.0	0.9	2.8	3.0	2.0	1.0	1.2	2.2	2.4
Syrian Arab Republic	-6.1	4.5	5.9	3.4	-6.3	-22.4	-16.9	-11.6	-0.8	-6.5	-5.0	-5.0
Turkey	3.3	0.7	-4.8	9.2	8.8	2.1	4.2	2.9	4.0	3.1	3.1	3.5
Latin America and the Caribbean	**2.3**	**4.1**	**-1.7**	**6.0**	**4.5**	**2.9**	**2.8**	**0.7**	**-0.6**	**-1.0**	**1.3**	**2.1**
South America	2.3	5.0	-1.0	6.5	4.7	2.5	3.2	0.1	-1.9	-2.3	0.9	2.0
Argentina	1.8	4.1	-6.0	10.4	6.1	-1.1	2.3	-2.6	2.4	-1.5	2.4	3.0
Bolivia (Plurinational State of)	5.1	6.1	3.4	4.1	5.2	5.1	6.8	5.5	4.8	4.6	4.2	4.1
Brazil	2.1	5.1	-0.1	7.5	3.9	1.9	3.0	0.1	-3.9	-3.2	0.6	1.6
Chile	3.4	3.3	-1.0	5.8	5.8	5.5	4.0	1.8	2.3	1.7	2.1	2.6
Colombia	4.0	3.5	1.7	4.0	6.6	4.0	4.9	4.4	3.1	1.9	2.5	3.0
Ecuador	4.0	6.4	0.6	3.5	7.9	5.6	4.6	3.7	0.3	-2.1	0.5	1.8
Paraguay	4.9	6.4	-4.0	13.1	4.3	-1.2	14.0	4.7	3.0	3.6	3.5	3.5
Peru	5.3	9.1	1.1	8.3	6.3	6.1	5.9	2.4	3.3	3.8	4.1	4.3
Suriname	3.2	4.1	3.0	5.1	5.3	3.1	2.8	1.8	0.1	-4.0	1.4	1.7
Uruguay	4.6	7.2	4.2	7.8	5.2	3.3	5.1	3.2	1.0	0.4	1.2	1.8
Venezuela (Bolivarian Republic of)	0.2	5.3	-3.2	-1.5	4.2	5.6	1.3	-3.9	-5.7	-8.0	-3.7	0.3
Mexico and Central America	2.2	1.7	-4.2	5.0	4.1	4.1	1.7	2.5	2.7	2.3	2.3	2.2
Belize	2.5	2.6	0.7	3.3	2.1	3.8	1.5	3.9	1.9	-0.9	1.2	1.5
Costa Rica	3.3	4.6	-1.0	5.0	4.3	4.8	2.0	3.0	3.7	4.1	4.0	4.3
El Salvador	1.2	1.3	-3.1	1.4	2.2	1.9	1.8	1.4	2.5	2.4	2.3	2.3
Guatemala	3.2	3.3	0.5	2.9	4.2	3.0	3.7	4.2	4.1	3.6	3.7	3.7
Honduras	2.9	4.2	-2.4	3.7	3.8	4.1	2.8	3.1	3.6	3.8	4.1	3.8
Mexico	1.9	1.4	-4.7	5.2	3.9	4.0	1.4	2.2	2.5	2.0	2.0	1.9
Nicaragua[e]	3.6	2.9	-2.8	3.2	6.2	5.6	4.5	4.6	4.9	4.3	4.1	4.3
Panama	6.9	8.6	1.6	5.8	11.8	9.2	6.6	6.1	5.8	5.4	5.3	5.0

Table A.3

Developing economies: rates of growth of real GDP, 2008–2018 *(continued)*

Annual percentage change

	2008–2015[a]	2008	2009	2010	2011	2012	2013	2014	2015	2016[b]	2017[c]	2018[c]
Caribbean	2.5	2.8	-0.4	3.2	2.4	2.4	3.0	3.1	4.0	2.7	2.7	2.8
Bahamas	-0.5	-2.3	-4.2	1.5	0.6	3.1	0.0	-0.5	-1.7	0.5	1.0	1.2
Barbados	-0.2	0.4	-4.0	0.3	0.8	0.3	-0.1	0.2	0.5	1.4	1.9	2.0
Cuba	2.7	4.1	1.4	2.4	2.8	3.0	2.7	1.0	4.3	1.0	1.5	2.0
Dominican Republic	4.6	3.1	0.9	8.3	2.8	2.6	4.8	7.3	7.0	6.8	5.1	4.5
Guyana	4.0	2.0	3.3	4.4	5.4	4.8	5.2	3.8	3.1	4.4	5.0	5.1
Haiti[e]	1.8	0.8	3.1	-5.5	5.5	2.9	4.2	2.7	1.0	1.5	1.4	2.1
Jamaica	-0.4	-0.7	-4.3	-1.5	1.7	-0.6	0.5	0.7	1.0	1.5	1.7	2.0
Trinidad and Tobago	0.5	3.4	-4.4	-0.1	0.0	1.4	1.7	1.9	0.0	-2.3	0.5	1.1
Latin America and the Caribbean - net fuel exporters	2.1	4.7	-1.1	1.0	5.3	4.9	3.1	0.3	-1.3	-2.9	-0.3	1.8
Latin America and the Caribbean - net fuel importers	2.3	4.0	-1.9	6.9	4.3	2.5	2.8	0.8	-0.5	-0.6	1.6	2.1
Memorandum items:												
Least developed countries	5.5	7.1	4.8	6.3	4.8	6.1	5.4	5.7	3.7	4.5	5.2	5.5
Africa (excluding Libya)	4.1	5.1	3.2	5.2	4.1	4.1	4.1	4.3	3.2	1.8	3.1	3.7
North Africa (excluding Libya)	3.4	4.7	3.6	3.5	2.6	2.8	2.8	3.2	3.6	2.7	3.3	3.5
East Asia (excluding China)	4.0	3.4	0.9	7.7	4.5	4.2	4.0	4.0	3.4	3.5	3.8	3.9
South Asia (excluding India)	3.1	3.3	2.8	5.0	4.7	0.4	1.0	4.2	3.3	4.9	5.1	5.1
Western Asia (excluding Israel and Turkey)	3.8	6.0	-0.4	4.5	7.0	5.4	3.2	2.4	2.1	1.5	2.1	2.7
Arab States[g]	3.3	5.9	0.8	4.3	3.1	6.3	1.4	2.3	2.4	1.9	2.5	3.0
Landlocked developing economies	5.9	6.8	4.4	7.6	6.5	5.8	6.9	5.5	3.5	2.6	3.6	4.2
Small island developing economies	3.7	2.7	-0.2	9.0	4.7	3.3	3.9	3.4	3.0	2.1	2.6	2.7

Source: UN/DESA, based on data of the United Nations Statistics Division and individual national sources.

Note: Regional aggregates calculated at 2010 prices and exchange rates.

a Average percentage change.

b Partly estimated.

c Baseline scenario forecasts, based in part on Project LINK and the UN/DESA World Economic Forecasting Model.

d Covering countries that account for 98 per cent of the population of all developing countries.

e Fiscal year basis.

f Special Administrative Region of China.

g Currently includes data for Algeria, Bahrain, Comoros, Djibouti, Egypt, Iraq, Jordan, Kuwait, Lebanon, Libya, Mauritania, Morocco, Oman, Qatar, Saudi Arabia, Somalia, Sudan, Syrian Arab Republic, Tunisia, United Arab Emirates, and Yemen.

Table A.4

Developed economies: consumer price inflation, 2008–2018

Annual percentage change[a]

	2008	2009	2010	2011	2012	2013	2014	2015	2016[b]	2017[c]	2018[c]
Developed economies	3.5	0.0	1.8	2.8	1.9	1.3	1.4	0.2	0.7	1.6	2.0
United States	4.4	-0.8	2.4	3.8	2.1	1.2	1.6	0.1	1.2	2.3	2.4
Canada	2.4	0.3	1.8	2.9	1.5	0.9	1.9	1.1	1.6	2.2	2.1
Japan	1.4	-1.3	-0.7	-0.3	0.0	0.4	2.7	0.8	-0.1	0.6	1.4
Australia	4.4	1.8	2.9	3.3	1.8	2.5	2.5	1.5	1.2	1.9	2.3
New Zealand	4.0	2.1	2.3	4.0	1.1	1.1	1.2	0.3	0.6	1.2	1.8
European Union	3.5	0.8	1.9	3.0	2.6	1.5	0.6	0.0	0.3	1.4	1.9
EU-15	3.3	0.7	1.9	2.9	2.5	1.5	0.6	0.1	0.3	1.4	1.9
Austria	3.2	0.4	1.7	3.6	2.6	2.1	1.5	0.8	0.6	1.7	2.4
Belgium	4.5	0.0	2.3	3.4	2.6	1.2	0.5	0.6	1.3	1.8	2.2
Denmark	3.6	1.0	2.2	2.7	2.4	0.5	0.4	0.2	0.2	1.2	2.0
Finland	3.9	1.6	1.7	3.3	3.2	2.2	1.2	-0.2	0.3	1.1	1.9
France	3.2	0.1	1.7	2.3	2.2	1.0	0.6	0.1	0.3	1.1	1.7
Germany	2.7	0.2	1.2	2.5	2.1	1.6	0.8	0.1	0.4	1.3	1.7
Greece	4.2	1.3	4.7	3.1	1.0	-0.9	-1.4	-1.1	-0.3	0.5	1.4
Ireland	3.2	-1.7	-1.6	1.2	1.8	0.5	0.3	0.0	0.3	1.2	1.8
Italy	3.5	0.8	1.6	2.9	3.2	1.3	0.2	0.1	-0.1	0.9	1.7
Luxembourg	4.1	0.0	2.8	3.7	2.9	1.7	0.7	0.1	0.3	0.8	1.8
Netherlands	2.2	1.0	0.9	2.5	2.8	2.6	0.3	0.2	0.6	1.0	1.6
Portugal	2.7	-0.9	1.4	3.6	2.8	0.4	-0.1	0.5	0.6	1.3	1.9
Spain	4.1	-0.2	2.1	3.0	2.4	1.5	-0.2	-0.6	-0.4	1.3	1.6
Sweden	3.3	1.9	1.9	1.4	0.9	0.4	0.2	0.7	1.1	1.9	2.2
United Kingdom	3.5	2.2	3.2	4.5	2.9	2.5	1.5	0.0	0.9	2.4	2.5
EU-13	6.1	3.1	2.7	3.8	3.7	1.5	0.2	-0.4	-0.5	1.7	2.2
Bulgaria	12.3	2.8	2.4	4.2	3.0	0.9	-1.4	-0.1	-0.2	1.6	1.8
Croatia	6.1	2.4	1.0	2.3	3.4	2.2	-0.2	-0.5	-0.9	1.2	2.3
Cyprus	4.7	0.4	2.4	3.3	2.4	-0.4	-1.4	-2.1	-0.8	0.7	1.6
Czech Republic	6.3	0.5	1.2	2.2	3.6	1.3	0.5	0.2	0.8	1.7	2.0
Estonia	10.6	0.2	2.7	5.1	4.2	3.2	0.5	0.1	0.8	2.1	2.5
Hungary	6.0	4.0	4.7	3.9	5.7	1.7	0.0	0.1	0.1	1.6	2.2
Latvia	15.4	3.5	-1.1	4.4	2.3	0.0	0.6	0.2	-0.3	1.5	2.1
Lithuania	10.9	4.4	1.3	4.1	3.1	1.0	0.1	-0.9	0.4	1.6	2.3
Malta	4.3	2.1	1.5	2.7	2.4	1.4	0.3	1.1	1.8	2.5	2.9
Poland	4.2	4.0	2.7	3.9	3.6	0.8	0.1	-0.7	-1.1	1.9	2.2
Romania	7.8	5.6	6.1	5.8	3.3	4.0	1.1	-0.6	-1.2	1.9	2.6
Slovakia	3.9	0.9	0.7	4.1	3.7	1.5	-0.1	-0.3	-0.8	0.8	1.7
Slovenia	5.5	0.9	2.1	2.1	2.8	1.9	0.4	-0.8	-0.2	1.4	2.1
Other Europe	2.9	0.8	1.4	0.7	-0.2	0.9	0.9	0.4	1.1	1.0	1.3
Iceland	12.8	16.3	7.5	4.2	6.0	4.1	1.0	0.3	1.6	2.5	3.2
Norway	3.5	2.3	2.3	1.3	0.3	2.0	1.9	2.0	3.1	2.0	2.1
Switzerland	2.3	-0.7	0.6	0.1	-0.7	0.0	0.1	-0.9	-0.4	0.2	0.6
Memorandum items											
North America	4.2	-0.7	2.4	3.7	2.1	1.2	1.6	0.2	1.2	2.2	2.4
Developed Asia and Pacific	2.0	-0.7	0.0	0.5	0.3	0.8	2.7	0.9	0.2	0.9	1.6
Europe	3.5	0.8	1.9	2.8	2.4	1.5	0.6	0.0	0.3	1.4	1.9
Major developed economies	3.4	-0.3	1.7	2.8	1.9	1.2	1.5	0.3	0.7	1.7	2.1
Euro area	3.3	0.3	1.6	2.7	2.5	1.4	0.4	0.0	0.2	1.2	1.7

Sources: UN/DESA, based on OECD, *Main Economic Indicators*; Eurostat; and individual national sources.

a Data for country groups are weighted averages, where weights for each year are based on 2010 GDP in United States dollars.

b Partly estimated.

c Baseline scenario forecasts, based in part on Project LINK and the UN/DESA World Economic Forecasting Model.

Table A.5
Economies in transition: consumer price inflation, 2008–2018

Annual percentage change[a]

	2008	2009	2010	2011	2012	2013	2014	2015	2016[b]	2017[c]	2018[c]
Economies in transition	15.7	11.1	7.0	9.7	6.3	6.4	7.9	15.8	8.1	7.0	5.3
South-Eastern Europe	9.4	4.2	4.1	7.2	4.8	4.4	1.0	0.8	0.5	1.7	2.4
Albania	3.4	2.3	3.6	3.5	2.0	1.9	1.6	1.9	1.1	2.3	2.8
Bosnia and Herzegovina	7.4	-0.4	2.2	3.7	2.0	-0.1	-0.9	-0.9	-0.9	0.5	1.0
Montenegro	8.8	3.5	0.7	3.5	4.1	2.2	-0.7	1.6	-0.2	1.2	2.0
Serbia	12.4	8.1	6.1	11.1	7.3	7.7	2.1	1.4	1.2	2.1	3.0
The former Yugoslav Republic of Macedonia	8.3	-0.7	1.5	3.9	3.3	2.8	-0.3	-0.3	-0.3	1.5	1.9
Commonwealth of Independent States and Georgia[d]	16.0	11.4	7.2	9.8	6.3	6.4	8.2	16.4	8.4	7.2	5.4
Net fuel exporters	**15.3**	**11.1**	**7.0**	**8.6**	**5.2**	**6.7**	**7.7**	**14.1**	**8.0**	**6.7**	**5.0**
Azerbaijan	20.8	1.4	5.7	7.9	1.0	2.4	1.4	4.2	10.5	7.1	5.8
Kazakhstan	17.2	7.3	7.1	8.3	5.1	5.8	6.7	6.6	15.0	8.0	6.5
Russian Federation	14.0	11.7	6.8	8.4	5.1	6.8	7.9	15.5	7.2	6.6	4.7
Turkmenistan	59.7	9.8	0.3	15.1	8.3	5.8	6.0	6.1	4.2	5.7	5.9
Uzbekistan	26.3	17.2	16.5	16.6	14.9	12.5	12.6	9.0	9.0	9.1	9.0
Net fuel importers	**20.9**	**13.2**	**8.7**	**19.0**	**14.7**	**4.7**	**12.4**	**33.5**	**12.2**	**10.8**	**8.2**
Armenia	8.9	3.4	8.2	7.7	2.6	5.8	3.0	3.7	0.2	1.5	3.0
Belarus	14.8	12.9	7.7	53.2	59.2	18.3	18.1	13.5	11.8	10.9	10.0
Georgia[d]	10.0	1.7	7.1	8.5	-0.9	-0.5	3.1	4.0	3.0	3.2	3.2
Kyrgyzstan	24.5	6.9	8.0	16.5	2.7	6.6	7.5	6.5	1.2	3.9	5.5
Republic of Moldova	12.9	-0.1	7.4	7.6	4.6	4.6	5.1	9.7	7.1	6.5	5.7
Tajikistan	20.5	6.4	6.4	12.4	5.8	5.0	6.1	5.7	6.3	4.8	4.3
Ukraine[e]	25.2	15.9	9.4	8.0	0.6	-0.3	12.2	48.7	14.7	12.7	8.6

Source: UN/DESA, based on data of the Economic Commission for Europe.

a Data for country groups are weighted averages, where weights for each year are based on 2010 GDP in United States dollars.

b Partly estimated.

c Baseline scenario forecasts, based in part on Project LINK and the UN/DESA World Economic Forecasting Model.

d Georgia officially left the Commonwealth of Independent States on 18 August 2009. However, its performance is discussed in the context of this group of countries for reasons of geographic proximity and similarities in economic structure.

e Starting in 2010, data for the Ukraine excludes the temporarily occupied territory of the Autonomous Republic of Crimea and Sevastopol.

Table A.6

Developing economies: consumer price inflation, 2008–2018

Annual percentage change[a]

	2008	2009	2010	2011	2012	2013	2014	2015	2016[b]	2017[c]	2018[c]
Developing countries by region[d]	**8.3**	**3.8**	**5.3**	**6.4**	**5.5**	**5.7**	**5.0**	**4.3**	**5.2**	**4.7**	**4.5**
Africa	**11.7**	**8.1**	**7.5**	**8.7**	**8.9**	**6.8**	**7.0**	**7.0**	**10.0**	**10.1**	**9.6**
North Africa	**10.8**	**7.0**	**6.7**	**8.6**	**8.8**	**7.3**	**8.3**	**7.8**	**8.7**	**8.4**	**7.9**
Algeria	4.9	5.7	3.9	4.5	8.9	3.3	2.9	4.8	7.0	6.0	5.5
Egypt	18.3	11.8	11.3	10.1	7.1	9.4	10.1	10.4	11.9	12.5	12.2
Libya	10.4	2.5	2.8	15.5	6.1	2.6	6.6	10.0	11.5	9.5	7.4
Mauritania	7.3	2.2	6.3	5.6	4.9	4.1	3.5	0.5	0.5	3.2	5.0
Morocco	3.7	1.0	1.0	0.9	1.3	1.9	0.4	1.6	1.7	2.4	2.8
Sudan	14.3	11.2	13.2	22.1	37.4	30.0	36.9	16.9	13.1	11.2	10.0
Tunisia	4.9	3.5	4.4	3.5	5.1	5.8	4.9	4.9	3.4	3.7	3.6
East Africa	**21.7**	**9.5**	**5.8**	**17.2**	**13.4**	**5.9**	**5.5**	**5.9**	**5.3**	**5.3**	**5.3**
Burundi	24.1	11.0	6.4	9.7	18.0	8.0	4.4	5.6	4.9	4.3	3.9
Comoros	1.7	4.4	3.4	1.8	1.8	2.3	0.6	-8.1	1.8	3.5	3.6
Democratic Republic of the Congo	17.3	2.8	7.1	15.3	9.7	1.6	1.0	1.0	1.2	1.8	2.5
Djibouti	12.0	1.7	4.0	5.1	3.7	2.4	2.9	2.1	3.1	3.5	4.0
Eritrea	16.9	32.4	15.2	25.3	20.7	8.1	14.8	11.2	11.5	7.5	6.0
Ethiopia	44.4	8.5	8.1	33.2	22.8	8.1	7.4	10.1	7.8	7.5	7.5
Kenya	26.2	9.2	4.0	14.0	9.4	5.7	6.9	6.6	5.9	5.5	5.2
Madagascar	9.2	9.0	9.2	9.5	6.4	5.8	6.1	7.4	6.5	6.8	6.4
Rwanda	15.4	10.4	2.3	5.7	6.3	4.2	1.8	2.5	4.1	4.8	5.2
Somalia	1.5	2.7	-15.3	-3.0	-2.0	-3.2	-4.2	-2.1	-0.7	0.4	0.9
Uganda	12.1	13.0	4.0	18.7	14.0	5.5	4.3	5.2	5.1	5.5	5.6
United Republic of Tanzania	10.3	12.1	6.2	12.7	16.0	7.9	6.1	5.6	5.2	5.3	5.4
Central Africa	**6.7**	**4.5**	**2.6**	**1.4**	**4.3**	**2.0**	**3.2**	**5.3**	**2.3**	**2.7**	**3.1**
Cameroon	5.3	3.0	1.3	2.9	2.9	1.9	1.9	2.7	2.3	2.3	2.3
Central African Republic	9.3	3.5	1.5	1.3	5.8	1.5	25.3	37.1	24.0	16.5	11.1
Chad	10.3	10.0	-2.1	-3.7	14.0	0.1	1.7	3.7	-1.7	0.3	2.0
Congo	7.3	5.3	5.0	1.3	3.9	6.0	0.1	5.1	3.5	4.0	3.8
Equatorial Guinea	6.6	4.7	7.8	2.5	1.0	1.2	4.8	11.7	1.5	2.2	3.5
Gabon	5.3	1.9	1.5	1.3	2.7	0.5	4.7	0.6	1.8	2.5	2.8
Sao Tome and Principe	32.0	17.0	13.3	14.3	10.6	8.1	7.0	5.3	5.5	4.6	3.9
West Africa	**11.4**	**10.3**	**11.6**	**9.7**	**10.6**	**7.6**	**7.3**	**8.3**	**13.0**	**15.7**	**15.7**
Benin	7.9	2.2	2.3	2.7	6.8	1.0	-1.1	0.3	1.1	3.1	3.3
Burkina Faso	10.7	2.6	-0.8	2.8	3.8	0.5	-0.3	1.0	0.7	1.5	2.1
Cabo Verde	6.8	1.0	2.1	4.5	2.5	1.5	-0.2	0.1	-1.5	0.6	1.6
Côte D'Ivoire	6.3	1.0	1.2	4.9	1.3	2.6	0.5	1.2	1.7	3.1	4.0
Gambia (Islamic Republic of the)	4.4	4.6	5.0	4.8	4.3	5.7	5.9	6.7	5.0	4.6	4.1
Ghana	16.5	19.3	10.7	8.7	9.2	11.6	15.5	17.1	18.1	12.5	10.2
Guinea	18.4	4.7	15.5	21.4	15.2	11.9	9.7	8.2	8.2	8.8	7.6
Guinea Bissau	10.5	-1.7	2.5	5.0	2.1	1.2	-1.5	1.4	1.5	2.3	2.8
Liberia	17.5	7.4	7.3	8.5	6.8	7.6	9.8	5.2	6.4	6.0	5.2
Mali	9.2	2.5	1.1	2.9	5.4	-0.6	0.9	1.4	-1.3	1.2	2.6
Niger	11.3	0.6	0.8	2.9	0.5	2.3	-0.9	1.0	0.7	1.8	2.3
Nigeria	11.6	11.5	13.7	10.8	12.2	8.5	8.1	9.0	15.2	18.8	18.9
Senegal	5.8	-2.2	1.2	3.4	1.4	0.7	-1.1	0.1	-0.6	1.7	2.6
Sierra Leone	14.8	9.3	16.6	16.2	12.9	10.3	7.3	8.0	9.7	9.2	8.6
Togo	8.7	3.3	1.8	3.6	2.6	1.8	0.2	1.8	2.6	2.1	2.0

Table A.6
Developing economies: consumer price inflation, 2008–2018 *(continued)*

Annual percentage change

	2008	2009	2010	2011	2012	2013	2014	2015	2016[b]	2017[c]	2018[c]
Southern Africa	**10.8**	**7.6**	**6.1**	**6.6**	**6.7**	**6.4**	**6.3**	**5.6**	**11.4**	**9.8**	**8.2**
Angola	12.5	13.7	14.5	13.5	10.3	8.8	7.3	10.3	33.7	28.3	21.9
Botswana	12.7	8.0	6.9	8.5	7.5	5.9	4.4	3.1	3.3	3.6	3.8
Lesotho	10.7	7.4	3.6	5.0	6.1	4.9	5.3	3.2	7.3	6.5	6.2
Malawi	8.7	8.4	7.4	7.6	21.3	27.3	23.8	21.9	23.5	16.1	11.9
Mauritius	9.7	2.5	2.9	6.5	3.9	3.5	3.2	1.3	1.0	2.4	3.2
Mozambique	10.3	3.3	12.7	10.4	2.7	4.3	2.6	3.6	18.0	12.5	8.5
Namibia	9.1	9.5	4.9	5.0	6.7	5.6	5.3	3.4	6.5	5.8	5.7
South Africa	10.1	7.3	4.1	5.0	5.8	5.8	6.1	4.5	6.6	6.0	5.6
Swaziland	12.7	7.4	4.5	6.1	8.9	5.6	5.7	5.0	8.5	6.8	6.0
Zambia	12.4	13.4	8.5	6.4	6.6	7.0	7.8	10.1	20.5	14.5	9.7
Zimbabwe	21.9	-39.9	3.0	3.3	3.9	1.6	-0.2	-2.4	-0.6	1.0	1.5
Africa - net fuel exporters	**11.7**	**9.5**	**9.9**	**10.1**	**10.4**	**7.9**	**8.4**	**8.7**	**13.1**	**13.8**	**13.0**
Africa - net fuel importers	**11.7**	**6.4**	**4.5**	**7.1**	**6.9**	**5.4**	**5.4**	**4.9**	**6.2**	**5.6**	**5.3**
East and South Asia	**7.5**	**2.5**	**4.9**	**6.4**	**4.7**	**5.3**	**3.5**	**2.7**	**2.8**	**3.1**	**3.4**
East Asia	**6.2**	**0.4**	**3.3**	**5.2**	**2.8**	**2.8**	**2.3**	**1.6**	**1.9**	**2.3**	**2.7**
Brunei Darussalam	2.1	1.0	0.4	2.0	0.5	0.4	-0.2	-0.4	-0.3	0.9	1.2
Cambodia	25.0	-0.7	4.0	5.5	2.9	2.9	3.9	1.2	2.8	3.0	2.9
China	5.9	-0.7	3.2	5.6	2.6	2.7	2.0	1.4	2.0	2.1	2.7
Fiji	7.7	3.2	3.7	7.3	3.4	2.9	0.5	1.4	3.1	2.5	2.6
Hong Kong SAR[e]	4.3	0.6	2.3	5.3	4.1	4.4	4.5	3.0	2.6	2.7	2.7
Indonesia	10.2	4.4	5.2	5.4	4.3	6.4	6.4	6.4	3.8	4.3	4.4
Kiribati	7.9	0.5	1.5	2.9	0.9	0.7	3.1	2.2	1.2	1.8	2.0
Lao People's Democratic Republic	7.6	0.0	6.0	7.6	4.3	6.4	4.1	1.3	1.3	2.1	2.8
Malaysia	5.4	0.6	1.7	3.2	1.7	2.1	3.1	2.1	2.0	2.4	2.5
Mongolia	25.1	6.3	10.1	9.5	15.0	8.6	13.0	5.8	3.0	4.3	4.9
Myanmar	26.8	1.5	7.7	5.0	1.5	5.5	5.5	10.8	9.6	8.7	7.7
Papua New Guinea	10.8	6.9	6.0	4.4	4.5	5.0	5.2	6.0	6.7	7.5	7.3
Philippines	8.3	4.2	3.8	4.6	3.2	3.0	4.1	1.4	1.7	2.8	3.3
Republic of Korea	4.7	2.8	2.9	4.0	2.2	1.3	1.3	0.7	1.0	1.8	2.0
Samoa	11.6	6.3	0.8	5.2	2.0	0.6	-0.4	0.7	0.8	1.5	2.0
Singapore	6.5	0.6	2.8	5.3	4.5	2.4	1.0	-0.5	-0.7	1.3	2.3
Solomon Islands	17.3	7.1	1.1	7.3	5.9	5.4	5.2	-0.6	2.3	3.4	4.1
Taiwan Province of China	1.7	-1.0	1.1	1.1	1.1	0.6	0.3	-0.6	1.1	1.2	1.5
Thailand	5.5	-0.8	3.3	3.8	3.0	2.2	1.9	-0.9	0.4	1.9	2.8
Timor-Leste	9.1	0.7	6.8	13.5	11.8	11.2	0.4	0.6	-1.0	1.9	3.3
Vanuatu	4.8	4.3	2.8	0.9	1.4	1.4	0.8	2.5	2.1	2.8	3.2
Viet Nam	23.1	7.1	8.9	18.7	9.1	6.6	4.1	0.9	2.5	4.0	4.5
South Asia	**12.9**	**11.0**	**11.4**	**11.3**	**12.4**	**15.6**	**8.4**	**6.9**	**6.2**	**6.4**	**6.1**
Afghanistan	30.6	-8.3	0.9	10.2	7.2	7.7	4.6	-1.5	6.0	6.5	6.5
Bangladesh	8.9	5.4	8.1	10.7	6.2	7.5	7.0	6.2	5.7	5.8	5.5
Bhutan	8.3	4.4	7.0	8.8	10.9	7.0	8.2	4.5	4.0	4.5	5.0
India	8.4	10.9	12.0	8.9	9.3	10.9	6.3	5.9	5.9	5.7	5.4
Iran (Islamic Republic of)	25.5	13.5	10.1	20.6	27.4	39.3	17.2	13.7	8.5	9.3	9.2
Maldives	12.3	4.0	6.6	12.8	12.1	2.3	2.1	1.0	2.5	3.0	3.9

Table A.6
Developing economies: consumer price inflation, 2008–2018 *(continued)*

Annual percentage change

	2008	2009	2010	2011	2012	2013	2014	2015	2016[b]	2017[c]	2018[c]
Nepal	9.9	11.1	9.3	9.3	9.5	9.0	8.4	7.9	8.5	8.3	8.0
Pakistan	20.3	13.6	13.9	11.9	9.7	7.7	7.2	2.5	4.0	5.2	5.5
Sri Lanka	22.6	3.5	6.2	6.7	7.5	6.9	3.3	0.9	4.9	5.0	5.3
East and South Asia - net fuel exporters	16.4	7.7	7.1	11.6	12.4	17.4	9.8	8.3	5.2	5.9	6.0
East and South Asia - net fuel importers	6.5	1.9	4.6	5.8	3.8	3.9	2.8	2.0	2.5	2.7	3.1
Western Asia	**10.6**	**4.1**	**4.9**	**4.9**	**5.6**	**6.3**	**4.9**	**4.9**	**5.9**	**5.5**	**5.1**
Net fuel exporters	11.5	3.3	3.3	4.4	2.8	2.8	2.7	3.2	3.5	3.3	3.3
Bahrain	3.5	2.8	2.0	-0.4	2.8	3.3	2.7	1.8	2.9	2.0	2.5
Iraq	12.7	6.9	2.9	5.8	6.1	1.9	2.2	1.4	0.5	2.0	3.0
Kuwait	10.6	4.6	4.5	4.9	3.2	2.7	2.9	3.3	3.0	3.4	3.9
Oman	12.1	3.9	3.2	4.1	2.9	1.2	1.0	0.1	1.4	3.0	2.9
Qatar	15.0	-4.9	-2.4	1.9	1.9	3.1	3.1	1.9	2.9	2.3	2.6
Saudi Arabia	10.0	5.0	5.4	5.8	2.9	3.5	2.7	2.2	3.7	3.2	3.2
United Arab Emirates	12.3	1.6	0.9	0.9	0.7	1.1	2.3	4.1	1.7	2.4	2.5
Yemen	19.0	5.4	11.2	19.5	9.9	11.0	8.1	30.0	35.0	22.5	17.5
Net fuel importers	9.6	5.1	6.8	5.6	8.8	10.5	7.5	7.0	8.9	8.1	7.2
Israel	4.6	3.3	2.7	3.5	1.7	1.6	0.5	-0.6	-0.3	1.1	2.3
Jordan	14.9	-0.7	5.0	4.2	4.5	4.8	2.9	-0.9	-0.7	1.5	2.6
Lebanon	10.2	1.2	4.0	3.8	7.8	5.5	0.8	-3.7	-1.4	1.8	2.2
Syrian Arab Republic	15.7	2.9	4.4	4.8	36.7	87.4	24.3	38.2	63.5	45.0	33.2
Turkey	10.5	6.2	8.6	6.5	9.0	7.5	8.9	7.7	8.2	7.8	7.0
Latin America and the Caribbean[d]	**7.6**	**5.0**	**5.5**	**6.3**	**5.9**	**6.0**	**7.8**	**7.1**	**9.2**	**6.1**	**4.8**
South America[d]	8.2	5.1	6.0	7.1	6.6	6.9	9.3	8.9	11.7	7.4	5.6
Argentina	20.6	9.4	17.2	14.8	17.2	17.6	32.8	15.7	36.0	21.0	14.0
Bolivia (Plurinational State of)	14.0	3.3	2.5	9.8	4.6	5.7	5.8	4.1	3.6	4.0	4.2
Brazil	5.7	4.8	5.0	6.6	5.4	6.2	6.3	9.1	8.9	5.8	4.6
Chile	8.7	1.5	1.5	3.3	3.0	1.8	4.7	4.3	3.9	3.1	2.7
Colombia	7.0	4.2	2.3	3.4	3.2	2.0	2.9	5.0	7.7	4.4	3.5
Ecuador	8.4	5.2	3.6	4.5	5.1	2.7	3.6	4.0	1.7	2.1	2.4
Paraguay	10.2	2.6	4.7	8.3	3.7	2.7	5.0	3.1	4.1	4.2	4.4
Peru	5.8	2.9	1.5	3.4	3.7	2.8	3.2	3.6	3.4	3.1	3.1
Suriname	14.7	-0.2	6.9	17.7	5.0	1.9	3.4	6.9	53.0	21.0	10.0
Uruguay	7.9	7.1	6.7	8.1	8.1	8.6	8.9	8.7	9.9	8.3	7.6
Venezuela (Bolivarian Republic of)	29.8	27.1	28.2	26.1	21.1	40.6	62.2	121.7	350.0	280.0	150.0
Mexico and Central America	5.9	5.1	4.1	3.7	4.1	3.9	4.0	2.5	2.6	2.9	2.9
Belize	6.4	-1.1	5.6	-3.6	1.3	0.5	1.2	-0.9	0.5	1.1	1.6
Costa Rica	13.4	7.8	5.7	4.9	4.5	5.2	4.5	0.8	0.3	2.8	3.3
El Salvador	6.7	1.1	0.9	5.1	1.7	0.8	1.1	-0.7	1.1	1.5	1.8
Guatemala	11.4	1.9	3.9	6.2	3.8	4.3	3.4	2.4	4.5	4.4	4.2
Honduras	11.4	5.5	4.7	6.8	5.2	5.2	6.1	3.2	2.6	3.7	4.3
Mexico	5.1	5.3	4.2	3.4	4.1	3.8	4.0	2.7	2.7	2.9	2.8
Nicaragua	19.8	3.7	5.5	8.1	7.2	7.1	6.0	4.0	3.6	4.5	4.7
Panama	8.8	2.4	3.5	5.9	5.7	4.0	2.6	0.1	0.7	1.9	2.3

Table A.6

Developing economies: consumer price inflation, 2008–2018 *(continued)*

Annual percentage change

	2008	2009	2010	2011	2012	2013	2014	2015	2016[b]	2017[c]	2018[c]
Caribbean	7.6	2.0	4.8	8.7	5.3	3.4	4.9	3.0	3.2	3.5	3.8
Bahamas	4.5	2.1	1.3	3.2	2.0	0.3	1.5	1.9	-0.3	1.0	1.3
Barbados	8.1	3.6	5.8	9.4	4.5	1.8	1.9	-1.1	0.5	1.5	2.3
Cuba	0.2	-0.8	0.5	11.1	5.6	0.6	6.4	4.0	4.3	4.0	4.5
Dominican Republic	10.6	1.4	6.3	8.5	3.7	4.8	3.0	0.8	1.7	2.6	2.9
Guyana	8.1	2.9	2.1	5.0	2.4	1.8	0.9	-1.0	0.7	1.0	1.5
Haiti	15.5	0.0	5.7	8.4	6.3	5.9	4.6	9.0	13.0	9.9	7.3
Jamaica	22.0	9.6	12.6	7.5	6.9	9.3	8.3	3.7	2.4	3.8	4.3
Trinidad and Tobago	12.0	7.0	10.5	5.1	9.3	5.2	5.7	4.7	3.2	3.5	3.9
Latin America and the Caribbean - net fuel exporters	7.9	4.5	2.9	4.0	3.9	2.5	3.3	4.7	6.2	3.9	3.4
Latin America and the Caribbean - net fuel importers	7.6	5.0	5.8	6.5	6.1	6.3	8.2	7.3	9.4	6.3	5.0
Memorandum items:											
Least developed countries	14.6	7.0	8.3	12.1	10.8	8.6	8.3	8.6	11.8	10.2	8.7
East Asia (excluding China)	6.8	2.1	3.4	4.6	3.1	3.0	2.9	1.9	1.8	2.5	2.8
South Asia (excluding India)	21.5	11.3	10.3	15.9	18.3	24.3	12.2	8.9	6.8	7.5	7.5
Western Asia (excluding Israel and Turkey)	11.7	3.2	3.4	4.4	4.4	6.5	3.5	4.4	5.8	5.0	4.6
Arab States[f]	11.4	4.4	4.4	5.7	5.8	6.8	5.1	5.5	6.7	6.1	5.6
Landlocked developing economies	19.9	6.0	6.3	10.3	7.5	6.0	6.0	5.8	9.0	6.7	6.0
Small island developing economies	7.1	1.4	3.7	6.4	4.8	2.9	2.7	1.2	1.7	2.5	3.1

Source: UN/DESA

a Data for country groups are weighted averages, where weights are based on GDP in 2010 prices and exchange rates.

b Partly estimated.

c Baseline scenario forecasts, based in part on Project LINK and the UN/DESA World Economic Forecasting Model.

d Regional aggregates exclude Venezuela (Bolivarian Republic of), due to the potential distortionary impacts of very high inflation in a single country.

e Special Administrative Region of China.

f Currently includes data for Algeria, Bahrain, Comoros, Djibouti, Egypt, Iraq, Jordan, Kuwait, Lebanon, Libya, Mauritania, Morocco, Oman, Qatar, Saudi Arabia, Somalia, Sudan, Syrian Arab Republic, Tunisia, United Arab Emirates and Yemen..

Table A.7

Developed economies: unemployment rates,[a,b] 2008–2018

Percentage of labour force

	2008	2009	2010	2011	2012	2013	2014	2015	2016[c]	2017[d]	2018[d]
Developed economies	6.1	8.4	8.8	8.5	8.6	8.5	7.8	7.1	6.6	6.4	6.2
United States	5.8	9.3	9.6	8.9	8.1	7.4	6.2	5.3	4.9	4.8	4.8
Canada	6.1	8.4	8.1	7.5	7.3	7.1	6.9	6.9	7.0	7.1	6.9
Japan	4.0	5.1	5.1	4.6	4.3	4.0	3.6	3.4	3.1	3.1	3.0
Australia	4.2	5.6	5.2	5.1	5.2	5.7	6.1	6.1	5.7	5.6	5.5
New Zealand	4.0	5.8	6.2	6.0	6.4	5.8	5.4	5.3	5.1	4.9	5.0
European Union	7.0	8.9	9.6	9.7	10.5	10.9	10.2	9.4	8.7	8.3	8.1
EU-15	7.2	9.1	9.5	9.6	10.6	11.0	10.5	9.8	9.2	8.8	8.6
Austria	4.1	5.3	4.8	4.6	4.9	5.4	5.6	5.7	6.1	5.9	6.0
Belgium	7.0	7.9	8.3	7.1	7.6	8.5	8.6	8.5	8.2	8.1	8.0
Denmark	3.5	6.0	7.5	7.6	7.5	7.0	6.5	6.2	6.1	5.8	5.4
Finland	6.4	8.1	8.4	7.8	7.8	8.2	8.7	9.3	8.9	8.8	8.6
France	7.4	9.1	9.3	9.2	9.8	10.3	10.3	10.4	10.2	9.9	9.7
Germany	7.4	7.7	6.9	5.9	5.4	5.2	5.0	4.6	4.2	4.0	3.8
Greece	7.8	9.6	12.7	17.9	24.6	27.5	26.6	25.0	23.7	23.4	22.9
Ireland	6.4	12.0	13.9	14.7	14.7	13.1	11.3	9.5	8.2	10.0	10.7
Italy	6.7	7.7	8.3	8.4	10.7	12.1	12.6	11.9	11.6	11.2	10.9
Luxembourg	4.9	5.2	4.6	4.8	5.1	5.8	6.0	6.5	6.3	6.4	6.5
Netherlands	3.7	4.4	5.0	5.0	5.8	7.3	7.4	6.9	6.2	5.9	5.7
Portugal	8.8	10.7	12.0	12.9	15.8	16.4	14.1	12.7	11.4	11.0	10.7
Spain	11.3	17.9	19.9	21.4	24.8	26.1	24.5	22.1	20.0	18.8	18.1
Sweden	6.2	8.3	8.6	7.8	8.0	8.0	7.9	7.4	7.0	6.6	6.2
United Kingdom	5.6	7.6	7.8	8.1	7.9	7.6	6.1	5.3	5.0	4.8	4.6
EU-13	6.5	8.4	9.8	9.8	10.0	10.1	9.0	7.9	6.7	6.4	6.2
Bulgaria	5.6	6.9	10.3	11.3	12.3	12.9	11.4	9.1	7.9	7.5	7.1
Croatia	8.6	9.2	11.7	13.7	16.0	17.3	17.3	16.3	13.5	13.0	12.5
Cyprus	3.7	5.4	6.3	7.9	11.9	15.9	16.2	14.9	12.5	12.6	12.4
Czech Republic	4.4	6.7	7.3	6.7	7.0	7.0	6.1	5.1	4.2	4.0	3.8
Estonia	5.7	13.6	16.7	12.4	10.0	8.6	7.4	6.2	6.7	6.3	5.9
Hungary	7.8	10.0	11.2	11.1	11.0	10.1	7.8	6.8	5.4	5.2	5.0
Latvia	7.8	17.6	19.5	16.2	15.0	11.8	10.8	9.9	9.6	9.3	8.9
Lithuania	5.8	13.8	17.8	15.4	13.4	11.8	10.7	09.2	8.4	8.2	7.5
Malta	6.0	6.9	6.9	6.4	6.3	6.4	5.8	5.4	4.9	5.0	4.9
Poland	7.1	8.2	9.6	9.7	10.1	10.4	9.0	7.5	6.2	5.9	5.7
Romania	5.6	6.5	7.0	7.1	6.8	7.1	6.8	6.8	6.2	6.1	5.8
Slovakia	9.6	12.1	14.5	13.7	14.0	14.2	13.2	11.5	9.9	8.9	8.0
Slovenia	4.4	5.9	7.3	8.2	8.9	10.2	9.7	9.0	8.0	7.9	7.6
Other Europe	3.1	3.8	4.3	3.9	3.9	4.1	4.2	4.5	4.7	4.7	4.6
Iceland	3.4	6.8	7.5	7.1	6.0	5.5	4.9	3.9	3.0	3.1	3.1
Norway	2.6	3.2	3.6	3.3	3.2	3.5	3.5	4.4	4.8	4.6	4.6
Switzerland	3.4	4.1	4.5	4.0	4.2	4.4	4.5	4.5	4.7	4.8	4.7
Memorandum items:											
Major developed economies	5.8	8.0	8.1	7.7	7.4	7.1	6.4	5.8	5.5	5.4	5.3
Euro area	7.6	9.6	10.2	10.2	11.4	12.0	11.6	10.9	10.2	9.8	9.5

Source: UN/DESA, based on data of the OECD and Eurostat.

a Unemployment data are standardized by the OECD and Eurostat for comparability among countries and over time, in conformity with the definitions of the International Labour Organization (see OECD, Standardized Unemployment Rates: Sources and Methods (Paris, 1985)).

b Data for country groups are weighted averages, where labour force is used for weights.

c Partly estimated.

d Baseline scenario forecasts, based in part on Project LINK and the UN/DESA World Economic Forecasting Model.

Table A.8

Economies in transition and developing economies: unemployment rates,[a] 2007–2016

Percentage of labour force

	2007	2008	2009	2010	2011	2012	2013	2014	2015	2016[b]
South-Eastern Europe[c]										
Albania	13.4	13.1	13.8	14.0	14.0	13.4	15.9	17.5	17.1	*16.0*
Bosnia and Herzegovina	29.0	23.4	24.1	27.2	27.6	28.0	27.5	27.5	27.7	*25.4*
Montenegro	19.4	16.8	19.1	19.7	19.7	19.7	19.5	18.0	17.6	*17.3*
Serbia	18.1	13.6	16.1	19.2	23.0	23.9	22.1	19.2	17.7	*17.5*
The former Yugoslav Republic of Macedonia	34.9	33.8	32.2	32.0	31.4	31.0	29.0	28.0	26.1	*23.4*
Commonwealth of Independent States and Georgia[c, d]										
Armenia	28.7	16.4	18.7	19.0	18.4	17.3	16.2	17.6	18.5	*18.3*
Azerbaijan	6.3	5.9	5.7	5.6	5.4	5.2	5.0	4.9	5.0	*5.5*
Belarus	1.0	0.8	0.9	0.8	0.7	0.6	0.5	0.5	0.9	*1.9*
Georgia[d]	13.3	16.5	16.9	16.3	15.1	15.0	14.6	12.4	12.0	*12.0*
Kazakhstan	7.3	6.6	6.6	5.8	5.4	5.3	5.2	5.0	5.0	*5.0*
Kyrgyzstan	8.2	8.2	8.4	8.6	8.5	8.4	8.3	8.0	7.6	*7.6*
Republic of Moldova	5.1	4.0	6.4	7.4	6.7	5.6	5.1	3.9	4.9	*5.2*
Russian Federation	6.0	6.2	8.3	7.3	6.5	5.5	5.5	*5.2*	*5.6*	*5.6*
Tajikistan	2.4	2.2	2.0	2.1	2.3	2.4	2.3	2.4	*2.4*	*2.4*
Turkmenistan[e]	10.4	10.4	10.5	10.4	10.3	10.3	10.2	10.1	*10.1*	*10.1*
Ukraine[f]	6.4	6.4	8.8	8.2	8.0	7.6	7.3	9.3	9.1	*9.1*
Uzbekistan	5.0	4.9	5.0	5.4	5.0	4.9	4.9	5.1	*5.1*	*5.2*
Africa[e]										
Algeria	13.8	11.3	10.2	10.0	10.0	11.0	9.8	10.6	11.3	*11.6*
Botswana	17.7	20.0	19.1	17.9	17.8	17.7	17.4	17.9	18.2	*18.1*
Egypt	8.9	8.7	9.4	9.0	12.0	12.7	13.2	13.0	12.5	*12.6*
Mauritius	8.5	7.2	7.3	7.7	7.9	8.7	7.6	7.7	7.5	*7.3*
Morocco	9.8	9.6	9.1	9.1	8.9	9.0	9.2	9.9	9.8	*9.7*
South Africa	22.3	22.4	23.5	24.7	24.6	24.7	24.6	24.9	25.2	*25.9*
Tunisia	12.4	12.4	13.3	13.0	18.3	17.6	15.9	15.3	15.0	*14.0*
Developing America[g]										
Argentina	8.5	7.9	8.7	7.7	7.2	7.2	7.1	7.3	6.5	*7.8*
Barbados	7.4	8.1	10.0	10.8	11.2	11.6	11.6	12.3	11.3	*10.6*
Bolivia (Plurinational State of)	7.7	4.4	4.9	*4.1*	3.8	3.2	4.0	3.5	*3.5*	*3.5*
Brazil[e]	9.3	7.9	8.1	6.7	6.0	8.2	8.0	7.8	9.3	*12.0*
Chile	7.1	7.8	9.7	8.2	7.1	6.4	5.9	6.4	6.2	*6.7*
Colombia	10.7	11.0	12.3	11.8	10.9	10.6	10.1	9.5	9.2	*9.8*
Costa Rica	4.8	4.8	8.5	7.1	7.7	9.8	9.1	9.5	9.7	*9.3*
Dominican Republic	5.4	5.3	5.8	5.7	6.7	7.2	7.9	7.2	6.9	*6.3*
Ecuador	7.4	6.9	8.5	7.6	6.0	4.9	4.7	5.1	5.4	*7.4*
El Salvador	5.8	5.5	7.1	6.8	6.6	6.2	5.6	6.7	*6.5*	*6.4*
Guatemala	..	..	..	4.8	3.1	4.0	3.8	4.0	2.8	*2.9*
Honduras	4.0	4.1	4.9	6.4	6.8	5.6	6.0	7.5	8.8	*8.9*
Jamaica	6.0	6.9	7.5	8.0	8.4	9.3	10.3	9.4	9.5	*10.1*
Mexico[h]	3.7	4.0	5.5	5.4	5.2	5.0	4.9	4.8	4.4	*4.0*
Nicaragua	5.9	6.1	7.9	7.8	5.9	5.9	5.6	6.6	*6.9*	*7.0*

Table A.8
Economies in transition and developing economies: unemployment rates,[a] 2007–2016 *(continued)*

Percentage of labour force

	2007	2008	2009	2010	2011	2012	2013	2014	2015	2016[b]
Developing America *(continued)*										
Panama	5.8	5.0	6.3	5.8	3.6	3.6	3.7	4.1	4.5	*4.0*
Paraguay	7.2	7.4	8.2	7.2	7.1	8.1	8.1	8.0	6.8	*7.4*
Peru	8.4	8.4	8.4	7.9	7.7	6.8	5.9	5.9	6.5	*6.5*
Trinidad and Tobago	5.6	4.6	5.3	5.9	5.1	5.0	3.7	3.3	3.5	*3.5*
Uruguay	9.8	8.3	8.2	7.5	6.6	6.7	6.7	6.9	7.8	*8.1*
Venezuela (Bolivarian Republic of)	8.4	7.3	7.9	8.7	8.3	8.1	7.8	7.2	7.0	*17.1*
Developing Asia[e]										
China	3.8	4.4	4.4	4.2	4.3	4.5	4.6	4.6	4.6	*4.6*
Hong Kong SAR[i]	4.0	3.6	5.2	4.3	3.4	3.3	3.4	3.3	3.3	*3.3*
India	3.7	4.2	3.9	3.5	3.5	3.6	3.6	3.5	3.5	*3.4*
Indonesia	9.1	8.4	7.9	7.1	6.6	6.1	6.2	5.9	6.1	*5.8*
Iran (Islamic Republic of)	10.6	10.5	11.9	13.5	12.5	12.7	10.4	10.6	10.8	*11.2*
Israel	7.3	6.1	7.6	6.7	5.6	6.9	6.2	5.9	5.3	*5.3*
Jordan	13.1	12.7	12.9	12.5	12.9	12.2	12.6	11.9	11.7	*11.5*
Korea, Republic of[h]	3.3	3.2	3.7	3.7	3.4	3.2	3.1	3.5	3.6	*3.8*
Malaysia	3.2	3.3	3.7	3.4	3.1	3.0	3.1	2.9	3.2	*3.2*
Pakistan	5.1	5.0	5.2	5.3	5.7	5.7	6.0	5.6	5.4	*5.4*
Philippines	7.4	7.3	7.5	7.3	7.0	7.0	7.1	6.6	6.1	*5.8*
Saudi Arabia	5.7	5.1	5.4	5.6	5.8	5.6	5.6	5.9	5.9	*5.9*
Singapore	3.0	3.2	4.3	3.1	2.9	2.8	2.8	2.8	2.8	*2.9*
Sri Lanka	6.0	5.2	5.9	4.9	4.2	4.0	4.4	4.3	4.3	*4.3*
Taiwan Province of China	3.9	4.1	5.9	5.2	4.4	4.2	4.2	4.0	3.8	*3.9*
Thailand	1.2	1.2	1.5	1.0	0.7	0.7	0.8	0.8	0.9	*0.7*
Turkey[h]	9.1	10.1	13.0	11.1	9.1	8.4	9.0	9.9	10.3	*10.3*
Viet Nam	2.1	2.4	2.6	2.6	2.0	1.8	2.0	1.9	2.2	*2.3*

Source: UN/DESA, based on data of the Economic Commission for Europe (ECE); ILO KILM 9th edition; Economic Commission for Latin America and the Caribbean (ECLAC) and OECD. UN/DESA estimates indicated in italics.

a As a percentage of labour force. Reflects national definitions and coverage. Not comparable across economies.

b Partly estimated.

c Sourced from UNECE Statistical Database.

d Georgia officially left the Commonwealth of Independent States on 18 August 2009. However, its performance is discussed in the context of this group of countries for reasons of geographic proximity and similarities in economic structure.

e Sourced from ILO KILM 9th edition.

f Starting in 2010, data for the Ukraine excludes the temporarily occupied territory of the Autonomous Republic of Crimea and Sevastopol.

g Sourced from CEPALSTAT Database, ECLAC.

h Sourced from OECD Short-Term Labour Market Statistics.

i Special Administrative Region of China.

Table A.9
Major developed economies: financial indicators, 2007–2016

Percentage

	2007	2008	2009	2010	2011	2012	2013	2014	2015	2016[a]
Short-term interest rates[b]										
Canada	4.63	3.31	0.69	0.78	1.17	1.16	1.17	1.17	0.82	0.82
Euro area[c]	4.28	4.63	1.23	0.81	1.39	0.57	0.22	0.21	-0.02	-0.25
Japan	0.75	0.85	0.58	0.38	0.33	0.33	0.24	0.20	0.17	0.08
United Kingdom	5.96	5.49	1.20	0.69	0.89	0.84	0.49	0.54	0.55	0.53
United States	5.27	2.96	0.56	0.31	0.30	0.28	0.17	0.12	0.23	0.60
Long-term interest rates[d]										
Canada	4.3	3.6	3.2	3.2	2.8	1.9	2.3	2.2	1.5	1.2
France	4.3	4.2	3.6	3.1	3.3	2.5	2.2	1.7	0.8	0.4
Germany	4.2	4.0	3.2	2.7	2.6	1.5	1.6	1.2	0.5	0.1
Italy	4.5	4.7	4.3	4.0	5.4	5.5	4.3	2.9	1.7	1.4
Japan	1.7	1.5	1.3	1.1	1.1	0.8	0.7	0.5	0.4	-0.1
United Kingdom	5.0	4.6	3.6	3.6	3.1	1.9	2.4	2.6	1.9	1.3
United States	4.6	3.7	3.3	3.2	2.8	1.8	2.4	2.5	2.1	1.7
General government financial balances[e]										
Canada	1.8	0.2	-3.9	-4.7	-3.3	-2.5	-1.9	-0.5	-1.7	-3.0
France	-2.5	-3.2	-7.2	-6.8	-5.1	-4.8	-4.0	-4.0	-3.5	-3.3
Germany	0.3	0.0	-3.0	-4.1	-0.9	0.0	-0.2	0.3	0.7	0.7
Italy	-1.5	-2.7	-5.3	-4.2	-3.5	-2.9	-2.7	-3.0	-2.6	-2.6
Japan	-2.1	-4.1	-10.4	-9.3	-9.8	-8.8	-8.5	-6.1	-5.2	-6.0
United Kingdom	-3.0	-5.0	-10.7	-9.6	-7.7	-8.3	-5.7	-5.7	-4.3	-4.1
United States	-2.9	-6.7	-13.1	-10.9	-9.6	-7.9	-4.4	-4.1	-3.7	-3.7

Source: UN/DESA, based on OECD, Economic Outlook; OECD, Main Economic Indicators.

a Average for the first nine months for short- and long-term interest rates.

b Three-month Interbank or money market rate.

c Three-month Euro Interbank Offered Rate (EURIBOR).

d Yield on 10-year government bonds.

e Surplus (+) or deficit (-) as a percentage of nominal GDP. Estimates for 2016.

Table A.10
Selected economies: real effective exchange rates, broad measurement,[a, b] 2007–2016

	2007	2008	2009	2010	2011	2012	2013	2014	2015	2016[c]
Developed economies										
Australia	93.4	91.5	87.0	100.0	106.8	108.5	103.4	97.9	89.3	89.0
Bulgaria	91.3	99.1	103.4	100.0	101.7	100.1	100.8	100.2	97.1	97.3
Canada	99.1	97.0	91.1	100.0	101.1	100.6	97.2	91.3	84.1	82.0
Croatia	97.9	102.4	103.5	100.0	97.2	94.5	95.6	95.0	92.5	92.6
Czech Republic	91.0	104.9	100.9	100.0	101.8	97.6	96.0	90.6	87.7	89.9
Denmark	100.7	101.9	104.7	100.0	99.0	96.2	96.8	97.8	94.2	95.5
Euro area	106.2	108.2	108.9	100.0	98.6	93.5	96.4	97.4	88.9	90.5
Hungary	103.0	106.1	99.6	100.0	99.7	96.5	96.2	92.2	88.5	88.6
Japan	82.6	87.8	99.5	100.0	101.5	100.5	79.7	75.1	69.6	78.8
New Zealand	107.3	100.0	91.6	100.0	104.0	106.9	109.9	112.8	104.3	103.2
Norway	99.9	99.9	95.8	100.0	100.4	99.5	98.5	93.3	84.6	84.0
Poland	103.6	113.7	96.2	100.0	98.4	94.7	95.6	96.2	91.5	87.8
Romania	114.0	107.3	100.1	100.0	102.7	96.5	101.2	102.0	98.3	96.9
Sweden	108.2	105.6	94.5	100.0	105.7	105.1	106.1	100.7	93.5	94.8
Switzerland	89.9	93.2	96.4	100.0	110.1	105.5	103.6	104.7	109.8	108.8
United Kingdom	128.5	112.0	100.0	100.0	100.3	104.2	102.6	109.6	114.4	105.4
United States	105.7	100.2	104.8	100.0	94.7	96.7	96.6	98.5	108.8	112.3
Economies in transition										
Russian Federation	94.1	99.7	93.7	100.0	103.7	104.6	106.9	98.0	80.1	75.9
Ukraine[d]	128.5	112.0	100.0	100.0	100.3	104.2	102.6	109.6	114.4	105.4
Developing economies										
Argentina	83.0	92.1	94.3	100.0	106.2	122.9	127.6	120.1	153.8	133.9
Brazil	86.9	90.1	87.4	100.0	103.2	92.9	87.2	84.2	69.6	71.1
Chile	99.0	99.7	94.7	100.0	100.6	102.0	101.0	90.8	88.8	88.7
China	89.9	96.8	101.7	100.0	102.2	108.1	114.6	117.1	128.1	124.0
Colombia	92.0	94.8	90.3	100.0	98.9	103.9	100.3	95.4	77.9	73.5
Ecuador	97.7	95.0	101.8	100.0	97.1	100.3	101.3	104.8	118.1	121.8
Egypt	73.8	81.4	94.3	100.0	97.1	102.9	97.1	104.0	116.9	118.1
Hong Kong SAR[e]	107.5	100.6	103.0	100.0	95.8	98.0	100.4	104.1	112.3	116.4
India	91.0	86.2	87.7	100.0	101.2	96.4	95.4	96.2	104.0	104.8
Indonesia	106.8	93.7	88.3	100.0	100.5	97.1	93.3	86.6	88.6	91.4
Israel	88.9	98.2	96.0	100.0	100.5	95.8	101.3	102.9	102.1	103.7
Korea, Republic of	130.5	106.6	91.9	100.0	99.7	99.2	103.6	109.3	109.5	107.8
Kuwait	92.5	99.5	100.4	100.0	100.6	103.9	104.3	106.6	112.4	115.3
Malaysia	98.4	98.3	95.0	100.0	99.9	99.5	99.9	98.8	91.7	87.5
Mexico	109.4	106.1	93.3	100.0	99.2	95.9	101.7	100.6	91.2	80.3
Morocco	102.9	102.8	104.7	100.0	97.3	94.8	96.1	96.5	96.3	98.0
Nigeria	93.2	100.0	93.5	100.0	99.8	109.6	116.0	119.9	115.9	111.8
Pakistan	102.8	98.0	96.9	100.0	102.2	103.7	100.7	107.7	116.6	118.8

Table A.10
Selected economies: real effective exchange rates, broad measurement,[a, b] 2007–2016 *(continued)*

	2007	2008	2009	2010	2011	2012	2013	2014	2015	2016[c]
Developing economies *(continued)*										
Peru	92.6	95.0	97.9	100.0	97.7	105.0	104.2	101.7	101.3	98.8
Philippines	95.3	98.4	96.1	100.0	100.2	104.9	109.0	108.4	115.8	112.8
Saudi Arabia	90.7	91.0	99.7	100.0	97.8	100.4	102.7	104.9	113.9	121.1
Singapore	92.4	96.9	97.3	100.0	105.3	110.1	112.2	112.0	110.2	109.8
South Africa	93.4	81.0	86.4	100.0	98.4	91.9	82.4	76.0	74.8	67.3
Taiwan Province of China	107.0	104.6	99.9	100.0	100.3	100.0	100.3	98.9	100.3	99.4
Thailand	98.0	97.7	95.0	100.0	99.0	99.1	104.7	101.1	103.1	99.1
Turkey	97.0	98.0	91.7	100.0	89.4	92.2	91.4	85.7	84.1	83.4
Uruguay	82.2	88.4	89.6	100.0	101.4	104.3	110.1	106.1	106.5	105.7
Venezuela, Bolivarian Republic of	92.2	110.4	147.0	100.0	107.1	128.8	124.4	183.9	397.4	903.9
Viet Nam	90.4	99.9	103.9	100.0	100.9	108.1	114.0	117.3	123.1	123.9

Source: JPMorgan Chase.

a Year 2010=100.

b CPI-based indices. The real effective exchange rate gauges the effect on international price competitiveness of the country's manufactures owing to currency changes and inflation differentials. A rise in the index implies a fall in competitiveness and vice versa.

c Average for the first ten months.

d Starting in 2010, data for the Ukraine excludes the temporarily occupied territory of the Autonomous Republic of Crimea and Sevastopol.

e Special Administrative Region of China.

Table A.11
Indices of prices of primary commodities, 2007–2016

Index: Year 2000=100

	Non-fuel commodities					Combined index				
	Food	Tropical beverages	Vegetable oilseeds and oils	Agricultural raw materials	Minerals and metals	Dollar	SDR	Manufactured export prices	Real prices of non-fuel commodities[a]	Crude petroleum[b]
2007	164	148	226	164	313	207	178	135	153	250.4
2008	234	178	298	198	332	256	213	142	180	342.2
2009	220	181	213	163	232	213	182	134	159	221.2
2010	230	213	262	226	327	256	222	136	188	280.6
2011	265	270	333	289	375	302	253	150	201	389.3
2012	270	212	307	223	322	277	239	146	190	396.6
2013	255	174	269	206	306	258	225	149	173	383.6
2014	240	214	253	186	280	243	211	148	164	348.9
2015	204	197	203	161	218	202	190	133	152	179.3
2013										
I	266	186	280	216	332	273	237	152	180	396.7
II	260	176	262	202	297	259	228	150	173	365.6
III	251	169	258	202	296	252	220	148	170	387.4
IV	243	164	274	203	297	250	215	151	165	385.7
2014										
I	244	198	279	198	289	249	214	151	165	379.6
II	245	220	270	191	281	248	212	150	165	383.6
III	238	220	237	181	285	242	210	149	162	365.2
IV	233	219	227	172	265	232	209	142	164	265.8
2015										
I	218	201	215	164	235	214	201	134	160	182.3
II	204	196	210	166	236	207	196	134	154	217.0
III	200	197	194	160	209	196	185	134	147	174.5
IV	195	194	193	153	193	189	179	132	143	143.9
2016										
I	193	180	204	148	189	186	177	130	143	108.5
II	212	186	230	157	198	200	188	132	152	153.3
III	218	197	231	157	206	206	195	...	...	155.4

Source: UNCTAD, *Monthly Commodity Price Bulletin*; United Nations, *Monthly Bulletin of Statistics*; and data from the Organization of the Petroleum Exporting Countries (OPEC) website, available from http://www.opec.org.

a Combined index of non-fuel commodity prices in dollars, deflated by manufactured export price index.

b The new OPEC reference basket, introduced on 16 June 2005, currently has 14 crudes. Indonesian (Minas) and Gabon (Rabi Light) crudes were added, in January and July 2016, respectively.

Table A.12
World oil supply and demand, 2008–2017

	2008	2009	2010	2011	2012	2013	2014	2015	2016[a]	2017[b]
World oil supply[c, d] *(millions of barrels per day)*	84.7	83.9	85.6	86.9	89.0	89.3	91.6	94.3	93.6	94.9
Developed economies	15.5	15.7	15.9	16.1	17.0	18.1	20.1	21.3	20.7	20.9
Economies in transition	12.9	13.4	13.7	13.7	13.7	13.9	14.0	14.1	14.2	14.4
Developing economies	54.3	52.8	53.8	55.0	56.2	55.1	55.3	56.6	56.3	57.2
OPEC	35.6	34.2	34.7	35.8	37.5	37.7	37.7	39.0	39.3	40.2
Non-OPEC	18.7	18.6	19.1	19.2	18.7	17.4	17.6	17.6	17.1	17.0
Processing gains[e]	2.0	2.0	2.1	2.1	2.1	2.2	2.2	2.2	2.3	2.3
Global biofuels[f]	1.4	1.6	1.8	1.9	1.9	2.0	2.2	2.3	2.4	2.5
World total demand[g]	86.7	85.5	88.5	89.5	90.7	92.0	93.2	95.0	96.3	97.5
Oil prices *(dollars per barrel)*										
OPEC basket[h]	94.5	61.1	77.5	107.5	109.5	105.9	96.3	49.5	39.6	..
Brent oil	97.6	61.9	79.6	110.9	112.0	108.9	98.9	52.4	43.4	52.4

Source: UN/DESA, International Energy Agency; U.S. Energy Information Administration; and OPEC.

a Partly estimated.

b Baseline scenario forecasts.

c Including global biofuels, crude oil, condensates, natural gas liquids (NGLs), oil from non-conventional sources and other sources of supply.

d Totals may not add up because of rounding.

e Net volume gains and losses in the refining process (excluding net gain/loss in the economies in transition and China) and marine transportation losses.

f Global biofuels comprise all world biofuel production including fuel ethanol from Brazil and the United States.

g Including deliveries from refineries/primary stocks and marine bunkers, and refinery fuel and non-conventional oils.

h The new OPEC reference basket, introduced on 16 June 2005, currently has 14 crudes.

Table A.13

World trade:[a] changes in value and volume of exports and imports, by major country group, 2008–2018

Annual percentage change

	2008	2009	2010	2011	2012	2013	2014	2015	2016[b]	2017[c]	2018[c]
Dollar value of exports											
World	14.1	-19.5	19.6	18.2	1.5	2.7	1.8	-10.9	0.7	6.5	7.0
Developed economies	**11.0**	**-19.6**	**14.1**	**15.5**	**-1.5**	**3.3**	**2.7**	**-10.0**	**2.2**	**5.5**	**6.0**
North America	9.6	-16.7	17.4	14.3	3.7	2.4	3.8	-6.4	0.5	7.2	8.8
Europe	11.0	-19.9	10.7	16.5	-3.0	5.1	2.6	-11.0	2.4	4.9	5.1
Developed Asia and Pacific	13.7	-23.2	31.2	11.6	-2.5	-6.8	1.0	-12.2	5.1	5.8	4.9
Economies in transition	**32.7**	**-32.3**	**27.9**	**31.0**	**2.8**	**-0.4**	**-5.4**	**-28.4**	**-6.7**	**14.1**	**12.2**
South-Eastern Europe	22.2	-18.8	14.3	21.2	-6.4	16.3	4.6	-10.7	6.9	8.7	8.1
Commonwealth of Independent States and Georgia[d]	33.2	-32.8	28.5	31.4	3.2	-1.0	-5.8	-29.2	-7.4	14.5	12.4
Developing economies	**17.6**	**-18.0**	**27.2**	**20.9**	**5.2**	**2.2**	**1.3**	**-10.5**	**-0.7**	**7.3**	**7.9**
Latin America and the Caribbean	14.9	-20.5	31.3	17.8	1.7	0.2	0.9	-11.3	0.7	10.5	10.3
Africa	26.5	-25.7	26.4	16.9	9.8	-12.2	-3.3	-23.8	-4.6	11.4	10.6
East Asia	13.8	-15.2	28.3	18.4	4.7	4.8	3.3	-5.3	-0.7	5.7	6.6
South Asia	16.2	-6.1	25.9	23.9	-0.6	4.7	-1.0	-14.1	1.0	7.8	7.8
Western Asia	30.6	-26.0	20.1	35.4	10.5	1.1	-2.5	-22.3	-1.4	9.6	10.7
Dollar value of imports											
World	14.6	-19.7	19.0	18.4	1.1	2.4	1.7	-10.5	2.2	7.5	7.1
Developed economies	**11.5**	**-21.9**	**14.5**	**16.2**	**-1.9**	**1.6**	**2.5**	**-10.6**	**2.8**	**7.0**	**7.2**
North America	7.6	-22.0	19.7	13.6	3.0	0.1	3.3	-4.5	0.5	9.0	10.2
Europe	11.9	-21.4	11.1	16.2	-5.1	3.5	2.5	-12.2	4.7	6.2	5.9
Developed Asia and Pacific	20.4	-24.7	24.0	23.1	5.4	-5.4	1.0	-17.1	-2.7	6.3	6.7
Economies in transition	**30.0**	**-30.4**	**22.3**	**28.5**	**7.7**	**3.3**	**-9.0**	**-27.5**	**-6.9**	**10.1**	**9.2**
South-Eastern Europe	27.0	-27.0	2.4	20.0	-6.7	5.4	3.7	-13.5	6.9	7.2	7.8
Commonwealth of Independent States and Georgia[d]	30.3	-30.7	24.3	29.2	8.8	3.2	-9.9	-28.5	-8.1	10.4	9.3
Developing economies	**19.1**	**-14.8**	**26.2**	**21.0**	**5.0**	**3.5**	**1.5**	**-9.1**	**1.9**	**8.0**	**7.0**
Latin America and the Caribbean	21.6	-20.5	27.6	19.9	5.6	4.9	1.7	-11.3	-4.3	5.0	5.9
Africa	23.1	-8.0	10.8	16.3	3.6	0.6	2.3	-13.2	6.3	6.6	7.2
East Asia	16.7	-15.8	32.5	21.8	4.6	4.4	1.7	-8.7	1.6	7.5	7.5
South Asia	19.7	-2.6	21.7	23.8	5.1	-4.2	-1.5	-8.8	-0.7	7.9	7.1
Western Asia	23.3	-15.5	13.7	20.2	7.2	5.1	2.0	-5.6	9.1	13.8	5.5
Volume of exports											
World	2.9	-10.0	11.5	7.1	3.4	3.4	4.1	2.8	1.3	2.6	3.3
Developed economies	**1.9**	**-11.9**	**11.4**	**5.6**	**2.3**	**2.7**	**4.3**	**4.4**	**1.6**	**2.7**	**3.1**
North America	3.3	-9.7	10.8	6.4	3.3	2.6	4.5	0.8	0.4	2.0	2.5
Europe	1.5	-11.6	10.5	6.3	2.2	2.8	3.7	5.7	2.2	3.0	3.3
Developed Asia and Pacific	1.7	-17.8	19.0	-0.2	1.2	2.3	7.7	3.7	0.5	2.3	3.0
Economies in transition	**1.6**	**-6.5**	**6.8**	**2.8**	**1.0**	**2.8**	**0.0**	**0.7**	**0.4**	**2.0**	**2.5**
South-Eastern Europe	5.3	-6.9	15.7	7.3	0.5	12.0	7.6	6.0	6.0	6.0	5.2
Commonwealth of Independent States and Georgia[d]	1.5	-6.5	6.5	2.6	1.0	2.4	-0.4	0.4	0.1	1.7	2.3

Table A.13

World trade[a]: changes in value and volume of exports and imports, by major country group, 2008–2018 *(continued)*

Annual percentage change

	2008	2009	2010	2011	2012	2013	2014	2015	2016[b]	2017[c]	2018[c]
Developing economies	**4.4**	**-7.6**	**12.0**	**9.4**	**5.1**	**4.4**	**4.2**	**0.9**	**0.9**	**2.5**	**3.6**
Latin America and the Caribbean	0.8	-9.4	8.7	6.7	2.5	1.2	1.5	4.2	2.0	2.4	3.0
Africa	5.9	-9.8	10.0	1.3	7.4	-4.9	3.4	1.1	0.7	2.9	3.9
East Asia	4.6	-7.5	14.7	10.2	4.8	7.1	5.2	1.1	0.8	2.6	3.9
South Asia	7.3	0.0	11.4	12.0	3.2	5.0	8.0	-4.4	1.4	1.9	3.0
Western Asia	5.3	-8.0	6.0	12.2	8.8	0.7	0.6	0.1	0.4	2.2	3.2
Volume of imports											
World	3.0	-10.7	12.7	7.3	2.7	3.0	3.5	2.2	1.1	2.8	3.3
Developed economies	**0.4**	**-12.1**	**10.8**	**5.0**	**1.0**	**1.9**	**4.2**	**4.7**	**1.8**	**2.6**	**2.9**
North America	-2.0	-13.5	12.9	5.5	2.5	1.1	3.9	3.8	0.3	1.5	2.4
Europe	1.1	-11.1	9.7	4.4	-0.4	2.2	4.1	5.9	2.8	3.2	3.2
Developed Asia and Pacific	2.5	-14.2	12.0	7.2	5.4	2.0	5.2	0.7	-0.6	2.0	2.4
Economies in transition	**12.0**	**-26.6**	**16.6**	**16.0**	**8.3**	**2.6**	**-6.7**	**-17.5**	**-7.2**	**6.6**	**6.5**
South-Eastern Europe	10.5	-16.2	3.6	6.1	0.9	1.4	8.9	3.6	5.6	4.0	5.3
Commonwealth of Independent States and Georgia[d]	12.2	-27.3	17.7	16.8	8.8	2.7	-7.7	-19.1	-8.4	6.9	6.6
Developing economies	**6.5**	**-6.7**	**15.5**	**10.0**	**4.7**	**4.5**	**3.4**	**0.4**	**0.8**	**2.8**	**3.7**
Latin America and the Caribbean	9.1	-14.6	21.2	11.2	4.5	3.1	0.1	-2.0	-2.6	2.0	2.6
Africa	4.8	-2.2	7.4	2.2	5.5	2.0	3.4	-0.5	1.7	2.6	4.0
East Asia	4.8	-5.7	18.3	10.7	4.8	6.8	4.4	2.1	1.5	3.4	4.1
South Asia	12.2	1.3	8.5	12.2	2.9	-6.0	1.5	-2.9	1.1	2.6	3.5
Western Asia	8.5	-10.2	8.1	9.2	5.4	4.6	4.3	-1.7	0.6	1.5	3.0

Source: UN/DESA.

a Includes goods and non-factor services.

b Partly estimated.

c Baseline scenario forecasts, based in part on Project LINK.

d Georgia officially left the Commonwealth of Independent States on 18 August 2009. However, its performance is discussed in the context of this group of countries for reasons of geographic proximity and similarities in economic structure.

Table A.14

Balance of payments on current accounts, by country or country group, summary table, 2007–2015

Billions of dollars

	2007	2008	2009	2010	2011	2012	2013	2014	2015
Developed economies	-552.5	-773.7	-266.1	-195.3	-240.9	-191.9	-4.8	-20.2	15.9
Japan	212.1	142.6	145.3	221.0	129.8	59.7	45.9	36.5	135.6
United States	-718.6	-690.8	-384.0	-442.0	-460.4	-446.5	-366.4	-392.1	-463.0
Europe[a]	15.6	-165.0	61.7	131.7	188.2	333.5	430.3	424.7	455.8
EU-15	26.5	-128.9	20.3	49.1	122.9	231.6	299.4	306.4	336.4
EU-13	-108.4	-120.9	-41.7	-49.6	-48.9	-29.5	0.1	-4.0	7.8
Economies in transition[b]	54.8	89.8	35.5	63.4	99.8	59.1	12.5	49.5	50.6
South-Eastern Europe	-11.6	-18.6	-7.5	-6.0	-8.5	-8.5	-5.9	-6.5	-4.5
Commonwealth of Independent States[c]	62.9	103.5	40.0	66.4	104.7	63.2	15.2	51.8	51.0
Developing economies[d]	735.3	729.6	363.6	373.8	438.2	455.6	363.8	376.7	180.8
Net fuel exporters	306.3	395.8	58.7	191.1	469.6	442.4	360.9	180.6	-183.2
Net fuel importers	429.0	333.8	305.0	182.8	-31.4	13.2	2.9	196.1	364.0
Latin America and the Caribbean	4.5	-40.5	-32.4	-95.7	-114.1	-136.2	-164.9	-186.8	-181.4
Net fuel exporters	16.0	37.1	-1.5	0.3	9.2	-6.1	-6.0	-15.1	-44.6
Net fuel importers	-11.5	-77.6	-30.9	-95.9	-123.3	-130.2	-158.9	-171.6	-136.8
Africa	38.4	23.9	-49.4	-20.1	-15.7	-44.0	-66.0	-98.8	-146.8
Net fuel exporters	100.8	112.8	1.3	41.8	48.3	58.1	25.5	-33.9	-94.5
Net fuel importers	-62.4	-88.9	-50.8	-61.9	-64.0	-102.1	-91.5	-64.9	-52.3
Western Asia	148.4	225.4	42.3	100.6	276.4	342.1	279.9	173.9	-79.9
Net fuel exporters	184.0	268.4	53.4	148.3	353.9	404.1	349.1	221.5	-47.5
Net fuel importers	-35.5	-42.9	-11.1	-47.7	-77.5	-62.0	-69.2	-47.5	-32.4
East and South Asia	543.9	520.7	403.2	388.9	291.7	293.8	314.9	488.3	589.0
Net fuel exporters	37.2	16.6	16.6	26.4	68.6	13.9	8.9	3.3	-7.0
Net fuel importers	506.7	504.1	386.6	362.5	223.0	279.8	305.9	484.9	595.9
World residual[e]	237.5	45.7	133.1	241.9	297.1	322.7	371.5	406.0	247.3

Source: International Monetary Fund (IMF), *World Economic Outlook* database, October 2016.

Note: IMF-WEO has adopted the sixth edition of the Balance of Payments Manual (BPM6).

a Europe consists of the EU-15, the EU-13 and Iceland, Norway and Switzerland (Table A).

b Includes Georgia.

c Excludes Georgia, which left the Commonwealth of Independent States on 18 August 2009.

d Libya has been excluded in the calculation due to unavailability of data.

e Statistical discrepancy.

Table A.15

Balance of payments on current accounts, by country or country group, 2007–2015

Billions of dollars

	2007	2008	2009	2010	2011	2012	2013	2014	2015
Developed economies									
Trade balance	-707.0	-815.9	-409.3	-495.9	-674.3	-632.9	-500.4	-540.9	-423.2
Services, net	313.8	304.2	279.5	311.5	401.4	413.9	487.4	543.8	508.8
Primary income	180.7	110.8	227.9	364.2	424.0	413.0	416.4	396.5	308.8
Secondary income	-340.0	-372.6	-364.0	-375.0	-391.9	-385.7	-408.2	-419.5	-378.3
Current-account balance	-552.5	-773.7	-266.1	-195.3	-240.9	-191.9	-4.8	-20.2	15.9
Japan									
Trade balance	120.9	55.6	57.8	108.5	-4.5	-53.9	-90.0	-99.9	-5.3
Services, net	-37.0	-38.0	-34.9	-30.3	-35.0	-47.8	-35.7	-28.8	-14.0
Primary income	139.8	138.1	134.6	155.1	183.1	175.6	181.6	184.2	170.8
Secondary income	-11.5	-13.1	-12.3	-12.4	-13.8	-14.2	-10.0	-19.0	-16.0
Current-account balance	212.1	142.6	145.3	221.0	129.8	59.7	45.9	36.5	135.6
United States									
Trade balance	-821.2	-832.5	-509.7	-648.7	-740.6	-741.2	-702.2	-752.2	-762.6
Services, net	115.8	123.8	125.9	154.0	192.0	204.4	240.4	262.0	262.2
Primary income	100.6	146.1	123.6	177.7	221.0	215.8	219.0	224.0	182.4
Secondary income	-113.9	-128.2	-123.8	-125.0	-132.7	-125.5	-123.5	-125.9	-145.0
Current-account balance	-718.6	-690.8	-384.0	-442.0	-460.4	-446.5	-366.4	-392.1	-463.0
Europe[a]									
Trade balance	-26.2	-70.4	52.5	40.4	45.4	185.6	292.8	305.0	383.4
Services, net	246.0	237.4	203.5	212.8	275.1	291.9	319.0	339.9	284.1
Primary income	8.4	-101.8	30.0	110.7	107.0	95.1	87.0	50.1	1.4
Secondary income	-212.5	-230.1	-224.3	-232.3	-239.3	-239.2	-268.6	-270.1	-213.0
Current-account balance	15.6	-165.0	61.7	131.7	188.2	333.5	430.3	424.7	455.8
EU-15									
Trade balance	0.9	-47.0	38.1	4.0	0.2	110.8	191.9	217.4	311.6
Services, net	175.9	158.7	141.4	151.2	207.3	225.8	248.0	266.1	215.9
Primary income	60.6	-14.9	56.5	118.8	146.2	123.1	112.9	69.7	6.3
Secondary income	-210.9	-225.7	-215.8	-224.9	-230.7	-228.0	-253.3	-246.7	-197.3
Current-account balance	26.5	-128.9	20.3	49.1	122.9	231.6	299.4	306.4	336.4
EU-13									
Trade balance	-103.1	-128.7	-45.6	-47.6	-51.3	-34.6	-13.9	-16.3	-9.3
Services, net	40.7	45.3	36.0	36.3	45.0	45.6	52.9	56.7	52.8
Primary income	-54.1	-46.6	-36.9	-45.7	-50.0	-45.0	-44.3	-47.3	-39.5
Secondary income	8.2	9.1	4.8	7.4	7.5	4.4	5.4	3.0	3.9
Current-account balance	-108.4	-120.9	-41.7	-49.6	-48.9	-29.5	0.1	-4.0	7.8
Economies in transition[b]									
Trade balance	113.9	176.3	105.3	155.5	222.3	205.7	181.9	203.7	137.0
Services, net	-23.6	-27.8	-24.1	-31.2	-36.7	-52.9	-63.2	-64.9	-41.0
Primary income	-47.3	-72.3	-59.0	-74.4	-100.3	-106.0	-115.9	-96.3	-56.0
Secondary income	11.8	13.6	13.3	13.5	14.5	12.2	9.7	7.1	10.4
Current-account balance	54.8	89.8	35.5	63.4	99.8	59.1	12.5	49.5	50.6

Table A.15
Balance of payments on current accounts, by country or country group, 2007–2015 *(continued)*

Billions of dollars

	2007	2008	2009	2010	2011	2012	2013	2014	2015
Economies in transition[b] *(continued)*									
South-Eastern Europe									
Trade balance	-22.7	-29.8	-19.8	-17.5	-20.8	-19.4	-17.0	-18.2	-14.9
Services, net	2.0	2.3	2.3	2.4	3.1	2.9	3.0	3.7	3.8
Primary income	-0.4	-0.6	-0.3	-0.9	-1.1	-1.5	-1.8	-2.0	-2.0
Secondary income	9.6	9.6	10.3	10.0	10.3	9.6	9.8	9.9	8.5
Current-account balance	-11.6	-18.6	-7.5	-6.0	-8.5	-8.5	-5.9	-6.5	-4.5
Commonwealth of Independent States[c]									
Trade balance	133.8	202.2	122.7	170.5	239.6	220.9	195.4	217.6	147.6
Services, net	-25.4	-30.1	-26.0	-33.1	-39.0	-54.6	-64.8	-67.4	-43.4
Primary income	-46.9	-71.5	-58.7	-73.3	-98.8	-104.4	-113.8	-94.1	-53.6
Secondary income	1.5	2.9	2.0	2.4	2.9	1.2	-1.6	-4.3	0.4
Current-account balance	62.9	103.5	40.0	66.4	104.7	63.2	15.2	51.8	51.0
Developing economies[d]									
Trade balance	832.4	890.4	543.4	678.5	845.8	862.3	885.8	849.2	643.8
Services, net	-165.6	-216.0	-180.7	-209.8	-240.7	-270.8	-306.6	-378.1	-340.0
Primary income	-154.4	-189.4	-214.8	-315.7	-385.4	-336.7	-401.7	-307.2	-314.5
Secondary income	222.8	244.6	215.7	220.8	218.6	200.7	186.3	212.7	191.5
Current-account balance	735.3	729.6	363.6	373.8	438.2	455.6	363.8	376.7	180.8
Net fuel exporters									
Trade balance	485.5	665.3	322.0	517.7	861.1	845.2	784.5	622.2	180.5
Services, net	-156.1	-206.9	-189.7	-210.3	-238.8	-252.2	-263.7	-297.9	-247.1
Primary income	-30.1	-68.7	-67.1	-96.7	-122.8	-117.1	-115.8	-104.2	-70.5
Secondary income	6.9	6.1	-6.5	-19.7	-29.9	-33.6	-44.0	-39.5	-46.1
Current-account balance	306.3	395.8	58.7	191.1	469.6	442.4	360.9	180.6	-183.2
Net fuel importers									
Trade balance	346.9	225.1	221.5	160.8	-15.3	17.1	101.3	227.1	463.3
Services, net	-9.5	-9.1	9.0	0.5	-1.9	-18.6	-42.8	-80.1	-92.9
Primary income	-124.4	-120.7	-147.7	-219.0	-262.7	-219.6	-285.9	-203.0	-244.0
Secondary income	215.9	238.5	222.2	240.6	248.5	234.3	230.3	252.2	237.6
Current-account balance	429.0	333.8	305.0	182.8	-31.4	13.2	2.9	196.1	364.0
Latin America and the Caribbean									
Trade balance	65.3	36.8	48.1	41.8	60.4	30.0	-6.4	-25.0	-65.5
Services, net	-23.6	-29.9	-33.5	-48.1	-63.4	-67.1	-71.3	-70.9	-48.4
Primary income	-104.3	-114.9	-104.8	-151.2	-174.5	-161.5	-149.7	-156.4	-135.4
Secondary income	67.2	67.5	57.9	61.9	63.4	62.3	62.6	65.6	67.9
Current-account balance	4.5	-40.5	-32.4	-95.7	-114.1	-136.2	-164.9	-186.8	-181.4
Africa									
Trade balance	61.0	68.4	-17.9	29.1	53.7	17.3	-2.1	-53.0	-124.9
Services, net	-32.5	-52.2	-44.4	-51.9	-64.7	-62.3	-60.3	-68.8	-50.1
Primary income	-47.9	-59.3	-49.9	-67.8	-80.2	-80.8	-87.6	-77.3	-57.0

Table A.15

Balance of payments on current accounts, by country or country group, 2007–2015 *(continued)*

Billions of dollars

	2007	2008	2009	2010	2011	2012	2013	2014	2015
Africa *(continued)*									
Secondary income	57.9	67.0	62.8	70.5	75.5	81.7	84.0	100.4	85.2
Current-account balance	38.4	23.9	-49.4	-20.1	-15.7	-44.0	-66.0	-98.8	-146.8
Western Asia									
Trade balance	217.7	346.9	168.9	265.6	461.0	540.8	491.3	413.4	129.1
Services, net	-63.8	-84.4	-74.0	-90.1	-99.3	-109.0	-115.2	-143.4	-121.3
Primary income	21.5	-6.0	-12.1	-16.9	-15.3	-9.4	-5.8	1.1	5.7
Secondary income	-26.9	-31.1	-40.5	-58.0	-70.1	-80.3	-90.3	-97.1	-93.4
Current-account balance	148.4	225.4	42.3	100.6	276.4	342.1	279.9	173.9	-79.9
East Asia									
Trade balance	541.4	533.0	474.7	476.3	438.3	488.8	563.0	685.1	870.9
Services, net	-47.1	-55.9	-51.6	-52.1	-67.7	-86.4	-123.8	-161.9	-181.3
Primary income	-14.3	3.0	-33.6	-56.8	-94.8	-58.3	-128.6	-43.4	-95.1
Secondary income	52.8	64.9	48.4	53.5	39.5	20.2	11.3	22.0	10.3
Current-account balance	532.8	545.0	437.9	420.9	315.3	364.3	321.9	501.8	604.9
South Asia									
Trade balance	-52.9	-94.6	-130.3	-134.4	-167.6	-214.5	-159.9	-171.1	-165.9
Services, net	1.4	6.3	22.9	32.5	54.4	53.9	64.1	67.0	61.1
Primary income	-9.4	-12.3	-14.3	-23.1	-20.7	-26.7	-30.0	-31.2	-32.6
Secondary income	71.9	76.3	87.1	93.0	110.3	116.8	118.7	121.8	121.5
Current-account balance	11.1	-24.3	-34.7	-32.0	-23.6	-70.6	-7.1	-13.5	-15.9
World residual[e]									
Trade balance	239.4	250.8	239.4	338.1	393.7	435.1	567.3	512.0	357.6
Services, net	124.6	60.4	74.8	70.5	124.0	90.3	117.6	100.9	127.8
Primary income	-21.0	-150.9	-46.0	-26.0	-61.8	-29.7	-101.1	-7.0	-61.7
Secondary income	-105.4	-114.5	-135.0	-140.7	-158.8	-172.8	-212.2	-199.8	-176.3
Current-account balance	237.5	45.7	133.1	241.9	297.1	322.7	371.5	406.0	247.3

Source: International Monetary Fund (IMF), *World Economic Outlook* database, October 2016.

Note: IMF-WEO has adopted the sixth edition of the Balance of Payments Manual (BPM6).

a Europe consists of the EU-15, the EU-13 and Iceland, Norway and Switzerland (Table A).

b Includes Georgia.

c Excludes Georgia, which left the Commonwealth of Independent States on 18 August 2009.

d Libya has been excluded in the calculation due to unavailability of data.

e Statistical discrepancy.

Table A.16

Net ODA from major sources, by type, 1994–2015

Donor group or country	Growth rate of ODA (2014 prices and exchange rates)					ODA as a percentage of GNI	Total ODA (millions of dollars)	Percentage distribution of ODA by type, 2015			
								Bilateral	Multilateral		
	1994-2004	2004-2012	2013	2014	2015	2015	2015	Total	Total (United Nations & Other)	United Nations	Other
Total DAC countries	0.9	4.5	5.5	1.5	6.9	0.30	131586	71.7	28.3	5.8	22.5
Total EU	0.8	4.4	6.2	3.6	12.7	0.47	73477	65.1	34.9	6.3	28.6
Austria	8.4	4.6	1.0	3.8	15.4	0.32	1207	55.4	44.6	2.3	42.3
Belgium	5.5	3.6	-5.1	5.8	-7.8	0.42	1894	59.3	40.7	7.6	33.1
Denmark	1.5	0.9	3.9	1.8	0.8	0.85	2566	73.2	26.8	9.7	17.1
Finland	1.6	7.2	2.6	12.2	-5.7	0.56	1292	53.6	46.4	13.1	33.3
France[a]	-2.1	3.5	-9.4	-6.8	2.8	0.37	9226	57.9	42.1	4.3	37.7
Germany	-0.9	5.7	4.3	14.4	25.9	0.52	17779	78.3	21.7	3.0	18.8
Greece	..	-1.5	-27.7	6.4	38.7	0.14	282	40.5	59.5	2.7	56.8
Ireland	15.6	4.7	0.1	-3.6	1.9	0.36	718	59.8	40.2	12.1	28.1
Italy	-4.0	-0.3	19.8	16.0	14.2	0.21	3844	42.8	57.2	6.0	51.2
Luxembourg	13.6	3.8	1.6	-2.2	-1.2	0.93	361	68.9	31.1	11.4	19.8
Netherlands	2.5	1.8	-6.0	1.8	24.4	0.76	5813	73.1	26.9	6.3	20.6
Portugal	4.5	-1.8	-20.4	-12.6	-16.1	0.16	306	46.6	53.4	3.5	49.9
Spain	2.7	4.1	11.0	-19.7	1.5	0.13	1604	35.8	64.2	4.1	60.1
Sweden	1.6	5.5	5.9	11.0	36.8	1.41	7092	68.0	32.0	17.6	14.4
United Kingdom	4.6	7.9	27.8	0.9	3.2	0.71	18700	62.9	37.1	5.6	31.5
Australia	0.6	7.8	-5.0	-3.5	-11.1	0.27	3222	82.5	17.5	4.8	12.7
Canada	-1.7	4.7	-10.9	-9.7	17.1	0.28	4287	69.6	30.4	5.5	25.0
Japan	-1.7	-0.7	33.0	-13.8	12.4	0.22	9320	67.4	32.6	7.8	24.8
New Zealand	3.0	4.9	-2.2	7.1	1.7	0.27	438	81.3	18.7	10.0	8.7
Norway	2.8	2.9	15.6	-2.8	8.7	1.05	4278	77.3	22.7	11.4	11.3
Switzerland	1.7	4.6	3.7	9.4	6.7	0.52	3538	77.2	22.8	7.6	15.2
United States	2.5	5.7	0.4	4.1	-7.0	0.17	31076	86.1	13.9	3.0	11.0

Source: UN/DESA, based on OECD/DAC online database, available from http://www.oecd-ilibrary.org/statistics.

a Excluding flows from France to the Overseas Departments, namely Guadeloupe, French Guiana, Martinique and Réunion.

Table A.17
Total net ODA flows from OECD Development Assistance Committee countries, by type, 2006–2015

	Net disbursements at current prices and exchange rates (billions of dollars)									
	2006	2007	2008	2009	2010	2011	2012	2013	2014	2015
Official Development Assistance	105.4	104.9	122.8	120.6	128.4	135.0	126.9	134.7	137.2	131.6
Bilateral official development assistance	77.5	73.7	87.1	83.9	90.6	94.8	88.4	93.4	94.7	94.4
in the form of:										
Technical cooperation	22.4	15.1	17.3	17.6	18.6	18.0	18.2	16.9	17.3	..
Humanitarian aid	6.8	6.5	8.8	8.6	9.3	9.7	8.5	10.5	13.1	..
Debt forgiveness	18.9	9.7	11.1	2.0	4.2	6.3	3.3	6.1	1.4	..
Bilateral loans	-2.4	-2.2	-1.1	2.5	3.8	1.9	2.6	1.4	5.2	..
Contributions to multilateral institutions[a]	27.9	31.2	35.7	36.6	37.8	40.2	38.5	41.3	42.6	37.2
of which are:										
UN agencies	5.3	5.9	5.9	6.2	6.5	6.5	6.6	6.9	6.8	7.6
EU institutions	10.1	12.0	13.5	14.2	13.6	13.7	12.0	12.8	13.3	12.0
World Bank	7.2	6.2	8.6	7.6	8.8	10.2	8.6	9.3	9.8	8.6
Regional development banks	2.5	2.4	3.2	3.1	3.2	4.1	3.9	3.9	4.0	3.2
Others	2.7	4.7	4.4	5.4	5.7	5.8	7.5	8.4	8.7	..
Memorandum item										
Bilateral ODA to least developed countries	17.4	19.7	23.5	24.3	28.2	30.7	27.4	30.0	26.3	..

Source: UN/DESA, based on OECD/DAC online database, available from http://www.oecd.org/dac/stats/idsonline.

a Grants and capital subscriptions. Does not include concessional lending to multilateral agencies.

Table A.18

Commitments and net flows of financial resources, by selected multilateral institutions, 2006–2015

Billions of dollars

	2006	2007	2008	2009	2010	2011	2012	2013	2014	2015
Resource commitments[a]	64.7	74.5	135.2	193.7	245.4	163.8	189.8	130.8	185.0	119.9
Financial institutions, excluding International Monetary Fund (IMF)	55.7	66.6	76.1	114.5	119.6	106.8	96.5	98.8	99.2	99.9
Regional development banks[b]	23.8	31.9	36.7	55.1	46.2	46.9	43.0	45.8	41.1	46.9
World Bank Group[c]	31.9	34.7	39.4	59.4	73.4	59.9	53.5	53.0	58.1	53.0
International Bank for Reconstruction and Development	14.2	12.8	13.5	32.9	44.2	26.7	20.6	15.2	18.6	23.5
International Development Association	9.5	11.9	11.2	14.0	14.6	16.3	14.8	16.3	22.2	19.0
International Financial Corporation[d]	8.2	10.0	14.6	12.4	14.6	16.9	9.2	11.0	10.0	10.5
International Fund for Agricultural Development	0.7	0.6	0.6	0.7	0.8	1.0	1.0	0.8	0.7	1.3
International Monetary Fund	1.0	2.0	48.7	68.2	114.1	45.7	82.5	19.6	72.7	6.2
United Nations operational agencies[e]	8.3	6.3	10.5	11.0	11.6	11.3	10.8	12.4	13.1	13.7
Net flows	-24.7	-4.4	43.4	54.6	64.6	78.7	35.1	8.8	-5.1	17.7
Financial institutions, excluding IMF	6.3	13.6	24.5	22.6	27.2	38.0	26.3	22.2	25.0	35.5
Regional development banks[b]	3.2	6.2	21.4	15.7	9.9	10.5	8.6	5.7	11.2	15.4
World Bank Group[c]	3.1	7.4	3.1	6.9	17.2	27.6	17.7	16.5	13.8	20.1
International Bank for Reconstruction and Development	-5.1	-1.8	-6.2	-2.1	8.3	17.2	8.0	7.8	6.4	9.0
International Development Association	7.3	7.2	6.8	7.0	7.0	9.1	7.8	7.0	7.4	9.9
International Financial Corporation	0.9	1.9	2.4	2.1	1.9	1.2	1.9	1.6	0.1	1.3
International Fund for Agricultural Development	0.2	0.2	0.2	0.2	0.2	0.3	0.3	0.2	0.2	0.2
International Monetary Fund	-31.0	-18.0	18.9	32.0	37.4	40.7	8.9	-13.4	-30.1	-17.9

Source: Annual reports of the relevant multilateral institutions, various issues.

a Loans, grants, technical assistance and equity participation, as appropriate; all data are on a calendar-year basis.

b African Development Bank (AfDB), Asian Development Bank (ADB), Caribbean Development Bank (CDB), European Bank for Reconstruction and Development (EBRD), Inter-American Development Bank (IaDB) and the International Fund for Agricultural Development (IFAD).

c Data is for fiscal year.

d Effective 2012, data does not include short-term finance.

e United Nations Development Programme (UNDP), United Nations Population Fund (UNFPA), United Nations Children's Fund (UNICEF), and the World Food Programme (WFP).

Bibliography

Aizenman, Joshua and Yothin Jinjarak (2010). De facto fiscal space and fiscal stimulus: Definition and assessment. *NBER Working Paper*, No. 16539.

Altshuler, Clive, Dawn Holland, Pingfan Hong and Hung-Yi Li (2016). The World Economic Forecasting Model at the United Nations. Available from http://www.un.org/en/development/desa/policy/wefm/documents/wefm1_overview.pdf

Alvarez, Roberto and Ricardo López (2005). Exporting and performance: evidence from Chilean plants. *Canadian Journal of Economics*, Vol. 38(4), pp. 1384-1400.

Alvarez, Roberto and Sebastian Vergara (2010). Exit in Developing Countries: Economic Reforms and Plant Heterogeneity. *Economic Development and Cultural Change*, Vol. 58(3), pp. 537-561.

Amiti, Mary and Jozef Konings (2007). Trade Liberalization, Intermediate Inputs, and Productivity: Evidence from Indonesia. *American Economic Review*, Vol. 97, No. 5, pp. 1611-1638.

Ariyoshi, Akira, Karl Habermeier, Bernard Laurens, Inci Otker-Robe, Jorge Iván Canales-Kriljenko and Andrei Kirilenko (2000). *Capital controls: country experiences with their use and liberalization*. Occasional Paper No. 190. Washington, D.C.: International Monetary Fund.

Aw, Bee Yan, Mark J. Roberts and Daniel Yi Xu (2011). R&D Investment, Exporting, and Productivity Dynamics. *American Economic Review*, Vol. 101, No. 4, pp. 1312–44.

Bank for International Settlements (2016a). *Quarterly Review*, September 2016.

Bank for International Settlements (2016b). BIS international banking statistics at end-December 2015. Available from http://www.bis.org/statistics/rppb1604.pdf

Bernard, Andrew B., J. Bradford Jensen, Stephen J. Redding, and Peter K. Schott (2011). The Empirics of Firm Heterogeneity and International Trade. *NBER Working Paper*, No. 17627, November.

Bhatia, Karan, Simon Evenett and Gary Hufbauer (2016). Why General Electric is localising production. VOX, CEPR's Policy Portal, 21 June 2016. Available from http://voxeu.org/article/why-general-electric-localising-production

Bitsch, Florian, Axel Buchner and Christoph Kaserer (2010). Risk, return and cash flow characteristics of infrastructure fund investments. *EIB Papers*, vol.15, No.1, pp. 106. European Investment Bank, Economics Department. Available from http://www.eib.org/attachments/efs/eibpapers/eibpapers_2010_v15_n01_en.pdf#page=108

Bloom, Nicholas, Mirko Draca and John Van Reenen (2011). Trade Induced Technical Change? The Impact of Chinese Imports on Innovation, IT and Productivity. *NBER Working Paper*, No. 16717, January.

Bollerslev, Tim (1986). Generalized autoregressive conditional heteroskedasticity. *Journal of Econometrics*, vol. 31, issue 3, pp. 307-327.

Bolton, Patrick, Roger Guesnerie and Frederic Samama (2010). Towards an international green fund. September. Available from http://cgt.columbia.edu/wp-content/uploads/2014/01/Towards-an-International-Green-Fund.pdf

Broner, Fernando, Tatiana Didier, Aitor Erce and Sergio L. Schmukler (2013). Gross capital flows: Dynamics and crises. *Journal of Monetary Economics*, vol. 60, Issue 1 (January), pp. 113-133.

Bussière, Matthieu, Giovanni Callegari, Fabio Ghironi, Giulia Sestieri and Norihiko Yamano (2013). Estimating Trade Elasticities: Demand Composition and the Trade Collapse of 2008-2009. *American Economic Journal: Macroeconomics* 5(3): 118-151.

Bustos, Paula (2011). Trade liberalization, exports and technology upgrading: evidence on the impact of MERCOSUR on Argentinean firms. *American Economic Review*, Vol. 101, No. 1, pp. 304–340.

Collier, Paul, Lani Elliott, Håvard Hegre, Anke Hoeffler, Marta Rynal-Querol and Nicholas Sambanis (2003). *Breaking the Conflict Trap: Civil War and Development Policy*. The World Bank and Oxford University Press.

Constantinescu, Cristina, Aaditya Mattoo and Michele Ruta (2015). The Global Trade Slowdown: Cyclical or Structural? *IMF Working Paper*, WP/15/6, January 2015.

Dasgupta, Dipak, Marc Uzan and Dominic Wilson, eds. (2001). *Capital Flows Without Crisis? Reconciling Capital Mobility and Economic Stability*. Abingdon and New York: Routledge.

Datt, Guarav and Martin Ravallion (1992). Growth and redistribution components of changes in poverty measures: A decomposition with application to Brazil and India in the 1980s. *Journal of Development Economics*, Vol. 38(2), pp. 275-295.

De Loecker, Jan (2007). Do exports generate higher productivity? Evidence from Slovenia. *Journal of International Economics*, Vol. 73, pp. 69–98.

de Luna-Martínez, José and Carlos Leonardo Vicente (2012). Global survey of development banks. *Policy Research working paper*, No. WPS 5969. Washington, D.C.: World Bank. http://documents.worldbank.org/curated/en/313731468154461012/Global-survey-of-development-banks

De Paula, Luis Fernando R., and Antonio José Alves, Jr. (2000). External financial fragility and the 1998-1999 Brazilian currency crisis. *Journal of Post Keynesian Economics*, vol. 22, No. 4 (Summer), pp. 589−617.

Della Croce, Raffaele (2012). Trends in Large Pension Fund Investment in Infrastructure. *OECD Working Papers on Finance, Insurance and Private Pensions*, No.29. Paris: Organszation for Economic Cooperation and Development. November. Available from http://www.oecd.org/daf/fin/private-pensions/trendsinlargepensionfundinvestmentininfrastructure.pdf

Deutsche Bank (2011). Solvency II and Basel III: Reciprocal effects should not be ignored. *Deutsche Bank Research Current Issues*. 22 September. Frankfurt am Main. Available from http://www.dbresearch.com/PROD/DBR_INTERNET_EN-PROD/PROD0000000000278734.PDF

Eichengreen, Barry, and Poonam Gupta (2015). Tapering talk: The impact of expectations of reduced Federal Reserve security purchases on emerging markets. *Emerging Markets Review*, vol.25, pp. 1-15.

Eichengreen, Barry, and Poonam Gupta (2016). Managing sudden stops. *World Bank Policy Research Working Paper*, No. 7639. Washington, D.C.: World Bank.

European Central Bank (2016). Understanding the weakness in global trade: What is the new normal? *Occasional Papers Series*, No. 178, September.

European Commission (2016). Report from the Commission to the Council and the European Parliament on Trade and Investment Barriers and Protectionist Trends. Brussels. 20 June. Available from http://trade.ec.europa.eu/doclib/docs/2016/june/tradoc_154665.pdf

Evenett, Simon and Johannes Fritz (2016). FDI Recovers? The 20th Global Trade Alert Report. CEPR Press, London. Available from http://www.globaltradealert.org/sites/default/files/GTA20_0.pdf

Federal Reserve Bank of New York (2016). Effective federal funds rate, overnight banking funding rate data. Available from https://apps.newyorkfed.org/markets/autorates/obfr-search-page

Federal Reserve Bank of St. Louis (2016). 3-Month London Interbank Offered Rate (LIBOR), based on U.S. Dollar. Available from https://fred.stlouisfed.org/series/USD3MTD156N#0

Forbes, Kristin, and Francis E. Warnock (2012). Capital flow waves: Surges, stops, flight, and retrenchment. *Journal of International Economics*, vol.88, Issue 2, pp. 235-251.

Frankfurt School-UNEP Centre/BNEF (2016). Global Trends in Renewable Energy Investment 2016. Frankfurt am Main. Available from http://www.fs-unep-centre.org

Gates, Scott, Håvard Hegre, Håvard Mokleiv Nygård and Håvard Strand (2010). Consequences of Armed Conflict in the Middle East and North Africa Region. Background paper for the World Bank. 23 November. Available from http://folk.uio.no/haavarmn/MENA_Cons_Conflict.pdf.

Ghosh, Atish R., Jun I. Kim, Enrique G. Mendoza, Jonathan D. Ostry and Mahrash S. Qureshi (2013). Fiscal fatigue, fiscal space and debt sustainability in advanced economies. *The Economic Journal*, 123(566), F4-F30.

Gordon, Robert (2012). Is U.S. Economic Growth Over? Faltering Innovation Confronts the Six Headwinds. *NBER Working Paper*, No. 18315, August.

Heller, S. P. (2005). Back to Basics — Fiscal Space: What It Is and How to Get It. *Finance and Development*, 42 (2), June.

Helpman, Elhanan (1981). International trade in the presence of product differentiation, economies of scale and monopolistic competition: A Chamberlin-Heckscher-Ohlin approach. Journal of International Economics, Vol. 11, Issue 3, pp. 305-334.

Holland, Dawn and Arjun Jayadev (2016). Linking inequality and poverty in macroeconomic models. Presentation at Project LINK Meeting 2016, Toronto, October. Available from http://www.rotman.utoronto.ca/FacultyAndResearch/ResearchCentres/ProjectLINK/LINKconferences/LINK-2016-Agenda.

Hoy, Chris and Andy Sumner (2016). Gasoline, Guns, and Giveaways: Is There New Capacity for Redistribution to End Three Quarters of Global Poverty? *Center for Global Development Working Paper*, No. 433. Institute of International Finance (2016). Capital Flows to Emerging Markets, November.

International Development Association (2014). Additions to IDA resources: seventeenth replenishment - IDA17: maximizing development impact. Washington, D.C.: World Bank Group. Available from http://documents.worldbank.org/curated/en/410401468160173357/Additions-to-IDA-resources-seventeenth-replenishment-IDA17-maximizing-development-impact.

International Energy Agency (2009). *The impact of the Financial Crisis and Economic Crisis on Global Energy Investment*. Paris: Organisation for Economic Cooperation and Development/ International Energy Agency. Available from https://www.iea.org/publications/freepublications/publication/impact.pdf.

International Energy Agency (2016). *World Energy Investment 2016*.

International Labour Organization (2016). *World Economic and Social Outlook: Trends 2016*, Geneva.

International Monetary Fund (2013). Staff Guidance Note for Public Debt Sustainability Analysis in Market-Access Countries. Prepared by the Strategy, Policy, and Review Department in collaboration with the Fiscal Affairs Department.

International Monetary Fund (2015). World Revenue Longitudinal Data. Available from http://data.imf.org/revenues

International Monetary Fund (2016a). World Economic Outlook database, October 2016.

International Monetary Fund (2016b). *Global Financial Stability Report*, October 2016. Available from http://www.imf.org/external/pubs/ft/gfsr/2016/02/pdf/text.pdf

International Monetary Fund (2016c). *World Economic Outlook: Subdued Demand: Symptoms and Remedies*. Washington, D.C., October.

International Monetary Fund (2016d). Currency composition of reserves. International Financial Statistics. Available from http://data.imf.org/?sk=E6A5F467-C14B-4AA8-9F6D-5A09EC4E62A4

International Monetary Fund (2016e). *World Economic Outlook: Too Slow for Too Long*. Washington, D.C., April.

ITU (2016). ICT Facts and Figures 2016, Core indicators on access to and use of ICT by households and individuals. Available from http://www.itu.int/en/ITU-D/Statistics/Pages/stat/default.aspx

Kleintop, Jeffrey (2012). Weekly Market Commentary, LPL Financial Research. 6 August. Available from http://moneymattersblog.com/login/login/wp-content/uploads/2012/08/WMC080712.pdf

Krugman, Paul (1981). Intra-industry Specialization and the Gains from Trade. *The Journal of Political Economy*, Vol. 89, No. 5, pp. 959-973.

Kwan, Simon (2009). Behavior of Libor in the Current Financial Crisis. *Federal Reserve Bank of San Francisco Economic Letter (2009-04)*, 23 January. Available from http://www.frbsf.org/economic-research/publications/economic-letter/2009/january/libor-financial-crisis

Lane, Philip R., and Gian Maria Milesi-Ferretti (2001). The external wealth of nations: measures of foreign assets and liabilities for industrial and developing countries. *Journal of International Economics*, vol. 55, Issue 2, pp. 263-294.

Lane, Philip R., and Gian Maria Milesi-Ferretti (2007). The external wealth of nations mark II: revised and extended estimates of foreign assets and liabilities, 1970–2004. *Journal of International Economics*, vol. 73, Issue 2 (November), pp. 223–250.

Lileeva, Alla (2008). Trade Evidence and Productivity Dynamics: Evidence from Canada. *Canadian Journal of Economics* 41(2): 360–90.

Lileeva, Alla and Daniel Trefler (2010). Improved Access to Foreign Markets Raises Plant-level Productivity...For Some Plants". *Quarterly Journal of Economics* 125 (3), 1051–1099.

Lipton, David (2016). Rebalancing China: International Lessons in Corporate Debt. Keynote address. Shenzhen. 10 June. Available from https://www.imf.org/en/News/Articles/2015/09/28/04/53/sp061016

López-Calva, Luis F. and Nora Lustig (2010). Explaining the decline in inequality in Latin America: Technological change, educational upgrading and democracy. In *Declining Inequality in Latin America: A decade of progress?*, López-Calva, Luis F. and Nora Lustig (eds.), Brookings Institution Press, pp. 1-24.

Melitz, Marc J. (2003). The Impact of Trade on Intra-Industry Reallocations and Aggregate Industry Productivity. *Econometrica*, Vol. 71, No. 6, pp. 1695-1725.

Low, Patrick (2013). The Role of Services in Global Value Chains, *Working Paper FGI-2013-1*, Fung Global Institute, June.

Low, Patrick (2015). Economic Development in Africa: Role of Services, presentation at UNCTAD in September 2015, Asia Global Institute.

Melitz, Marc J. and Daniel Trefler (2012). Gains from Trade when Firms Matter. *Journal of Economic Perspectives,* Vol. 26, No. 2, pp. 91–118.

Melitz, Marc J. and Stephen J. Redding (2015). Heterogeneous Firms and Trade. *Handbook of International Economics*, Vol. 4, Elsevier: North Holland.

Muchhala, Bhumika, ed. (2007). *Ten Years After: Revisiting the Asian Financial Crisis.* Washington, D.C.: Woodrow Wilson International Center for Scholars, Asia Program. Available from https://www.wilsoncenter.org/sites/default/files/Asia_TenYearsAfter_rpt.pdf

Mukim, Megha (2011). Does exporting increase productivity? Evidence from India. *London School of Economics Working Paper*, June 20.

Multilateral Development Banks (2016). MDB Response to the G20 Action Plan for MDB Balance Sheet Optimisation. July. Available from http://www.g20.org/English/Documents/Current/201608/P020160815361155807206.pdf

National Association of Insurance Commissioners (2011). *Capital Markets Bureau Special Report*. Available from http://www.naic.org/capital_markets_archive/110819.htm

Nicita, Alessandro and Julia Seiermann (2016). G20 Policies and Export Performance of Least Developed Countries. *Policy Issues in International Trade and Commodities Study Series*, No. 75. UNCTAD.

Novy, Dennis and Alan M. Taylor (2014). Trade and Uncertainty. *NBER Working Paper*, No. 19941, February. Available from http://www.nber.org/papers/w19941

Organisation for Economic Cooperation and Development (2014). Targeting ODA towards countries in greatest need. 29 April. DCD/DAC(2014)20. Available from https://www.oecd.org/dac/financing-sustainable-development/DAC(2014)20.pdf

Organisation for Economic Cooperation and Development (2015a). *The future of productivity*. OECD Publishing, Paris.

Organisation for Economic Cooperation and Development (2015b). Providers of development co-operation beyond the DAC: Trends and profiles. In *Development Co-operation Report 2015: Making Partnerships Effective Coalitions for Action*. Paris. Available from http://dx.doi.org/10.1787/dcr-2015-en

Organisation for Economic Cooperation and Development (2016a). Development aid in 2015 continues to grow despite costs for in-donor refugees. 13 April. Paris. Available from http://www.oecd.org/dac/stats/ODA-2015-detailed-summary.pdf

Organisation for Economic Cooperation and Development (2016b). 2016 Global aid prospects and projections: from words to action. Paris. Available from http://www.oecd.org/dac/financing-sustainable-development/development-finance-standards/FSS%202016%20flyer.pdf

Prichard, Wilson, Alex Cobham and Andrew Goodall (2014). The ICTD Government Revenue Dataset. *ICTD Working Paper*, 19, Brighton: International Centre for Tax and Development.

Prosser, David (2013). Special Report An alternative way to invest. *Pensions Insight*. 5 August. Available from http://www.engagedinvestor.co.uk/special-report-an-alternative-way-to-invest/1472270.article

Ravallion, Martin (2009). Do poorer countries have less capacity for redistribution? *Policy Research working paper*, No. WPS 5046. Washington, D.C.: World Bank Group.

Ravallion, Martin (2013). How long will it take to lift one billion people out of poverty? *Policy Research working paper*, No. WPS 6325. Washington, D.C.: World Bank Group.

Roy, Rathin, Antoine Heuty and Emmanuel Letouzé (2009). Fiscal space for what? Analytical issues from a human development perspective. In *Fiscal Space: Policy Options for Financing Human Development*, Roy, R. and A. Heuty (eds.), 33-68.

TheCityUK (2013a). Sovereign Wealth Funds. March. London.

TheCityUK (2013b). Pension markets. *Financial markets series*. March. London.

TheCityUK (2015). UK Fund Management: An attractive proposition for international funds. November, London.

Thorton, Daniel (2009). What the Libor-OIS Spread Says. *Economic SYNOPSES*, Number 24, 2009. Available from https://research.stlouisfed.org/publications/es/09/ES0924.pdf

Towers Watson (2013). Global Pension Assets Study 2013. January. Available from https://www.towerswatson.com/en/Insights/IC-Types/Survey-Research-Results/2013/01/Global-Pensions-Asset-Study-2013

United Nations (1986). *World Economic Survey 1986: Current Trends and Policies in the World Economy*. Sales No. E.86.II.C.1.

United Nations (1990). *World Economic Survey 1990: Current Trends and Policies in the World Economy*. Sales No. E.90.II.C.1.

United Nations (2011). Fourth United Nations Conference on the Least Developed Countries, Programme of Action for the Least Developed Countries for the Decade 2011-2020. A/CONF.219/3/Rev.1.

United Nations (2014). Report of the Intergovernmental Committee of Experts on Sustainable Development Financing. A/69/315. 14 August.

United Nations (2015). World Population Prospects: The 2015 Revision. DVD Edition. Department of Economic and Social Affairs, Population Division.

United Nations (2016a). *World Economic Situation and Prospects 2016*. Sales No. E16. II.C.2.

United Nations (2016b). Committee for Development Policy. Report on the eighteenth session (14-18 March 2016). Supplement No. 13. E/2016/33. Available from http://www.un.org/en/development/desa/policy/cdp/cdp_ecosoc/E_2016_33_en.pdf

United Nations (2016c). International trade and development, Report of the Secretary-General. A/71/275.

United Nations Conference on Trade and Development (2012). *Services, Development and Trade: The Regulatory and Institutional Dimension of Infrastructure Services, Vol. I and Vol. II*, UNCTAD/DITC/TNCD/2010/4/Vol. I and UNCTAD/DITC/TNCD/2010/4/Vol. II.

United Nations Conference on Trade and Development (2013a). *Maximising the development impact of remittances*. UNCTAD/DITC/TNCD/2011/8.

United Nations Conference on Trade and Development (2013b). Recent Trends in Infrastructure FDI. Input to the UNTT on Financing for Sustainable Development.

United Nations Conference on Trade and Development (2014a). Report of the Expert Meeting on the Impact of Access to Financial Services, including by Highlighting Remittances on Development: Economic Empowerment of Women and Youth, TD/B/C.I/EM.6/3.

United Nations Conference on Trade and Development (2014b). Impact of access to financial services, including by highlighting remittances on development: Economic empowerment of women and youth, Note by the UNCTAD secretariat, TD/B/C.I/EM.6/2.

United Nations Conference on Trade and Development (2015a). *Information Economy Report 2015*. UNCTAD/IER/2015.

United Nations Conference on Trade and Development (2015b). Access to financial services as a driver for the post-2015 development agenda, *Policy Brief*, No. 35.

United Nations Conference on Trade and Development (2015c), The Continental Free Trade Area: Making it work for Africa, *Policy Brief No. 44*.

United Nations Conference on Trade and Development (2016a). *Trade and Development Report, 2016: Structural transformation for inclusive and sustained growth*. United Nations publication. Sales No. E.16.II.D.5. New York and Geneva.

United Nations Conference on Trade and Development (2016b). *World Investment Report 2016. Investor Nationality: Policy Challenges.* Sales No. E.16.II.D.4.

United Nations Conference on Trade and Development (2016c). Services, development and trade: the regulatory and institutional dimension. Note by the UNCTAD secretariat, TD/B/C.I/MEM.4/11.

United Nations Conference on Trade and Development (2016d). Report of the Multi-year Expert Meeting on Trade, Services and Development on its fourth session. TD/B/C.I/MEM.4/12.

United Nations Conference on Trade and Development (2016e). UNCTAD B2C E-commerce Index 2016. *UNCTAD Special Notes on ICT for Development,* No. 7. TN/UNCTAD/ICT4D/07.

United Nations Conference on Trade and Development, (2016f). *Commodities at a Glance: Special Issue on Gold.* UNCTAD/SUC/2015/3.

United Nations Conference on Trade and Development (2016g). Nairobi Maafikiano, From decision to action: Moving towards an inclusive and equitable global economic environment for trade and development. TD/519/Add.2.

United Nations Conference on Trade and Development (2016h). Nairobi Azimio. TD/519/Add.1.

United Nations Conference on Trade and Development (2016i). Ministerial round table: Where next for the multilateral trading system. TD/INF.53.

United Nations Conference on Trade and Development (2016j). Trading into Sustainable Development: Trade, Market Access, and the Sustainable Development Goals. UNCTAD/DITC/TAB/2015/3.

United Nations Environment Programme (2015). Designing a Sustainable Financial System in Bangladesh. October. Available from http://unepinquiry.org/publication/bangladesh/

United Nations Environment Programme (2016). The United Kingdom: Global Hub, Local Dynamics: Mapping the Transition to a Sustainable Financial System. January. Available from http://unepinquiry.org/publication/united-kingdom/

United Nations, Economic Commission for Africa (2015). *Illicit Financial Flow: Report of the High Level Panel on Illicit Financial Flows from Africa.* Available from http://www.uneca.org/sites/default/files/PublicationFiles/iff_main_report_26feb_en.pdf

United Nations, Economic Commission for Latin America and the Caribbean (2016a). *Economic Survey of Latin America and the Caribbean 2016: The 2030 Agenda for Sustainable Development and the challenges of financing for development.* Santiago de Chile.

United Nations, Economic Commission for Latin America and the Caribbean (2016b). *Panorama Fiscal 2016.* United Nations, Santiago de Chile.

United Nations, Economic and Social Commission for Western Asia (2016). *Survey of Economic and Social Developments in the Arab Region 2015-2016.* United Nations, Beirut.

United Nations, Economic and Social Council (2016). Report of the Secretary-General on Trends and progress in international development cooperation. 10 May. E/2016/65.

United Nations, General Assembly (2016a). Comprehensive High-level Midterm Review of the Implementation of the Istanbul Programme of Action for the Least Developed Countries for the Decade 2011-2020. 23 May. A/CONF.228/L.1.

United Nations, General Assembly (2016b). Report of the Secretary-General on External debt sustainability and development. 2 August. A/71/276.

UNWTO (2016a). *UNWTO Tourism Highlights, 2016 edition*. World Tourism Organization. Available from: http://mkt.unwto.org/highlights

UNWTO (2016b). *UNWTO World Tourism Barometer*, Volume 14, November. World Tourism Organization. Available from: http://mkt.unwto.org/barometer

Van Biesebroeck, James (2006). Exporting raises productivity in Sub-Saharan African manufacturing firms. *Journal of International Economics* 67 (2), 373–391.

Willis Towers Watson (2016). Global pension assets study 2016. February. Available from https://www.willistowerswatson.com/en/insights/2016/02/global-pensions-asset-study-2016

World Bank (2015). *Global Economic Prospects, January 2015: Having Fiscal Space and Using It*. Washington, D.C.: World Bank.

World Bank (2016a). *World Development Report 2016: Digital Dividends*. Washington, D.C.: World Bank. doi:10.1596/978-1-4648-0671-1. License: Creative Commons Attribution CC BY 3.0 IGO

World Bank (2016b). Migration and Remittances Data, updated as of April 2016. Available from http://www.worldbank.org/en/topic/migrationremittancesdiasporaissues/brief/migration-remittances-data

World Bank (2016c). Annual Report. Available from http://www.worldbank.org/en/about/annual-report

World Bank (2016d). World Bank International Debt Statistics. Available from http://data.worldbank.org/data-catalog/international-debt-statistics

World Bank (2016e). *World Bank Quarterly Bulletin on External Debt*. June. Available from http://datatopics.worldbank.org/debt/QuarterlyBulletin-June2016

World Economic Forum (2011). The future of Long-term investing. A World Economic Forum report in conjunction with Oliver Wyman. Available from http://www3.weforum.org/docs/WEF_FutureLongTermInvesting_Report_2011.pdf

World Gold Council (2016). *Gold Demand Trends: Second quarter 2016*.

World Trade Organization (2016a). *Report on G20 Trade Measures*, 21 June. Available from https://www.wto.org/english/news_e/news16_e/g20_wto_report_june16_e.pdf

World Trade Organization (2016b). General Council, Minutes of the meeting, 27 July. WT/GC/M/163.WTO (2016c). The shifting regulatory landscape for ICT convergence. Presentation at UNCTAD's MYEM on Trade, Services and Development.

Yao W., F. Benzimra, F. Cheung and I. Sheffuding (2016). Asia cross asset focus: Restructuring China Inc. *Société Générale Cross Asset Research*. 23 May. Paris.

Yoshida, N., H. Uematsu, and C. E. Sobrado (2014). Is extreme poverty going to end? An analytical framework to evaluate progress in ending extreme poverty. *Policy Research working paper*, No. WPS 6740. Washington, D.C.: World Bank Group.

www.ingramcontent.com/pod-product-compliance
Lightning Source LLC
Chambersburg PA
CBHW061209240926
51846CB00006B/1165
* 9 7 8 9 2 1 1 0 9 1 7 5 5 *